The SQL Server Handbook

A Guide to Microsoft Database Computing

The SQL Server Handbook

A Guide to Microsoft Database Computing

Ken England and Nigel Stanley

Digital Press

Boston • Oxford • Melbourne • Singapore • Toronto • Munich • New Delhi • Tokyo

A member of the Reed Elsevier group

Digital Press™ is an imprint of Butterworth–Heinemann, Publisher for Digital Equipment Corporation.

Recognizing the importance of preserving what has been written, Butterworth-Heinemann prints its books on acid-free paper whenever possible.

Library of Congress catalog card number: 95-071210

ISBN: 1-55558-152-8

The publisher offers discounts on bulk orders of this book. For information, please write:
Manager of Special Sales, Digital Press
Butterworth–Heinemann
313 Washington Street
Newton, MA 02158–1626

Order number: EY–T818E–DP

10 9 8 7 6 5 4 3 2

Composition: P.K. McBride, Southampton, UK

Printed in the United States of America

To Margaret, Michael and Katy
for all their help and encouragement

Ken

To Rue,
for being there

Nigel

Foreword

Microsoft SQL Server has grown in importance with the rapid take-up of Windows NT as a platform for small to medium size database applications. Commercially, its popularity has much to do with its excellent price performance, and it is often assumed by the less well-informed that this is its major virtue. However, anyone who has followed the evolution of the database from its initial release will be aware that it has become a powerful and sophisticated product.

With the ending of the partnership between Microsoft and Sybase, whose SQL Server database formed the original kernel of the product, Microsoft SQL Server has diverged significantly from its origins and with Version 6.0 it is delivering a very distinctive set of capabilities. Version 6.0 is a major release by any measure. It moves Microsoft SQL Server up market by offering support for SMP hardware and includes some parallel database administration capabilities such as parallel back-up and recovery. Performance has also been improved in other areas, for example, by support for bi-directional cursors. Particularly interesting is its distributed management capabilities which are clearly targeted at enterprise wide usage.

It is not surprising then that this product is now attracting the attention of database managers and administrators across the globe, and the need for a volume which defines, illustrates and explains its latest incarnation is obvious. England and Stanley are both UK based consultants with international reputations and long experience in the field of database. They have done an excellent job explaining and clarifying the many features of the product and their relevance. They provide advice for the database designer, the administrator and the programmer and they do so in an easily accessible and readable way.

This book is an essential reference to those who use, intend to use, or simply wish to understand Microsoft SQL Server.

Robin Bloor
CEO ButlerBloor

Contents

Preface

This book is based on Version 6.0 of Microsoft SQL Server, which was released in June 1995. This version provides a technically sophisticated and fully functional database management system for the Microsoft Windows NT operating system which can be running on Intel based platforms or Risc computers such as Digital Equipment Corporation's 64 bit AXP processor commonly known as Alpha.

Microsoft first shipped SQL Server on Windows NT in September 1993 with SQL Server 6.0 shipping in June 1995. SQL Server 6.0 excels in the area of distributed management where its distributed management object layer and graphical management tools enable a database administrator to manage a set of SQL Servers in remote locations on the network as easily as if they were local. With the new replication facilities present in SQL Server 6.0, Microsoft are supplying a product that can be used to build distributed systems that can be comprised of a number of geographically distributed servers but can still be managed practically.

The growing popularity of Windows NT and SQL Server 6.0 among customers, software development companies, and consulting firms has prompted us to write this book. It is intended to be a comprehensive introduction to the extensive capabilities offered by SQL Server and a text in which we can impart some of our experience.

This book is definitely not intended to be a re-hash of the documentation set. It is intended to be a text where readers, whether they be developers, database administrators, people performing a technical database evaluation or computer professionals looking to broaden their horizons, can gain a good overview of the product in one place and can also find thorough explanations of subjects such as locking, performance tuning and database administration.

This book is also not intended to focus on SQL Server alone but to position SQL Server within the rest of the Microsoft database family and to look at scenarios such as upsizing from Microsoft Access.

SQL Server 6.0 provides a much more powerful and easy to use graphical management tool known as the SQL Enterprise Manager. It is now possible to almost completely forget about the system stored procedures that can be found in earlier versions of SQL Server and also pervade Sybase SQL Server. In this book, however, we have chosen to provide numerous examples of the use of system stored procedures as well as the SQL Enterprise Manager. We have done this because we believe that this will be useful for readers who have worked with earlier versions of SQL Server and also readers who are familiar with Sybase SQL Server.

Written ready for the initial release of SQL Server 6.0, the subject matter of this book is very up to date. However, this can present the occasional challenge as syntax and features may sometimes change slightly. For these cases we apologise in advance.

The chapters are written to follow one another in a logical fashion, building on some of the topics introduced in previous chapters. The structure of the chapters is as follows:

- Chapter 1 introduces the components of Microsoft SQL Server and the Microsoft database family as well as the product history of SQL Server.
- Chapter 2 describes the SQL Server architecture and the creation and modification of databases, dump devices, segments and removable media.
- Chapter 3 presents the data definition features, such as the creation of tables, user-defined datatypes and views.
- Chapter 4 introduces the data manipulation features, including how to retrieve and store data, multistatement procedures, stored procedures and external functions.
- Chapter 5 introduces advanced data manipulation features, such as flow control, stored procedures and extended stored procedures.
- Chapter 6 presents the data integrity features in SQL Server, including defaults, rules, triggers, transactions and referential integrity constraints.
- Chapter 7 describes indexed access, the function of the optimizer as well as techniques to observe and influence its strategy. The database cache is also described.

- Chapter 8 introduces SQL Server locking mechanisms and strategies and the methods and tools available for monitoring locking.
- Chapter 9 explores the physical design, tuning and optimization of a SQL Server and its databases.
- Chapter 10 introduces database administration.The backing up and restoration of databases and transaction logs is examined as is the setting up of security and permissions.
- Chapter 11 explores some of the distributed features of SQL Server such as replication.
- Chapter 12 introduces Microsoft Open Database Connectivity (ODBC), components and the application programming interface.
- Chapter 13 discusses the components of Microsoft Object Linking and Embedding (OLE).
- Chapter 14 describes the architecture of Microsoft Joint Engine Technology (Jet).
- Chapter 15 explores how Microsoft Access may be used with SQL Server especially with reference to upsizing Microsoft Access applications to SQL Server using the upsizing wizard.
- Chapter 16 discusses using Visual Basic for Applications with SQL Server and SQL Distributed Management Objects (DMO).
- Chapter 17 speculates on the future direction of Microsoft SQL Server.

6.0 To enable SQL Server users of versions prior to SQL Server 6.0 to be able to easily spot new features introduced in this version, we have highlighted new SQL Server 6.0 functionality with this symbol.

Acknowledgements

Most of all, we would like to thank Margaret England and Rue Stanley for their long suffering while we were writing this text. Writing about databases is, unfortunately, not an activity in which most of the family can join in. Because of this, writing and being sociable are usually mutually exclusive! We also would like to thank them for the great favor they did us in proof-reading.

Margaret had to spend many a weekend anchored to the house. Michael England is too young to understand databases but old enough to understand computer games and he was very patient while his dad kept disappearing in front of a PC for protracted periods of time! Katy England is too young to understand or care about computer games!

Although not a database expert, Rue's enthusiasm for the book has been enormous. The all important task of encouraging its completion will never be forgotten, nor the lost evenings and weekends that could have been spent together.

As well as the friends and colleagues who helped us with the book, we would like to give an extra special thanks to the following people.

A very special thank you to Keith Burns who patiently explained SQL Server topics on a number of occasions, and to Stephen J. Cartland whose help with Windows NT has been invaluable. Another special thank you goes to Mike Cash and the folk at Butterworth Heinemann and Mac Bride our typesetter. Many thanks to our other friends in Microsoft, without whose skill and hard work SQL Server 6.0 would not have seen the light of day.

Ken England
Nigel Stanley
June 1995

1 Microsoft Database Computing

1.1 INTRODUCTION

This chapter is designed to introduce the reader to the Microsoft database family. Although primarily concerned with Microsoft's Back Office database product, SQL Server, this book will discuss some of Microsoft's other database products as many SQL Server users will, no doubt, use products such as Microsoft Access and Microsoft Visual Basic in conjunction with Microsoft SQL Server. This chapter will briefly look at the database family and associated product history to enable the reader to position the products.

1.2 THE DATABASE PRODUCTS

Founded in 1975 Microsoft is one of the computing industry's success stories. The introduction of Microsoft Windows and Microsoft DOS lead to the explosive growth of the personal computer as one of the key tools in today's information technology world.

Database computing on the personal computer has evolved over the past decade. The increased price performance of computer hardware coupled with easier to use software has fueled the demand for business solutions that are practical and cost effective. Client server computing, whilst not a new concept, was able to benefit from the explosive growth in personal computers. Computer companies such as Microsoft have continually developed new tools and products aimed at increasing the productivity and performance of both developers and users.

In the early days of the personal computer, word processor and spreadsheet development happened in leaps and bounds, meanwhile, databases were somewhat neglected. The early database management systems were little more than glorified file management systems and these were aimed at developers rather than end users. Ease of use was not a major design goal!

One of the most valuable assets of any company, however, is data and so vendors came to realize that customers wanted personal computer based database management systems that were powerful but were also easy to use. Performance, the ability to maintain data integrity and good interoperability with mini computer and mainframe platforms also became increasingly important.

A number of vendors brought out personal computer based database products to address these needs and one of these was Microsoft. After what some would consider a long wait, Microsoft Access was launched. If it was a long wait then it was worth it as Microsoft Access became an immediate success. Highly integrated with their widely used Microsoft Windows graphical user interface (GUI), aimed at power users (see below) and end users, it had something for everyone. It was easy to use, and development using Access could be performed at a number of levels. Quite sophisticated databases could be developed using drag and drop techniques in conjunction with a form and report development tool.

For the more adventurous user, more sophisticated features could be added with macros and, for the developer, a programming language known as Access Basic could be used. Microsoft Access databases could also be used by multiple users simultaneously although the product is not optimized for simultaneous access by large user populations. This is where Microsoft SQL Server comes into its own.

Microsoft Access is not the only database product provided by Microsoft. In fact, Microsoft has a family of database products designed to fit together to provide a consistent environment for computer users and developers as shown in Figure 1-1.

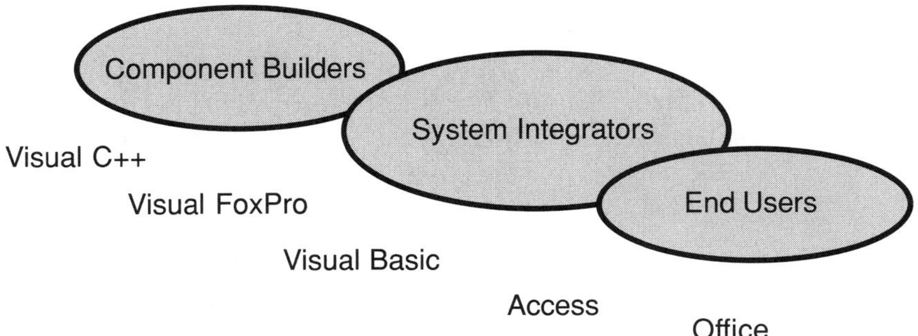

Figure 1-1 Microsoft Database and Developer Tools Cover a Range of Users

Briefly looking at the product family:

- Microsoft Access is designed for the power user – an individual who is reasonably computer literate and maybe uses spreadsheets of word processors to store information. At the time of writing Access is at Version 2.0, with Version 3.0 proposed for the end of 1995. Version 3.0 is cited as being fully 32 bit, further details remain unspecified.
- Microsoft FoxPro is designed for the xBASE developer – an individual who's main task is to create personal computer database applications for users. xBASE is the generic term for dBASE type languages and may include products such as Clipper and CA Visual Objects. Microsoft FoxPro was purchased from Fox Software in 1992 and at the time of writing is just in the process of being updated to Version 3.0, Visual FoxPro. This is designed to update FoxPro and bring it in line with other Microsoft developer products with full object orientation, 32 bit code base and the use of reusable add-in components based on Object Linking and Embedding (OLE) called OCXs.
- Microsoft Visual Basic (VB) is designed for the Basic language developer. Currently at Version 3.0, Version 4.0 is in beta test at the time of writing.

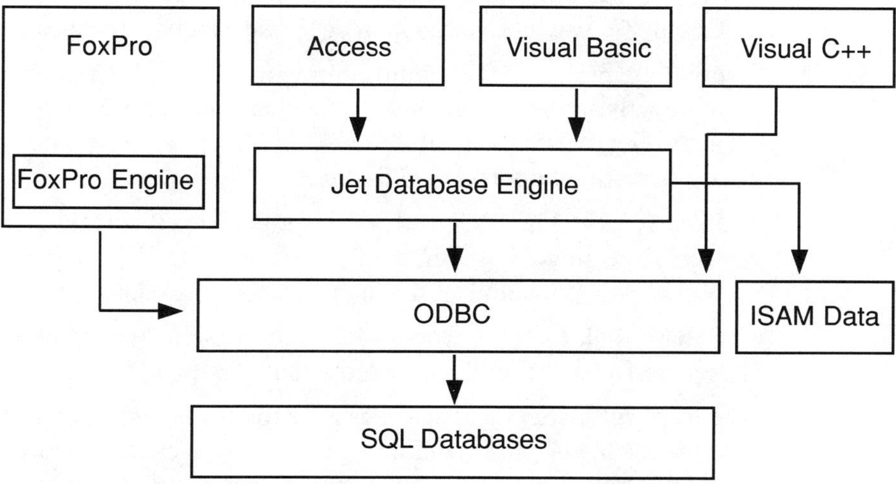

Figure 1-2 Microsoft Current Database and Developer Tools Architecture

1.3 MICROSOFT SQL SERVER

Microsoft SQL Server is Microsoft's server hosted relational database management system (RDBMS) and is a component of Microsoft's Back Office suite of products.

1.3.1 Some SQL Server History

In 1987 Microsoft and Sybase announced a long term strategic relationship to develop and market a relational database management system (RDBMS) for Microsoft operating systems. Sybase licensed the SQL Server RDBMS and other related technology components to Microsoft for use on the OS/2 and up and coming Windows NT platforms.

Microsoft developed other technologies in line with this announcement including SQL Bridge, which enabled OS/2 hosted SQL Servers transparent connectivity to Sybase SQL Servers on UNIX, the SQL Object Manager, and Administrator utilities to graphically administer a SQL Server database.

Microsoft also developed DB-Library, the SQL Server programming interface, for use on OS/2, Windows, Windows NT and MS-DOS operating systems. This technology was then licensed by Sybase and sold under the name "Open Client" for use on UNIX, OpenVMS and Macintosh platforms.

Over the period of the relationship with Sybase, Microsoft started to take a more active role in the technology development side of SQL Server, culminating in the fact that the original Windows NT SQL Server was engineered entirely at Microsoft Corporation in Redmond, WA.

In early 1994 Microsoft and Sybase announced that their strategic directions were diverging. However, both companies agreed to maintain some level of backwards compatibility, that is applications could interoperate, to Version 4.21.

Sybase took the SQL Server 4.21 code base, added some refinements and released a line of products called Sybase System 10. This included:

- **Replication Server.** This is designed for distributed server applications where the use of two phase commit would not be practical due to server or network down time. For a two phase commit to complete, all server components need to be available during the transaction. In reality this is not always possible, so replication is seen as a useful alternative. Instead of data being committed in one transaction, copies of the data (which can be down to the row level) are effectively moved across the network in real time, updating remote servers. In most real life scenarios this asynchronous propagation of data is more than adequate for most applications.

- **Navigation Server.** At the time of writing this is generally available on selected AT&T systems. It is designed to be a high-end parallel relational database based on Sybase's SQL Server.
- **Omni-SQL Gateway**. This enables heterogeneous database servers, distributed around the network to transparently appear as one virtual database.
- Other components to provide better backup and server monitoring.

The release of the System 10 product line was seen to counter Oracle's presence in the enterprise computing arena with their large scale distributed database servers.

Microsoft moved the SQL Server 4.21 code base forward with their release of SQL Server on the Windows NT platform. Windows NT is the strategic server platform for Microsoft, and although at the time of writing the OS/2 SQL Server product is still available from Microsoft the authors believe there will be little if any further development on this product.

When engineering Microsoft SQL Server for Windows NT, Microsoft's philosophy was to use native Windows NT capabilities as much as possible, for example, threading and scheduling. In this way, instead of re-inventing the wheel, the SQL Server engineers used the facilities provided by Windows NT. This then enabled them to focus on database functionality and to produce a product that is highly integrated with the operating system, indeed, it is sometimes easy to forget that SQL Server is not actually part of it!

As it was being re-engineered for Windows NT, SQL Server was improved in a number of areas, those listed below being just a few:

- Scaleability and increased system capacity
- Very powerful symmetric multiprocessing support
- Multiple hardware platform support – Intel, Risc
- An improved query optimizer
- Asynchronous I/O
- Better lock management

All these improvements come together to mean a fast and highly scaleable database engine.

2 SQL Server Architecture

2.1 INTRODUCTION

This chapter will give the reader a good understanding of the general *make up* of Microsoft SQL Server. The installation process is covered, and then we examine the process of building the devices which hold the databases. The creation of databases and transaction logs and how they are expanded is also covered. The final section of this chapter covers a topic in SQL Server new in Version 6.0, the creation of databases on removable media.

By the end of this chapter a reader should have a good grasp of the SQL Server architecture and feel happy about starting the steps of installing and building a server. It is not the intention of this chapter to give a blow by blow account of product installation, more an expansion of areas which may be of interest to the database administrator.

2.1.1 Overview of Windows NT

Although this is a book about Microsoft SQL Server and related technologies, Windows NT technology is a crucial foundation stone. All examples and experiences related in this book refer to the Windows NT SQL Server product.

Windows NT shipped to the market place on 31st August 1993 to mixed reviews. The release of the product followed nearly seven years of tough development, lead by operating system *guru* Dave Cutler, late of Digital Equipment Corporation where he led the development team for the OpenVMS operating system.

Windows NT is the most powerful member of the Microsoft Windows family designed for high end workstation or multiprocessor servers. The key features of Windows NT are:

- **Manageability** – The use of the Windows 3.1 graphical user interface gives users a familiar environment. For the database user this is useful as graphical tools have been built to manage SQL Server and remove a lot of the tedium of writing SQL scripts. Later versions of Windows NT will have the new Windows 95 User Interface.

- **Security** – Windows NT is designed to be certified to US Department of Defense C2 level security. At the time of writing the certification process is nearing completion. SQL Server can integrate into the Windows NT security model with single stage logon saving the system administrator time in setting up groups of users.
- **Multithreading** – any application can be written to take advantage of this, so that an application's processes can be multitasked, for example executing one query whilst building another and printing a third. Windows NT also supports pre-emptive multitasking so that applications are forced to yield processor time as opposed to co-operative multiprocessing in 16 bit versions of Windows which rely upon the application yielding processor time to other applications. A poorly written Windows 3.1 application can consume all system resources and prevent other applications from operating.
- **Symmetric Multiprocessing** – With micro computers that support multiple processors Windows NT can 'load balance' work across multiple processors to give improved performance. A query's performance can be improved by threading it across processors balanced with other work.

2.1.2 SQL Server Architecture

SQL Server can very much be thought of as a family of products, tightly integrated to offer a good suite of complimentary services. This is shown in Figure 2-1.

Client Applications			
DB-Library	Embedded SQL	Open Data Services	ODBC
SQL DMO	SQL Executive	Replication Engine	Host Gateways
SQL Server RDBMS			

Figure 2-1 The SQL Server Family

The *SQL Server RDBMS* component is the database engine responsible for data storage, security and integrity.

On top of the RDBMS engine we have, the *SQL Distributed Management Objects (DMO)* component which is an *Object Linking and Embedding (OLE)* layer of objects used for the distributed management of servers. These objects interface to the graphical management tools. The *SQL Executive* is responsible for the management of administrative tasks such as the alerting of operators. *Replication* is the component that is responsible for sending data to remote servers that have requested it. *Host gateways* are used to access remote data in non SQL Server format.

DB-Library is the client/server interface to SQL Server normally used by developers using the C programming language. *Embedded SQL* is used with the COBOL interface to SQL Server. *Open Data Services (ODS)* is another application programming interface (API) which enables gateways to be constructed to interoperate across the data enterprise and *ODBC* is the Microsoft Open Database Connectivity interface which we will discuss in more detail in Chapter 12.

There are in excess of 200 client applications which can combine with Microsoft SQL Server to create client server based solutions. These include the popular *Office* type applications from Microsoft including Access, Excel and Word and from other vendors products such as Forest and Trees, Paradox and dBASE.

SQL Enterprise Manager	Visual Tools and Scripting
SQL DMO	
SQL Executive	SQL Server RDBMS

Figure 2-2 The SQL Server Distributed Management Framework

Figure 2-2 shows the Distributed Management Framework (DMF). This is an architecture for managing the many components that may be found in a large, distributed SQL Server environment.

The SQL Enterprise Manager tool is used for day to day administration duties, including setting up and configuring stored procedures, triggers, tables and other SQL objects and can be thought of as the graphical interface to the DMF. Because the DMO is a set of documented objects with properties and methods it can easily be used with Visual Basic and so powerful administration scripts can be written.

A unique advantage of using SQL Server on Windows NT is the native integration of the product in such areas of security and performance tuning. We will cover these in later chapters.

2.2 SQL SERVER INSTALLATION

SQL Server installation is generally a straight forward process, assuming the user has the appropriate hardware to support Windows NT and SQL Server. As in any installation routines there are some areas which require special consideration, which we will move onto in a moment.

Hardware Requirements for Microsoft SQL Server:

- Intel 486 or Pentium or Risc-based chip such as DEC Alpha or MIPS
- 16Mb RAM minimum, 32Mb or 64Mb recommended
- 35Mb free disk space
- CDROM drive

Networks supported include:

- Novell Netware IPX/SPX
- Microsoft Named Pipes
- TCP/IP Sockets
- Banyan Vines
- DECnet
- AppleTalk
- Multiprotocol networks

Some quick facts on system capacities:

- Supports up to 2Gb memory
- 8 terabytes disk storage
- 32,767 databases per server
- 32,767 connections per server
- Unlimited database objects
- Database can span multiple physical disks

The authors are yet to find any SQL Server system hitting any of these limits!

Remote installation is possible across the network and is useful for the centralized database administrator.

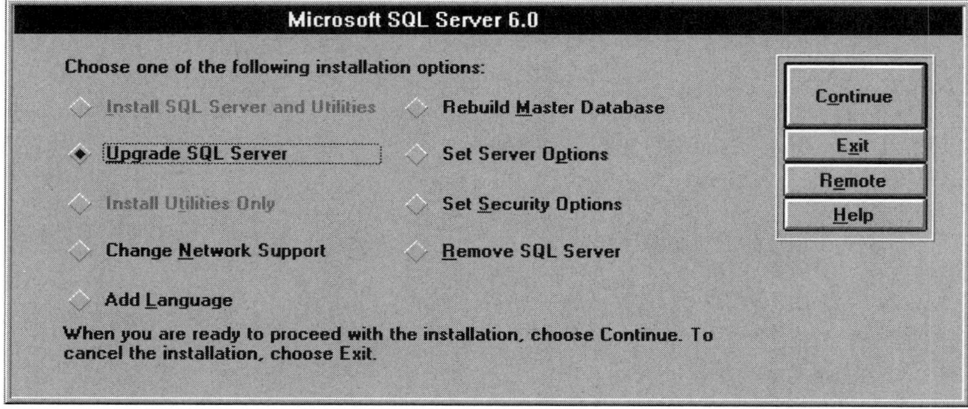

Figure 2-3 SQL Server Setup Options

2.2.1 SQL Server Character Sets

The installation process will need to know which character set to use. The choice of character set determines which types of character SQL Server will recognise in the stored data. If the incorrect character set is chosen on installation then databases will need to be rebuilt and the data reloaded.

A character set contains 256 characters, of which the first 128 are identical for each character set but the remaining 128, called the *extended character set*, are different. The extended characters contain the language specific characters such as diacritical marks and specialized accents. If databases are to use these extended characters, the same character set must be chosen on the client and the server. SQL Server 6.0 has the choice of three character sets:

- Multilingual
- US English
- Latin 1 or ANSI

Multilingual is generally the character set of choice for European, North American and South American installations.

The installation process will need to know which sort order is required. The sort order governs the collation and presentation of data produced by a query. If the incorrect sort order is selected on installation and a change is needed then the databases will need to be rebuilt and the data reloaded. A choice of sort orders is provided by SQL Server. The *Binary* sort order is the simplest and fastest sort order to use as the collating sequence is based on the numeric value of the characters in the installed character set. A *dictionary* sort order will not perform as quickly as one based on binary character sorting.

The default character set and sort order for SQL Server 6.0 is *ANSI* and *dictionary order case insensitive*.

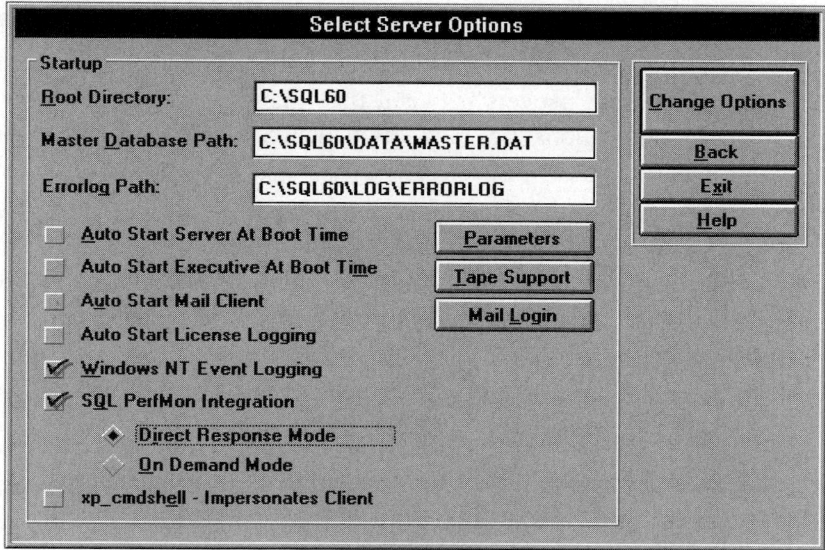

Figure 2-4 SQL Server 6.0 Server Set Up Installation Options

During the installation of SQL Server a number of Transact-SQL scripts are run. A sample of these are listed below:

- CONFIG.SQL to set the SQL Server configuration options.
- INSTCAT.SQL to install the catalog stored procedures.
- INSTMSTR.SQL to install the master database.

Other scripts are available as options. A sample of these are listed below:

- INSTPUBS.SQL to install the *pubs* (short for publishers, not the British drinking establishments!) sample database.
- INSTSUPL.SQL to install supplemental stored procedures.
- ADMIN2.SQL and OBJECT2.SQL for the SQL Tools stored procedures used by the version 4.21 SQL Object Manager and SQL Administrator.
- HELPSQL.SQL to install the SQL Help script and create the stored procedure *sp_help* used for syntax checking.

It is advisable to install these remaining options, except maybe the pubs database, unless disk space is at an absolute premium.

Through out this book the authors have used the *pubs* database for the examples, so it may be an idea to install it if you wish to follow our examples.

SQL Server will use network libraries (Net-Libraries) to pass data and information packets between the client and the SQL server. Inter-process communications (IPC) supported include NWLink IPX/SPX and TCP/IP. SQL Server will always listen on named pipes irrespective of the IPC used.

SQL Server can integrate its own security model with that of Windows NT so that separate logon and SQL passwords do not have to be maintained. This also allows SQL Server applications to utilise the Windows NT C2 level certifiable security features such as encrypted passwords and domain wide accounts.

2.3 SQL SERVER SYSTEM DATABASES

During installation of SQL Server three system databases are created:

- Master

- Model
- Tempdb

SQL Server 6.0 will also install the *msdb* database as described below.

2.3.1 The Master Database

The *master* database is the *controller* of the databases and operations within a SQL Server. It contains, amongst other things, the system stored procedures, user login ids and system tables which maintain the database statistics. The default database for users following logon is master and so this should be changed to another database which the user is likely to need on a regular basis. There is no need for most users to access the master database – indeed this must be discouraged to prevent problems that may affect the entire SQL Server installation. The system administrator (SA) login id will still require the master database as its default.

Hint: Due to its critical nature, it is recommended that the master database is backed up each time a database object contained within it is changed or created.

2.3.2 The Model Database

The *model* database is effectively a template used for each new database that is created on a SQL Server system. Contained within the model database are all of the system tables that are required for each database, and if changes are made to the model database then they will be reflected in every database created after that change. Typical changes to the model database can include the addition of user defined datatypes, rules and default privileges. Again care must be taken as to who actually accesses the model database as the changes they make will be perpetuated throughout the system.

2.3.3 The Tempdb Database

The *tempdb* database is a shared work area that is used by all databases in a SQL Server system. With a default size of 2Mb this temporary area is cleared each time the system is closed down and, when users log out, temporary tables will automatically be removed from *tempdb*. It may be necessary to increase the size of *tempdb* if large sorts are undertaken, or subqueries frequently use the GROUP BY function or users undertake a lot of activity directly on the temporary tables. For increased performance, the database administrator may specify that *tempdb* is held in memory. This is described in Chapter 9.

2.3.4 The Pubs Database

The *pubs* database is installed optionally at install time and is used for demonstration and example work. It might be advisable to install this database if you wish to follow the examples that can be found throughout this book. Chapter 3 describes the *pubs* database in more detail.

6.0

For those of you who are familiar with the pubs database provided with SQL Server 4.21, the pubs database has been updated to reflect the new product enhancements in SQL Server 6.0:

- Addition of international data to test sorts and character sets.
- Three new tables *employees*, *jobs* and *pub_info*.
- The *publishers* table has a new country column.
- Referential integrity is now enforced with primary and foreign key constraints.
- More complex triggers have been provided.
- The *pub_info* table contains text and graphics data.
- All defaults and rules have been changed to use the DEFAULT and CHECK constraints respectively.

2.3.5 The Msdb Database

SQL Server 6.0 uses a new database called *msdb* which provides support for the *SQL Executive*. During installation two devices are created – a 2Mb device MSDBDATA which contains the data and a 1Mb device MSDBLOG which contains the transaction log. These devices are created on the same disk drive as the master database.

2.4 CREATING & MANAGING DEVICES, DATABASES & SEGMENTS

The creation and subsequent management of *devices*, the fundamental SQL Server storage components, is an important area for the database administrator to understand. Although not designed to supplant the product documentation, this chapter will discuss device architecture and the process of creating and then subsequently managing devices which in the authors' opinion is often poorly understood.

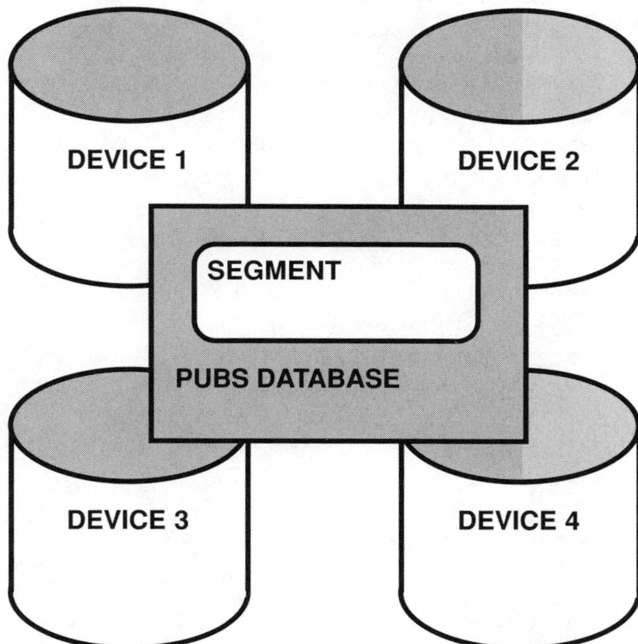

Figure 2-5 Devices, Databases and Segments

2.4.1 Creating Devices

All databases are stored on *database devices* which can be considered to be disk files which reside on disk. As well as the databases themselves, database *transaction logs* are also stored on database devices. A second class of device is known as a *dump device*. Dump devices may be stored on disk, diskette or tape and are used for database and transaction log backups. Figure 2-5 shows a database that is spread over four devices and a *segment* that is spread over two devices. Segments will be discussed shortly.

With versions prior to SQL Server 6.0, once created a device size could not be increased – an important factor that needed to be taken into consideration by the database administrator prior to deciding upon the initial database device sizing. The minimum size of a device is 1Mb, which is sufficient space for a transaction log backup, but for database storage the device will need to be at least 2Mb. This is the absolute minimum, and naturally this size will need to be increased depending on the size of the database and the potential growth of the SQL Server system.

2.4.2 Device Number

Before adding a device to a database the administrator needs to obtain a device number using the system procedure *sp_helpdevice*. Once executed this procedure will supply a list of used device numbers. Any device number that has not been allocated can then be used.

Below is a typical display from *sp_helpdevice* showing the device names and physical attributes within a typical SQL Server system:

```
sp_helpdevice

device_name    physical_name          description
-----------    ---------------------- -------------------------------------
diskdump       nul                    disk, dump device
diskettedumpa  a:sqltable.dat         diskette, 1.2 MB, dump device
diskettedumpb  b:sqltable.dat         diskette, 1.2 MB, dump device
master         C:\SQL\DATA\MASTER.DAT special, default disk, physical disk,25 MB

(1 row(s) affected)
```

and the following columns:

```
Status          cntrltype  device_number    low   high
16        2         0                0     20000
16        3         0                0     19
16        4         0                0     19
3         0         0                0     12799
```

The *device_name* column is the logical device name, *physical_name* is the physical device name, *description* gives device information and the type of dump device and *status* specifies the type of device as shown in Table 1.

Number	Description
1	Default device disk
2	Physical disk
4	Logical Disk
8	Skip header
16	Disk or tape dump device
32	Serial writes
64	Device mirrored
128	Reserved
256	Reserved
512	Mirror enabled

Table 1 The Device Status Column

The *cntrltype* column specifies the type of controller as a bit field as shown in Table 2.

Number	Description
0	Database device dsk
2	Dump device
3-4	Diskette device
5	Tape dump device

Table 2 The Cntrltype Column

The *low* column gives the first virtual page number for a database device, with this value always being 0 for a dump device. The *high* column is the last virtual page number for a database device.

Armed with a new device number, the database administrator can now create a device.

Hint: If the SQL Enterprise Manager is used to create devices the device number is specified for you and you need not concern yourself with it.

2.4.3 DISK INIT

The Transact-SQL syntax to create a device is fairly straightforward:

```
disk init
name = 'authors'
physname = 'c:\sql\data\aut.dat'
vdevno= 2,
size = 10240
```

This will create a disk with the logical name of *authors*, a physical name of *aut.dat*, device number 2 with a size of 10240 2Kb blocks giving a device size of 20Mb.

- The logical name will be truncated to 30 characters, although it is possible to name it longer, but standard SQL naming conventions must be adhered to.
- The physical name specifies the path to the physical file location.
- The virtual device number is a unique identifier for the device, which must be between 0 and 255.
- The size of database is determined in numbers of 2Kb blocks, with 512 2Kb blocks per Megabyte. Database devices must be the same or a greater size than the model database.
- There is also a parameter *vstart* to specify the starting virtual address for SQL Server to begin using the device.

SQL Server 6.0 allows the size of devices to be increased with the DISK RESIZE Transact-SQL statement:

```
disk resize
name = 'authors'
size = 20480
```

This will resize the *authors* device to 40Mb.

The execution speed of DISK INIT has been increased as it now takes advantage of the fact that, with Windows NT, a FAT file is created by zeroing all of the required bytes and an NTFS file is created by presenting the application with a zeroed image of the required file.

The CNTRLTYPE parameter of DISK INIT and DISK REINIT has now been removed as Windows NT can now automatically detect this information.

Hint: The *sysdevices* table in the master database contains the logical and physical names of each device in the system. If a device is dropped then it is automatically removed from the *sysdevices* table. Here is the result of a SELECT on our *sysdevices* table:

```
use master
go
select * from sysdevices

low high   status cntrltype name           phyname
--- ----   -----  -------   -----          --------
0   20000  16     2         diskdump       nul
0   19     16     3         diskettedumpa  a:sqltable.dat
0   19     16     4         diskettedumpb  b:sqltable.dat
0   12799  3      0         master         C:\SQL\DATA\MASTER.DAT

(4 row(s) affected)
```

As a device is being created it will automatically be split into 256 2Kb pages known as *allocation units*. The DISK INIT statement initializes the first page which will subsequently contain information concerning the remaining 255 pages. This architecture is somewhat similar to the FAT or *file allocation table* data used in the MS-DOS PC operating system.

A simpler way to create a database device may be to use the SQL Enterprise Manager. Figure 2-6 shows the same device created via its interactive dialogue. The name, pathname and size can be specified along with a graphical representation of the available free space.

2.4.4 Default Database Devices

If no database device is specified when a database is created then the default device is used which is normally the master device on a standard installation of SQL Server. This default should be changed by the database administrator after the SQL Server installation.

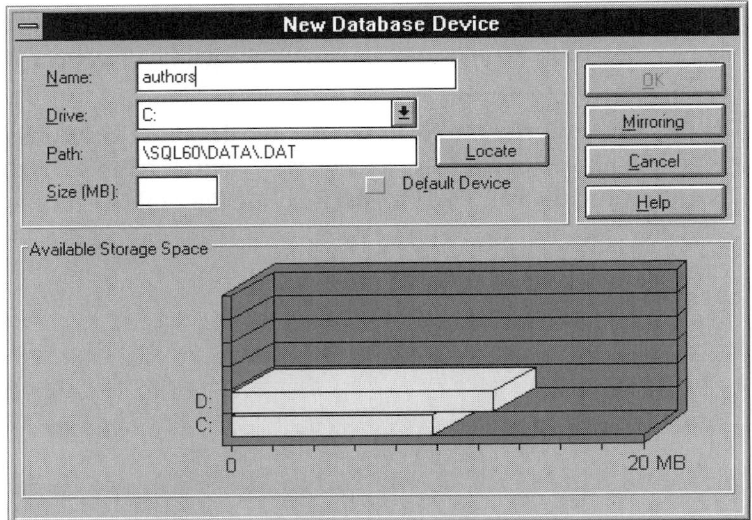

Figure 2-6 Creating a Device with the SQL Enterprise Manager

This example shows how to add a database device to a pool of default database devices:

```
sp_diskdefault authors, defaulton
```

And to remove it is just as simple:

```
sp_diskdefault authors, defaultoff
```

The device is called by its logical name, with *defaulton* and *defaultoff* adding or removing the device to or from the default pool.

Hint: As a careful systems administrator you should immediately dump the master database once a default has been specified.

To see how much space is available for use in a device, the SQL Enterprise Manager can be used as shown in Figure 2-7.

2.4.5 Dump Devices

Dump devices are the storage medium used for database and transaction log backups. These devices may be diskette or tape as well as normal fixed disk giving the administrator a number of options to ensure secure back up. Once added, a dump device's physical and logical names are stored in the *sysdevices* table.

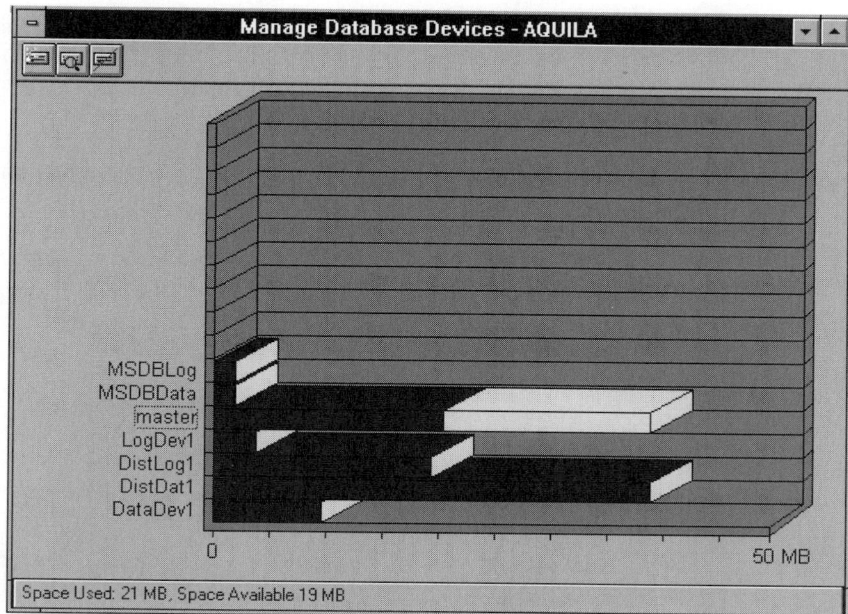

Figure 2-7 Checking Device Space with the SQL Enterprise Manager

---

Hint: As with normal devices, it is best practice to create separate physical dump devices for a database and its associated transaction log.

If a tape is to be used as a dump device then the physical name given is that allocated by Windows NT during tape installation, otherwise dump devices follow standard device naming conventions.

```
sp_addumpdevice 'diskette', 'autdumpa', 'a:\autdump.dat'
```

- Either *disk, diskette* or *tape* can be specified as the dump media.
- Specify the name of the dump device using the logical name, again the same naming conventions apply as for creating database devices.
- There are also options to specify the controller number. Disk dump devices must be 2, diskette devices must be 3 or 4 and tape device 5. If tape devices are used then an extra command of *skip* or *noskip* can be used to specify if tape labels are to be ignored.

Earlier versions of SQL Server were not able to detect the end of removable device media and the storage capacity had to be specified when dump devices were being created. This option is still available, but used for backward compatibility reasons only.

In SQL Server 6.0 the CNTRLTYPE and MEDIA_CAPACITY options for the *sp_addumpdevice* statement have now been removed.

The SQL Enterprise Manager can be used to add dump devices. Figure 2-8 shows the above dump device being created with the SQL Enterprise Manager.

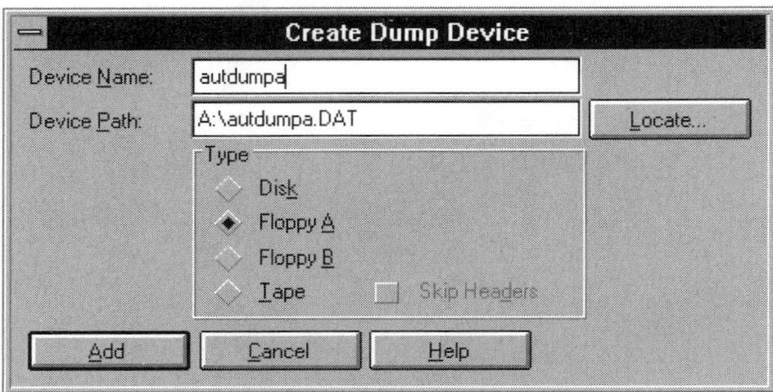

Figure 2-8 Adding a Dump Device with the SQL Enterprise Manager

2.4.6 Dropping Devices

The system administrator (SA) is the only user with the access rights to drop databases and dump devices. Before dropping a device which contains databases the databases need to be dropped first, and then the device. Once dropped a device is removed from the *sysdevices* table. The system stored procedure *sp_dropdevice* is used to drop a device with the device being referred to by its logical name:

```
sp_dropdevice  authors
```

The SQL Enterprise Manager can also be used to remove devices.

Hint: Interestingly, the associated operating system file is not automatically removed when a device is dropped. This must be done manually by the system administrator.

2.4.7 Segments

The use of multiple disks can give substantial performance improvements to a SQL Server database. SQL Server on Windows NT allows three types of database *spanning*:

- SQL Server segments
- Windows NT RAID 0 or RAID 5 striping
- Hardware disk arrays

SQL Server segments give very good control over table and index placement. This can yield significant performance improvements but managing segments is not always simple and in a large database with many tables and indexes it can become complex. With each SQL Server database containing up to 32 segments the database administrator can fine tune read and write operations to a precise degree.

Typical examples of using segments include the storing of *text* and *image* data on separate physical devices, splitting very large and heavily accessed tables across two devices and the splitting of a table and its non clustered indexes on separate devices.

When a database is created 3 segments are automatically created:

- SYSTEM
- LOGSEGMENT
- DEFAULT

The *system* segment stores the system tables, the *logsegment* segment stores the transaction log and the *default* segment stores all the remaining database objects unless extra segments are created.

2.4.8 Creating a Segment

Segments can only be created after the database device has been built. Here is an example of adding a segment:

```
sp_addsegment auth_seg, authors
```

This will create the logically named segment *auth_seg* on the logical device name *authors* which we created earlier. The *syssegments* and *sysusages* system tables are automatically updated to map to the new segment.

Database tables and indexes can now be created on the named segment, with the system table *sysindexes* recording the number of the segment where the individual object physically exists. Here we create a table *authors* onto the *auth_seg*, and then create an associated index which is placed on a separate segment *auth_seg2* :

```
create table authors
    (au_id          id,
    au_lname        varchar(40)   not null,
    au_fname        varchar(20)   not null,
    phone           char(12),
    address         varchar(40)   null,
    city            varchar(20)   null,
    state           char(2)       null,
    zip             char(5)       null,
    contract        bit)
    on auth_seg
```

A nonclustered index on the *au_lname* column is placed on another segment:

```
create index auth_lname_index on authors (au_lname) on auth_seg2
```

Creating tables and indexes is discussed in detail in Chapter 3. Segment sizes may need to be increased as tables or indexes grow in size. As the segment is extended it may be mapped onto other database devices. Here is an example of increasing the size of the segment *auth_seg*:

```
sp_extendsegment auth_seg, authors2
```

This will extend the *auth_seg* segment and place it onto the device *authors2*. As you can see the logical name of the database device is used. The *sysusages* system table is updated with the new space mapping.

If we decide to change the data storage segment for our table *auth_name* for future data input then the system procedure *sp_placeobject* can be used:

```
sp_placeobject auth_seg3, auth_name
```

All future data written to the table *auth_name* will be stored on the segment *auth_seg3*.

Hint: Splitting indexes across devices using *sp_placeobject* is not recommended as system performance may be degraded. A simple solution is to drop the index and then recreate it on the new segment. Clustered indexes are always on the same segment as the data because the bottom level of the index is the data anyway. This is discussed in Chapter 7.

2.4.9 Determining Segment Configuration

There are two system procedures that enable a database administrator to look at the segment configuration of a SQL Server: These are *sp_helpsegment* and *sp_helpdb*. Executing *sp_helpsegment* will produce a result similar to this:

```
sp_helpsegment

segment   name                 status
-------   ------------------   -----
0         system               0
1         default              1
2         logsegment           0
```

The segment number is displayed, with the logical name and the status of the segment. By explicitly naming the segment further information is given:

```
sp_helpsegment 'default'

segment   name                 status
-------   ------------------   -----
1         default              1

device                     size
------                     ----------------------
master                     3MB
master                     5MB
table_name                 index_name                indid
-------------------        --------------------      ---
MSlast_monitor             MSlast_monitor            0
MSscheduled_backups        MSscheduled_backups       0
MSscheduled_backups        sched_idx                 2
Msscheduled_backups_log    Msscheduled_backups_log   0
helpsql                    helpsql_index             2
          :
          :
```

Hint: Don't forget that 'default' is a reserved word so needs to be enclosed in inverted commas!

To determine segment configuration in a specific database then use the system procedure *sp_helpdb* followed by the database name:

```
sp_helpdb master

name      db_size  owner  dbid  created      status
------    -------  ------ ----- --------     -------------
master    8MB      sa     1     Mar 2 1994   trunc. log on
chkpt.

device_fragments    size    usage
---------------     -----   -------
master              3MB     data and log
master              5MB     data and log

device       segment
-------      ----------
master       default
master       logsegment
master       system
```

2.4.10 Dropping Segments

Segments can only be dropped once they are empty, that is, they contain no database objects. As well as dropping a segment in its entirety, they can also be dropped from individual devices. Space is still allocated to a database if a segment has been dropped, and this space will not be available for use until the default segment is mapped onto the database device or another segment is created on the device. The *sysusages* and *syssegments* tables will automatically be updated when the segments have been dropped.

```
sp_dropsegment auth_seg
```

This will drop the segment *auth_seg* which we created earlier on.

Hint: Given the extra management complexity involved with segments and the more widespread use of RAID technology, less database administrators are using segments to explicitly place tables and indexes. We suspect that the use of segments will diminish dramatically during the lifetime of SQL Server 6.0.

2.4.11 Creating Databases

A database is the *container* in which objects such as tables, views, indexes, triggers and stored procedures are placed. Databases can also be thought of as a *unit of administration*. It is individual databases that are backed up, restored and integrity checked.

Databases are created with the CREATE DATABASE statement which will allocate space to a database on one or more devices. The database size will default to 2MB, which is the size of the *model* database, unless otherwise specified. Once allocated to a certain size it is difficult to reclaim any storage space unless the database is dropped, so some care has to be taken with the initial sizing.

SQL Server 6.0 has introduced a new Database Consistency Checker (DBCC) utility command *shrinkdb*. This will enable a database administrator to reduce the size of a database.

Extending the size of a database is fairly straightforward using the ALTER DATABASE statement which will be covered later.

It is a wise idea to store the associated transaction log on a separate device by using the LOG ON clause in the CREATE DATABASE command. This will ensure a much easier time in the event of media failure and is good practice anyway. Transaction log size will vary depending on the size of the database, however, as a start point, the transaction log should occupy about 25% of the size of the database.

To create a database you will need to be in the master database, and by default SA is the only login id with sufficient rights to create databases unless permissions have been granted to other users:

```
create database pubs
on default  = 8
log on publog
```

This will create a database named *pubs* which will be 8 Mb in size and stored on the default device. The LOG ON clause places the transaction log onto the database device *publog*.

The *sysdatabases* and *sysusages* system tables are both updated with details of the newly created database.

If a database has been created without using the LOG ON clause then it is possible to move the transaction log to a new device using the system procedure *sp_logdevice*:

```
sp_logdevice pubs, publog
```

This example will move the *pubs* transaction log onto the *publog* device. After using this system procedure always backup the master database.

The SQL Enterprise Manager can be used to create a database as shown in Figure 2-9.

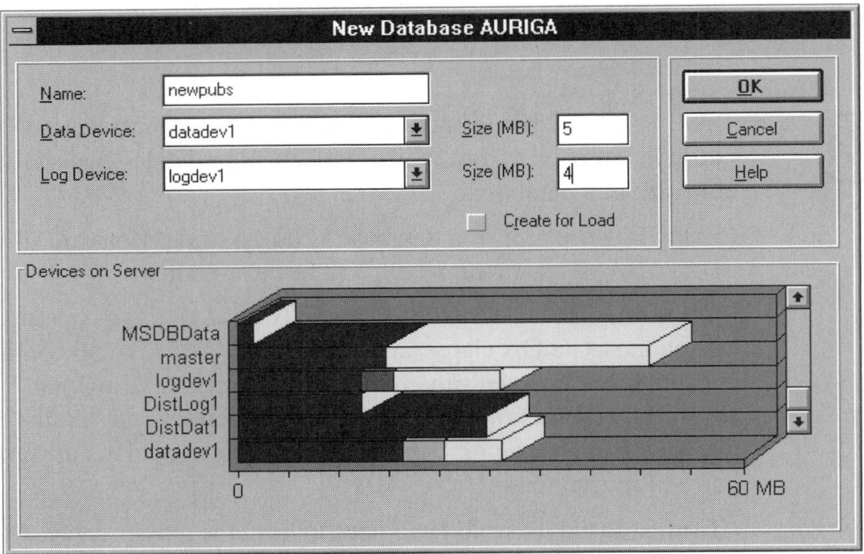

Figure 2-9 Creating a Database with the SQL Enterprise Manager

In SQL Server 6.0, the CREATE DATABASE command is now more intelligent as SQL Server will determine if the devices are new and if so will not reinitialize them, saving considerable time.

2.4.12 Increasing Database Size

To extend a database, the ALTER DATABASE statement can be used. The permission to use ALTER DATABASE travels with the database owner and transferring ownership of a database will transfer the ability to increase the database size.

To display information about the database sizes on a SQL Server the *sp_helpdb* command can be used:

```
use pubs
go
sp_helpdb
```

```
name     db_size  owner  dbid  created        status
-----    -------  -----  ----  ---------      ---------------
master   8MB      sa     1     Mar 2 1994     trunc.log on chkpt.
model    2MB      sa     3     Mar 2 1994     no options set
pubs     2MB      sa     4     Mar 2 1994     no options set
tempdb   2MB      sa     2     Feb 11 1995    select into/bulkcopy
```

The storage space can be displayed by using *sp_spaceused*:

```
use pubs
go
sp_spaceused
```

```
database_name  database_size  reserved  data    index_size  unused
-------------  -------------  --------  ------  ----------  ------
pubs           2MB            1984KB    1350KB  62KB        572KB
```

The space usage of the databases on a server can be easily checked with the SQL Enterprise Manager as shown in Figure 2-10.

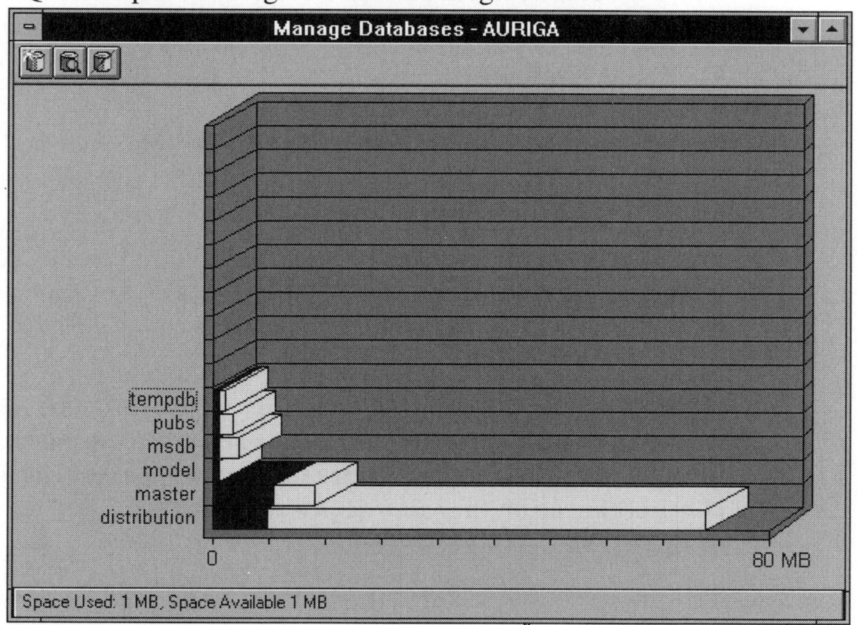

Figure 2-10 Checking Databases with the SQL Enterprise Manager

The size of the database will increase in 2Mb units by default, with 1Mb being the minimum increase that can be specified. If there is a problem with disk space then SQL Server will allocate as much space as possible in 0.5Mb units.

```
alter database pubs
on datadev1 = 5
```

This will increase the size of the *pubs* database by 5Mb, on the device *datadev1*. The *sysusages* system table will be updated with a new row for each new allocation of space.

Hint: Always back up the master database once ALTER DATABASE has been used.

2.4.13 Increasing Transaction Log Sizes

As a good database administrator you will no doubt have your transaction logs placed on separate devices to your databases. To increase the size of these logs you can also use the ALTER DATABASE statement:

```
alter database pubs
on logdev1 = 4
```

This will increase the *pubs* transaction log available space by 4 Mb. The SQL Enterprise Manager can be used to increase the size of a database and its transaction log as shown in Figure 2-11.

If the log is not on a separate device, the space for it can be increased by creating a new device, using the ALTER DATABASE statement and moving the transaction log across using *sp_logdevice*.

Hint: Using CREATE DATABASE with the LOG ON extension immediately puts the entire transaction log onto the separate device. Using *sp_logdevice* will only affect future space allocation and will leave the initial pages of the log on the same device as the data.

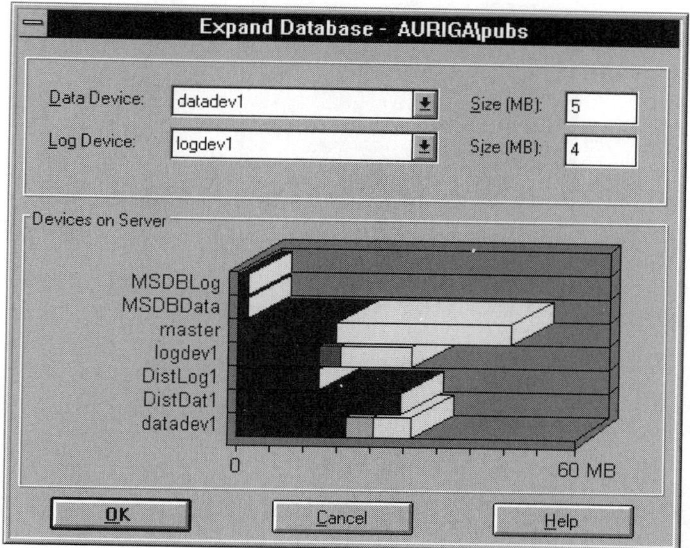

Figure 2-11 Increasing the Size of a Database with the SQL Enterprise Manager

2.4.14 Dropping a Database

A database can only be dropped by the SA login id or the database owner and these permissions cannot be transferred. Before dropping it, ensure that the database is not in use by anyone and that it is not open for reading or writing:

```
drop database pubs
```

This will drop the *pubs* database. Multiple databases can be dropped in the same statement by separating the database name by a comma:

```
drop database pubs, customers, orders
```

Again, always back up the master database after dropping a database. Once dropped, all references to the database will be removed from the system tables.

Dropping a database with the SQL Enterprise Manager tool will double check the action as shown in Figure 2-12.

Figure 2-12 Dropping a Database Confirmation with the SQL Enterprise Manager

In this case we declined as we wish to use the *pubs* database further on in the book!

Databases which have been marked as suspect or offline can now be dropped using the DROP DATABASE command.

2.5 SUPPORT FOR REMOVABLE MEDIA

SQL Server version 6.0 now supports the use and creation of databases for distribution on removable media such as CD-ROM, optical drives or floppy disks. The minimum database size has now been reduced to 1 MB which makes it suitable for most floppy media, although the 1MB size is not all available for data storage as the SQL Server system tables will automatically reserve 512K .

2.5.1 Creating a Removable Database

There are a number of points that the developer will need to be aware of whilst creating a database for later distribution on removable media:

- The database should be spread onto three devices, splitting up the transaction log, system catalog and data tables. The device for the transaction log is only used during development, and once development is completed the stored procedure *sp_certify_removable* is run to truncate the transaction log and move it to the system device, dropping the log device.
- The database must be created on a new device.
- No other databases can use the devices to ensure that the removable media database sits in contiguous sections.

To assist in this process there is a new system stored procedure *sp_create_removable* which will automatically create three or more devices as needed. Once created then database development can start but the following rules need to be adhered to:

- Do not make any reference to objects outside of the database as these will not be available once the database has been distributed.
- Do not add any users to the database and do not change user permissions.
- Keep the use of devices exclusive.
- Keep the SA login id as the owner of the database.

2.5.2 Preparing the Database for Distribution

Once you are happy with your database the next step is to prepare it for distribution. The *sp_certify_removable* stored procedure is run which undertakes a number of checks on the database:

- Checks there are no user-created users on the database.
- Checks there are no user-created permissions in the database and that the SA login id is the database owner.
- Ensures that the database is contiguous.
- Truncates the transaction log and drops the transaction log device.
- Sets the database to *offline*.

The AUTO option can be used with *sp_certify_removable* to automatically assign all object ownership to the SA login id and drop any user created database users and their permissions.

2.5.3 Installing a Removable Database

The stored procedure *sp_dbinstall* is run to install the database. Whether the database is left on the removable media or copied onto the local hard disk it will always remain read only. Once installed the database will need to be put *online* by using the *sp_dboption* stored procedure.

2.5.4 Setting a Database Online or Offline

The database can either be online and available or offline and unavailable. Prior to removing the database it must be placed offline, once offline it will not be automatically recovered at start time. Failure to turn the database offline will result in uncomfortable operating system error messages at a later date:

```
sp_dboption customer, offline, FALSE
sp_dboption customer, offline, TRUE
```

Setting *offline* to be FALSE will set the database *online* and setting *offline* to TRUE will set the database *offline*.

2.5.5 Deinstalling a Removable Database

To deinstall the database the stored procedure *sp_dbremove* is run. The *dropdev* extension updates *sysdevices* by removing all devices which were used exclusively by that database.

Hint: Always backup the master database after using *sp_dbremove*.

---

3 Defining Database Objects

3.1 INTRODUCTION

In this chapter we will look at the *Data Definition Language* (DDL) capabilities in SQL Server. DDL is used to define various objects that are typically found in a SQL Server database and include:

- Tables
- User-defined datatypes
- Views
- Indexes
- Defaults
- Rules
- Stored Procedures
- Triggers

In this chapter we will discuss tables, user-defined datatypes and views in detail. Indexes, defaults, rules, constraints, stored procedures and triggers will be explored in later chapters. The definition of these objects is held as data in system tables which reside in the master or user databases and is often known as *metadata* as it is data that describes data.

In the next chapter we will look at the *Data Manipulation Language* (DML) capabilities in SQL Server. DML is used manipulate the data that can be found in the tables in a SQL Server database. This is often user data although the DML can just as easily and consistently manipulate the metadata.

3.2 METHODS FOR CREATING SQL SERVER OBJECTS

Historically, database management systems used proprietary languages to create their data structures, such as tables and views. The disadvantage of this approach is that every database management system had its own unique way of describing its metadata and querying its user data. Knowledge gained using one product was not easily transportable to another product. In an effort to solve this problem, the standards bodies defined a standard language for relational database management systems known as *Structured Query Language* (SQL). This is defined by the American National Standards Institute (ANSI), the International Standards Organization (ISO) and standards bodies from other countries. It is adopted by most vendors of relational database management systems.

SQL Server is no exception and provides its version of SQL known as *Transact-SQL*. It should be noted that the SQL Standard is a *living* document and the standard is continually evolving. At any given point in time the database management system vendors will support subsets of the standard to greater or lesser extents. So beware, the SQL provided by vendors is likely to be very similar but not completely so.

Creating objects and manipulating them in SQL Server can be achieved with Transact-SQL and the examples in this book use Transact-SQL. It is not the only method, however, as SQL Server provides graphical tools that can also be used. Which method is used is a matter of preference and we will introduce both approaches. Database administrators who are already familiar with earlier versions of SQL Server will be used to typing Transact-SQL. New users will probably find that it is easier to use the SQL Enterprise Manager. The authors themselves, although familiar with Transact-SQL and other vendors' SQL implementations, are finding it more and more productive to use the SQL Enterprise Manager.

It should be noted that the Transact-SQL definitions of objects can be reverse-engineered from the objects themselves irrespective of the method used to create them.

Hint: It is worth keeping a textual Transact-SQL definition of the metadata present in SQL Server. This provides a means of recreating lost definitions and can form part of the database documentation as well as being a tool for recreating definitions on other database management systems.

The tools used to create and manage objects include:

- ISQL – a utility that accepts individual Transact-SQL statements or groups of them known as *batches*.
- ISQL/w – a graphical tool that accepts individual Transact-SQL statements or groups of them and also provides a graphical representation of the way SQL Server executes queries (a query plan). ISQL/w can be thought of as a graphical superset of ISQL and thus ISQL will not be described separately.
- SQL Enterprise Manager – a graphical tool that can be used for creating and managing SQL Server objects instead of using textual Transact-SQL statements. It is also used to administer local and remote servers.

There are other graphical tools such as the SQL Performance Monitor that are used for monitoring the performance of a database. These are discussed in other chapters.

3.2.1 ISQL/w

ISQL/w can be invoked by mouse clicking on the ISQL/w icon in the SQL Server for Windows NT program group or its equivalent can be mouse clicked from within the SQL Enterprise Manager. When it is selected the user is presented with a window as shown in Figure 3-1.

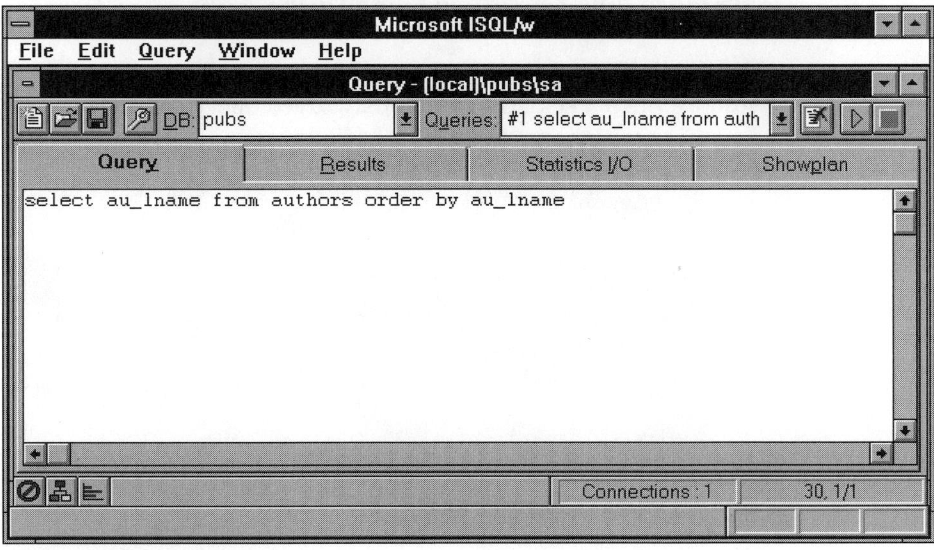

Figure 3-1 The ISQL/w Window

The window consists of a number of *tabs* such as the *Query* tab and the *Results* tab. The Transact-SQL queries can be entered by selecting the *Query* tab and the results of the Transact-SQL are then displayed in the *Results* tab. Once a query has been entered it can be executed by either clicking on the Execute button or entering ALT+X or CTRL+E. How the query is executed is down to personal preference, however, if the keyboard has just been used to enter a Transact-SQL statement it is often more convenient to enter ALT+X or CTRL+E. If the *Query* window contains a number of Transact-SQL statements and one statement or part of one needs to be executed, the relevant text can be selected prior to execution and only the selected text will be executed.

Both the Transact-SQL statements and the results can be cut, copied, pasted or printed. They can also be saved to a file which is useful if Transact-SQL statements are regularly executed.

Hint: If another database management system is being migrated to SQL Server, SQL statements from that database held in a text file can be edited to make them consistent with Transact-SQL and then easily executed by opening them as a saved query. As table and view definitions are generally similar across many relational database management systems a dump of the old definitions into a file for later execution under SQL Server can save much time, typing and minimize mistakes.

The familiar *New*, *Open* and *Save* buttons can be used to open a new query window, open an existing previously saved query and save a query.

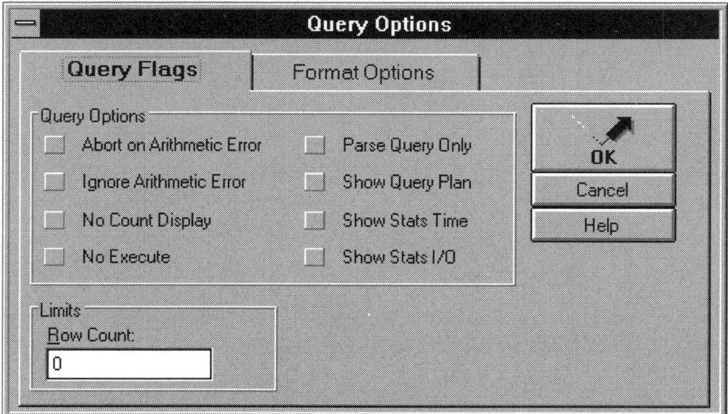

Figure 3- 2 The Query Options Window

The button to the right of the *New*, *Open* and *Save* buttons sets the *query options*, for example whether the count of affected rows is displayed after query execution. Figure 3-2 shows the Query Options window.

As can be seen, many options can be set that determine the way in which a Transact-SQL statement will execute and display output. The query execution mode, the graphical showplan and the graphical statistics buttons are very useful when investigating query performance and are described in Chapter 9.

To the right of the *query options* button are list boxes to allow the desired database and query to be selected. To the right of the list boxes are three buttons that control query execution: *Remove Current Query*, *Execute Query* and *Cancel Query*. In the lower left hand side of the window can be found another three buttons that are useful when analyzing queries. Using these, the *Execution Mode*, *Showplan* and *Statistics I/O* can be switched on and off.

3.2.2 SQL Enterprise Manager

The SQL Enterprise Manager, newly introduced with SQL Server 6.0, can be selected by clicking the SQL Enterprise Manager icon in the SQL Server for Windows NT program group. When it is selected the user is presented with a window as seen in Figure 3-3.

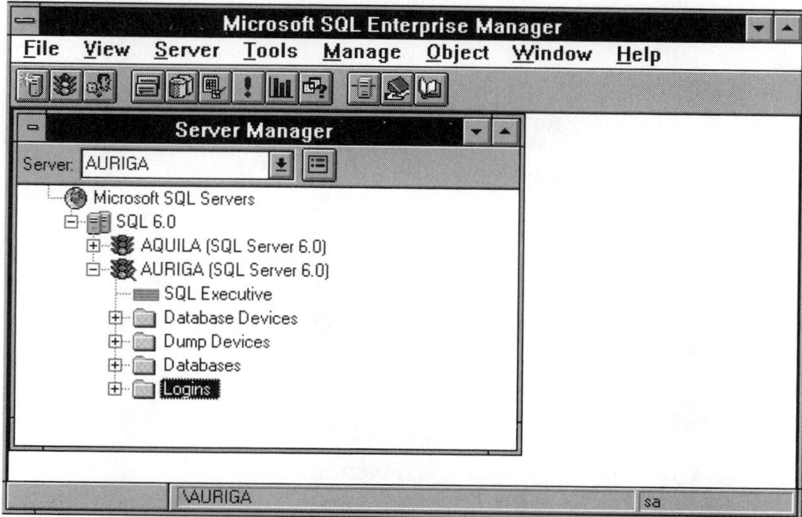

Figure 3-3 The SQL Enterprise Manager Window

There are various routes into the SQL Enterprise Manager to arrive at a window that will allow the database administrator to perform a particular task and we shall explore some of these. As can be seen from Figure 3-3, there are a number of menu options labeled *File*, *View*, *Server*, *Tools*, *Manage*, *Object*, *Window* and *Help*.

The *File*, *Window* and *Help* menus have the usual Windows NT functions such as *exiting*, *tiling* and providing assistance and the *View* menu has the function of turning off the *Toolbar* and *Status* displays. The *Status* display can be found at the bottom of the window and contains information such as the number of connections.

The *Server* menu allows server related functions to be performed such as server *configuration* and *registration*. The *Tools* menu provides access to various tools such as the *Task Scheduler* and the *Query Analyzer*.

The *Manage* menu displays a list of objects that can be managed such as *Logins, Databases, Tables, Indexes* and the *Object* menu provides a means of performing various activities against database objects such as *renaming, dropping* and specifying *permissions* and *dependencies*.

Below the menu bar is a set of buttons to make it easy and quick to activate various functions. From left to right these buttons allow the database administrator to:

- Register Servers
- Start/Stop/Pause Servers
- Manage Logins
- Manage Databases
- Schedule Tasks
- Manage Alerts
- Investigate Activity on a Server
- Analyze Queries
- Display the Replication Topology
- Manage Replication Publishing
- Manage Replication Subscribing

All in all, the SQL Enterprise Manager provides all the capabilities and more of the *SQL Administrator* and *SQL Object Manager* provided in previous versions of SQL Server.

Perhaps, though, most database administrators will tend to use point and click to manage objects by selecting and clicking on the various objects in the graphical display. The basic approach is to click on objects displaying a '+' to expand them and to double click the underlying objects to manage them. Figure 3-3 shows an unexpanded server named AQUILA and an expanded server named AURIGA. Figure 3-4 shows the display after the database folder has been expanded. The *Server Legend* has also been displayed.

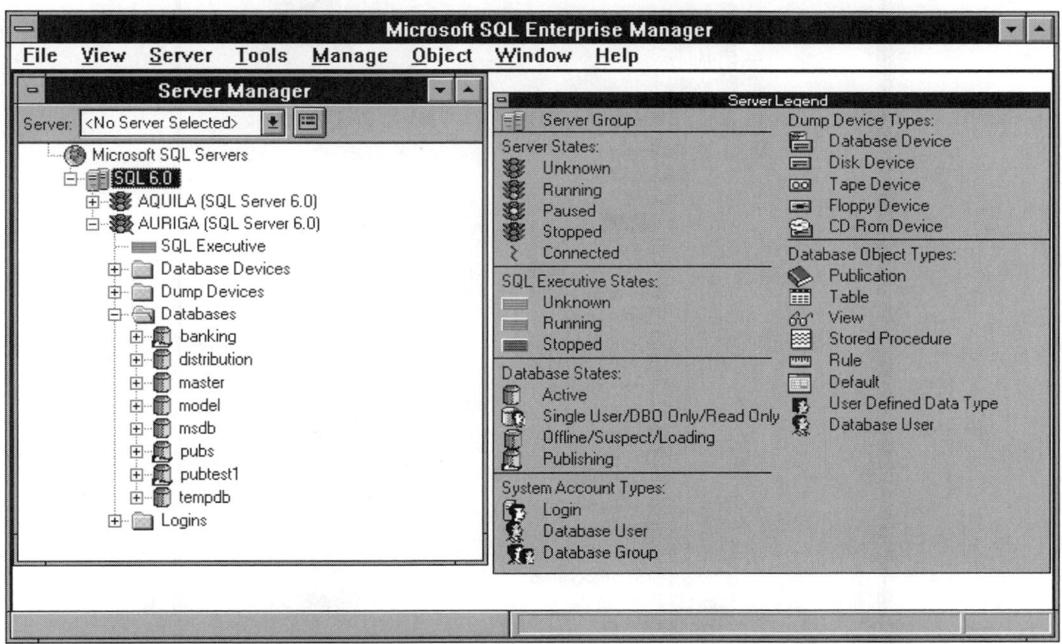

Figure 3-4 An Expanded Database Folder

This process can be continued as shown in Figure 3-5. The *pubs* database has been expanded and then its objects and its tables have also been expanded in a *drill down* fashion.

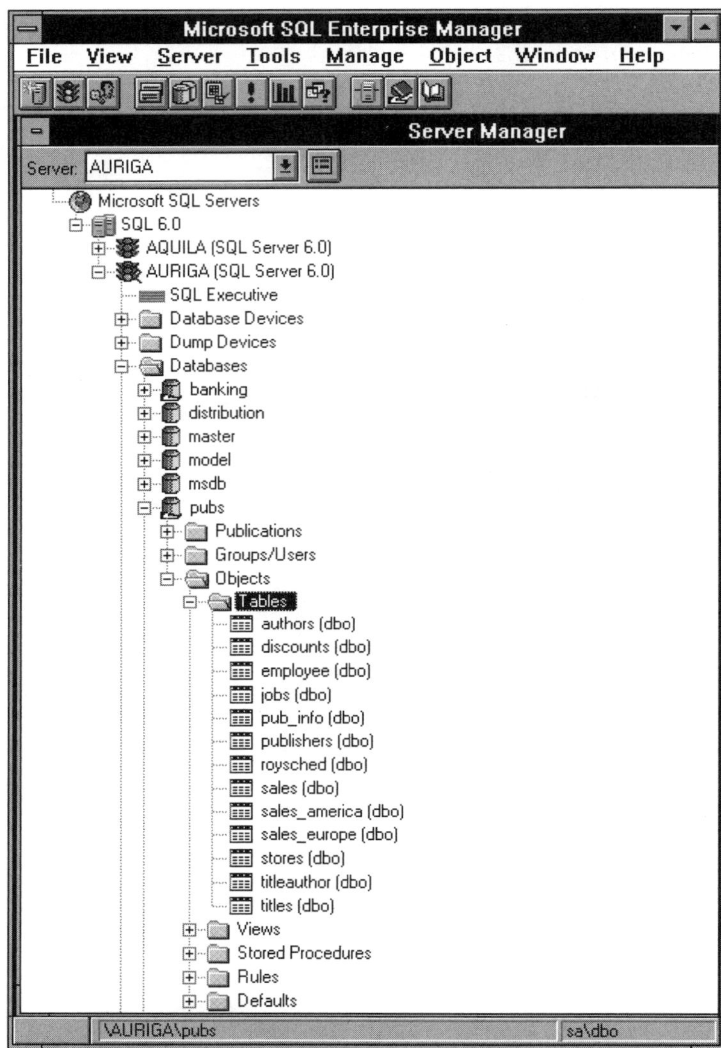

Figure 3-5 The Database Objects for the Pubs Database

The objects in the hierarchy can be double clicked or the right mouse button can be used with the desired object selected. For example, if the employee table is double clicked a window appears that enables the database administrator to manage the attributes of that table as shown in Figure 3-6.

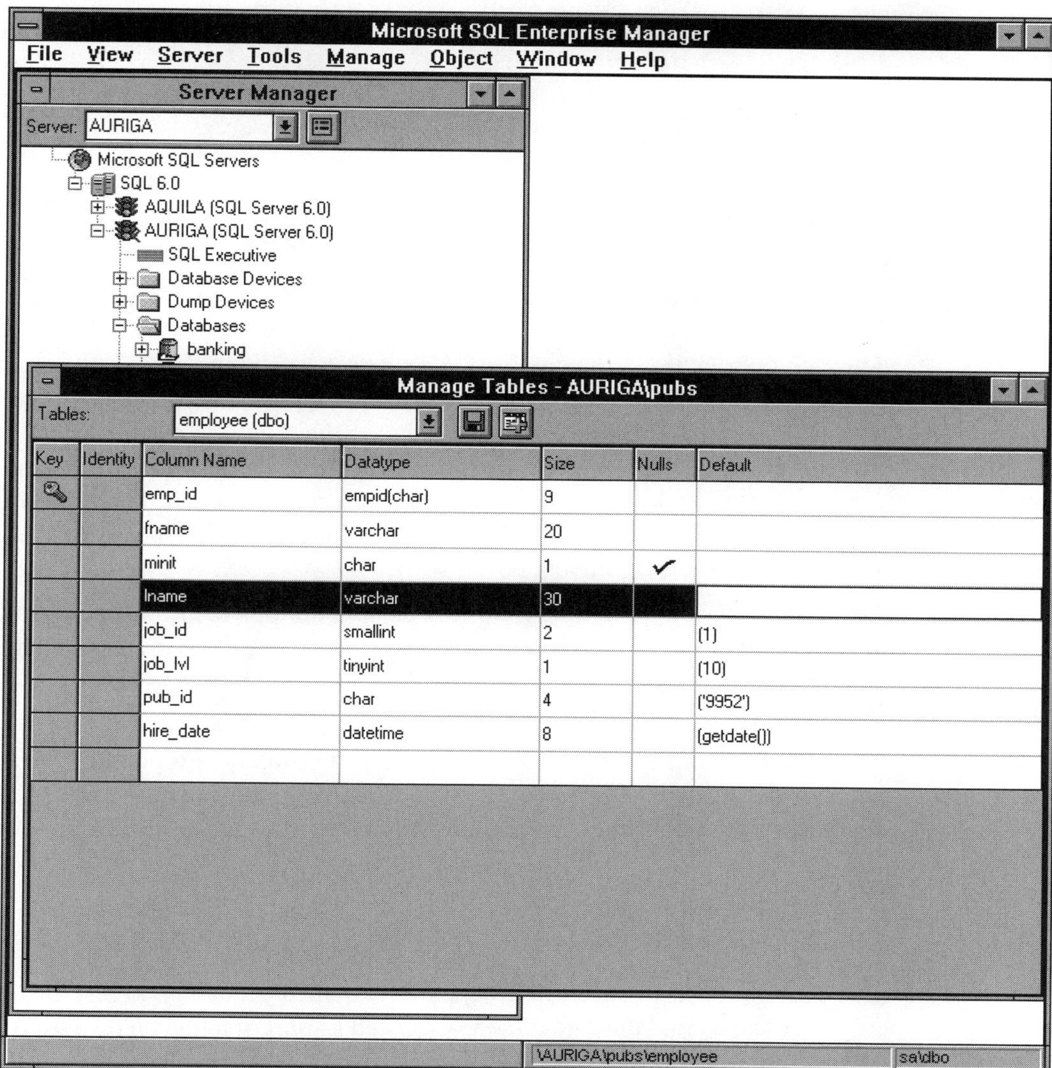

Figure 3-6 The SQL Enterprise Manager Manage Tables Window

If an object is selected by clicking the right mouse button a pop-up menu appears which shows the operations that can be performed on that object. The operations that are displayed depend on the objects selected, but for a table they include:

- Edit
- Drop
- Rename
- Indexes
- Triggers
- Permissions
- Dependencies

The *Edit* option allows the database administrator to alter certain table characteristics and is equivalent to double clicking the table with the left mouse button. The *Drop* and *Rename* option allows the database administrator to drop or rename the table. The *Indexes* and *Triggers* options display information on a table's indexes and triggers and the *Permissions* and *Dependencies* options allow the database administrator to manage permissions on the table and view the table's dependencies.

There are also *New Table* and *Generate Scripts* options to allow a new table to be created or provide options to allow the database administrator to create textual Transact-SQL scripts definitions for the selected table or various other objects.

The SQL Enterprise Manager is a very powerful graphical tool and we will look at various aspects of it as we discuss the definition of various objects. A detailed description can be found in the Microsoft SQL Server documentation.

3.3 CREATING TABLES, USER-DEFINED DATATYPES & VIEWS

At a point in the database design cycle it becomes necessary to physically create the tables that until now merely existed as part of a logical design. By now a number of decisions should have been made, such as:

- The tables that are to be created in the database
- The columns that comprise the tables
- The datatypes and size of those columns
- Default values for columns

- Legal values for columns
- The columns in a table that constitute the primary key
- The columns in a table that constitute the foreign keys
- The views that are to be created in the database
- The indexes that are to be created on a table

Assuming this is so, let us now look at how tables, user-defined datatypes and views are created. We will look at how to create these objects in Transact-SQL and the SQL Enterprise Manager.

3.3.1 Creating Tables

Tables are created with the CREATE TABLE Transact-SQL statement. Basically, it is simply a case of naming the table and listing the columns that it will be comprised of:

```
create table titleauthor
       (au_id      id,
       title_id    tid,
       au_ord      tinyint    null,
       royaltyper int         null)
```

The only items that need to be considered initially are the names ofthe columns and the table itself, the datatypes of the columns and whether the columns allow *null* values. There are a number of other attributes concerning, for example, database integrity and we shall meet these in later chapters.

In the above example the datatypes are *tinyint, int, id* and *tid*. Tinyint and int are known as *system-supplied datatypes* whereas id and tid are known as *user-defined datatypes*. These will be described shortly. By default, a column is flagged as *not null* which means that a value for the column must be supplied when the row is inserted into the table if a default value is not bound to the column or user-defined datatype or specified in some other way. If the attribute null is specified, the row can be inserted without a value in the column. Null represents the fact that a value is missing or undefined.

Hint: A table cannot contain more than 250 columns.

If a table is created, in what database does it reside? Prior to creating a table a database context must be created, that is, the database environment must be declared. In Transact-SQL this is achieved with the USE statement:

```
use pubs
```

Tables may now be created in the *pubs* database. To create a table in another database another USE statement can be issued:

```
use oldpubs
```

Tables can be created on specific device segments and this was discussed in Chapter 2.

The two classes of datatypes used for table columns are *system-supplied* and *user-defined* datatypes. As their names suggest, system-supplied datatypes are those datatypes that SQL Server provides whereas user-defined datatypes are defined by the database designer using the system-supplied datatypes as building blocks. User-defined datatypes can be specific to a database or, if they are created in the *model* database, to all the databases in a SQL Server.

How to create user-defined datatypes will be discussed shortly. First it is worth looking at the system-supplied datatypes of which there are the following groups:

- Character
- Binary
- Integer
- Floating Point
- Exact Numeric
- Money
- Date and Time
- Miscellaneous

Character

This datatype typically holds alphanumeric characters but can also hold symbols. Character datatypes can be specified as char(n), varchar(n) and text. A char(n) column can be considered to be a fixed length of 'n' characters up to a maximum of 255. If a char(80) column is created it will take up 80 bytes whether 8 or 80 characters are stored in it.

In contrast, a varchar(n) column can be considered to be a variable length of 'n' characters up to a maximum of 255. If a varchar(80) column is created it will take up only the space it actually needs. If 8 characters are stored in it, considerably less space will be used than if 80 characters are stored in it. Hence, a varchar column could save disk space if a column contained text that varied in length throughout the table, such as a person's lastname. However, a varchar(n) datatype requires more processing than its char(n) brother.

Text datatypes are less commonly used. They can hold up to 2^{31} - 1 characters which is rather a large number, in fact it is 2,147,483,647!

In SQL Server 6.0, the synonyms *character* and *character varying* can be used instead of *char* and *varchar* respectively.

Binary

This datatype holds binary data. In a similar way to the character datatypes described above there are binary(n), varbinary(n) and image datatypes. The binary(n) and varbinary(n) datatypes can hold a maximum of 255 bytes. The image datatype can hold up to 2,147,483,647 bytes of binary data! Binary is not that common in the commercial world, image even less so, although the growing spread of multimedia may change this as the image datatype can be used to hold multimedia objects.

Integer

The integer datatype is very common. It holds integer numbers, the range being determined by the actual integer datatype in use. The integer datatypes available are *tinyint*, *smallint* and *int*. The tinyint datatype can hold integers that fall in the range 0 to 255. The smallint datatype can hold integers in the range 2^{15} - 1 to - 2^{15}, that is, 32,767 to - 32,768. The int datatype can hold integers that the range 2^{31} - 1 to - 2^{31}, that is, 2,147,483,647 to - 2,147,483,648.

In SQL Server 6.0, the synonym *integer* can be used instead of *int*.

Floating Point

This datatype typically holds floating point numbers. Floating point datatypes can be specified as *real* or *float*. The real datatype uses four bytes of storage to hold floating point numbers in the range 3.4E-38 to 3.4E+38 with seven digit precision. The float datatype uses eight bytes of storage to hold floating point numbers in the range 1.7E-308 to 1.7E+308 with fifteen digit precision.

In SQL Server 6.0, the synonym *double precision* can be used instead of *float*.

Exact Numeric

The datatypes decimal and numeric are newly introduced with SQL Server 6.0. They can hold values in the range 10^{38} -1 and - 10^{38}.

A *precision* can be specified in the form decimal[(p[,s])] or numeric[(p[,s])] where *p* is the precision, that is the maximum number of digits stored on both sides of the decimal point and *s* is the *scale* which is the maximum number of digits stored right of the decimal point. For example, decimal (5,2) could represent 345.66.

The storage requirements of the exact numeric datatype depend on the precision, for example, a precision of 5 would need 4 bytes of storage whereas a precision of 15 would need 8 bytes of storage.

Money

This datatype typically holds money amounts. Money datatypes can be specified as *smallmoney* or *money*. The smallmoney datatype uses four bytes of storage to hold money amounts in the range +214,748.3647 to -214,748.3648 with ten-thousandth of a monetary unit precision. The money datatype uses eight bytes of storage to hold money amounts with ten-thousandth of a monetary unit precision in the range +922,337,203,685,477.5807 to -922,337,203,685,477.5808.

Date and Time

This datatype typically holds dates and times. The datetime datatype uses two four byte integers - one for the number of days since the base date and one for the number of milliseconds since midnight. The base date is defined as January 1st, 1900. There is also a smalldatetime datatype which uses four bytes of storage to hold date and time values with an accuracy of one minute.

Miscellaneous

There are a number of datatypes that cannot be conveniently grouped with the others. The *bit* datatype can hold the values 0 or 1 and uses a single bit to do so. The *timestamp* datatype holds a value that is updated every time a row containing it is updated or when the row is initially inserted. It holds a value that is unique in the database. Its main use is as a check to see if a row has been changed since a user last read it and is used in conjunction with *browse mode*. The *sysname* datatype is actually a user-defined datatype but is made available by *SQL Server*. It is used in *SQL Server*'s system tables and is created as varchar(30) not null.

Tables can also be created using the SQL Enterprise Manager. To do so double click the *Tables* folder for the database in which you want to create the table. In the *Manage* window ensure that *<New Table>* appears in the *Tables* Box. Add column names and datatypes. System-supplied and user-defined datatypes are listed in the properties box when the *Datatype* cell is clicked. The length of the datatype, whether nulls are allowed and defaults can also be specified. An example is shown in Figure 3-7.

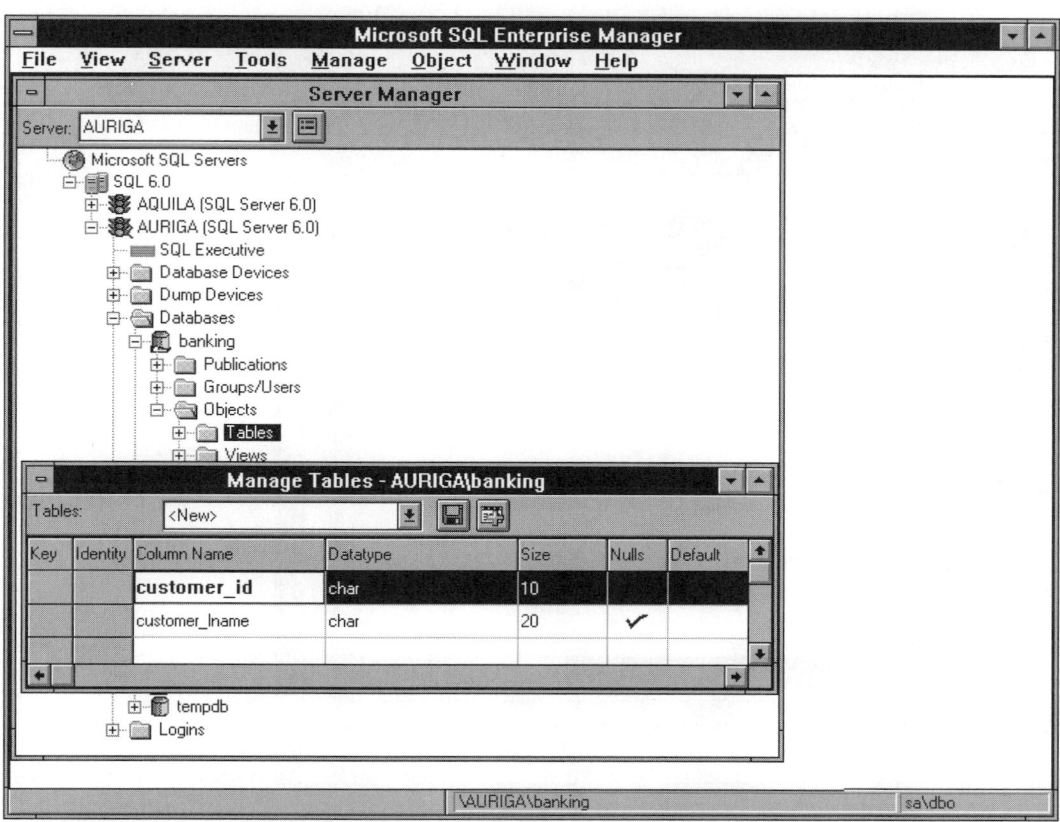

Figure 3-7 Using the SQL Enterprise Manager to Create a Table

3.3.2 Altering Tables

Once a table is created it may be subsequently altered with the ALTER TABLE Transact-SQL statement. There is little than can be done with the ALTER TABLE statement other than to add new columns to the table, for example:

```
alter table titles
    add best_seller_flag    char(1)    null
```

All of the system datatypes mentioned previously may be used with the exception of *bit*. The null attribute must be present otherwise what value would this new column take for rows that have already been inserted in the database?

Unfortunately, it is not possible currently in SQL Server to drop columns from a table or alter the characteristics of an existing column other than database integrity features which will be dealt with in Chapter 6.

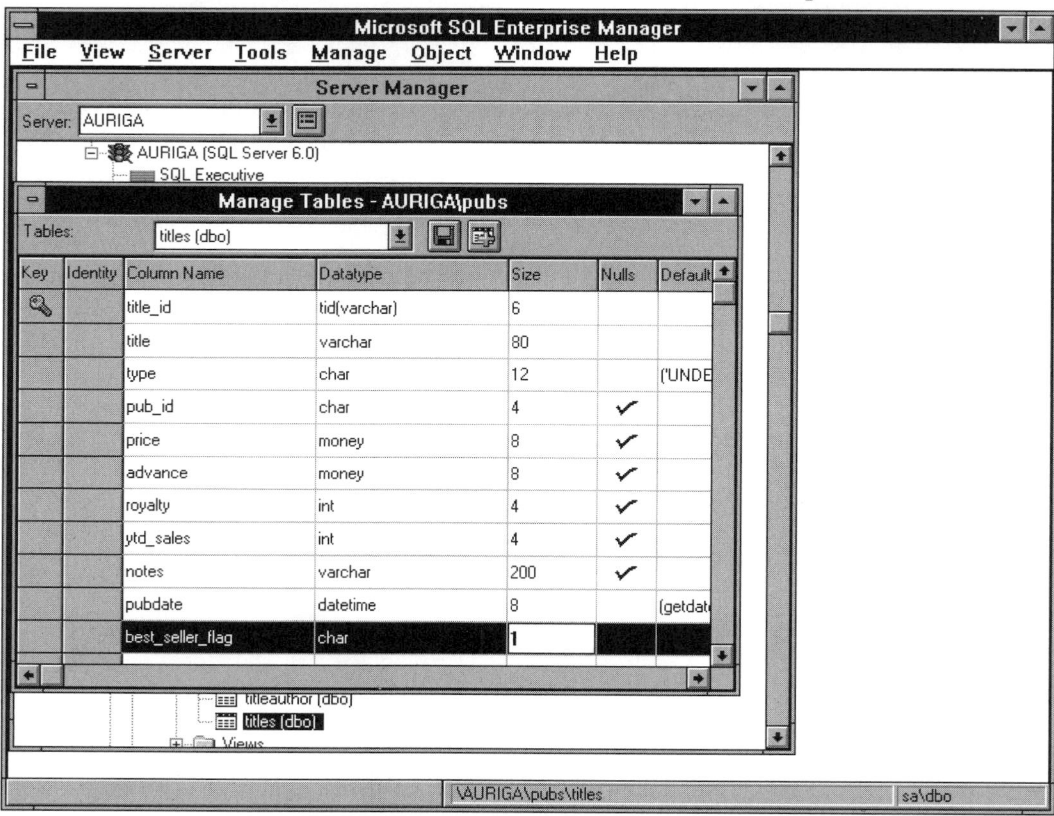

Figure 3-8 Adding a New Column to a Table

To add a column to an existing table using the SQL Enterprise Manager is merely a matter of appending to the columns displayed in the *Manage Tables* window that is displayed after double clicking the *Tables* folder. Adding a new column to a table is shown in Figure 3-8.

3.3.3 Renaming Tables

Occasionally it may become necessary to change the name of a table. This is accomplished with the system stored procedure *sp_rename*:

```
sp_rename authors, writers
```

Care should be taken when using this stored procedure as other objects that are based on the table and refer to it by name such as a view will be affected. They may appear to work fine but once SQL Server attempts to recompile the object a failure will occur. It is best to change any objects that depend on the table immediately after the name is changed.

To find which objects are dependent on the table use the *sp_depends* system stored procedure or click the right mouse button on the table name and then select *Dependencies* from the pop-up menu in the SQL Enterprise Manager as shown in Figure 3-9. To rename the table click the right mouse button on the table name and then select *Rename* from the pop-up menu.

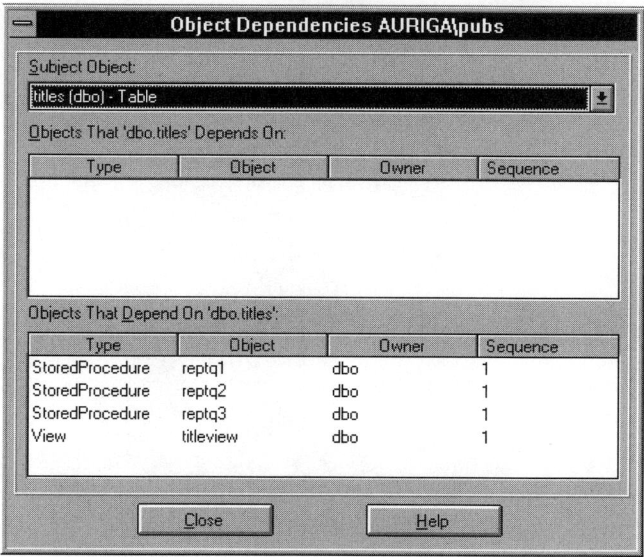

Figure 3-9 Checking Table Dependencies

3.3.4 Copying Tables

Often a number of tables inside a database have similar definitions and so the ability to copy a table's structure is useful. There are a number of methods of achieving this varying in ease of use and functionality. If the original table was created from a Transact-SQL script held in a file then this file can be modified and executed using ISQL/w to create the new table. If no script file is available then one can be generated with the script generation facility in the SQL Enterprise Manager.

If the right mouse button is clicked on the table name and then *Generate SQL Scripts* selected from the pop-up menu in the SQL Enterprise Manager, the scripts window appears as shown in Figure 3-10. The table whose Transact-SQL script is to be generated can be chosen along with the attributes of the table that can also be generated, such as permissions which are described in Chapter 10. The resulting Transact-SQL script file can be modified and executed using ISQL/w to create the new table.

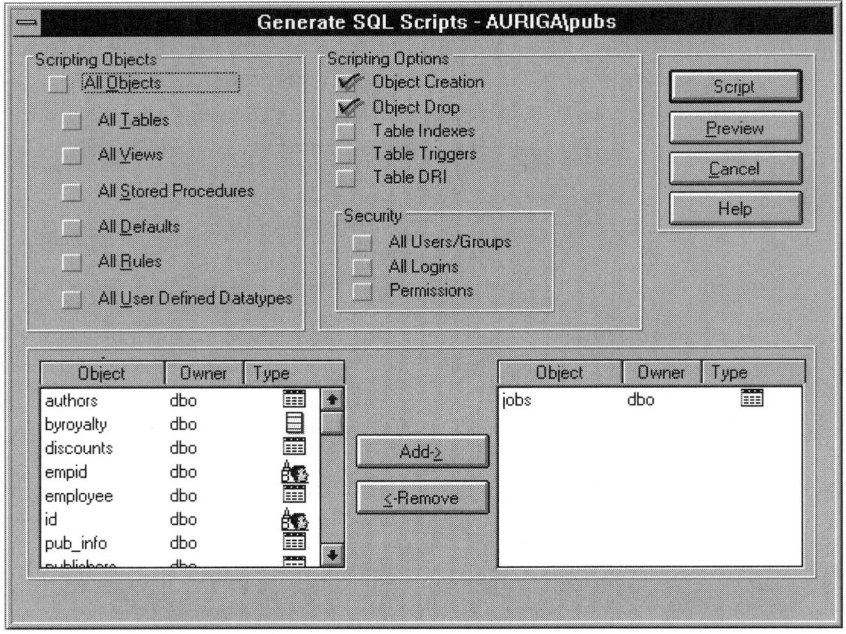

Figure 3-10 The Generate SQL Scripts Window

Copying user data between tables and files is usually performed using the *Bulk Copy Program (BCP)* utility or *SQL Transfer Manager* as described in Chapter 10.

3.3.5 Dropping Tables

To drop a table the DROP TABLE statement is used. This removes the table from the database and also any indexes or triggers created on the table as well as any permissions. No user can be accessing the table while it is being dropped. Disk space used by the table and its indexes will be released to be used by other database objects as required:

```
drop table authors
```

The SQL Enterprise Manager can be used to drop a table. To do so click the right mouse button on the table name and then select *Drop* from the pop-up menu.

Care should be taken when dropping tables as other objects that are based on the table and refer to the table by name, such as a view, will be affected.

3.3.6 Showing Table Details

A common requirement is to display details about a table, perhaps its columns or its indexes or maybe the space that it uses. There are a number of system stored procedures that are useful in this respect and the main ones are shown below.

```
sp_help

Name         Owner        Object_type
---------    ---------    -------------
titleview    dbo           view
authors      dbo           user table
discounts    dbo           user table
publishers   dbo           user table
roysched     dbo           user table
sales        dbo           user table
stores       dbo           user table
                 :
                 :
```

This is a widely used system stored procedure that displays information about objects in the current database. Entered with no parameters it will display information about all the objects in the current database. This is useful when a list of tables is required. The table name can also be entered as a parameter:

```
sp_help authors

Name        Owner           Object_type
---------   ---------       ------------
authors     dbo             user table

Data_located_on_segment     When_created
----------------------      ----------------
default                     24 Oct 1994 16:25

Column_name    Type     Length  Nulls  Default_name   Rule_name
---------      -------  ------  -----  ----------     ---------
au_id          id       11      0      (null)         (null)
au_lname       varchar  40      0      (null)         (null)
au_fname       varchar  20      0      (null)         (null)
phone          char     12      0      phonedflt      (null)
address        varchar  40      1      (null)         (null)
city           varchar  20      1      (null)         (null)
state          char     2       1      (null)         (null)
zip            char     5       1      (null)         ziprule
contract       bit      1       0      (null)         (null)

index_name index_description                      index_keys
---------- ----------------------------           -----------------
auidind    clustered,unique located on default    au_id
aunmind    nonclustered located on default        au_lname,au_fname

(1 row(s) affected)

keytype object      related_object object_keys   related_keys
------  -------     -----------    ------------  ---------------
primary authors     - none -       au_id,*,*,*,* *,*,*,*,*,*,*,*
foreign titleauthor authors        au_id,*,*,*,* au_id,*,*,*,*,*
```

The above display is from SQL Server 4.21.

The *sp_depends* system stored procedure can be used to display details about the dependencies associated with a table:

```
sp_depends authors
In the current database the specified object is referenced by
the following:
object                   type
-----------------------  ------------
dbo.titleview            view
dbo.reptq2               stored procedure

(1 row(s) affected)
```

The *sp_spaceused* system stored procedure can be used to display details about the space usage associated with a table:

```
sp_spaceused titles

name      rows    reserved  data    index_size unused
-----     -----   -------   -----   ---------  -------
titles    18      48KB      4KB     8KB        36KB
```

Catalog Stored Procedures

There are also a number of *catalog stored procedures* that have been added to SQL Server to provide a consistent catalog interface which is compatible with Microsoft Open Database Connectivity (ODBC). Microsoft Open Database Connectivity is discussed in Chapter 12. These include *sp_tables, sp_columns, sp_fkeys, sp_pkeys, sp_statistics* and *sp_table_privileges* and these can be used to obtain information about tables and their attributes. The *sp_tables* catalog stored procedure is shown below. It can be used to display a list of tables and views:

```
sp_tables

table_qualifier  table_owner table_name  table_type  remarks
---------------  ----------- ----------  ----------  -------
pubs             dbo         authors     TABLE       (null)
pubs             dbo         discounts   TABLE       (null)
pubs             dbo         publishers  TABLE       (null)
```

Using the SQL Enterprise Manager to Display Table Details

The SQL Enterprise Manager can be used to display table details. To do so click the right mouse button on the table name and then select *Edit* from the pop-up menu. We have already seen this window with respect to seeing the columns and their attributes in the table. However, if we select *Advanced*

Features, we can easily display information about integrity constraints. This is shown in Figure 3-11. Information on other aspects of the table, such as its indexes and triggers, can be displayed by clicking the right mouse button on the table name and then selecting the appropriate option from the pop-up menu.

The information displayed in these windows, most people would agree, is an order of magnitude more readable than the output from the system stored procedures!

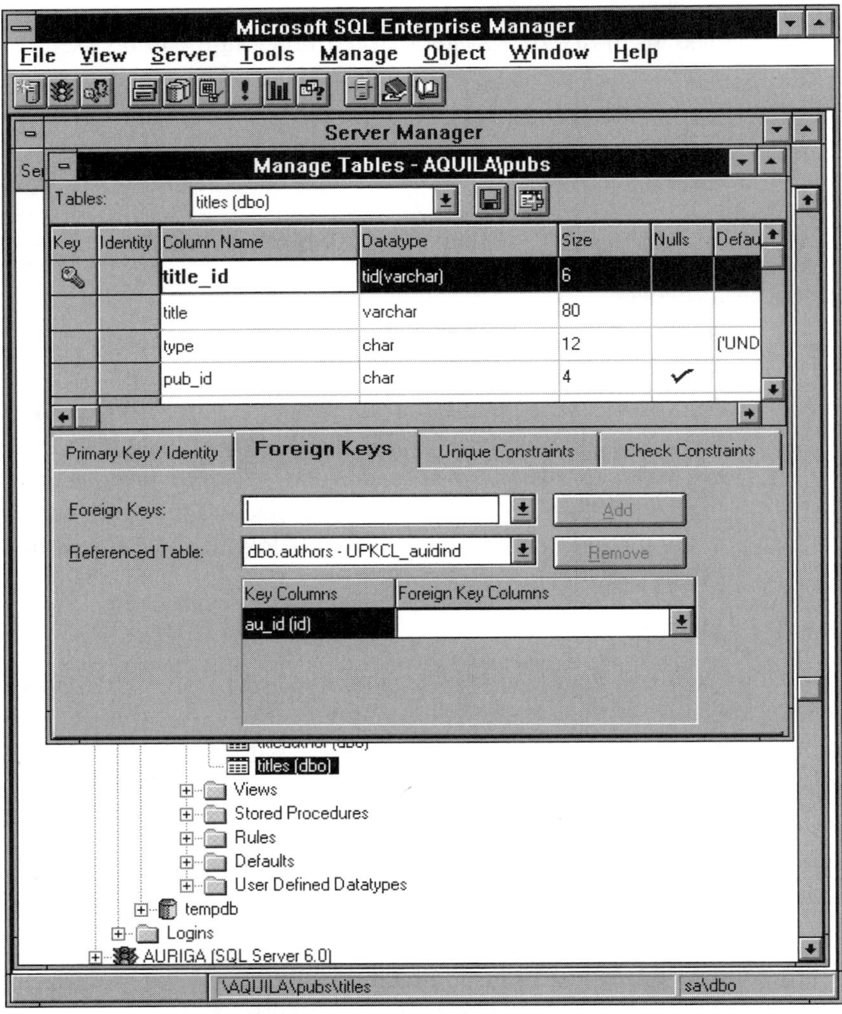

Figure 3-11 Displaying Table Information

3.3.7 Temporary Tables

In the same way that applications have used scratch files over the years, SQL Server provides the capability to create scratch tables. These are known as *temporary tables* and can be used to hold data that need not exist after the session in which they were created finishes. Temporary tables are created in the database known as *tempdb* and this is done merely by prefixing the table name in the CREATE TABLE statement with a # character, as shown below:

```
create table #not_for_long
    (id_num          char (9),
    num              integer)
```

In previous versions of SQL Server, temporary tables were only visible from the session in which they were created and were known as *local* temporary tables. SQL Server 6.0, however, also supports temporary tables that can be used by other sessions. These are known as *global* temporary tables. To create a global temporary table the # sign is merely replaced with ##:

```
create table ##can_u_see_me
    (id_num          char (9),
    num              integer)
```

3.3.8 Creating Views

Views are virtual tables which do not physically hold data, but rather act like a *window* into the physical tables that were defined with the CREATE TABLE statement. Views can be created in a database with the CREATE VIEW Transact-SQL statement or the SQL Enterprise Manager. To the end-user, a view looks like a table and generally can be treated as if it were a table, however, there are some restrictions concerning the updating of views. The physical tables on which views are based are called *base* tables.

Views can contain subsets of the rows or columns found in a base table or a combination of base tables and can be used to replace often used SELECT and JOIN operations. Views may also be used to enforce security. A user may be allowed to retrieve data through a view, but not from the underlying base table. Views also provide another level of abstraction in a database as a view can hide from the user the fact that it is comprised of a number of base tables. Because of this, a database administrator can often change the definition and number of base tables in a view without the user being aware that the change has occurred.

Suppose we wish to create a view that limits the number of columns that are displayed from the authors table. Perhaps we only want to provide a view that displays the author id, last name and first name. This is shown pictorially in Figure 3-12.

AUTHORS TABLE

AU_ID	AU_LNAME	AU_FNAME	PHONE	ADDRESS	CITY	STATE	ZIP	CONTRACT
472-77-451	ENGLAND	KEN	415 765-9966	23 ROPLEY BOULEVARD	PALO ALTON	NH	98776	1
986-54-7332	STANLEY	NIGEL	415 751-8809	2 EPSOM DRIVE	SAN SPA	NH	98776	1
556-44-8799	CASH	MIKE	913 223-5566	11 OXFORD PLACE	LOS BOOKOS	KS	66726	1
:	:	:		: :	:	:	:	

AU_ID	AU_LNAME	AU_FNAME
472-77-451	ENGLAND	KEN
986-54-7332	STANLEY	NIGEL
556-44-8799	CASH	MIKE
:	:	:

AUTHORS_NAMES VIEW

Figure 3-12 The authors_names View

To see how such a view is created in Transact-SQL we need to look at the definition of the table first:

```
create table authors
    (au_id          id,
    au_lname        varchar(40)         not null,
    au_fname        varchar(20)         not null,
    phone           char(12),
    address         varchar(40)         null,
    city            varchar(20)         null,
    state           char(2)             null,
    zip             char(5)             null,
    contract        bit)
```

Creating this view is simple, we merely have to list the columns we require:

```
create view authors_names
    as select au_id, au_lname, au_fname
    from authors
```

If we used a Transact-SQL SELECT statement to query this view we would see the following data returned:

```
au_id          au_lname        au_fname
-----------    ------------    -----------
172-32-1176    White           Johnson
213-46-8915    Green           Marjorie
664-21-9866    Hobbs           Lilian
238-95-7766    Carson          Cheryl
557-23-7623    England         Ken
648-92-1872    Blotchet-Halls  Reginald
672-71-3249    Yokomoto        Akiko
876-56-3221    Stanley         Nigel
    :
    :
998-72-3567    Ringer          Albert

(26 row(s) affected)
```

In fact, we can change the names of the columns if we wish. This can be useful if we are creating views for different groups of users who might use different names to refer to the same piece of data:

```
create view authors_names
    (badge_num,
    last_name,
    first_name)
    as select au_id, au_lname, au_fname
    from authors
```

We would now see more meaningful columns headings:

```
badge_num      last_name       first_name
----------     ----------      --------
172-32-1176    White           Johnson
213-46-8915    Green           Marjorie
    :
    :
(26 row(s) affected)
```

The above views have limited the number of columns from the authors table that can be seen. Suppose that we often wanted to see details for authors who lived in the state of New Hampshire. We would use a select statement in the view to filter the rows returned.

```
create view authors_names_nh
    as select au_id, au_lname, au_fname
    from authors
    where state = "NH"
```

A Transact-SQL SELECT statement using this view would in fact now only return three rows:

```
au_id          au_lname       au_fname
-----------    -----------    -----------
664-21-9866    Hobbs          Lilian
557-23-7623    England        Ken
876-56-3221    Stanley        Nigel

(3 row(s) affected)
```

If we wished to rename the columns again we would create the view in the following way:

```
create view authors_names_nh
    (badge_num,
    last_name,
    first_name)
    as select au_id, au_lname, au_fname
    from authors
    where state = "NH"
```

View can contain mathematical expressions such as the following view that displays the difference between the high royalty range and low royalty range from the *roysched* table:

```
create view royalty_range_size
    (id,
    range_size)
    as select title_id, (hirange - lorange)
    from roysched
```

Built-in functions may also be used:

```
create view royalty_range_size
    (range_size)
    as select avg(hirange - lorange)
    from roysched
```

Often views are defined as the combination of more than one base table. If we look at the sales table we find a column *stor_id* which identifies a book store. However, it is merely a four character identifier. If we look at the stores table we also find the stor_id column together with the name and address of the store. We can create a view that combines these two tables using the stor_id column. The definitions of the base tables are as follows:

```
create table sales
    (stor_id      char(4),
    ord_num       varchar(20),
    date          datetime,
    qty           smallint,
    payterms      varchar(12),
    title_id      tid)

create table stores
    (stor_id      char(4),
    stor_name     varchar(40)  null,
    stor_address  varchar(40)  null,
    city          varchar(20)  null,
    state         char(2)      null,
    zip           char(5)      null)
```

Suppose we wish to create a view that lists the quantity of titles sold to each store displaying the store name, the quantity sold, the sale date and the title id of the book. We could use the following Transact-SQL statement to create the view that performed a join of the two base tables sales and stores:

```
create view sales_by_store
    (store_name,
    quantity_sold,
    date_of_sale,
    book_id)
    as select stor_name, qty, date, title_id
    from sales, stores
    where sales.stor_id = stores. stor_id
```

This view will return the following data:

```
store_name          quantity_sold date_of_sale           book_id
---------------     ------------  -----------------      ---------
Barnum's            75            13 Sep  1985  0:00 PS2091
Barnum's            50            24 May  1987  0:00 PC8888
News & Brews        10            14 Sep  1985  0:00 PS2091
News & Brews        40            15 Jun  1987  0:00 TC3218
News & Brews        20            15 Jun  1987  0:00 TC4203
News & Brews        20            15 Jun  1987  0:00 TC7777
                    :
```

```
Eric the Read Books  5            14 Sep  1985  0:00 BU1032
Fricative Bookshop  35            21 Feb  1988  0:00 BU2075
Fricative Bookshop  15            28 Oct  1987  0:00 BU7832
Fricative Bookshop  10            12 Dec  1987  0:00 MC2222

(21 row(s) affected)
```

We can now see a meaningful store name instead of an identifier, however, we still have to suffer an identifier for the title. We can enhance the view so it also combines rows from the titles table. This is called a 3-way join as three tables are joined. The definition of the titles base table is as follows:

```
create table titles
    (title_id   tid,
    title       varchar(80)   not null,
    type        char(12),
    pub_id      char(4)       null,
    price       money         null,
    advance     money         null,
    royalty     int           null,
    ytd_sales   int           null,
    notes       varchar(200)  null,
    pubdate     datetime)
```

The view definition now becomes:

```
create view sales_by_store
    (store_name,
    quantity_sold,
    date_of_sale,
    book_name)
    as select stor_name, qty, date, title
    from sales, stores, titles
    where
    sales.stor_id = stores.stor_id and
    sales.title_id = titles.title_id
```

This view will return the following data:

```
store_name quantity_sold date_of_sale      book_name
---------- ------------- ----------------  ----------------
Barnum's   75            13 Sep 1985 0:00  Is Anger the Enemy?
Barnum's   50            24 May 1987 0:00  Secrets of Silicon Valley
           :
           :

(21 row(s) affected)
```

Again, we can filter the number of rows. If we are only interested in book stores in Ohio we can specify a WHERE clause on the SELECT statement:

```
create view sales_by_store_oh
    (store_name,
    quantity_sold,
    date_of_sale,
    book_name)
    as select stor_name, qty, date, title
    from sales, stores, titles
    where
    sales.stor_id = stores.stor_id and
    sales.title_id = titles.title_id and
    state = "OH"
```

The SQL Enterprise Manager can be used to create views. To do so double click the *Views* folder for the database in which you want to create the view.

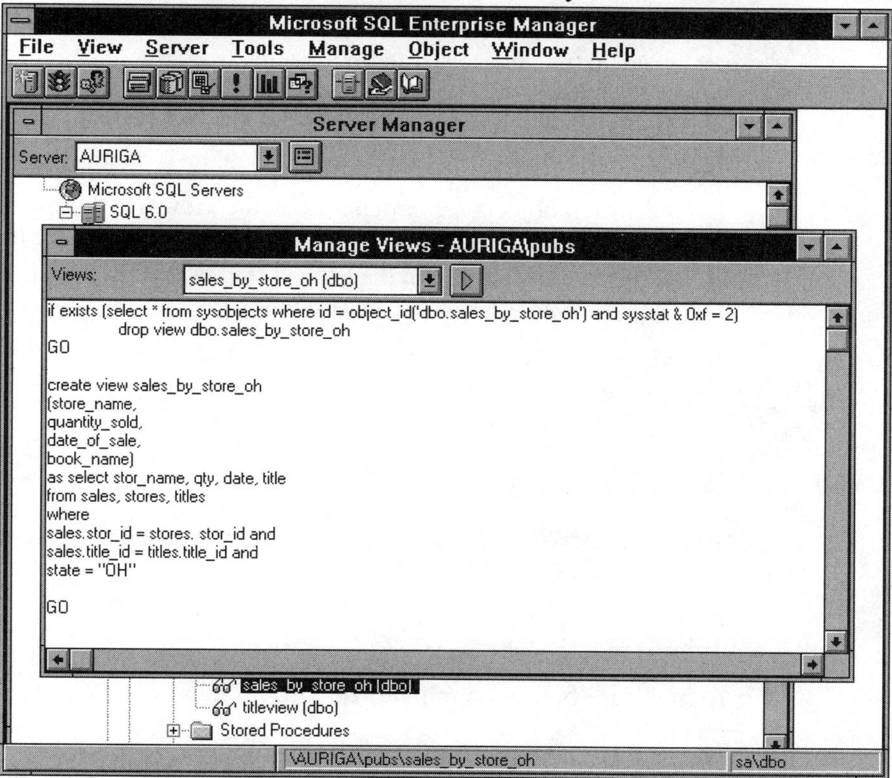

Figure 3-13 Editing a View Definition

In the *Manage* window ensure that *<New>* appears in the *Views* Box. The definition of the view can be added into the text area.

The SQL Enterprise Manager can also be used to edit existing views. To do so double click the name of the view. A textual Transact-SQL view definition will then be displayed as in Figure 3-13 which can be edited and the Transact-SQL then executed. Of course, this can also be achieved using ISQL/w but the operation is more easily performed in the SQL Enterprise Manager.

3.3.9 Renaming Views

Like a table, it may become necessary to change the name of a view. This is accomplished with the system stored procedure *sp_rename*:

```
sp_rename sales_by_store_oh, sales_by_store_ohio
```

Care should be taken when using this stored procedure as other objects that are based on the view and refer to the view by name such as another view will be affected. They may appear to work fine but once SQL Server attempts to recompile the object a failure will occur. It is best to change any objects that depend on the view immediately after the name is changed.

To find which objects are dependent on the view use the *sp_depends* system stored procedure or in the SQL Enterprise Manager click the right mouse button on the view name and then select *Dependencies* from the pop-up menu. This is a similar display as was shown for the table in Figure 3-9.

To rename the view click the right mouse button on the view name and then select *Rename* from the pop-up menu.

3.3.10 Dropping Views

To drop a view the DROP VIEW statement is used. This removes the view from the database:

```
drop view authors_names
```

The SQL Enterprise Manager can be used to drop a view. To do so click the right mouse button on the view name and then select *Drop* from the pop-up menu.

Care should be taken when dropping views as other objects that are based on the view and refer to the view by name will be affected.

3.3.11 Showing View Details

A common requirement is to display details about a view. There are a number of system stored procedures that are useful in this respect, the main ones being *sp_help* and *sp_helptext*:

```
sp_help authors_names

Name                Owner               Type
------------------  ----------------    ----------
authors_names       dbo                 view
Data_located_on_segment                 When_created
-----------------------                 ---------------
not applicable                          6 Nov 1994 18:53
Column_name  Type     Length  Nulls  Default_name  Rule_name
-----------  -------  ------  -----  ------------  ----------
au_id        id       11      0      (null)        (null)
au_lname     varchar  40      0      (null)        (null)
au_fname     varchar  20      0      (null)        (null)
No defined keys for this object.
```

The system stored procedure *sp_helptext* can be used to display the definition of the CREATE VIEW Transact-SQL statement:

```
sp_helptext authors_names

text
----------------------------------------------------------
create view authors_names as select au_id, au_lname, au_fname from authors

(1 row(s) affected)
```

Using the SQL Enterprise Manager to Display View Details

The SQL Enterprise Manager can be used to display details about a view. To do so click the right mouse button on the view name and then select the desired information category such as *Permissions*.

3.3.12 Extra Considerations when Dealing with Views

On the whole, views can be treated like tables. There are, however, a few idiosyncrasies that need to be mentioned. The first is concerned with the updating of data in a view. If the select statement that is used to define the view contains a *subquery* it is not possible to update the view. Subqueries will be covered in Chapter 3. Other idiosyncrasies involve the use of functions such as SUM and the GROUP BY clause. Care is also needed with the use of *outer joins* in a view. The GROUP BY clause and outer joins are also covered in Chapter 3.

3.3.13 User-Defined Datatypes

As discussed in Chapter 3, SQL Server provides a number of system-supplied datatypes. In addition, SQL Server enables a database designer to define his or her own datatypes known as *user-defined datatypes*. This is achieved with the *sp_addtype* system stored procedure. In practice, this provides the capability to give frequently used datatypes in the database more meaningful names. It does not provide the capability to define *abstract datatypes* such as, for example, map co-ordinates. Using *sp_addtype* is very simple. The name of the user-defined datatype is specified together with its system-supplied datatype and, optionally, whether it can hold null values:

```
sp_addtype badge_number, 'char(8)', 'not null'
sp_addtype height, tinyint, null
```

Note that the parentheses and the space in the not null in the first example generate a requirement to use single quotation marks. This can be irritating trying to remember to use single quotation marks for different datatypes. It may be easier to use single quotation marks all the time for consistency:

```
sp_addtype height, 'tinyint', 'null'
```

Once a user-defined datatype has been defined it can be used in a table definition:

```
create table employee
    (badge         badge_number,
    last_name      char(20)        not null,
    first_name     char(20)        not null)
```

If required, the null and not null option of the user-defined datatype can be overridden in the table definition:

```
create table employee
    (badge         badge_number    null,
    last_name      char(20)        not null,
    first_name     char(20)        not null)
```

User-defined datatypes can have defaults and rules associated with them. Defaults and rules will be discussed in Chapter 6.

User-defined datatypes can be created using the SQL Enterprise Manager. To do so double click on the *User Defined Datatypes* folder. The *Manage User-Defined Datatypes* window is displayed as shown in Figure 3-14.

Details of existing user-defined datatypes are displayed in the window and the characteristics of the new user-defined datatype can be typed in.

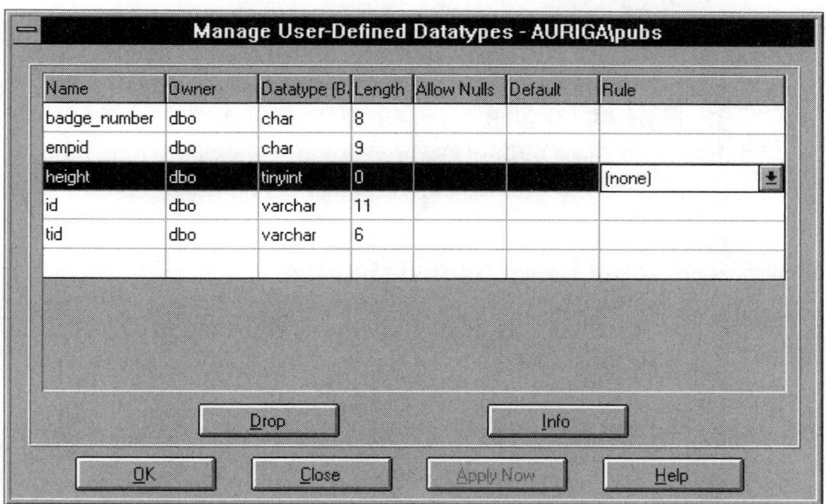

Figure 3-14 Creating User-Defined DataTypes

Hint: Suppose a user-defined datatype is going to be used in many databases. It can be defined in the *model* database. As the model database is effectively a template from which user databases are created the user-defined datatype will automatically be created in future user databases on the server. This can help to enforce a company's internal database standards.

3.3.14 Dropping User-Defined Datatypes

To remove a user-defined datatype from a database the *sp_droptype* system stored procedure can be used:

```
sp_droptype height
```

If the user-defined datatype is being used in a table definition it cannot be dropped:

```
sp_droptype  badge_number

Type is being used. You cannot drop it.
object          type     owner    column          datatype
----------      -----    ------   -------         -------------
employee        U        dbo      badge           badge_number

(1 row(s) affected)
```

User-defined datatypes can be dropped using the SQL Enterprise Manager. To do so double click on the user-defined datatypes folder. This displays the *Manage User-Defined Datatypes* window as shown in 3-14. The user-defined datatype to be dropped can be selected and the *Drop* button clicked.

3.3.15 Renaming User-Defined Datatypes

Occasionally it may become necessary to change the name of a user-defined datatype. This is accomplished with the system stored procedure *sp_rename*:

```
sp_rename badge_number, badge_no
```

SQL Server takes care of the fact that a table might be using the user-defined datatype. If the table EMPLOYEE created previously was now examined we would see the new user-defined datatype name:

```
sp_help employee

Name            Owner            Object_type
---------       ---------        --------------
employee        dbo              user table

Data_located_on_segment          When_created
-------------------              ------------------

default        11 Nov 1994 15:24

Column_name      Type      Length Nulls Default_name Rule_name
------------     --------  ------ ----- -----------  ---------
badge            badge_no  8      1     (null)       (null)
last_name        char      20     0     (null)       (null)
first_name       char      20     0     (null)       (null)
Object does not have any indexes.
No defined keys for this object.
```

The SQL Enterprise Manager may be used to rename user-defined datatypes. To rename the user-defined datatype click the right mouse button on its name and then select *Rename* from the pop-up menu.

3.3.16 Showing User-Defined Datatype Details

The *sp_help* system stored procedure can be used to display details about a user-defined datatype:

```
sp_help badge_no

Type_name    Storage_type Length Nulls Default_name Rule_name
----------   ---------    -----  ----- ----------   --------
badge_no     char         8      0     (null)       (null)
```

Information concerning user-defined datatypes can be displayed using the SQL Enterprise Manager. To do so double click on the *User Defined Datatypes* folder. This displays the *Manage User-Defined Datatypes* window as shown in Figure 3-14.

Select the required user-defined datatype and click the *Info* button. The information shown in Figure 3-15 is displayed.

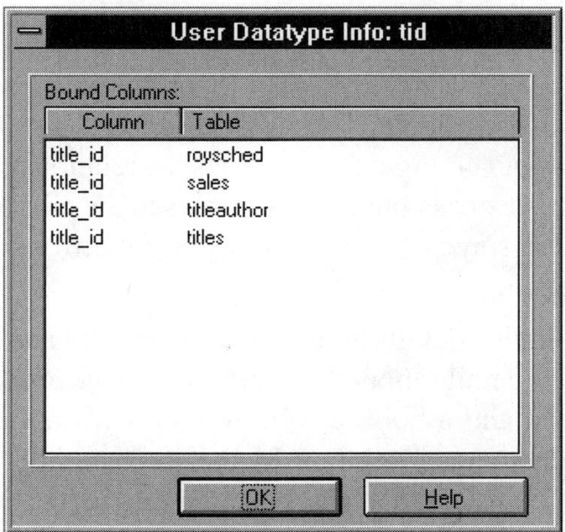

Figure 3-15 Displaying Column Binding Information for a User-Defined Datatype

3.4 THE PUBS EXAMPLE DATABASE

Now we have discussed tables, views and user-defined datatypes we can introduce the *pubs* database. This is an example database that Microsoft use in their SQL Server documentation and is an ideal database with which to demonstrate SQL Server concepts.

There are eleven tables in the pubs database (eight prior to SQL Server 6.0):

- authors
- discounts
- employee
- jobs
- pub_info
- publishers
- roysched
- sales
- stores
- titles
- titleauthor

These tables are described in detail in the *Microsoft SQL Server for Windows NT* documentation, however, Figure 3-16 shows the relationships between the tables. Note that we have occasionally added rows to the pubs database and so the results displayed in some of our examples might differ slightly from the results you might obtain.

The *authors* table contains details about the authors held in the database and the *titles* table contains details about the books held in the database. An author can write many books and a book can be written by a number of authors. Hence, there is a many to many relationship between authors and titles. This is resolved by using the *titleauthor* table which participates in a one to many relationship with the authors and titles tables. The titleauthor table also holds extra information such as the order in which the authors are named and their royalty split.

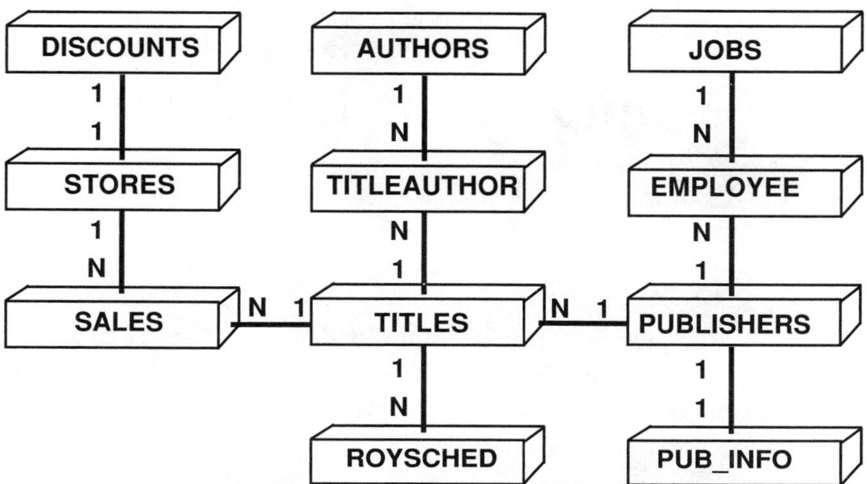

Figure 3-16 The Pubs Database

The *stores* table contains details about the book stores that stock books. A store can sell many books and a book can be sold in a number of stores. Hence, there is a many to many relationship between stores and titles. This is resolved by using the *sales* table which participates in a one to many relationship with the stores and titles tables. The sales table represents all the sales for bookstores of a given book. It also holds information such as the quantity of the book sold. Participating in a one to one relationship with stores is the *discounts* table which represents discount levels awarded to individual stores.

Participating in a one to many relationship with titles is the *publishers* table as a publisher publishes many books and participating in a one to many relationship with titles is the *roysched* table which holds royalty details. Each publisher has an entry in the *pub_info* table which holds details about the publisher and their logo in text and image datatypes.

Participating in a one to many relationship with publishers is the *employees* table representing people employed by the publisher. Each employee has a *job_id* column which relates the *jobs* table to the employee. The jobs table contains job information such as the job description.

4 Manipulating Database Data

4.1 INTRODUCTION

The previous chapter discussed elements of the *Data Definition Language* (DDL) capabilities in SQL Server. As we saw, DDL is used to define various objects that are typically found in a SQL Server database including tables and views.

In this chapter we will discuss the *Data Manipulation Language* (DML) capabilities in SQL Server. DML is used to manipulate the user data in the database, typically inserting it into tables, updating it, querying it and deleting it. Note that although we usually think of DML as manipulating user data it can also be also used to manipulate system data that is stored in SQL Server system tables.

In this chapter we will cover the following DML topics:

- Querying and sorting data
- Joining tables
- Aggregates
- Built-in functions
- Inserting data into tables
- Updating data in tables
- Removing data from tables

The intention of this chapter is not be a definitive reference book on using the Transact-SQL SELECT statement, rather it is to give the reader a taste of some of the possibilities. For a definitive text, the *Microsoft SQL Server Transact-SQL Reference* manual should be consulted. Advanced topics such as multi-statement Transact-SQL and stored procedures will be covered in the next chapter.

It was seen in Chapter 3 that the SQL Enterprise Manager is used to manipulate database objects and it is frequently used for this purpose. It is not, however, used as frequently to manipulate user data. Typically this would be performed with ISQL/w or perhaps another tool such as Microsoft Access or a programming language such as Visual Basic or Microsoft Visual C++. In this chapter we will give our examples in Transact-SQL executing under ISQL/w.

4.2 BASIC RELATIONAL TERMS

This chapter will not attempt to describe relational concepts as it is assumed that the reader will be familiar with these. However it is worth just revising a few points.

In relational databases, such as SQL Server, data is stored in tables. Examples of tables are those in the pubs database including the titles and authors tables. Usually, a table represents some real-world object that is relevant to a company's business. A table may contain a number of rows that are instances of table elements. For example, the authors table contains a number of rows, one for each author. The rows consist of columns, which are data elements and represent attributes of the table element. For example, the authors table consists of a number of columns that are attributes of the entity author, such as the author's name and address.

In the relational model, a column or number of columns is designated as a *primary key*. A row must be uniquely identified by its primary key, therefore, a primary key value cannot occur more than once in a table. This also means that a primary key cannot contain null values, that is, a column that constitutes a primary key must contain a value. In the titles table, the primary key is the unique identifier of a book represented by the column title_id. Each book's title_id value is unique throughout the database. No two books may have the same value for title_id.

Columns in one table usually do not also appear in another table, other than to establish a relationship between tables. These columns are called *foreign keys*. In the pubs database, the sales table contains a column title_id. This is a foreign key and establishes a relationship between the titles table and the sales table.

Other common terms that are often found in the relational world are *selection*, *projection* and *join*. A selection operation forms a subset of the rows in a table usually by applying some condition such as the authors who live in New Hampshire. A projection operation removes columns from the rows being retrieved by forming a stream of rows with only specified columns present.

A *join*, probably one of the most powerful relational operators, allows data from more than one table to be combined. Typically, data from more than one table is joined by relating certain meaningful columns from the tables. In the pubs database a common operation would be the joining of the title and sales tables over the title_id column to produce a report about book sales.

4.3 QUERYING AND SORTING DATA

The most frequently used Transact-SQL keyword is almost certainly SELECT. It is used to query the data in the database tables and to return subsets of the rows and columns based on specified criteria. In this chapter we will explore the many select options. First, though, we must choose the database which holds the data we need to query. To do this we simply issue the Transact-SQL USE statement:

```
use pubs
```

Once we have selected our database we can begin to query data. The simplest form of the SELECT statement is that used to query all the rows and all the columns in a table:

```
select * from discounts

discounttype        stor_id    lowqty    highqty    discount
-----------------   ------     -----     -------    --------
Initial Customer    (null)     (null)    (null)     10.5
Volume Discount     (null)     100       1000       6.7
Customer Discount   8042       (null)    (null)     5.0

(3 row(s) affected)
```

Care should be taken with case sensitivity. Suppose we had entered the table name as DISCOUNTS:

```
select * from DISCOUNTS

Msg 208, Level 16, State 1
Invalid object name 'DISCOUNTS'.
```

SQL Server would not have found a table of this name. The * character is a short hand way of saying that all the columns in the table should be displayed. All the columns could be listed but for a large table this might be tedious.

Hint: When writing production applications it is good practice to list all the columns. This assists in documentation and makes the SELECT statement independent of any future addition of columns to the table.

4.3.1 Working with Columns

To limit the number of columns returned we can list them instead of using the * character:

```
select discounttype, stor_id, discount from discounts

discounttype        stor_id      discount
---------------     ------       ---------
Initial Customer    (null)       10.5
Volume Discount     (null)       6.7
Customer Discount   8042         5.0

(3 row(s) affected)
```

Note that the full name of a database object such as a column is more complex than that implied above. It is in fact:

```
database_name.owner_name.table_name.column_name
```

The fuller version is used to resolve ambiguity and if there is none a shorter version can be used. If we are working in the context of a specific database and in that database the table names are unique, we can refer to a column by *table_name.column_name*. If we are only manipulating one table then we can dispense with *table_name*. We can also dispense with *table_name* if we are dealing with multiple tables and the column name is unique amongst these tables.

A column name like *stor_id* might not be meaningful to some users, so a SELECT statement has syntax to allow the columns to be given different names:

```
select discounttype, stor_id bookstore, discount from discounts
```

```
discounttype        bookstore    discount
---------------     ---------    --------
Initial Customer    (null)       10.5
Volume Discount     (null)       6.7
Customer Discount   8042         5.0

(3 row(s) affected)
```

Text can be added to the SELECT statement:

```
select 'The Answer is: ', discounttype, stor_id bookstore,
discount from discounts
              discounttype         bookstore   discount
------------  -----------------    ---------   --------
The Answer is: Initial Customer    (null)      10.5
The Answer is: Volume Discount     (null)      6.7
The Answer is: Customer Discount   8042        5.0

(3 row(s) affected)
```

Even mathematical expressions can be placed in the list of columns:

```
select discounttype, stor_id bookstore, discount,
discount * 1.75 from discounts

discounttype        bookstore   discount
----------------    ---------   --------    -------
Initial Customer    (null)      10.5        18.375
Volume Discount     (null)      6.7         11.725
Customer Discount   8042        5.0         8.75

(3 row(s) affected)
```

As before, we can name the column but this time we have more than one word in the column name so we must enclose it in single quotation marks:

```
select discounttype, stor_id bookstore, discount,
discount * 1.75 'Inc UK VAT' from discounts

discounttype        bookstore   discount    Inc UK VAT
----------------    ---------   --------    -------
Initial Customer    (null)      10.5        18.375
Volume Discount     (null)      6.7         11.725
Customer Discount   8042        5.0         8.75

(3 row(s) affected)
```

To readers from the United Kingdom this column will be familiar!

So far we have always returned every row from the table. We might wish to remove duplicate rows. We can do this with the DISTINCT keyword. Suppose we wish to list the *title_id* column from the *sales* table to obtain a list of books that have been sold:

```
select title_id from sales

title_id
--------
PS2091
PS2091
PS2091
MC3021
MC3021
BU1032
PS2091
BU1032
BU1111
BU2075
BU7832
MC2222
PC1035
PC8888
PS1372
PS2106
PS3333
PS7777
TC3218
TC4203
TC7777

(21 row(s) affected)
```

SQL Server displays 21 rows but some of them, for example PS2091 appear more than one time. We can use the DISTINCT keyword to remove multiple occurrences of a value from the *title_id* column:

```
select distinct title_id from sales

title_id
--------
BU1032
BU1111
BU2075
BU7832
```

```
MC2222
MC3021
PC1035
PC8888
PS1372
PS2091
PS2106
PS3333
PS7777
TC3218
TC4203
TC7777

(16 row(s) affected)
```

Now only 16 rows have been returned and they are all distinct values.

4.3.2 Working with Rows

To return a subset of the rows in a table based on some criteria the WHERE clause is used. This is a very common form of the SELECT statement and there are many operators that can be used in the WHERE clause.

Simple WHERE Conditions

By using the operators supplied with SQL Server various conditions may be specified on a SELECT statement. Simple comparisons may be performed as in the following examples:

```
select title from titles where title_id = 'MC2222'

title
-----------------------------------------------
Silicon Valley Gastronomic Treats

(1 row(s) affected)

select title_id from sales where qty > 30

title_id
--------
PS2091
BU2075
```

```
PC8888
TC3218

(4 row(s) affected)

select title_id from sales where qty/1.175 < 30

title_id
--------
PS2091
PS2091
MC3021
MC3021
BU1032
PS2091
BU1032
BU1111
BU2075
BU7832
MC2222
PC1035
PS1372
PS2106
PS3333
PS7777
TC4203
TC7777

(18 row(s) affected)
```

Specification of a range of values may be made with the BETWEEN operator:

```
select title_id, qty from sales where qty between 10 and 15

title_id      qty
--------      ---
PS2091        10
MC3021        15
BU1032        10
BU7832        15
MC2222        10
PS3333        15

(6 row(s) affected)
```

Note that BETWEEN 10 AND 30 includes the values 10 and 15:

```
select title_id, qty from sales where qty not between 10 and 50

title_id       qty
--------       ---
PS2091         75
PS2091         3
BU1032         5

(3 row(s) affected)
```

A check can be made to see if a value is in a list. A common example is US states:

```
select pub_name from publishers where state in ('NH', 'MA')

pub_name
----------------------
New Moon Books

(1 row(s) affected)

select pub_name from publishers where state
not in ('NH', 'DC')

pub_name
----------------------
New Moon Books
Algodata Infosystems

(2 row(s) affected)
```

Simple text matching is provided:

```
select title_id, title from titles where title like '%oo%'

title_id  title
-------   --------------------------------------------
BU1111    Cooking with Computers: Surreptitious Balance Sheets
MC3026    The Psychology of Computer Cooking
TC3218    Onions, Leeks, and Garlic: Cooking Secrets of the
          Mediterranean

(3 row(s) affected)
```

In this example the % wildcard is used which represents any string of zero or more characters.

A column that allows NULL values can be tested to see if a NULL value is present:

```
select title from titles where price is null

title
--------------------------------------------
The Psychology of Computer Cooking
Net Etiquette

(2 row(s) affected)
```

More Complex WHERE Conditions

Simple WHERE clauses can be combined with the logical operators AND, OR and NOT to enable more complex SELECT statements to be written. For example, it might not be sufficient that we specify the name of a city in a WHERE clause as there may be more than one city with the same name in different states. Instead we might choose to specify the state as well as the city:

```
select pub_name from publishers where city = 'Boston' and
state = 'MA'

pub_name
-----------------------
New Moon Books

(1 row(s) affected)
```

Note that both these conditions must be true so only publishers who are based in Boston and Massachusetts are displayed. The OR logical operator can be used to display rows when any of the conditions are true as opposed to all of them being true using the AND operator. If we wished to display the publishers that were based in the state of California or the city of Washington we could use the OR operator:

```
select pub_name from publishers where city = 'Washington' or
state = 'CA'

pub_name
-----------------------
Binnet & Hardley
Algodata Infosystems

(2 row(s) affected)
```

Suppose we wished to display all the publishers except those based in California. In this case we could use the NOT operator which effectively reverses the condition following it:

```
select pub_name from publishers where not state = 'CA'

pub_name
----------------------
New Moon Books
Binnet & Hardley

(2 row(s) affected)
```

The logical operators AND, OR and NOT can be combined in a WHERE clause. Knowing which logical operator is executed first can be confusing and so the authors strongly recommend that parentheses are used to clarify the order in which the operators are evaluated.

Displaying Data in Order

The relational model does not stipulate in what order data is returned from a query unless a specific order is requested. If a specific order is not requested, the order in which the table rows are returned is undefined and is often governed by the order in which data was inserted into a table or the access method chosen by the query optimizer to retrieve it.

This fact is easily forgotten and so it is important to ask SQL Server to sort the data before returning it by the use of the ORDER BY clause:

```
select au_lname, au_fname from authors order by au_lname

au_lname          au_fname
---------------   --------
Bennet            Abraham
Blotchet-Halls    Reginald
Carson            Cheryl
DeFrance          Michel
Dull              Ann
England           Ken
Green             Marjorie
Greene            Morningstar
Gringlesby        Burt
Hobbs             Lilian
Hunter            Sheryl
Karsen            Livia
```

```
Locksley        Charlene
MacFeather      Stearns
McBadden        Heather
O'Leary         Michael
Panteley        Sylvia
Ringer          Albert
Ringer          Anne
Smith           Meander
Stanley         Nigel
Straight        Dean
Stringer        Dirk
White           Johnson
Yokomoto        Akiko
delCastillo     Innes

(26 row(s) affected)
```

In the above example, the table rows from the authors table are displayed in ascending order of their last name. Ascending order is the default but we could have explicitly specified that we wanted ascending order:

```
select au_lname, au_fname from authors order by au_lname asc
```

We could have asked for the results in descending order:

```
select au_lname, au_fname from authors order by au_lname desc
```

More than one column can be used in the ORDER BY clause:

```
select au_lname, au_fname from authors order by au_lname asc,
au_fname desc
```

In the above example the results will be sorted by ascending last name and, within the same last name, descending first name.

4.3.3 Combining Data From Multiple Tables

We have concentrated up until now on SELECT statements operating on a single table. As was mentioned in Chapter 3, it is very often the case that two or more tables must be operated on simultaneously. The idea is that the tables are combined to form a result that looks like a set of rows from one table. The operations that are often used to combine the rows from more than one table are the join and the union and these operations are described below. Another way of combining the results of more than one table is to use a subquery as described later in this chapter.

Combining Data by Joining Tables

Suppose we wished to display a list of books that each publisher publishes, containing the name of the publisher and the title of the book. These two pieces of information are not held in any one table. The publishers name is held in the *publishers* table and the title of the book is held in the *titles* table as shown from their definitions below:

```
create table publishers
    (pub_id      char(4)       not null,
    pub_name     varchar(40)   null,
    city         varchar(20)   null,
    state        char(2)       null)

create table titles
    (title_id    tid,
    title        varchar(80)   not null,
    type         char(12),
    pub_id       char(4)       null,
    price        money         null,
    advance      money         null,
    royalty      int           null,
    ytd_sales    int           null,
    notes        varchar(200)  null,
    pubdate      datetime)
```

We must combine the information in these two tables and we do this by using a join operation to bring the two tables together. How though do we know which book relates to which publisher? There must be some way of relating the rows in the two tables otherwise joining them will not produce a sensible result. There is, in each of the tables, a column named *pub_id* which is the identifier that uniquely identifies each publisher. It is this column that we will use to relate the rows from each table. Rows from each table with the same *pub_id* will be matched together:

```
select publishers.pub_id, pub_name, title
    from publishers, titles
    where publishers.pub_id = titles.pub_id

pub_id pub_name       title
-----  -------------- ------------------------------------
0736   New Moon Books You Can Combat Computer Stress!
0736   New Moon Books Is Anger the Enemy?
0736   New Moon Books Life Without Fear
0736   New Moon Books Prolonged Data Deprivation:Four Case Studies
```

```
0736    New Moon Books   Emotional Security:A New Algorithm
0877    Binnet & Hardley Silicon Valley Gastronomic Treats
0877    Binnet & Hardley The Gourmet Microwave
0877    Binnet & Hardley The Psychology of Computer Cooking
        :
        :
 (18 row(s) affected)
```

Note that the WHERE clause contains the statement that is used to relate the rows in the two tables, namely that a *pub_id* column from the row in one table must equal the *pub_id* from the row in the other table. Note that there is no need to display the *pub_id* column if that is not desired.

In this example, the columns that are used in the WHERE clause to relate the rows have the same name in both tables, namely *pub_id*. This is not always the case. Because they have the same name, mentioning just *pub_id* to name a column in the list of columns to be displayed would be ambiguous, therefore, the column name must be qualified with the table name.

The join operation can be thought of as a concatenation of rows from the publishers table with the appropriate matching rows from the titles table. It is therefore important to specify the correct relationship between the tables in the WHERE clause otherwise the wrong rows will be concatenated.

In many cases the operator that joins the table will be the equals sign (=), however, the greater than (>), greater than or equal to (>=), less than (<), less than or equal to (<=), not equal to (<> or !=), not greater than (!>) and not less than (!<) operators are also valid.

The WHERE clause, as well as containing the conditions required to relate the tables, is also likely to contain extra statements to filter the rows in the same way that rows are filtered in a single table as described previously:

```
select publishers.pub_id, pub_name, title from publishers,titles
  where publishers.pub_id = titles.pub_id and type = 'business'

pub_id  pub_name             title
------- -----------------    ------------------------------
1389    Algodata Infosystems The Busy Executive's Database Guide
1389    Algodata Infosystems Cooking with Computers: Surrepti-
                             tious Balance Sheets
0736    New Moon Books       You Can Combat Computer Stress!
1389    Algodata Infosystems Straight Talk About Computers

(4 row(s) affected)
```

The above SELECT statement will list the publishers who publish business books and the titles of those books. Note that the type column in the WHERE predicate is not qualified by a table name as it only appears in the titles table and so there is no ambiguity.

The above example is known as a *two-way join* because two tables are joined together. More than two tables can be joined together and doing this is merely a case of adding extra tables and the relevant conditions in the WHERE clause of the SELECT statement. For example, to find out information concerning the quantity of computer books sold at particular book stores the titles, sales and stores tables must be joined:

```
select stor_name, title, date, qty from stores, titles, sales
    where
         stores.stor_id = sales.stor_id and
         titles.title_id = sales.title_id and
         type = 'popular_comp'


stor_name  title                      date              qty
--------   -------------------        ---------------   ---
Bookbeat   But Is It User Friendly?   22 May 1987  0:00  30
Barnum's   Secrets of Silicon Valley  24 May 1987  0:00  50

(2 row(s) affected)
```

It is possible, in theory, to join many tables together. However, in practice doing this can adversely affect performance. Many tables must be accessed and the query optimizer must also work hard to look at the many options now available to it for efficient processing of the join. Alternative ways of formulating the query, perhaps in stages, may sometimes be preferable.

Outer Joins

Suppose we execute the join query as described previously:

```
select publishers.pub_id, pub_name, title from publishers,titles
    where publishers.pub_id = titles.pub_id
```

This join will only return rows when there exists matching publishers and titles. This is not unreasonable as a book will have a publisher and a publisher will publish a number of books. Suppose we now look at the join of the titles and sales tables:

```
select titles.title_id, date, qty from titles, sales where
titles.title_id = sales.title_id

title_id     date                       qty
---------    -------------------        ----
BU1032       14 Sep 1985   0:00         10
BU1032       14 Sep 1985   0:00         5
BU1111       11 Mar 1988   0:00         25
BU2075       21 Feb 1988   0:00         35
BU7832       28 Oct 1987   0:00         15
MC2222       12 Dec 1987   0:00         10
MC3021       14 Sep 1985   0:00         25
MC3021       14 Sep 1985   0:00         15
PC1035       22 May 1987   0:00         30
PC8888       24 May 1987   0:00         50
PS1372       29 May 1987   0:00         20
PS2091       13 Sep 1985   0:00         75
PS2091       14 Sep 1985   0:00         10
PS2091       14 Sep 1985   0:00         20
PS2091       13 Sep 1985   0:00         3
PS2106       29 May 1987   0:00         25
PS3333       29 May 1987   0:00         15
PS7777       29 May 1987   0:00         25
TC3218       15 Jun 1987   0:00         40
TC4203       15 Jun 1987   0:00         20
TC7777       15 Jun 1987   0:00         20

(21 row(s) affected)
```

It is possible that a book does not have any sales associated with it. In this case no information would be returned about the book. Only books with matching rows in the sales table would be displayed. This is probably not what we want as we may wish to also see the books that have not sold. To ensure that books that have no matching sales appear in the rows returned from the query alongside books that have matching sales we can use an *outer join*.

To specify an outer join we can use the outer join operators. A *left outer join* is represented by *= and a *right outer join* is represented by =*. A left outer join ensures that rows from the left (first) table are returned even if there are no matching rows in the right table. A right outer join ensures that rows from the right (second) table are returned even if there are no matching rows in the left table. Therefore a left outer join of the titles and sales table would return rows for books that had no sales:

```
select titles.title_id, date, qty from titles, sales where
titles.title_id *= sales.title_id

title_id     date                    qty
--------     ------------------      ----
BU1032       14 Sep 1985  0:00       10
BU1032       14 Sep 1985  0:00       5
BU1111       11 Mar 1988  0:00       25
BU2075       21 Feb 1988  0:00       35
BU7832       28 Oct 1987  0:00       15
MC2222       12 Dec 1987  0:00       10
MC3021       14 Sep 1985  0:00       25
MC3021       14 Sep 1985  0:00       15
MC3026       (null)                  (null)
PC1035       22 May 1987  0:00       30
PC6889       (null)                  (null)
PC8888       24 May 1987  0:00       50
PC9999       (null)                  (null)
PS1372       29 May 1987  0:00       20
PS2091       13 Sep 1985  0:00       75
PS2091       14 Sep 1985  0:00       10
PS2091       14 Sep 1985  0:00       20
PS2091       13 Sep 1985  0:00       3
PS2106       29 May 1987  0:00       25
PS3333       29 May 1987  0:00       15
PS7777       29 May 1987  0:00       25
TC3218       15 Jun 1987  0:00       40
TC4203       15 Jun 1987  0:00       20
TC7777       15 Jun 1987  0:00       20

(24 row(s) affected)
```

To obtain information on the columns in tables that are likely to give meaningful results if they are used as join criteria, the *sp_helpjoins* system stored procedure can be used:

```
sp_helpjoins titles, sales

first_pair
--------- ---   ------------
title_id        title_id

(1 row(s) affected)
```

Unions

Another way of combining data from multiple tables is to use the *union* operation. The union operation is not dissimilar to the operation of appending a file to another one only with the union operation we are dealing with relational tables. Suppose that instead of one sales table there is a sales table for American sales and one for European sales. There definitions might be identical except for their names:

```
create table sales_america
    (stor_id      char(4),
    ord_num       varchar(20),
    date          datetime,
    qty           smallint,
    payterms      varchar(12),
    title_id      tid)

create table sales_europe
    (stor_id      char(4),
    ord_num       varchar(20),
    date          datetime,
    qty           smallint,
    payterms      varchar(12),
    title_id      tid)
```

To combine data from the two tables in a query we could use the UNION operator:

```
select stor_id, title_id, qty from sales_america
union
select stor_id, title_id, qty from sales_europe

stor_id  title_id   qty
-------  ---------  ----
6380     PS209      13
6380     BU103      25
7066     PC8888     50
7067     TC4203     20
7067     TC7777     20
7067     TC3218     40
7131     PS3333     15
         :
         :
9055     PS7777     18
9820     MC222      27
```

```
9820        BU7832      11
9820        BU2075      26
9966        BU103       27
9966        MC3021      11
9966        BU1111      18
9966        PC1035      22

(38 row(s) affected)
```

There are a number of restrictions that apply to the use of the union operator. The SELECT statements should contain the same number columns in the select list (list of columns to be returned) and these should be in the same order for each select statement to be unioned. These restrictions are not unreasonable. Also we would expect that the columns in the select list of the select statements should have the same datatypes.

Transact-SQL is not, in fact, as restrictive as this. Columns that contain data to be unioned may have different datatypes as long as SQL Server can make an implicit conversion and there are rules that govern the results of such unions. One restriction that is unfortunate, however, is that a union operator may not appear in a view definition or a subquery.

4.3.4 Performing Calculations on Data

Transact-SQL has a number of useful functions that can be used to perform operations such as adding up the data in a column and finding the number of rows in a table. These are often known as *aggregate* functions. The use of aggregate functions is very common and Transact-SQL supplies the following:

- SUM – adds up the values in a column or expression
- AVG – averages the values in a column or expression
- COUNT – counts the number of values in a column or expression
- COUNT (*) – counts the number of rows returned from a query
- MIN – finds the smallest value in a column or expression
- MAX – finds the largest value in a column or expression

Find the total number of sales:

```
select sum(qty) from sales

-----
493

(1 row(s) affected)
```

It is probably more readable to give a decent column heading:

```
select Total = sum(qty) from sales

Total
-----
493

(1 row(s) affected)
```

Find the average number of sales:

```
select Average = avg(qty) from sales

Average
-----
23

(1 row(s) affected)
```

Find the total number of rows in the sales table with a non null value in the title_id column:

```
select 'Total Count' = count(title_id) from sales

Total Count
----------
21

(1 row(s) affected)
```

Find the total number of rows in the sales table with a distinct non null value in the title_id column:

```
select 'Distinct Count' = count(distinct title_id) from sales

Distinct Count
---------------
16

(1 row(s) affected)
```

Find the total number of rows in the authors table:

```
select 'Number of Authors' = count(*) from authors

Number of Authors
-----------------
26

(1 row(s) affected)
```

Find the lowest value in the price column in the titles table:

```
select 'Least Expensive Book' = min(price) from titles

Least Expensive Book
--------------------
2.99

(1 row(s) affected)
```

Find the highest value in the price column in the titles table:

```
select 'Most Expensive Book' = max(price) from titles

Most Expensive Book
-------------------
22.95

(1 row(s) affected)
```

Find the lowest value in the last name column in the authors table:

```
select Name = min(au_lname) from authors

Name
--------------------
Bennet

(1 row(s) affected)
```

Group By

It is often useful to use the above aggregate functions in conjunction with the GROUP BY clause. As its name suggests, this clauses groups data together when returning results.

Instead of returning the total number of authors we could return the number of authors in each state:

```
select state, count(*) from authors group by state

state
---- -------
CA   15
IN   1
KS   1
MD   1
MI   1
NH   3
OR   1
TN   1
UT   2

(9 row(s) affected)
```

Again, we could provide a more meaningful heading:

```
select state, Total = count(*) from authors group by state

state Total
----- -----
CA    15
IN    1
      :
      :
(9 row(s) affected)
```

The other aggregate functions can be used with GROUP BY:

```
select stor_id, Total = sum(qty) from sales group by stor_id

stor_id   Total
-------   -----
6380      8
7066      125
7067      90
7131      130
7896      60
8042      80

(6 row(s) affected)
```

Earlier we saw how to filter the rows returned from a SELECT statement with a WHERE clause. The WHERE clause may be used with SELECT statement involving the GROUP BY clause, however, to place conditions on the groups themselves, the HAVING clause is used:

```
select state, Total = count(*) from authors group by state
having count(*) > 2

state   Total
----    -----
CA      15
NH      3

(2 row(s) affected)
```

In the above example, the earlier SELECT statement is modified to limit the results to states where the number of book stores is greater than two.

Another clause that is typically used with the aggregate functions is COMPUTE:

```
select stor_id, qty from sales order by stor_id compute
sum(qty) by stor_id

stor_id   qty
-------   ------
6380      3
6380      5

          sum
          ====
          8

stor_id   qty
-------   ------
7896      10
7896      15
7896      35

          sum
          ====
          60
          :
          :
stor_id   qty
-------   ------
8042      10
8042      15
8042      25
8042      30

          sum
          ====
          80

(27 row(s) affected)
```

Unlike the previous examples we have seen using aggregate functions, the use of the COMPUTE clause causes the summary values to be displayed as extra rows. Also, we can see the detail lines which means that the display is more like a report.

4.3.5 Using Subqueries

So far we have looked at SELECT statements that manipulate data from one or more tables. It is permissible to nest a SELECT statement inside another SELECT statement and this is called a subquery. By using subqueries, more than one table can be manipulated in a similar way to using joins. In many instances the use of subqueries and joins is interchangeable.

```
select stor_name from stores where stor_id
in (select stor_id from sales)

stor_name
----------------------------------------
Barnum's
News & Brews
Doc-U-Mat: Quality Laundry and Books
Bookbeat
Eric the Read Books
Fricative Bookshop

(6 row(s) affected)
```

In the above example we are asking for the store name of every store that has sold a book, in other words, appears in the sales table. In essence we are replacing a hard-coded list with a dynamically created one.

```
select stor_name from stores where stor_id
in (select stor_id from sales where qty > 10)

stor_name
----------------------------------
Barnum's
News & Brews
Doc-U-Mat: Quality Laundry and Books
Bookbeat
Fricative Bookshop

(5 row(s) affected)
```

In the above example we are asking for the store name of every store that has sold more than 10 copies of any book (at a given date).

A common use of a subquery is in conjunction with the EXISTS clause:

```
select au_lname from authors where exists
    (select * from publishers
    where publishers.state = authors.state)
    and authors.state = 'KS'


au_lname
------------------

(0 row(s) affected)
```

Although there are authors who live in Kansas, there are no publishers who have addresses there.

4.3.6 Useful Functions

In SQL Server there are a number of functions that are available for use in Transact-SQL and SQL Server 6.0 has added to this list. As they are *built into* the product they are known as *built-in* functions. These built-in functions are useful in many different areas of application in the same way that Microsoft Excel functions are. Here follows a number of examples:

```
select object_name(16003088)

---------------
authors

(1 row(s) affected)
```

This is an example of a *system* function and a very useful one at that. It converts the identification number of an object to the object name. An object identification number would be returned, for example, by the *sp_lock* system stored procedure. Some system functions do not take parameter values:

```
select host_name(), db_name()

------------    -----------
AURIGA          pubs

(1 row(s) affected)
```

The *host_name* system function returns the workstation name and the *db_name* system function returns the database name.

```
select upper('usa')

----
USA

(1 row(s) affected)
```

This is an example of a *string* function that converts lowercase letters to uppercase. There are many useful string functions. There are also many useful *mathematical* functions:

```
select pi()

----------------
3.141592653589793

(1 row(s) affected)
```

What's the square root of 2,401?

```
select sqrt(2401)

------------
49.0

(1 row(s) affected)
```

Not to mention *date* functions also:

```
select getdate()

--------------
30 Dec 1994 17:22

(1 row(s) affected)
```

Perhaps, one of the functions of most practical value is the CONVERT function which converts between datatypes:

```
select convert(char(10), 67780)

------
67780

(1 row(s) affected)
```

```
select  convert(int,'67')

-----
67

(1 row(s) affected)
```

4.3.7 The CASE Expression

SQL Server 6.0 introduced the ANSI SQL 92 CASE expression. This can be used to allow conditional processing within, for example, a SELECT statement. There are two forms of the CASE expression – *simple* and *searched.* The simple case expression allows an equality or inequality test:

```
select au_id,
    "Contract Status" =
         case contract
              when 1 then 'Under Contract'
              when 0 then 'No Contract'
         end
from authors

au_id          Contract Status
----------     --------------
172-32-1176    Under Contract
213-46-8915    Under Contract
238-95-7766    Under Contract
267-41-2394    Under Contract
274-80-9391    Under Contract
409-56-7008    Under Contract
427-17-2319    Under Contract
472-27-2349    Under Contract
486-29-1786    Under Contract
672-71-3249    Under Contract
724-08-9931    No Contract
724-80-9391    Under Contract
756-30-7391    Under Contract
846-92-7186    Under Contract
893-72-1158    No Contract

(15 row(s) affected)
```

Instead of printing a fairly meaningless 0 or 1, the CASE expression substitutes meaningful text for these values. The searched CASE expression takes this concept a stage further and allows more powerful comparisons to be made:

```
select title_id,
    "Sales Comment" =
  case
    when ytd_sales is null then 'Not yet sold'
    when ytd_sales < 500 then 'Low Sales'
    when ytd_sales >= 500 and ytd_sales < 4000 then 'Good Sales'
    else 'Keep Authors Happy!'
  end
from titles
where type = 'psychology'

title_id      Sales Comment
---------     ---------------
PS1372        Low Sales
PS2091        Good Sales
PS2106        Low Sales
PS3333        Keep Authors Happy!
PS7777        Good Sales

(5 row(s) affected)
```

4.4 ADDING DATA TO A TABLE

There are various methods of putting new data into the database, that is, adding new rows to tables. In Transact-SQL this is usually accomplished with the INSERT statement but can also be accomplished with a variation of the SELECT statement. Before looking at these methods it is useful to introduce the concept of a transaction.

4.4.1 Working with Transactions

Transactions will be dealt with in more detail in Chapter 6, however, we need to introduce the concept of a transaction here as operations that change the data in a table, such as inserting, modifying and deleting rows, can be executed within the scope of a transaction. A transaction is an atomic unit of work, either all the operations within a transaction are performed or none are.

In Chapter 6 we will see how this rule applies to stored procedures and triggers, but for now let us consider that a transaction is an all or nothing event.

By default, if a statement such as INSERT is executed it will either succeed or fail. Once it succeeds the result of the insert is made permanent and the only way to remove the change made to the table by the insert is to execute a compensating verb such as a DELETE. If a series of inserts is made and one fails, perhaps because the server machine crashes, the inserts made prior to the failure will be unaffected – they will have succeeded as shown below:

```
insert row1      OK
insert row2      OK
insert row3      OK
insert row4      <====server crashes during this insert
```

The insert of row 4 will not execute partially, the statement itself will be rolled back. However, if these insertions formed part of a higher level business transaction it might not make sense to allow some of the inserts to succeed and some to fail. If money was being transferred between bank accounts, the integrity of the operation would normally require that debits and credits must all happen successfully or none of them must happen.

We will therefore introduce the concept of a database transaction which we shall refer to merely as a transaction. A database transaction is a group of statements that must all succeed or must all fail. If a failure occurs during a transaction, the database is restored to its state at the point at which the transaction started, in other words, all the statements in the transaction are rolled back. In the previous example, the server machine crashed during the insert of row 4. If these operations had been performed within a transaction, the insertion of rows 1, 2 and 3 would be subsequently rolled back.

```
start transaction
insert row1      OK
insert row2      OK
insert row3      OK
insert row4      <====server crashes during this insert
*** all inserts rolled back ***
```

To start a transaction in Transact-SQL the BEGIN TRANSACTION statement is used. To end a transaction and make the changes to the database permanent the COMMIT TRANSACTION statement is used and to force a transaction rollback during a transaction a ROLLBACK TRANSACTION statement is used. These may be abbreviated to BEGIN TRAN, COMMIT TRAN and ROLLBACK TRAN respectively.

4.4.2 Using INSERT to Add Rows to a Table

Now that the concept of a transaction has been introduced we can look at changing the database with various statements such as INSERT. If you execute a BEGIN TRANSACTION before changing the data in the database you can then execute a ROLLBACK TRANSACTION to remove the changes. This will allow you to *leave a database as you found it!*

Hint: Write locks are held on database objects for the length of a transaction, as discussed in Chapter 8. Be very careful when experimenting with changing data that you do not lock out other users. The authors suggest that your own test database is used.

The INSERT statement takes two main forms. The first is used when the values for the columns of the row to be inserted are explicitly specified, the second is used when the values for the columns of the row to be inserted are obtained from the result of a SELECT statement, that is, the values already exist somewhere. Let us look at the first form:

```
insert authors
  values
     ('674-23-8877','England','Ken','603-786-8877',
         '23 Acacia Av.','Nashua','NH','03055',1)
```

In this example we have specified a value for all the columns and because of this we did not need to provide a *column list.* The number of values we have specified is the same as the number of columns in the table and they are in the same order.

If we only wished to supply values for a subset of the columns we would need to provide a column list:

```
insert authors (au_id, au_lname, au_fname, phone, contract)
   values ('774-49-5653','Stanley','Nigel','415-332-5541',1)
```

Note that omitting columns can only be done if a table column was defined to allow NULL values or a default value was associated with it, otherwise an error would occur:

```
insert authors (au_id, au_lname, au_fname, phone)
  values ('569-32-7675','England','Margaret','301-999-8888')

Msg 233, Level 16, State 2
The column contract in table authors may not be null.
```

The second form of the INSERT statement uses a SELECT clause in order to retrieve rows from other tables or views and store them in the target table. Suppose we had created a new table to contain those authors who live in California and that new table was identical to the authors table:

```
create table ca_authors
    (au_id        id,
    au_lname      varchar(40)  not null,
    au_fname      varchar(20)  not null,
    phone         char(12),
    address       varchar(40)  null,
    city          varchar(20)  null,
    state         char(2)      null,
    zip           char(5)      null,
    contract      bit)
```

We could easily populate the new table with the following INSERT statement:

```
insert ca_authors
  select * from authors where state = 'CA'
```

Often the target table is not identical to the source table and so slightly different formats are used for the INSERT statement. For example, suppose we decide that the state column is now superfluous so it is not present in the ca_authors table. If we attempted to use the same INSERT statement as in the above example we would receive an error message:

```
insert ca_authors
  select * from authors where state = 'CA'

Msg 213, Level 16, State 5
Insert error: column name or number of supplied values does
not match table definition.
```

In this example we can specify a column list on the SELECT statement:

```
insert ca_authors
  select au_id, au_lname, au_fname, phone, address, city, zip, contract
  from authors where state = 'CA'
```

We might decide that the new table has an extra column that holds the number of books an author has published and that once the table is populated, this column will be updated as the information becomes available. We must, in this case, supply a column list on the INSERT statement or the column list in the table and the column list on the SELECT statement will no longer agree:

```
insert ca_authors
  (au_id, au_lname, au_fname, phone, address, city, zip, contract)
  select au_id, au_lname, au_fname, phone, address, city, zip, contract
  from authors where state = 'CA'
```

The new column must have been defined to allow NULL values.

4.4.3 Using SELECT INTO to Add Rows to a Table

A special form of the SELECT statement, SELECT INTO, can be used to load data from one table or view to another table and to automatically create the target table before inserting the data. This option, unlike operations using the INSERT statement, are not logged in SQL Server's transaction log and therefore there are important considerations for recovery when using this version of the SELECT statement.

Simply put, the database administrator will not be able to dump the transaction log. This is discussed in more detail in Chapter 10. Note also that SELECT INTO cannot be executed within a user specified transaction, that is, using BEGIN TRANSACTION.

To use the SELECT INTO statement, a special option must be set on the database using the *sp_dboption* system stored procedure. To use this procedure the database administrator must be using the master database, that is USE MASTER must have been previously executed or the default database for the user must be master. The only users who can change database options are the system administrator or the owner of the database.

The database option that needs to be set is *select into/bulkcopy.* First it is a good idea to check whether this option is already set for the pubs database.

This can be achieved by using the system stored procedure *sp_helpdb*:

```
sp_helpdb pubs

name   db_size  owner      dbid  created      status
-----  -------  ---------  ----- ----------   --------
pubs   15 MB    england    4     Oct 24 1994  no options set

device_fragments size        usage
---------------  -----       ------
db_dev_1         5 MB        data only
db_dev_2         5 MB        data only
log_dev_1        5 MB        log only
```

We can see immediately that there are 'no options set' in the *status* column. To see the options that can be set we can execute *sp_dboption* with no parameters:

```
sp_dboption

Settable database options:
--------------------
ANSI null default
dbo use only
no chkpt on recovery
offline
published
read only
select into/bulkcopy
single user
subscribed
trunc. log on chkpt.

(1 row(s) affected)
```

To set the database option we can use *sp_dboption* with one of the above options, the value for the option and the database name of the database for which we wish to set the option:

```
sp_dboption pubs, "select into/bulkcopy", true
```

We are now able to run the SELECT INTO statement in the pubs database:

```
select * into ca_authors from authors where state = 'CA'

(15 row(s) affected)
```

We can create an empty table by specifying a condition in the WHERE clause that will not result in any rows being returned:

```
select * into empty_authors from authors where state = 'ZZ'

(0 row(s) affected)
```

4.4.4 Modifying Data in a Table

It is often the case that one or more rows in a table need to be changed. This is achieved with the Transact-SQL UPDATE statement:

```
update authors
   set au_fname = 'Katy' where au_fname='Katie' and
                                    au_lname = 'England'

(1 row(s) affected)
```

It can be seen that the UPDATE statement has a WHERE clause like a SELECT statement and this is used to specify the rows that are to be changed. The UPDATE statement can use arithmetic expressions such as in the example below where all the book prices are increased by 10%:

```
update titles set price = price*1.1

(19 row(s) affected)
```

4.4.5 Deleting Data from a Table

The removal of data from a table is achieved with the Transact-SQL DELETE statement:

```
delete authors

(27 row(s) affected)
```

The above example removes all the rows from the authors table. Like the UPDATE statement, the DELETE statement has a WHERE clause which is used to specify the rows that are to be removed:

```
delete from authors where au_id = '267-41-2394'

(1 row(s) affected)
```

The DELETE statement, like the INSERT and UPDATE statements, logs each delete in the transaction log. If many rows are to be deleted this can cause the transaction log to grow significantly. Another means of deleting all the rows from a table is therefore provided in Transact-SQL with the TRUNCATE TABLE statement:

```
truncate table ca_authors
```

This removes all the rows from a table and deallocates space used by the table without logging the operation to the transaction log. It cannot be executed within a user specified transaction, that is, using BEGIN TRANSACTION and it will not fire a delete trigger. Triggers are discussed in Chapter 6.

5 Advanced Database Manipulation

5.1 INTRODUCTION

The previous chapter discussed elements of the *Data Manipulation Language* (DML). This chapter will take this subject further and look at some more advanced DML features. The features covered will be:

- Multistatement SQL
- Cursors
- Stored Procedures
- System Stored Procedures
- Extended Stored Procedures

5.2 MULTISTATEMENT SQL

As opposed to executing a single line of Transact-SQL, SQL Server supports the concept of batches of Transact-SQL statements. SQL Server also provides Transact-SQL language syntax to support flow control. These topics will now be discussed.

5.2.1 Transact-SQL Batches

It is possible with Transact-SQL to issue a group of Transact-SQL statements as a unit known as a *batch*. This is most commonly done when executing Transact-SQL from a file through ISQL or ISQL/w. SQL Server executes the statements in a file when it sees an *end-of-batch* terminator which by default is *go* but may be altered on the ISQL command line using the /c qualifier.

An example of a batch would be as follows:

```
select 'Max Price' = max(price) from titles
select 'Num Publishers' = count(*) from  publishers
go

Max Price
----------
22.95

(1 row(s) affected)

Num Publishers
----------
3

(1 row(s) affected)
```

There are various rules that specify what Transact-SQL statements are allowed in a batch alongside other Transact-SQL statements and what operations are allowed in the same batch. Statements that must be on their own in a batch are:

- CREATE PROCEDURE
- CREATE RULE
- CREATE DEFAULT
- CREATE TRIGGER
- CREATE VIEW

The following example violates this rule by placing two CREATE VIEW statements in a batch:

```
create view v1 as select * from authors
create view v2 as select * from titles
go

Msg 111, Level 15, State 3
 CREATE VIEW must be the first command in a query batch.
Msg 127, Level 15, State 1
  This CREATE may only contain 1 statement.
```

The correct form would be to use two batches:

```
create view v1 as select * from authors
go
create view v2 as select * from titles
go
```

The following CREATE statements are allowed in the same batch:

- CREATE DATABASE
- CREATE TABLE
- CREATE INDEX

Other considerations are that objects dropped cannot be created again in the same batch and an INSERT statement cannot be executed in a batch if it uses a rule or default created with *sp_bindrule* and *sp_bindefault* issued in the same batch. Also be aware that, prior to SQL Server 6.0, the USE Transact-SQL statement does not take effect until the batch completes and so it is no use issuing a USE *database-name* and then issuing a Transact-SQL statement that you wish to run in the context of *database-name*:

```
use master
select * from syslocks
go

Msg 208, Level 16, State 1
Invalid object name 'syslocks'.
```

This restriction does not apply in SQL Server 6.0. Apart from the above rules, for repetitive jobs, Transact-SQL statements can happily be placed in files and executed through ISQL or ISQL/w which is an extremely useful time-saving capability. The ISQL command line qualifier **/i** can be used to specify an inputfile containing batches of Transact-SQL statements to ISQL:

```
isql/U england /i script.sql /P
```

The above example executes a file named *script.sql* containing Transact-SQL statements.

5.2.2 Transact-SQL Flow Control

Like high level languages, Transact-SQL provides various statements to support flow control. These statements are most commonly used in stored procedures, described later in this chapter and triggers, described in Chapter 6. Transact-SQL also provides the ability to define both local and global variables. The flow control statements, in alphabetic order are:

- BEGIN...END
- GOTO
- IF...ELSE
- PRINT
- RAISERROR
- RETURN
- WAITFOR
- WHILE

In describing these statements the alphabetic order will be discarded in favor of a more logical order.

PRINT

This keyword is used all the time:

```
print 'Where is Dave?'
```

```
Where is Dave?
```

Sometimes the string you wish to print contains quotes:

```
print 'Dave's not here'
```

```
Msg 102, Level 15, State 1
Incorrect syntax near 's'.
Msg 105, Level 15, State 1
Unclosed quote before the character string ' '.
```

The solution is to add another quote:

```
print 'Dave''s not here'
```

```
Dave's not here
```

The PRINT statement can also be used with variables as described shortly.

IF...ELSE

The IF and ELSE keywords are used frequently to perform conditional processing. As in high level languages, the SQL statement following the IF is executed if the IF condition is true, otherwise the SQL statement following the ELSE is executed assuming that an ELSE has been specified:

```
if (select max(price) from titles) > 30
    print 'There are books costing more than $30'
else
    print 'There are no books costing more than $30'

(0 row(s) affected)

There are no books costing more than $30
```

Note that a single Transact-SQL statement follows the IF and the ELSE. It is possible to execute a number of Transact-SQL statements instead of just one and to do this the BEGIN and END keywords must be used.

BEGIN...END

A group of Transact-SQL statements can be delimited by the BEGIN and END keywords and such a group is known as a statement block:

```
if (select max(price) from titles) > 30
    print 'There are books costing more than $30'
else
  begin
    print 'There are no books costing more than $30'
    select 'Average price of a book' = avg(price) from titles
  end

(0 row(s) affected)


There are no books costing more than $30
Average price of a book
---------------
14.77

(1 row(s) affected)
```

WHILE

The WHILE keyword is used in a similar fashion to that found in most high level languages, with some action or group of actions being performed as long as some condition is true:

```
while (select min(price) from titles) > 1
  begin
    update titles set price = price - 1
  end
```

In the above example, as long as the price of the books stays above one dollar a dollar is subtracted from each price repeatedly, that is, first of all the test is made to see if the minimum price of the books is greater than one and, if it is, all the books will have their prices updated. The test will then be made again and so on until the minimum price is not greater than one dollar. Note that the resulting prices will have a minimum price less than one dollar.

One use you may find for the WHILE keyword is to facilitate the loading of test data into you tables.

The BREAK and CONTINUE keyword can be also used in conjunction with the WHILE keyword. The BREAK forces a premature exit from the WHILE loop whereas the CONTINUE causes a return to the beginning of the WHILE loop without executing subsequent Transact-SQL statements:

```
while (select min(price) from titles) > 1
  begin
    update titles set price = price - 1
    if (select price from titles where title_id = 'PS2106') = 6
     begin
      print 'Back to the WHILE test without doing the next step'
      continue
     end

  if (select avg(price) from titles where type = 'business') < 20
     begin
      print 'Exit stage right...'
      break
     end
   end
```

In the above example there are extra tests made. If the price of the book with *title_id* PS2106 becomes equal to six dollars the WHILE loop is continued without executing the second test. The second test checks to see if the average price of the business books has become less than twenty dollars and if it has the WHILE loop is immediately exited.

GOTO

The GOTO statement is used in a similar fashion to that found in most high level languages, with some code branch being taken if some condition is true:

```
if (select max (qty) from sales) > 1000
    goto hi_fi_shop
```

The label hi_fi_shop would appear in the Transact-SQL with a colon:

```
hi_fi_shop:
```

RETURN

This causes an exit and is normally used within a stored procedure as we shall see shortly:

```
    :
    :
stored procedure body
    :
if  (select count(*)  from authors) > 10
    return
    :
```

RAISERROR

The RAISERROR statement is similar to PRINT but a number can be placed in the global variable @@ERROR which will be described shortly:

```
raiserror 45456 'She''s breaking up captain'

Msg 45456, Level 16, State 1
She's breaking up captain
```

WAITFOR

The WAITFOR statement causes a wait to occur for a specified delta-time, for example, 10 minutes or an absolute time, for example, 10:23, or for some event such as a mirror device failure:

```
waitfor delay '00:00:10'
print 'Your 10 seconds is up...'
```

```
waitfor time '12:50'
print 'Lunchtime approaching...'
```

The first example waits for 10 seconds before displaying a message and the second waits until 12:50.

DECLARING VARIABLES

Transact-SQL provides the capability to define variables in a similar fashion to most programming languages. Variables, in conjunction with the flow control constructs we have seen, allow for a level of programming to be performed with Transact-SQL. There are two classes of variable known as *local* and *global*. Local variables are user defined whereas global variables are system supplied.

Local variables are found everywhere, for example they are often found in stored procedures and triggers. They are created with the DECLARE keyword:

```
declare @college char(30)

declare @counter_1 smallint
```

Note that the variable name must begin with a @ symbol. The single @ denotes a local variable whereas @@ denotes a global variable. A number of variables may be declared with one declare keyword:

```
declare @college    char(30),
        @counter_1  smallint,
        @prize      money
```

~~Hint: This is more efficient tha~~t using a separate DECLARE statement for each variable.

~~Variables are assigned values wi~~th a SELECT statement:

```
declare @college char(30)
select @college = 'Queen Elizabeth'
print @college

(1 row(s) affected)
Queen Elizabeth
```

A number of variables may be assigned values with one SELECT statement:

```
select @college    =  'Queen Elizabeth',
       @counter_1  =  0,
       @prize      =  1000
```

Hint: This is more efficient that using a separate SELECT statement for each variable.

Local variables must be used in the same procedure or batch where they are declared:

```
declare @planet char(30)
select  @planet = 'Pluto'
print   @planet
go
print   @planet
go

(1 row(s) affected)

Pluto
Msg 137, Level 15, State 2
Must declare variable '@planet'.
```

In the above example the second PRINT statement attempts to use the variable outside the batch in which it was declared.

Variables may be used in flow control statements:

```
declare @num_authors smallint
select  @num_authors = count(*) from authors
      if @num_authors < 100
        print '*** Recruit more authors ***'

(1 row(s) affected)


*** Recruit more authors ***
```

Global variables are created by SQL Server for the convenience of the Transact-SQL developer and are preceded by @@.

There are a number of global variables, currently around thirty and throughout this book we shall meet a number of them. Table 3 shows a small sample.

Global Variable	Content
@@ERROR	The last error number generated by the system for that user connection. Can be set by RAISERROR as described previously.
@@ROWCOUNT	The number of rows that the last Transact-SQL statement processed.
@@SERVERNAME	The name of the local SQL Server.
@@VERSION	The version number of the current Microsoft SQL Server.

Table 3 Some of the Global Variables Available in SQL Server

5.3 CURSORS

SQL Server 6.0 has introduced *server-based* cursors. This capability allows single row processing on a results set. A set of rows is stepped through one-by-one and processing can be performed against each. The result set can be stepped through forwards or backwards depending on how the cursor is declared:

```
declare publishers_cursor cursor for select * from publishers
go

    open publishers_cursor

         fetch next from publishers_cursor

         fetch next from publishers_cursor
              :
              :
         fetch next from publishers_cursor

    close publishers_cursor

deallocate publishers_cursor
```

In the above example the cursor is first defined and in this case it is defined as a simple SELECT statement. Next the cursor is opened and it is at this point that most of the work gets done as the query optimizer works out its strategy and the result set is formed.

Following the opening of the cursor the rows are retrieved one at a time with the FETCH statement and they can then be individually processed. When the required rows have been processed the cursor is closed. It can be re-opened but no fetches are possible while it is closed. Finally, the cursor is deallocated which deletes the cursor and removes any memory structures and resource associated with it.

The above cursor is a *forward only* cursor in that the FETCH statement can only move forward through the result set. To move about the result set a *scroll* cursor can be declared:

```
declare employee_cursor scroll cursor
for select lname, fname from employee order by lname
go

    open employee_cursor
                :
         fetch first from employee_cursor
         Accorti    Paolo
                :
         fetch last from employee_cursor
         Tonini     Daniel
                :
         fetch prior from employee_cursor
         Thomas     Gary
                :
         fetch absolute 5 from employee_cursor
         Brown      Lesley
                :
         fetch relative -3 from employee_cursor
         Afonso     Pedro
                :
    close employee_cursor

deallocate employee_cursor
```

Absolute N returns the *Nth* row within the results set. *N* can be negative in which case the row returned will be the *Nth* row counting backwards from the last row of the results set.

Relative N returns the *Nth* row after the row that has just been fetched. *N* can be negative in which case the row returned will be the *Nth* row counting backwards from the row that has just been fetched.

There are other keywords that can be used with DECLARE CURSOR. For example, the keyword INSENSITIVE specifies that the result set is placed in an intermediate temporary table. Because of this, changes made to the base table will not been seen.

A DECLARE CURSOR statement can also be created dynamically within a text string and executed. This facility in conjunction with stored procedures can provide very powerful run-time processing.

5.4 STORED PROCEDURES

Now that we have covered many aspects of Transact-SQL we can look at stored procedures. What is a stored procedure? A stored procedure is like a Transact-SQL program that is stored in a SQL Server database. It comprises of a number of Transact-SQL statements and often includes variables and flow control statements.

What is the advantage of using stored procedures? There are, in fact, a number of benefits in using stored procedures:

- Function encapsulation
- Performance
- Client/server processing
- Security

From an *encapsulation of function* perspective, stored procedures enable the designer to place an action or group of actions together in a database. This can effectively *hide* the complexity of the group of actions. Developers can then easily *re-use* procedures.

From a *performance* perspective, SQL Server processes a stored procedure when it is first executed and uses the query optimizer to create an efficient query execution plan which it then keeps in memory cache. The subsequent execution of that stored procedure therefore happens very quickly.

From an *client/server* perspective, by using stored procedures, complex SQL logic can be held at the server in the database. Holding one copy of the procedure definition can simplify maintenance and security can be implemented more easily. Less SQL code is passed between the client and the server.

From an *inheritance of privilege* perspective, users can execute stored procedures such that they can perform set actions in a database even though they have no access to the base objects, such as tables, referenced in the stored procedure.

Stored procedures are not unlike the procedures found in high level languages as they can be called with input and output parameters and they themselves can call other stored procedures. If required, stored procedures can return a status which may indicate the success or failure of the stored procedure.

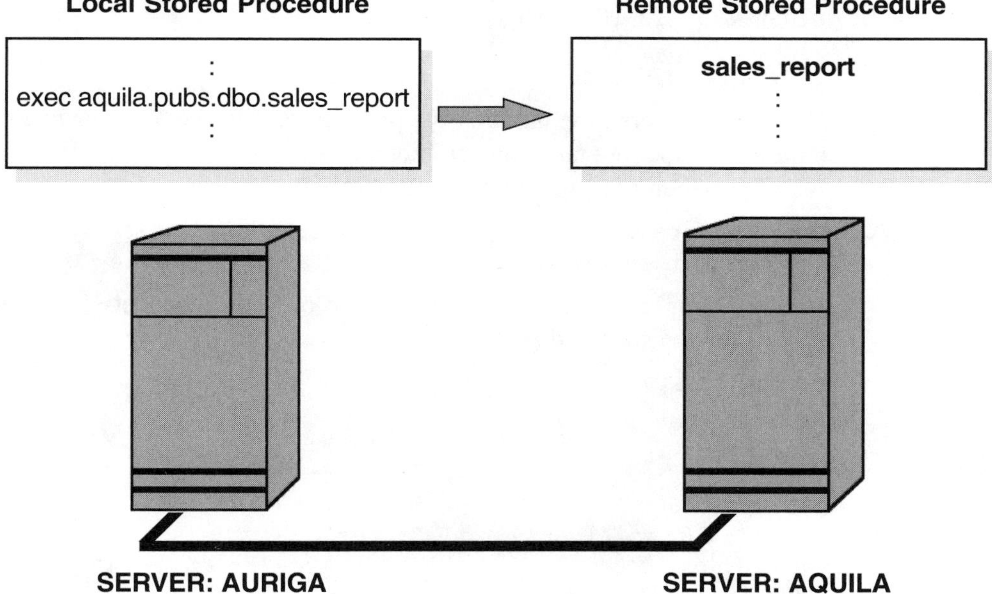

Figure 5-1 Calling Remote Stored Procedures

However, unlike the procedures found in most high level languages, stored procedures that reside on remote SQL Servers can also be called relatively easily. A typical configuration is shown in Figure 5-1.

5.4.1 Creating Stored Procedures

Stored procedures are defined in Transact-SQL with the CREATE PROCEDURE statement:

```
create procedure when as
select 'Date and Time Now' = getdate()
```

The simple example above creates a stored procedure named *when* that displays the current data and time. How do we execute this stored procedure?

There are a number of ways as we shall see shortly and here is one of them:

```
when

Date and Time Now
---------------
8 Jan 1995 12:15

(1 row(s) affected)
```

We merely entered the name of the procedure. The above procedure is very simple as it does not take any parameters. Stored procedures may take a number of parameters up to a maximum of 255:

```
create procedure author_in_state @state_code char(2) as
select au_id, au_fname, au_lname from authors where state = @state_code
```

In this example the author_in_state stored procedure accepts a single input parameter, the state code:

```
author_in_state UT

au_id          au_fname      au_lname
-------        ------------  --------------------
899-46-2035    Anne          Ringer
998-72-3567    Albert        Ringer

(2 row(s) affected)
```

Suppose that we were to omit the parameter?

```
author_in_state

Msg 201, Level 16, State 2
Procedure author_in_state expects parameter @state_name, which
was not supplied.
```

As we can see, SQL Server displays an error message. One way around this is to supply a default value for the parameter, another way around this is to test for the existence of any required parameters:

```
create procedure author_in_state @state_code char(2) = 'UT' as
select au_id, au_fname, au_lname from authors where state = @state_code
```

The above example assigns a default value of UT to the *@state_code* parameter.

```
author_in_state

au_id           au_fname      au_lname
-------         -----------   ----------------
899-46-2035     Anne          Ringer
998-72-3567     Albert        Ringer

(2 row(s) affected)
```

To test for the omission of a parameter it is convenient to give the parameter a value of null and to then test the parameter value for null:

```
create procedure author_in_state @state_code char(2) = null as
 if @state_code is null
  print '*** You forgot to enter a state code, please try again ***'
 else
  select au_id,au_fname,au_lname from authors where state = @state_code
```

If we now omit the parameter:

```
author_in_state

*** You forgot to enter a state code, please try again ***
```

If more than one parameter is needed by a stored procedure it is important to know the order in which parameters are specified on the call to execute the stored procedure. First, though, let us look at how a stored procedure is called and executed. We have shown one method which is to merely enter the name of the stored procedure specifying any parameters needed:

```
author_in_state UT
```

Another format is shown below:

```
execute author_in_state UT
```

or in its abbreviated form:

```
exec author_in_state UT
```

The simple format that does not require the EXECUTE keyword can only be used if it is the only or first statement in a batch and, if not, the batch will fail:

```
select count(*) from authors
author_in_state MI

Msg 102, Level 15, State 1
Incorrect syntax near 'MI'.
```

We will use the formats we have described interchangeably.

SQL Server 6.0 has introduced the ability to allow the execution of a character string that is dynamically created at execution time:

```
exec ("drop index " + @index_name)
```

Executing a stored procedure on a remote server is a simple matter. Merely, specify the server name:

```
exec aquila.pubs.dbo.author_in_state UT
```

Of course, the configuration of the local and remote server must have been set up to allow this remote stored procedure invocation to succeed.

Hint: There are important considerations for recovery when using remote stored procedures in that they cannot be rolled back as they are not treated as part of a transaction.

An alternative way of supplying parameters to a stored procedure is to use the following format:

```
author_in_state @state_code = MI

au_id          au_fname      au_lname
--------       -----------   ---------------
712-45-1867    Innes         delCastillo
```

This method of entering parameters removes the need to make sure that the position of the parameters is correct which is important when more than one parameter is used:

```
add_numbers @num1 = 10, @num2 = 7
```

is equivalent to specifying the parameters the other way around:

```
add_numbers @num2 =7, @num1 = 10
```

It is important for the Transact-SQL that called a stored procedure to be able to test if the stored procedure was successful or not and this is achieved by virtue of the fact that stored procedure can return a status value that may then be tested. The integer value returned may be set by SQL Server itself or by the stored procedure developer. SQL Server reserves the range of values -1 to -99 to indicate a failure and 0 to indicate success.

```
declare @return_status_code  int
exec @return_status_code = author_in_state KS
select 'Value of status variable' = @return_status_code
```

The above example declares a variable to receive the return status, executes the stored procedure and then the value of the variable is displayed to show if the stored procedure was successful:

```
au_id          au_fname       au_lname
--------       -----------    ---------------
341-22-1782    Meander        Smith

Value of status variable
----------------------
0

(1 row(s) affected)
```

To return a user specified parameter in the return status code the RETURN keyword is used with the return status code value:

```
create procedure author_in_state @state_code char(2) = null as
  if @state_code is null
   return 1
  else
   select au_id,au_fname,au_lname from authors where state = @state_code
```

Instead of printing a message as before, the *author_in_state* stored procedure now returns a status code of 1 if no parameter value is supplied. This can be tested by the calling Transact-SQL:

```
declare @return_status_code  int
exec @return_status_code = author_in_state
   if (@return_status_code = 1)
    print '*** Forgot again didn''t we!! ***'

*** Forgot again didn't we!! ***
```

Often when we call a stored procedure we want to get an answer back. SQL Server allows us to return values in parameters and these are known as *output parameters*. Output parameters are defined in the same way as the input parameters we have already seen but with the OUTPUT keyword which can be abbreviated to OUT.

```
create procedure add_numbers @num1 int, @num2 int, @answer int out as
select @answer = @num1 + @num2
```

To execute this stored procedure we could enter the following Transact-SQL.

```
declare @the_sum int
exec add_numbers @num1 = 5, @num2 = 18, @answer = @the_sum out
select @the_sum

-----
23

(1 row(s) affected)
```

Stored procedures can also be created using the SQL Enterprise Manager. To do so double click the *Stored Procedures* folder for the database in which you want to create the stored procedure.

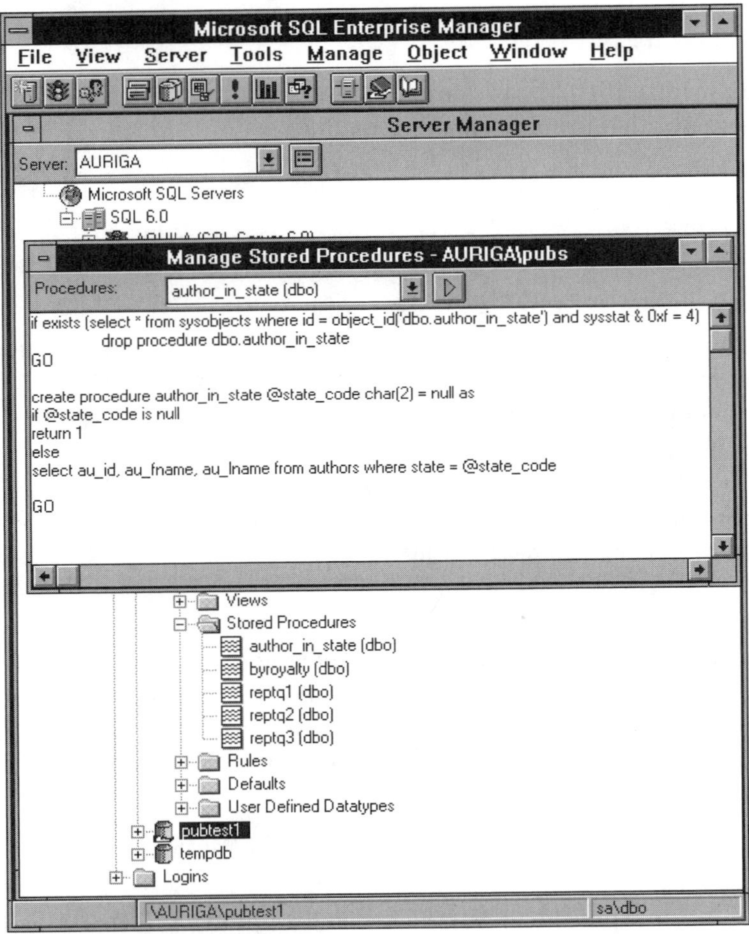

Figure 5-2 Editing Stored Procedures in the SQL Enterprise Manager

In the *Manage* window ensure that <*New*> appears in the *Procedures* Box. Add the stored procedure Transact-SQL statements as required.

Stored procedures can also be edited using the SQL Enterprise Manager. To do so click the stored procedure name with the right mouse button. In the pop-up menu select *Edit*. The current definition of the stored procedure is displayed and can be edited. This is shown in Figure 5-2.

With SQL Server 6.0, *local* and *global temporary procedures* can be created. As with temporary tables, discussed in Chapter 3, they are created by preceding the procedure_name with a # for local temporary procedures or a ## for global temporary procedures:

```
create procedure ##author_in_state @state_code char(2) as
select au_id, au_fname, au_lname from authors where state = @state_code
```

Again, as with temporary tables, local temporary procedures are visible in the current session only and global temporary procedures are visible to all sessions.

Also introduced with SQL Server 6.0 are *Auto Execution* stored procedures. These are stored procedures that are automatically executed when SQL Server starts after all the databases have been recovered.

To create an Auto Execution stored procedure, USE master must have been executed and the database administrator must be logged in as SA.

```
sp_makestartup  startup_tasks_proc

Procedure has been marked as 'startup'.
```

The above example shows a stored procedure *startup_tasks_proc* being flagged such that it will automatically execute when SQL Server starts. To see which stored procedures are to be automatically executed when SQL Server starts, the *sp_helpstartup* system stored procedure can be used:

```
sp_helpstartup

Startup stored procedures:
--------------------
startup_tasks_proc

(1 row(s) affected)
```

To stop a stored procedure from automatically executing when SQL Server starts, the *sp_unmakestartup* system stored procedure can be used:

```
sp_unmakestartup  startup_tasks_proc

Procedure is no longer marked as 'startup'.
```

Trace flags (4022) can be set to stop any Auto Execution stored procedures from automatically executing when SQL Server starts.

5.4.2 Dropping Stored Procedures

Stored procedures may be dropped with the DROP PROCEDURE statement which can be abbreviated to DROP PROC:

```
drop procedure author_in_state
```

If the dropped stored procedure is referenced by another stored procedure that tries to execute it an error message will be returned, for example, suppose the dropped stored procedure *author_in_state* is called by a stored procedure named *author_info* then the following example shows the result:

```
author_info

Msg 2812, Level 16, State 4
Stored procedure 'author_in_state' not found.
```

Stored procedures may also be dropped by using the SQL Enterprise Manager. To do so click the stored procedure name with the right mouse button. In the pop-up menu select *Drop*.

5.4.3 Renaming Stored Procedures

Stored procedures may be renamed by using the *sp_rename* system stored procedure:

```
sp_rename author_in_state, au_state
```

If another stored procedure executes *author_in_state* it will fail after the next time it is recompiled.

Stored procedures may also be renamed by using the SQL Enterprise Manager. To do so click the stored procedure name with the right mouse button. In the pop-up menu select *Rename*.

5.4.4 Showing Stored Procedure Details

The stored procedures that are present in a database can be listed by using the *sp_help* system stored procedure:

```
sp_help

Name             Owner         Object_type
-----------      ----------    ---------------
authors_names    dbo           view
                 :
                 :
add_numbers      dbo           stored procedure
author_in_state  dbo           stored procedure
author_info      dbo           stored procedure
byroyalty        dbo           stored procedure
```

Information can also be obtained about an individual stored procedure using *sp_help* with the stored procedure name:

```
sp_help author_in_state

Name              Owner          Type
--------------    ----------     -------------
author_in_state   dbo            stored procedure

Data_located_on_segment      When_created
---------------              ----------------
not applicable               8 Jan 1995 15:42
Parameter_name      Type     Length       Param_order
----------          -------- -----        ---------
@state_code         char     2            1
```

The Transact-SQL used to create a particular stored procedure can be obtained using *sp_helptext*:

```
sp_helptext author_in_state

text
------------------------------------------------------
create procedure author_in_state @state_code char(2) = null as
if @state_code is null
  print '*** You forgot to enter a state code, please try again ***'
else
  select au_id, au_fname, au_lname from authors where state =
@state_code
```

There are also two useful catalog stored procedures that can be used to obtain information about stored procedures, *sp_stored_procedures* and *sp_sproc_columns*. The catalog stored procedures *sp_stored_procedures* displays a list of stored procedures whereas *sp_sproc_columns* returns information about columns in a stored procedure.

To display information concerning the objects referenced by a stored procedure the system stored procedure *sp_depends* can be used:

```
sp_depends  author_in_state

Things the object references in the current database.
object              type          updated    selected
-------------       ---------     ------     -----
dbo.authors         user table    no         no

(1 row(s) affected)
```

Information about stored procedures may also be obtained by using the SQL Enterprise Manager. To do so click the stored procedure name with the right mouse button. In the pop-up menu select the information category required, for example *Dependencies*. The *Object Dependencies* window is shown in Figure 5-3.

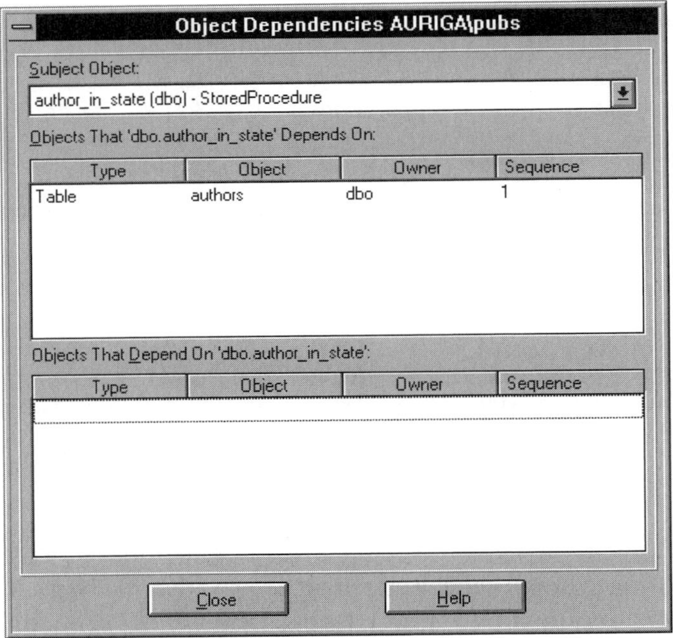

Figure 5-3 Stored Procedure Dependencies

5.5 SYSTEM STORED PROCEDURES

System stored procedures, often known as simply *system procedures*, are stored procedures that are supplied as part of SQL Server. The naming convention in SQL Server uses '*sp_*' to prefix the stored procedure name so that it is obvious that the procedure is a system stored procedure. In general, system stored procedures manipulate system tables as these should not be manipulated directly.

We have met system stored procedures already, for example, *sp_help, sp_depends* and *sp_rename*. There are many system stored procedures in SQL Server and there are also *extended stored procedures* and *catalog stored procedures*. Extended stored procedures will be discussed shortly. Catalog stored procedures are merely system stored procedures that provide a consistent interface to the system catalog (in practice the system tables) so that the routines present in Microsoft Open Database Connectivity (ODBC) can interrogate a SQL Server.

To obtain help about a particular system stored procedure the *sp_helpsql* system stored procedure can be used:

```
sp_helpsql  sp_rename

helptext
-----------------------------------------------------------
sp_rename
Changes the name of a user-created object in the current database.

   sp_rename <oldname>, <newname>
```

It is worth setting aside some time to browse through the documentation set to familiarize yourself with the system procedures so that you can make a mental note of which ones exist. It is also worth doing the same for the system tables. The system stored procedures supplied with SQL Server are the same as user-written stored procedures, the only difference being is that they access system tables. For most system tables there is no reason why you cannot write your own useful stored procedures to read information from them.

Hint: It is worth spending some time looking at how the system stored procedures are written. This is best accomplished using the SQL Enterprise Manager, and selecting the *Stored Procedures* folder in the master database. The definitions of selected system stored procedures can then easily be read.

Here is a simple example of a stored procedure that lists the stored procedures in the current database:

```
create procedure show_procs as
select 'Stored Procedures' = name from sysobjects
    where type = 'P' order by name

show_procs

Stored Procedures
-----------------
add_numbers
author_in_state
author_info
byroyalty
reptq1
reptq2
reptq3
show_procs

(8 row(s) affected)
```

The *SQL Server for Windows NT Transact-SQL Reference* manual lists all the system stored procedures and system tables.

5.6 EXTENDED STORED PROCEDURES

We have seen previously that SQL Server has many built-in functions, however, a designer may be limited by the scope of these. SQL Server therefore provides *extended stored procedures* which permit functions within a *dynamic link library* (DLL) to be executed. In essence this means that the functions available to SQL Server are limited only by a developer's imagination. Developers can write extended stored procedures using Microsoft' *Open Data Services* (ODS). As with conventional stored procedures, a return status and output parameters can be returned.

Microsoft provides a number of extended stored procedures with SQL Server. The extended stored procedures provided with SQL Server include the following to work with Windows NT groups and integrated security:

- xp_enumgroups
- xp_grantlogin

- xp_loginconfig
- xp_logininfo
- xp_revokelogin

xp_logininfo

Below is an example of using xp_logininfo:

```
exec xp_logininfo 'england','all'

account name    type  privilege mapped login name   permission path
-------------   ----  -------------    ---------    ----------------
AURIGA\england  user  admin             sa          BUILTIN\Administrators

(1 row(s) affected)
```

xp_logevent

The extended stored procedure *xp_logevent* allows messages to be logged to the SQL Server error log and/or the Windows NT Event Viewer:

```
exec xp_logevent 50023, "The truth is out there"
```

If we were to now look at the SQL Server error log we would see the following output:

```
      :
95/01/14 12:53:02.10 server    Error : 50023, Severity: 10, State: 1
95/01/14 12:53:02.10 server    The truth is out there
      :
```

If we looked in the Windows NT Event Viewer and double-clicked on our entry we would see the window displayed in Figure 5-4.

xp_cmdshell

The extended stored procedure *xp_cmdshell* allows any Windows NT command to be executed:

```
exec xp_cmdshell "print c:\feb_report.lis"

output
----------------------------------------------------
C:\feb_report.lis is currently being printed

(1 row(s) affected)
```

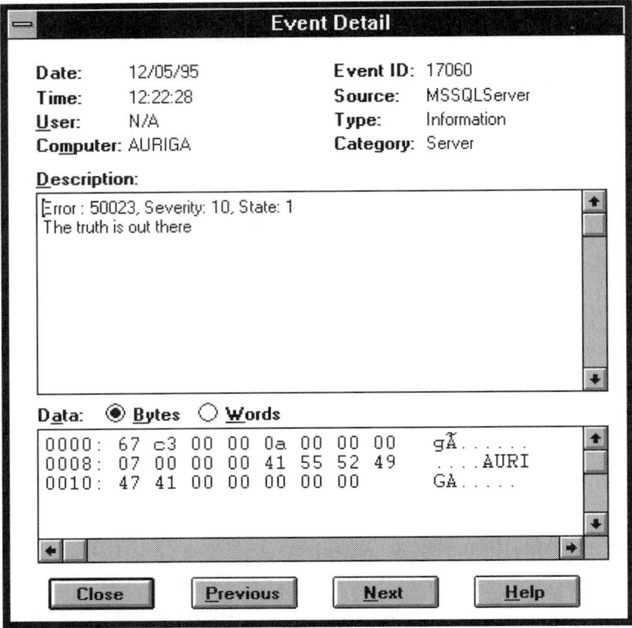

Figure 5-4 The Windows NT Event Viewer

xp_sendmail

The extended stored procedure *xp_sendmail* sends a message (or the result of a query) to the specified recipients:

```
xp_sendmail 'db_admin', 'Transaction log dumped OK.'

xp_sendmail 'england', @query = 'exec my_report'
```

This is a very useful extended stored procedure as it allows the database administrator to send messages from within a stored procedure or trigger:

sp_addextendedproc

A developer who develops extended stored procedures must add them to SQL Server. This is accomplished with the *sp_addextendedproc* stored procedure:

```
sp_addextendedproc xp_cpu_usage, cpucalc
```

In the above example, *cpucalc* is the name of the dynamic link library that contains the function *xp_cpu_usage*. Extended stored procedures are removed with the stored procedure *sp_dropextendedproc*.

The stored procedure *sp_helpextendedproc* displays information about extended stored procedures:

```
sp_helpextendedproc

name                 dll
-------------------  -------------------------
sp_cursor            cursor extended procedure
sp_cursorclose       cursorclose extended procedure
sp_cursorfetch       cursorfetch extended procedure
sp_cursoropen        cursoropen extended procedure
sp_cursoroption      cursoroption extended procedur
sp_replcmds          replcmds extended procedure
sp_replcounters      replcounters extended procedur
sp_repldone          repldone extended procedure
sp_replflush         replflush extended procedure
sp_replstatus        replstatus extended procedure
sp_repltrans         repltrans extended procedure
xp_availablemedia    xpstar.dll
xp_cmdshell          xpsql60.dll
xp_deletemail        sqlmap60.dll
xp_dirtree           xpstar.dll
xp_enumerrorlogs     xpstar.dll
xp_enumgroups        xplog60.dll
xp_enumqueuedtasks   xpstar.dll
xp_eventlog          xpstar.dll
     :
     :
```

6 Data Integrity

6.1 INTRODUCTION

Maintaining data integrity in a database is extremely important. Once data integrity is compromised the data begins to lose its value to the organization and whether the performance of the database is good or bad becomes irrelevant - bad data is no good to anyone. It should be noted that any attempt to enforce data integrity will usually result in a performance degradation, however small. If a parent table has to be read to ensure that a valid parent row exists for the row that is about to be inserted, extra disk I/O and CPU will be required as well as extra locking. Data integrity, therefore, is likely to be a trade-off between performance and reliable data.

Where should the integrity of the data in the database be enforced? As database servers are likely to provide data storage facilities for multiple clients residing on multiple platforms around the network, it seems reasonable to place integrity mechanisms at the database server level. This has a number of advantages:

- No matter what client generates input data and no matter where that client is, if integrity checking is done at the database server level, the input data can be validated and rejected if necessary.
- The integrity constraints are held in one place, that is, the database server. This can simplify maintenance considerably as a data integrity rule only has to be changed, added or removed in one place.

However, one also has to take network access into account. Some data checks may be sensibly done at the client even if they are also repeated in the database server, for example, is a US state code valid? There are no correct or incorrect approaches, the best approach depends upon the requirements of the application. It is unusual, however, not to have at least some data integrity checking. Let us now look at the facilities available within SQL Server that help the database designer enforce database integrity. These features are listed below:

- Defaults
- Rules
- Triggers
- Constraints
- Transactions

Prior to SQL Server 6.0, there were no constraints available in SQL Server. Integrity was accomplished with a mixture of defaults, rules and triggers. The introduction of ANSI/ISO SQL style constraints and column defaults with SQL Server 6.0 means that there is now a more standardized and elegant means of accomplishing database integrity. We will, however, describe all the database integrity enforcement features in SQL Server as the new constraints do not completely replace all of the previous methods, indeed, the powerful capabilities provided by triggers are by no means replaced by constraints.

6.2 DEFAULTS

When a user enters data into a table it is possible that not all the columns are provided with user-entered data. In Chapter 3 we saw that, when creating a table, a column may be created with the *NOT NULL* or *NULL* attribute. If a column is created with the NOT NULL attribute and an attempt is made to store a row in the table with no data for the column an error will occur. If a column is created with the NULL attribute and an attempt is made to store a row in the table with no data for the column, the value NULL will be assigned to the column.

This is not, in fact, the complete story. The database designer can specify that, if an attempt is made to store a row in the table with no data for a column, a *default* value is assigned to the column.

A default is created with the CREATE DEFAULT statement:

```
create default state_default as '??'
```

```
create default royalty_default as 100
```

As well as a constant a default may be a mathematical expression or a built-in function:

```
create default cost_default as 20.00*17.5

create default user_default as user_name()
```

Default values can be specified for a table column or a user-defined datatype using the system stored procedure *sp_bindefault* which binds the default previously created with the table column or user-defined datatype:

```
sp_bindefault state_default, 'authors.state'

Default bound to column.
```

There are some guidelines for assigning defaults to a table column or a user-defined datatype:

- The size of the default and the column must be such that the column can hold the default:

```
create default state_deflt as 'Missing State'

sp_bindefault city_deflt, 'publishers.city'

insert into publishers
    (pub_id, pub_name, city) values ('1622','Buttermann
Heinworth','Fresno')

(1 row(s) affected)

select * from publishers

pub_id    pub_name               city         state
------    -------------          ---------    -----
0736      New Moon Books         Boston       MA
0877      Binnet & Hardley       Washington   DC
1389      Algodata Infosystems   Berkeley     CA
1622      Buttermann Heinworth   Fresno       Mi

(4 row(s) affected)
```

The default value has clearly been truncated, this could cause problems in the future with the applications - what does 'Mi' actually mean?

- Datatypes must be compatible:

```
create default lowqty_deflt as 'Missing Qty'

sp_bindefault lowqty_deflt, 'discounts.lowqty'
insert into discounts (discounttype, highqty, discount) values
('Incentive',1200,7.0)

Msg 257, Level 16, State 1
Implicit conversion from datatype 'varchar' to 'smallint' is
not allowed. Use the CONVERT function to run this query.
```

When a default has been bound to a column any subsequent rows to be added to the table will use the default if no value is supplied for the column, however, existing rows are not affected by the binding of the default to the column.

In the case of user-defined datatypes the situation is a little more complex. A default is being bound to a user-defined datatype which is then being used in the definition of a number of columns in the database. To which columns does the default apply? The answer is that all the columns which were defined with the user-defined datatype become linked to the default. There are two exceptions to this behavior. First, if a column already has a default it is not affected by the default on the user-defined datatype. Second, if the *futureonly* parameter is specified with *sp_bindefault*, columns already in the database using that user-defined datatype are not linked to the default:

```
sp_bindefault my_deflt, my_datatype, futureonly
```

To unbind a default the system stored procedure *sp_unbindefault* should be used unless a new default is being bound in which case the old binding is removed automatically. Again, in the case of user-defined datatypes the situation is a little more complex.

Unless the *futureonly* parameter is specified, all the columns that are defined with the user-defined datatype are unbound from the default. If the *futureonly* parameter is specified, all existing columns that are defined with the user-defined datatype are left bound to the default. Again, if a column has been directly bound to a default it is not affected.

To drop a default the DROP DEFAULT statement should be used:

```
drop default state_deflt
```

To do this successfully the default must not be bound to any column otherwise an error will result:

```
drop default state_deflt

Msg 3716, Level 16, State 1
The default 'state_deflt' cannot be dropped because it is
bound to one or more column.
```

To obtain information about defaults use the system stored procedure *sp_help* to list the defaults and *sp_help* with a table name will list the defaults associated with any columns in the table:

```
sp_help discounts

Name                      Owner       Type
-------------------       ---------   ------
discounts                 dbo         user table
Data_located_on_segment               When_created
-----------------------               -------------------
default                                   24 Oct 1994 16:25
Column_name  Type       Length   Nulls  Default_name Rule_name
------------ -----      ------   ----   ------------ ----------
discounttype varchar    40       0      (null)        (null)
stor_id      char       4        1      (null)        (null)
lowqty       smallint   2        1      lowqty_deflt  (null)
highqty      smallint   2        1      (null)        (null)
discount     float      8        0      (null)        (null)
             :
             :
```

To see the definition of a default use the system stored procedure *sp_helptext*:

```
sp_helptext city_default

text
-----------------------------------
create default city_default as '??'

(1 row(s) affected)
```

Defaults may also be managed by using the SQL Enterprise Manager. Having selected the required database, click the on the '+' symbol next to the *Defaults* folder to expand it and then select the name of the default to be managed.

Click the right mouse button and from the pop-up menu choose *Edit* as shown in Figure 6-1.

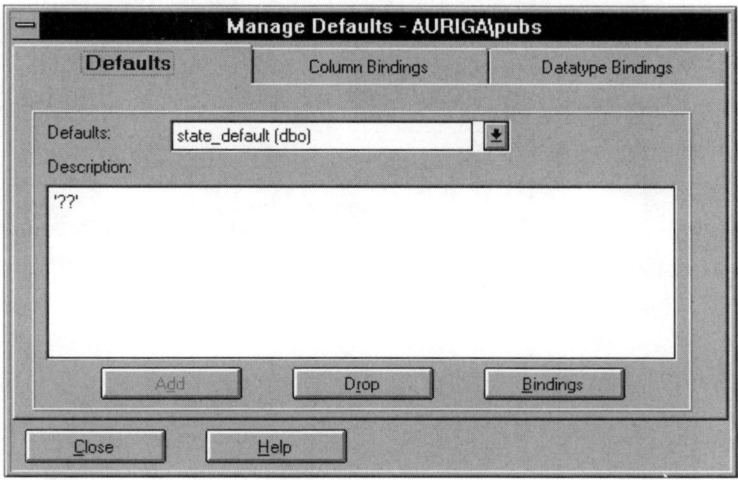

Figure 6-1 The Manage Defaults Window

This window allows the database administrator to create defaults and bind them to columns and user-defined datatypes as well as to drop them.

SQL Server 6.0 has introduced syntax in the CREATE TABLE and ALTER TABLE Transact-SQL statements to allow defaults to be specified directly for columns:

```
create table publishers
    (pub_id      char(4)      not null,
    pub_name     varchar(40)  null,
    city         varchar(20)  null,
    state        char(2)      null,
    country      varchar(30)  null       default ('USA'))
```

This capability considerably simplifies the management of default values. To manage default values using the SQL Enterprise Manager click the right mouse button on the required table name and then select Edit from the pop-up menu as shown in Figure 6-2.

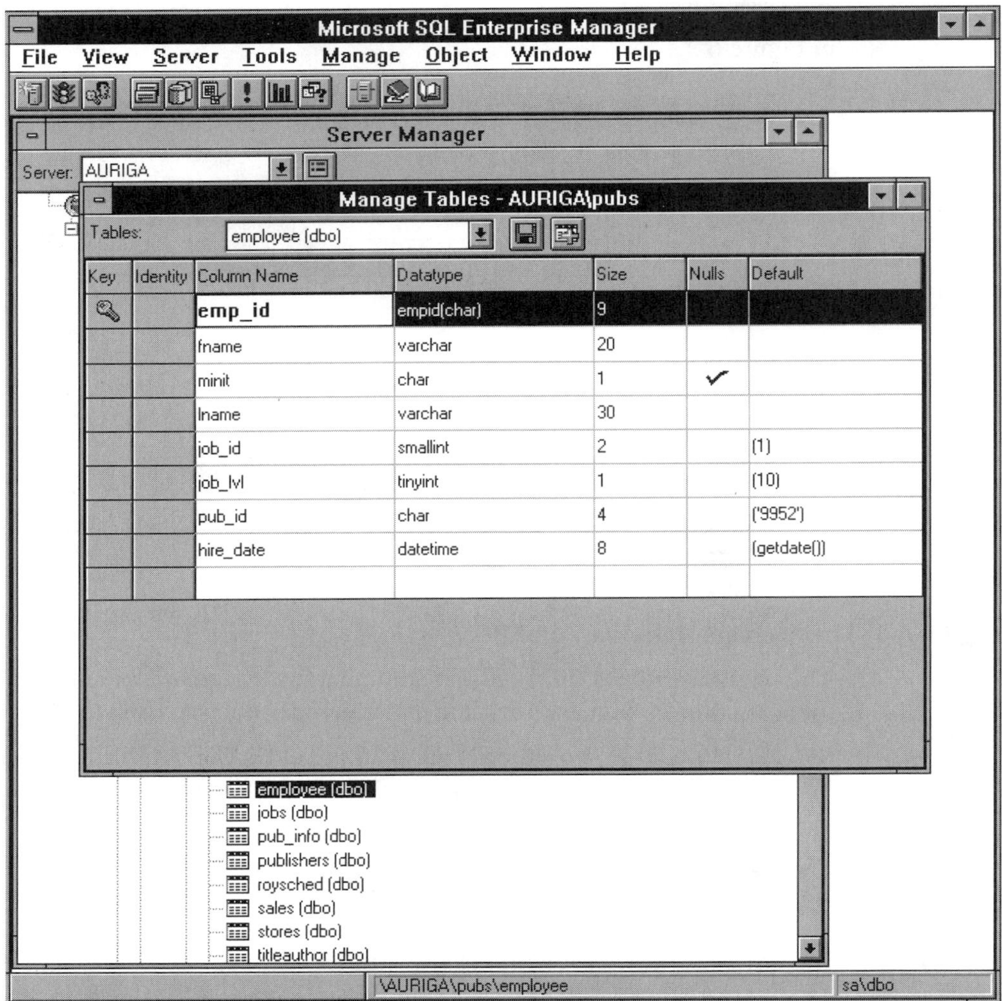

Figure 6-2 Managing Default Values

The default values for each column in the table are displayed and can be altered or new ones added to columns that do not have them. Note that the *hire_date* column has a default value of *getdate()* showing that default values can be functions as well as constants.

6.3 RULES

A rule can be used to apply data validation criteria to table columns or user-defined datatypes. For example a rule may ensure that a data value is within a certain range or data conforms to a particular format. The use of rules is not dissimilar to the use of defaults in the manner that they are implemented in SQL Server. First of all a rule is created and then it is bound to table columns or user-defined datatypes. In the following example a rule is created to place an upper limit on advances.

```
create rule top_advance as @advance_value < 20000
```

The rule is then bound to the table column advance:

```
sp_bindrule top_advance, 'titles.advance'

Rule bound to table column.
```

If an INSERT or UPDATE statement is executed that violates the rule, an error message is returned:

```
insert titles values
    ('MC9876','Incredible Curries','mod_cook','0877',$10.99,
     $21000,10,50,'Yummy','10/10/94')

Msg 513, Level 16, State 1
A column insert or update conflicts with a rule imposed by a previous
CREATE RULE command. The command was aborted. The conflict occurred in
database 'pubs', table 'titles', column 'advance'
Command has been aborted.

update titles set advance = advance + 15000

Msg 513, Level 16, State 1
A column insert or update conflicts with a rule imposed by a previous
CREATE RULE command. The command was aborted. The conflict occurred in
database 'pubs', table 'titles', column 'advance'
Command has been aborted.
```

When a rule is bound to a column or user-defined datatype, existing data is not checked. The example below shows an UPDATE statement that causes the advance column of eight rows from the titles table to become larger than 20000. The previous rule is then successfully bound:

```
update titles set advance = advance + 15000

(19 row(s) affected)
```

```
select title_id from titles where advance > 20000

title_id
------
BU2075
MC3021
PC1035
PC8888
PS1372
PS2106
TC3218
TC7777

(8 row(s) affected)

sp_bindrule top_advance, 'titles.advance'

Rule bound to table column.
```

This is an important consideration. It is easy to look at the rule on a column and think that data in the column must conform to the rule whereas it may not. It is good practice to always check the existing data first to get an idea whether it conforms to the new rule or not and whether, if it does not, it is an acceptable state of affairs.

If a rule is bound to a user-defined datatype, columns already created with the user-defined datatype will be associated with the rule unless the futureonly parameter is used:

```
sp_bindrule my_rule, my_datatype, futureonly
```

If a rule is already bound to a table column, the column will not be associated with a rule that is bound to the user-defined datatype with which the table column was created and rules on table columns will always override rules on user-defined datatypes.

To unbind a rule the *sp_unbindrule* system stored procedure is used:

```
sp_unbindrule 'titles.advance'

Rule unbound from table column.
```

Again, the futureonly parameter can be used to specify that existing columns created with the user-defined datatype will stay associated with the rule.

To drop a rule the DROP RULE statement should be used:

drop rule top_advance

To do this successfully the rule must not be bound to any column otherwise an error will result:

```
drop rule top_advance

Msg 3716, Level 16, State 1
The rule 'top_advance' cannot be dropped because it is bound
to one or more column.
```

To obtain information about rules use the system stored procedure *sp_help* to list the rules and *sp_help* with a table name will list the rules associated with any columns in the table:

```
sp_help titles

Name              Owner         Type
----------------  -----------   -----
titles            dbo           user table
Data_located_on_segment         When_created
-----------------------         ------------------
default                         24 Oct 1994 16:25
Column_name   Type        Length Nulls Default_name Rule_name
------------  -----       ------ ----  ------------ ----------
              :
price         money       8      1     (null)       (null)
advance       money       8      1     (null)       top_advance
royalty       int         4      1     (null)       (null)
              :
              :
```

To see the definition of a rule use the system stored procedure *sp_helptext*:

```
sp_helptext  top_advance

text
--------------------------------------------------
create rule top_advance as @advance_value < 20000

(1 row(s) affected)
```

Rules can also be created using the SQL Enterprise Manager. To do so double click the *Rules* folder for the database in which you want to create the rule. In the *Manage* window ensure that <*New*> appears in the *Rules* Box. Add the rule definition as required and then bind the rule to the appropriate columns or user-defined datatypes.

Rules can also be edited using the SQL Enterprise Manager. To do so click the rule name with the right mouse button. In the pop-up menu select *Edit*. The current definition of the rule is displayed and can be edited, as shown here.

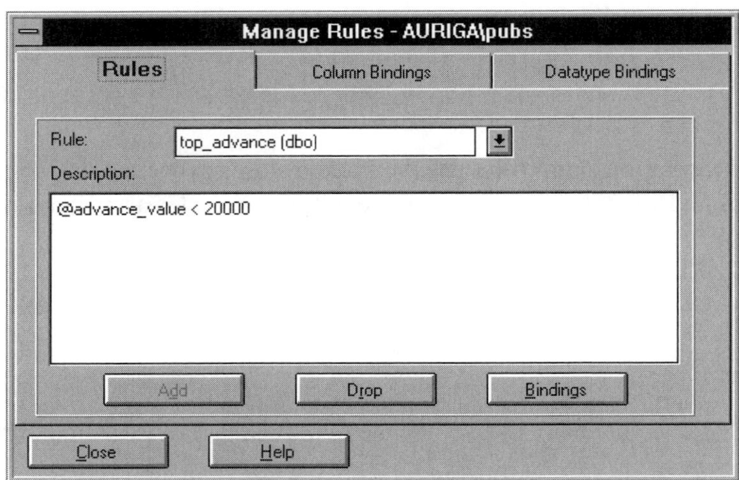

Figure 6-3 Editing a Rule Definition

The *Column Bindings* tab or *Datatype Binding* tab can be selected to edit bindings.

SQL Server 6.0 has introduced *check constraints*. These are an alternative means of applying tests on a data value that is being inserted or updated to ensure that it obeys a certain set of criteria. Check constraints may be added as part of the CREATE TABLE statement or as part of the ALTER TABLE statement. In the following example the ALTER TABLE statement is used to apply the same condition as specified in the top_advance rule defined previously:

```
alter table titles
    add constraint titles_advance_ck
    check (advance < 20000)
```

Suppose we now repeat our illegal INSERT statement:

```
insert titles values
   ('MC9876','Incredible Curries','mod_cook','0877',$10.99,
     $21000,10,50,'Yummy','10/10/94')
```

```
Msg 547, Level 16, State 2
INSERT statement conflicted with COLUMN CHECK constraint
'titles_advance_ck'. The conflict occurred in database 'pubs',
table 'titles', column 'advance'
Command has been aborted.
```

Note that the error message mentions the violated constraint by name. If we had not explicitly named the constraint SQL Server would have supplied a name for us:

```
alter table titles
    add check (advance < 20000)

insert titles values
   ('MC9876','Incredible Curries','mod_cook','0877',$10.99,
     $21000,10,50,'Yummy','10/10/94')

Msg 547, Level 16, State 2
INSERT statement conflicted with COLUMN CHECK constraint
'CK__titles__advance__57BD1053'. The conflict occurred in
database 'pubs', table 'titles', column 'advance'
Command has been aborted.
```

Not quite as readable but it is still easy to see that a check constraint in the titles table concerning the advance column has been violated.

Check constraints can compare columns within the table row being inserted or updated:

```
alter table titles
    add constraint titles_advance_ck
    check (advance < (6000 * price))

insert titles values ('MC5132','101 Curries','mod_cook','0877',
                      $3.99, $25000, 10,50,'OK','11/11/94')

Msg 547, Level 16, State 2
INSERT statement conflicted with TABLE CHECK constraint
'titles_advance_ck'. The conflict occurred in database 'pubs',
table 'titles'
Command has been aborted.
```

It is possible to add a check constraint to a table when existing data would violate the check constraint. This is achieved by using the WITH NOCHECK clause:

```
alter table titles
with nocheck
add constraint titles_advance_ck
check (advance < 20)
```

Obviously this can be dangerous. It is easy to look at a check constraint on a column and think that data in the column must conform to the check constraint whereas it may not. It is good practice to always check the existing data first to check whether it conforms to the new check constraint.

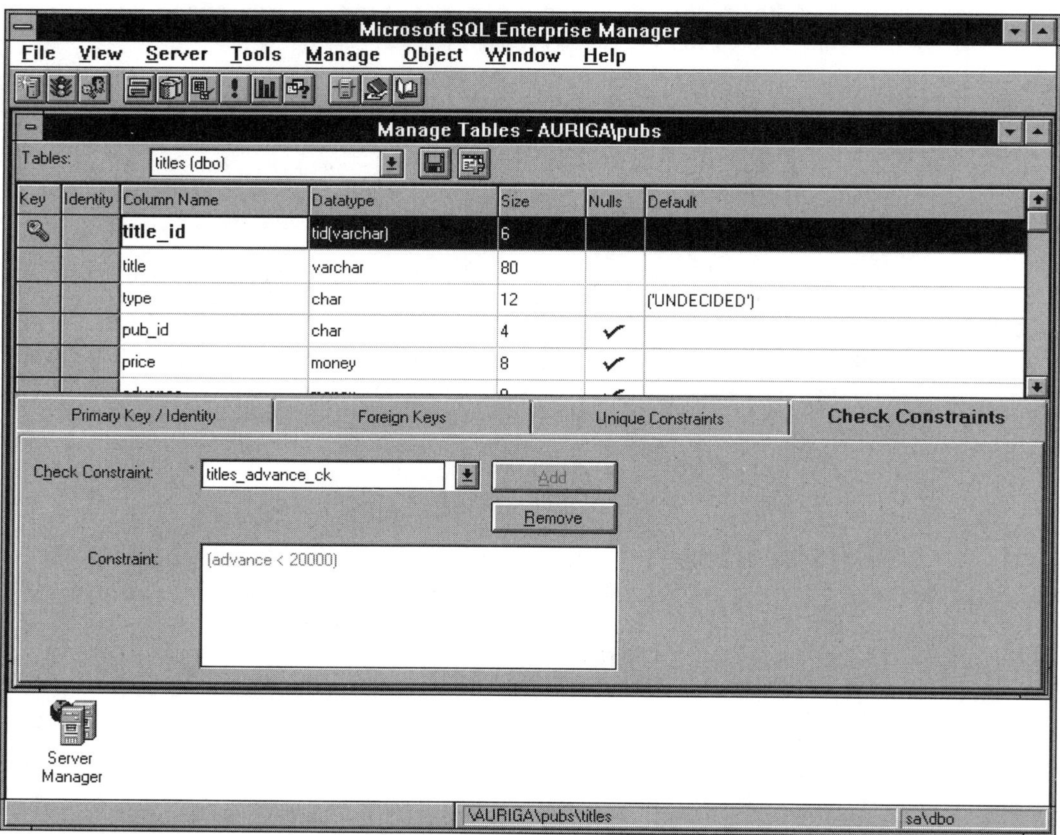

Figure 6-4 Editing Check Constraints

To drop a check constraint from a table, use the ALTER TABLE statement:

```
alter table titles
drop constraint titles_advance_ck
```

Check constraints can also be created and edited using the SQL Enterprise Manager. To do so click the table name with the right mouse button. In the pop-up menu select *Edit*. The current definition of the table is displayed. If the *Advanced Features* button is clicked and then the *Check Constraints* tab selected a window appears, as shown in Figure 6-4, which allows new check constraints to be created or existing ones to be edited.

Check constraints cannot compare values in columns in different tables. To do this triggers should be used.

6.4 TRIGGERS

It is possible in SQL Server to ensure that predefined actions take place when an event occurs such as an INSERT, UPDATE or DELETE statement being executed. The initiation of predefined actions is made possible through database objects known as *triggers*. A trigger can *fire* when, for example, a row from a particular table is deleted. The trigger then executes Transact-SQL statements as specified by the database designer.

One of the most useful aspects of triggers is that, no matter how an event is initiated, the trigger will always fire. For example, a row may be updated by the use of ISQL/w, a Microsoft Access client application, a Visual Basic program or whatever. The important fact is that the update of the row fires the trigger. This has important implications for the enforcement of database integrity as triggers make it possible to enforce database integrity outside of the applications in one central place - the database.

Triggers are created and stored in the database and are associated with particular tables. They are usually classified as one of three types:

- Insert
- Update
- Delete

Associated with one table can be a maximum of three triggers with one that fires when a row is inserted in the table, one that fires when an update is made to the table and one that fires when a row is deleted from the table. If desired a trigger may be fired when any combination of the above three events occurs, however, only one trigger may be fired for an event.

If a new trigger is created on a table that is associated with the same event, that is INSERT, UPDATE or DELETE, as an existing trigger on the table, then the new trigger takes over responsibility for that event and it will be the new trigger that fires.

For example, suppose we have a trigger named *trig1* that fires when an INSERT or UPDATE statement is executed and a trigger named *trig2* that fires when a DELETE statement is executed. If a new trigger *trig_upd* is created that fires when an UPDATE statement is executed and the table is updated, *trig_upd* would fire instead of *trig1*. *Trig1* would still fire if a row was inserted in the table.

Suppose now that a new trigger *trig_ins* is created that fires when an INSERT statement is executed. *Trig1* would now no longer be associated with either INSERT or UPDATE events and it would be dropped automatically from the database. This would happen without any accompanying warning message and so care should be taken when creating triggers that any existing ones are not accidentally destroyed.

Triggers are created with the CREATE TRIGGER statement:

```
create trigger publ_ins_trigger on publishers
    for insert
    as
    print 'A new publisher has been inserted'
```

The above trigger will fire when a row is inserted into the publishers table. Note that individual INSERT statements will each cause the trigger to fire whereas the single INSERT statement INSERT INTO ... SELECT * FROM will only cause the trigger to fire once.

```
create trigger publ_upd_trigger on publishers
    for update
    as
    print 'A publisher has been updated'
```

The above trigger will fire when a row is updated in the publishers table. Again, individual UPDATE statements will each cause the trigger to fire whereas a single UPDATE statement that updates many rows will only cause the trigger to fire once.

```
create trigger publ_del_trigger on publishers
    for delete
    as
    print 'A publisher has been deleted'
```

The above trigger will fire when a row is deleted from the publishers table, and again, note that individual DELETE statements will each cause the trigger to fire whereas a single DELETE statement that deletes many rows will only cause the trigger to fire once. Note also that a TRUNCATE TABLE statement will not cause the firing of a delete trigger.

```
create trigger publ_trigger on publishers
    for insert, update, delete
    as
    print 'A publisher has been inserted, updated or deleted'
```

The above trigger will fire when a row is inserted, updated or deleted from the publishers table. This trigger therefore fires when any event occurs and is useful when the same set of actions are to be performed whatever the event.

Note that in the above examples, even if the INSERT INTO ... SELECT * FROM, UPDATE or DELETE statements did not in fact process any rows the triggers would still have fired as in the example below:

```
delete publishers where state = 'NH'

A publisher has been inserted, updated or deleted

(0 row(s) affected)
```

In the above examples simple PRINT statements have been actioned. In practice, triggers would contain many Transact-SQL statements to execute complex actions, however, some Transact-SQL statements cannot be put inside a trigger including CREATE statements and DROP statements. Triggers may not be defined on views or temporary tables.

It is possible and common to access other tables in a trigger. There are some considerations to be made when writing triggers that do this. First, a user cannot access a table through a trigger in a way that conflicts with the privileges granted that user. If a user would normally not be able to insert data into a table then that user cannot then do so through a trigger.

Second, a trigger that accesses another table may cause a trigger to fire that is associated with that table. This is allowed in SQL Server but only to a maximum nesting of sixteen. This nesting can be disabled using the *sp_configure* system stored procedure:

```
sp_configure 'nested triggers', 0
```

Triggers can also be written that fire when a specific column or columns are affected by an UPDATE or INSERT statement:

```
create trigger publ_state_trigger on publishers
    for insert, update
    as
    if update (state)
    print 'The state has been updated'
```

The above trigger will fire if the state column is updated through the use of an INSERT or UPDATE statement:

```
insert into publishers values ('1622', 'England & Stanley',
'Boston', 'MA')

The state has been updated

(1 row(s) affected)
```

If the state column is not updated through the use of an INSERT or UPDATE statement, the trigger will not fire.

```
insert into publishers (pub_id, pub_name, city) values
('1756', 'Hobbs & Burns', 'Nashua')

(1 row(s) affected)
```

The trigger may involve multiple columns:

```
create trigger publ_state_city_trigger on publishers
    for insert, update
    as
    if update (state) or update (city)
    print 'The state or city has been updated'

update publishers set city = 'Alton' where pub_id = '1622'

The state or city has been updated

(1 row(s) affected)
```

6.4.1 Trigger Test Tables

It is often useful while actioning Transact-SQL statements inside a trigger to have access to column values that are potentially changed by the statement that caused the trigger to fire. For example, an UPDATE statement may change the values of one or more columns so there will be an old pre-update value for a column and a new post-update value.

To facilitate access to these old and new values from the Transact-SQL statements executing inside the trigger, SQL Server provides two tables. These tables are known as the *deleted* table and the *inserted* table and are written to by SQL Server during INSERT, UPDATE and DELETE statements. They can be read by the Transact-SQL statements executing inside the trigger. The way in which the tables are used is governed by the type of statement that fired the trigger, whether INSERT, UPDATE or DELETE.

The Deleted Table

The deleted table is written to when a DELETE statement causes the trigger to fire. It holds the rows that have been deleted from the user table. As an UPDATE statement is treated by SQL Server as a DELETE plus INSERT combination, it too writes the rows that have been deleted from the user table to the deleted table.

The INSERT statement does not access the deleted table.

The Inserted Table

The inserted table is written to when an INSERT statement causes the trigger to fire. It holds copies of the rows that have been inserted into the user table. Again, as an UPDATE statement is treated by SQL Server as a DELETE plus INSERT combination, it writes the rows that it inserts into the user table also into the inserted table.

The DELETE statement does not access the inserted table.

6.4.2 Using Triggers for Auditing

It is often useful to keep an audit trail by writing changes made to a table into an associated audit table together with perhaps the date and time the change was made and the person who made the change. The following trigger inserts a row into an audit table for every row that is inserted into the publishers table.

The definition of the audit table is as follows:

```
create table audit_publishers
    (pub_id         char (4),
    pub_name        varchar (40) null,
    city            varchar (20) null,
    state           char (2 )    null,
    change_date     datetime,
    change_user     sysname (30))
```

The definition of the trigger on publishers is as follows:

```
create trigger publ_audit_trigger on publishers
for insert
as
begin
   insert audit_publishers
      select pub_id, pub_name, city, state, getdate(),
             user_name() from inserted
   print 'Publisher audit row(s) inserted'
end
```

Again, this is a fairly simple trigger. The print statement would normally not appear but is a useful diagnostic feature. Even if the trigger fires once, such as in an INSERT INTO ... SELECT * FROM statement, each inserted row will be copied to the audit table. The above trigger only fires for inserted rows, however, updated rows and deleted rows should be captured in which case it would be useful to have an extra column in the audit_publishers table that held a code representing the event, for example, DEL for a delete and then the trigger could be made more general.

6.4.3 Using Triggers for Integrity Enforcement

We have discussed defaults, rules and check constraints as a means of enforcing database integrity. However, they are limited to controlling the data that can be entered into a column. This is important but we also need a means to enforce the integrity of data between the tables in a database. This is known as *referential integrity* and we can enforce this by the use of triggers. Shortly we shall see that SQL Server 6.0 has now introduced *primary* and *foreign* key constraints for enforcing referential integrity which are more in keeping with the ANSI/ISO SQL standard.

Central to the enforcement of referential integrity are the concepts of primary keys and foreign keys. A column or number of columns from a table can be designated as a *primary key*. A row must be uniquely identified by its primary key so a primary key value cannot occur more than once in a table. This also means that a primary key cannot contain null values, that is, a column that constitutes a primary key must contain a value. To establish a relationship between a master table and its dependent table requires a similar grouping of columns in the dependent table, called a *foreign key*, as the primary key in the master table.

This is often, but not only, seen in a parent-child hierarchy where there is a one-to-many relationship between a row in the parent table and rows in the child table. Common examples are a bank branch and its customers or an order header record and the order items. In the pubs database an example would be the titles and their sales or the stores and their sales.

To take the stores and sales example further, in the *stores* table, the primary key is the unique identifier of a store represented by the column *stor_id*. Each store's stor_id value is unique throughout the database. No two stores may have the same value. The *sales* table contains a column *stor_id*. This is a foreign key and establishes a relationship between the stores and sales tables.

Enforcing referential integrity between the stores and sales tables would require that, for example, the following could not occur:

1) A sales row is inserted into the sales table with a stor_id value that does not exist in the stores table.

2) A sales row is updated such that the stor_id value in it is given a value that does not exist in the stores table.

3) A store is deleted from the stores table while sales exist for that store.

4) A store has its stor_id changed while sales exist for that store.

If any of the above was allowed to happen the database would contain sales for a non-existent store which would indicate nonsensical data in the database. Note, however, these are business rules and it might be reasonable to record sales for a store that did not exist in the database, however strange!

Check on Insert

There are a number of tables in the database which are related, but we will just focus on the *stores* and *sales* tables. Let us first of all look at a trigger to ensure that (1) above does not occur. We will need to check that the appropriate store exists when we insert a sale:

```
create trigger sales_insert_trigger on sales
for insert
as
if (select count(*) from inserted, stores
    where inserted.stor_id = stores.stor_id) <> @@rowcount
```

```
begin
    rollback transaction
    print 'A stor_id does not exist in the stores table'
end

insert sales values ('2323', 'TZ2323', '10/10/94',30, 'Net 30',
'MC2222')

A stor_id does not exist in the stores table
```

How does this trigger work? The SELECT statement performs a join between the inserted table and the stores table using the common *stor_id* column. The inserted table contains copies of all the inserted rows and therefore contains the same number of rows as the number of rows inserted which is held in the global variable @@ROWCOUNT supplied by SQL Server.

However, if the stor_id of any of the rows in the inserted table does not have a corresponding row in the stores table then the number of rows returned from the join will be less that the number of rows inserted. Therefore, the COUNT(*) result will not equal the value of the number of rows inserted that is held in @@ROWCOUNT and the IF statement will be evaluated as TRUE. The transaction will be rolled back and all the inserts performed by the INSERT statement that fired the trigger will be canceled.

This is a little coarse in the fact that we might have inserted many sales and only had one insertion that compromised integrity but the trigger still cancels all the inserts. The trigger can be fine tuned to allow the inserts that do not compromise integrity to succeed:

```
create trigger sales_insert_trigger on sales
for insert
as
if (select count(*) from inserted, stores
   where inserted.stor_id = stores.stor_id) <> @@rowcount
begin
   delete sales from sales, inserted
    where inserted.stor_id = sales.stor_id and
          inserted.stor_id not in (select stor_id from stores)
end
```

The above trigger does not impede the inserts that do not compromise integrity but it deletes the inserts that do. The trigger does not cause the transaction to rollback.

Check on Update

Now let us look at a trigger to ensure that integrity violation (2) listed previously does not occur. We will need to check that the appropriate store exists when we update the stor_id in a row held in the sales table:

```
create trigger sales_update_trigger on sales
for update
as
if (select count(*) from inserted, stores
    where inserted.stor_id = stores.stor_id) <> @@rowcount
begin
    rollback transaction
    print 'A stor_id does not exist in the stores table'
end

update sales set stor_id = '2323' where ord_num = 'N914008'

A stor_id does not exist in the stores table
```

How does this trigger work? It works in a similar fashion to the INSERT trigger we looked at earlier. The SELECT statement performs a join between the *inserted* table and the *stores* table using the common *stor_id* column. The inserted table contains copies of all the inserted rows that resulted from the update and therefore contains the same number of rows as the number of rows updated which is held in the global variable @@ROWCOUNT supplied by SQL Server.

However, if the stor_id of any of the rows in the inserted table does not have a corresponding row in the stores table then the number of rows returned from the join will be less that the number of rows updated. Therefore, the COUNT(*) result will not equal the value of the number of rows updated that is held in @@ROWCOUNT and the IF statement will be evaluated as TRUE. The transaction will be rolled back and all the changes made by the UPDATE statement that fired the trigger will be canceled.

Again, this is a little coarse in that we might have updated many sales and only had one update that compromised integrity but the trigger still cancels all the updates. This trigger can also be fine tuned to allow the updates that do not compromise integrity to succeed in a similar way to the INSERT trigger.

Check on Delete

Now let us look at a trigger to ensure that integrity violation (3) listed previously does not occur. We can deal with this by either disallowing the DELETE statement and rolling it back if any sales exist for the store we are deleting or we could *cascade* the delete operation, that is, we can remove any rows in the sales table that reference the store we are deleting.

The following trigger disallows the delete operation if any sales exist for the store we are deleting:

```
create trigger store_delete_trigger on stores
for delete
as
if (select count(*) from deleted, sales
    where deleted.stor_id = sales.stor_id) > 0
begin
    rollback transaction
    print 'Sales exist for the stor_id that is to be deleted'
end
```

This trigger works in the following way. The SELECT statement performs a join between the *deleted* table and the *sales* table using the common *stor_id* column. The deleted table contains copies of all the deleted rows that resulted from the DELETE statement. If the stor_id of any of the rows in the deleted table have a corresponding row in the sales table then the number of rows returned from the join will be greater than zero. Therefore, the IF statement will be evaluated as TRUE. The transaction will be rolled back and the changes made by the DELETE statement that fired the trigger will be canceled.

Again, this is a little coarse in the fact that we might have deleted many stores and only had one delete that compromised integrity but the trigger still cancels all the deletes. Again, the trigger can be fine tuned to allow the deletes that do not compromise integrity to succeed.

The following trigger cascades the delete operation if any sales exist for the store we are deleting:

```
create trigger store_casc_delete_trigger on stores
for delete
as
delete sales from deleted, sales
where sales.stor_id = deleted.stor_id
```

In practice we would need to put in a little more effort than this. First of all a DELETE trigger on stores would need to delete any rows from the discount table that referenced the stores that were being removed from the stores table. Second we would probably want to audit some information from the deleted rows into an audit table so that information about sales involving the deleted store could be kept.

Triggers can be, and typically are, much more complex that the examples shown above. However, it is only a matter of using the Transact-SQL constructs we have already seen and perhaps stored procedures to create very powerful triggers. A trigger can even include an extended stored procedure as shown below:

```
create trigger example_xp_delete_trigger on discounts
for delete
as
exec master.dbo.xp_cmdshell "print c:\feb_report.lis"
```

Triggers can also be created and edited using the SQL Enterprise Manager. To do so click the table name with the right mouse button. In the pop-up menu select *Triggers*. The *Manage Triggers* window is displayed. In the *Triggers* box <*New*> can be selected or a trigger name which allows new triggers to be created or existing ones to be edited. This is shown in Figure 6-5.

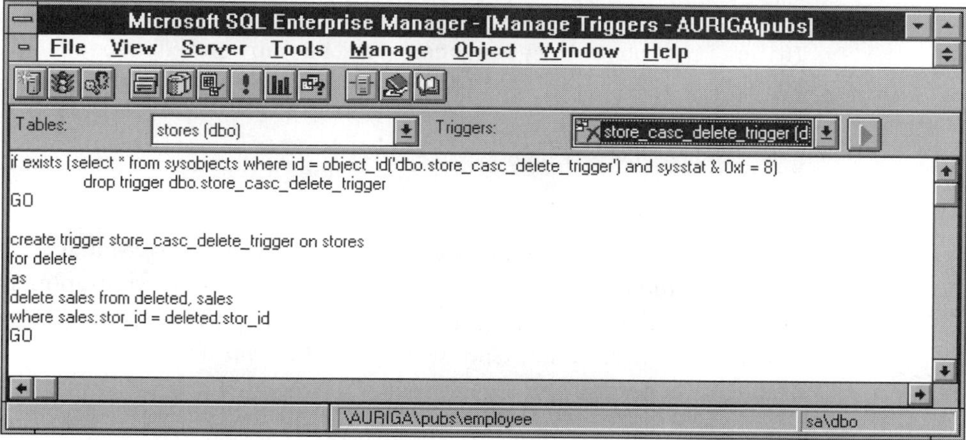

Figure 6-5 Managing Triggers in the SQL Enterprise Manager

6.4.4 Dropping Triggers

If a table that has triggers associated with it is dropped then the triggers are also dropped. Triggers may be dropped explicitly with the DROP TRIGGER statement:

```
drop trigger store_casc_delete_trigger
```

Triggers can also be dropped using the SQL Enterprise Manager. To do so click the table name with the right mouse button. In the pop-up menu select *Triggers*. The *Manage Triggers* window is displayed. In the *Triggers* box selected a trigger name. Choose *Object...Drop* from the SQL Enterprise Manager menu bar.

6.4.5 Renaming Triggers

Triggers may be renamed with the *sp_rename* system stored procedure:

```
sp_rename publ_trigger, publisher_trigger
```

Like stored procedures, triggers may be affected if the objects they reference are renamed. To display information concerning the objects referenced by a trigger the system stored procedure *sp_depends* can be used:

```
sp_depends publ_audit_trigger

Things the object references in the current database.
object                 type       updated   selected
------------------     ---------  -----     ------
dbo.audit_publishers   user table yes       no

(1 row(s) affected)
```

Triggers can also be renamed using the SQL Enterprise Manager. To do so click the table name with the right mouse button. In the pop-up menu select *Triggers*. The *Manage Triggers* window is displayed. In the *Triggers* box selected a trigger name. Choose *Object...Rename* from the SQL Enterprise Manager menu bar.

6.4.6 Showing Trigger Details

The system stored procedure *sp_help* provides a list of the triggers in the current database:

```
sp_help

Name                 Owner      Object_type
--------------       -------    ------------
publ_audit_trig      dbo        trigger
publ_state_city      dbo        trigger
publisher_trigg      dbo        trigger
sales_insert_tr      dbo        trigger
```

The name of the trigger may also be specified:

```
Name                 Owner      Type
------------------   -------    -------
publ_audit_trigger   dbo        trigger

Data_located_on_segment   When_created
------------              ---------------
not applicable            21 Jan 1995 11:13
```

The system stored procedure *sp_helptext* displays the Transact-SQL used to create the trigger:

```
sp_helptext  publ_audit_trigger

text
----------------------------------------------------------
create trigger publ_audit_trigger on publishers
for insert
as
begin
insert  audit_publishers
select pub_id, pub_name, city, state, getdate(), user_name()
from inserted
print 'A publisher audit has been inserted'
end
```

Information about trigger *dependencies* and *permissions* may also be obtained by using the SQL Enterprise Manager. To do so click the table name with the right mouse button. In the pop-up menu select *Triggers*. The *Manage Triggers* window is displayed. In the *Triggers* box selected a trigger name. Choose *Object..Dependencies* or *Object..Permissions* from the SQL Enterprise Manager menu bar.

6.5 PRIMARY, FOREIGN & UNIQUE KEY CONSTRAINTS

As previously mentioned, SQL Server 6.0 has introduced *primary, foreign* and *unique* key constraints. These establish referential integrity rules in the database for single tables or between multiple database tables. Primary, foreign and unique key constraints can be defined on the CREATE TABLE or ALTER TABLE statements.

```
create table publishers
  (pub_id char(4)      not null
          constraint pk_publishers_pub_id primary key clustered,
  pub_name varchar(40)  null,
  city     varchar(20)  null,
  state    char(2)      null,
  country  varchar(30)  null         default ('USA'))
```

The above example creates the *publishers* table and defines a primary key constraint on the *pub_id* column. As a primary key cannot contain null the column pub_id must be defined as not null. To ensure that the primary key contains only unique values, SQL Server automatically creates a unique clustered index on the column or columns that constitute the primary key. If desired, a nonclustered index can be created instead.

```
insert into publishers values
   ('1622', 'Five Lakes Publishing', 'Chicago', 'IL', 'USA')

Msg 2627, Level 14, State 1
Violation of PRIMARY KEY constraint 'pk_publishers_pub_id':
Attempt to insert duplicate key in object 'publishers'.
Command has been aborted.
```

The above example shows that the primary key constraint will stop any attempt to insert a row that will result in the primary key column holding non-unique values.

```
create table pub_info
  (pub_id  char(4)   not null
           constraint fk_publishers references publishers(pub_id)
           constraint pk_pub_info primary key clustered,
  logo     image     null,
  pr_info  text      null)
```

The above example creates the *pub_info* table and defines a primary key constraint on the *pub_id* column. However, it also defines the *pub_id* column to be a foreign key referencing the primary key, *pub_id*, in the *publishers* table.

Let us now see how this primary and foreign key relationship can enforce referential integrity. First let us try to delete a row from the *publishers* table that has a corresponding row in the pub_info table:

```
delete from publishers where pub_id = '1622'

Msg 547, Level 16, State 2
DELETE statement conflicted with COLUMN REFERENCE constraint
'fk_publishers'. The conflict occurred in database 'pubs',
table 'pub_info', column 'pub_id'
Command has been aborted.
```

Next, let us attempt to change the value of the *pub_id* column for a row in the *pub_info* table to a value that does not exist in the publishers table:

```
update pub_info set pub_id = '1066' where pub_id = '1622'

Msg 547, Level 16, State 2
UPDATE statement conflicted with COLUMN FOREIGN KEY constraint
'fk_publishers'. The conflict occurred in database 'pubs',
table 'publishers', column 'pub_id'
Command has been aborted.
```

Again, SQL Server forbids this operation in order to prevent an orphaned row in the *pub_info* table. Can we insert a row into the *pub_info* table with a *pub_id* that does not exist in the *publishers* table?

```
insert into pub_info (pub_id) values ('2323')

Msg 547, Level 16, State 2
INSERT statement conflicted with COLUMN FOREIGN KEY constraint
'fk_publishers'. The conflict occurred in database 'pubs',
table 'publishers', column 'pub_id'
Command has been aborted.
```

Again, SQL Server also forbids this operation for similar reasons.

We have said that a primary key constraint enforces the fact that the primary key must be a unique value. In doing this it also ensures that there are no null values stored in the column or columns that constitute the primary key. It may be that we require the uniqueness property for a column but wish to allow null values. In this case we can use a *unique key constraint.* In this case a single null value is allowed to be stored but two nulls are considered as duplicates.

The Identity Statement

While discussing constraints, particularly primary key constraints, it is worth mentioning another new SQL Server 6.0 feature, the *identity* statement. The identity statement may be included as part of a CREATE or ALTER table statement and it specifies that a table column will receive a value generated by SQL Server. This is known as an *identity column.*

When a row is inserted into a table with an identity column, SQL Server automatically generates a value for it so the INSERT statement would not typically supply one. Identity columns are useful when a key value needs to be specified for the rows in a table and there is no obvious real-life value that can be used. There can be only one identity column defined for a table and the column must be defined with the datatype int, smallint, tinyint, or numeric with scale of zero.

As rows are inserted into a table, SQL Server increments the value of the identity column by the *increment* specified. The first row in the table will be given the value of the *seed* specified. Both the seed and the increment have default values of one:

```
create table jobs
    (job_id    smallint   identity(1,1),
    job_desc   varchar(50)     not null)


insert into jobs (job_desc) values ('Nuclear Physicist')
insert into jobs (job_desc) values ('Brain Surgeon')
insert into jobs (job_desc) values ('Astronaut')
insert into jobs (job_desc) values ('Database Administrator')

select * from jobs


job_id    job_desc
------    ------------------------
1         Nuclear Physicist
2         Brain Surgeon
3         Astronaut
4         Database Administrator


(4 row(s) affected)
```

If we were to specify a seed of 10 and an increment of 5, that is, identity(10,5):

```
select * from jobs

job_id    job_desc
------    ------------------------
10        Nuclear Physicist
15        Brain Surgeon
20        Astronaut
25        Database Administrator

(4 row(s) affected)
```

When referring to the identity column in a SELECT statement it is not necessary to know its name as a keyword IDENTITYCOL can be used instead:

```
select IDENTITYCOL from jobs

job_id
-----
10
15
20
25

(4 row(s) affected)
```

Primary, foreign and unique key constraints can also be created and edited using the SQL Enterprise Manager. To do so click the table name with the right mouse button. In the pop-up menu select *Edit*. The current definition of the table is displayed. If the *Advanced Features* button is clicked a number of tabs are displayed such as *Primary Key/Identity*, *Foreign Keys, Unique Constraints* and *Check Constraints*. If a tab is selected a window appears which allows a new constraint to be created or existing ones to be edited. Figure 6-6 shows the Primary Key/Identity tab.

The use of the SQL Enterprise Manager considerably simplifies the creation and management of constraints and identity columns.

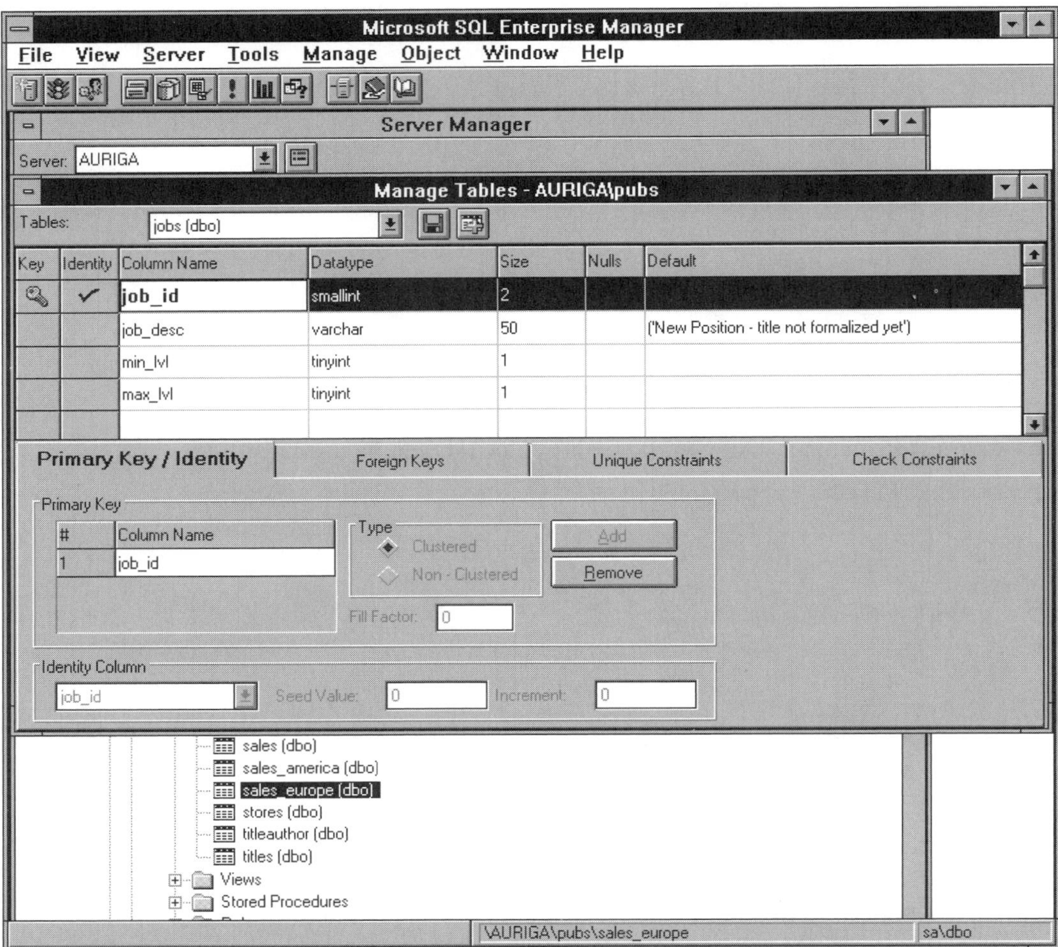

Figure 6-6 Editing a Primary Key Constraint

From Figure 6-6 it can be seen that the SQL Enterprise Manager is all you need to display information about the constraints associated with a table. However, information can also be obtained using Transact-SQL:

```
sp_help jobs
```

```
Name                                      Owner      Type
---------                                 -----      -------
jobs                                      dbo        user table

Data_located_on_segment                   When_created
------------------------                  -----------------
default                                   2 Apr 1995  9:51

Column_name          Type        Length  Prec  Scale  Nullable  Identity
------------         -------     ------  ---   ----   --------  --------
job_id               smallint    2       5     0      no        yes
job_desc             varchar     50                   no        no
min_lvl              tinyint     1       3     0      no        no
max_lvl              tinyint     1       3     0      no        no

index_name         index_description                              index_keys
------------------ --------------------------------------         --------
PK_jobs_job_id_24  clustered,unique,primary key located on default job_id

constraint_type              constraint_name              constraint_keys
------------------------     --------------------------   -------------
PRIMARY KEY (clustered)      PK_jobs_job_id_243D6C4D      job_id
DEFAULT on column job_desc   DF_jobs_job_desc_25319086    ('New Position - title
                                                          not formalized yet')
CHECK on column min_lvl      CK_jobs_min_lvl_2625B4BF     (min_lvl >= 10)
CHECK on column max_lvl      CK_jobs_max_lvl_2719D8F8     (max_lvl <= 250)

Table is referenced by
employee:  FK__employee__job_id__2CD2B24E
```

We think you will agree that the SQL Enterprise Manager display is a little more friendly!

6.6 TRANSACTIONS

The concept of a transaction being an *atomic* unit of work was introduced in Chapter 4. We will revisit transactions here as they are essential for maintaining database integrity. The fact that all the Transact-SQL statements that change the database in some way can be grouped together, such that all the changes succeed or none do, is clearly an important feature. For example, we can debit one bank account and credit another confident that, should a failure occur, we will not be in a position where only one account has been changed.

To achieve this, as was mentioned in Chapter 4, Transact-SQL statements are grouped within a BEGIN TRANSACTION statement and a COMMIT TRANSACTION statement. The COMMIT TRANSACTION ends a transaction successfully whereas a ROLLBACK TRANSACTION statement is used to force a transaction rollback which will undo all the changes made to the database since the BEGIN TRANSACTION statement. These may be abbreviated to BEGIN TRAN, COMMIT TRAN and ROLLBACK TRAN respectively and transactions that are specified with these statements are usually called a *user transaction* or *user-specified transaction*:

```
begin transaction
    select price from titles where title_id = 'MC2222'
    update titles set price = $10.99 where title_id = 'MC2222'
    select price from titles where title_id = 'MC2222'
rollback transaction
select price from titles where title_id = 'MC2222'

price
------------
19.99

(1 row(s) affected)

(1 row(s) affected)

price
------------
10.99

(1 row(s) affected)

price
------------
19.99

(1 row(s) affected)
```

In the above example of a user transaction, it can be seen that the ROLLBACK TRANSACTION statement has returned the price changed by the UPDATE statement to its original value.

Pairs of BEGIN TRANSACTION and COMMIT TRANSACTION statements can be nested although the successful ending of the transaction is caused by the outermost COMMIT TRANSACTION. This nesting usually occurs when a trigger or stored procedure that is executed within a user transaction itself has a pair of BEGIN TRANSACTION and COMMIT TRANSACTION statements.

To check the user transaction nesting level the global variable @@TRANCOUNT may be accessed. SQL Server sets the nesting level in @@TRANCOUNT automatically:

```
begin transaction
    begin transaction
        begin transaction
        select @@trancount
        commit transaction
    commit transaction
commit transaction

-------
3

(1 row(s) affected)
```

The behavior of user transactions that call stored procedures and fire triggers needs a little further discussion. Suppose a trigger or stored procedure executes a ROLLBACK TRANSACTION statement - how will this affect other Transact-SQL statements in the batch?

```
create procedure roll_them_back as
begin transaction
rollback transaction
```

In the example below the stored procedure *roll_them_back* issues a ROLLBACK TRANSACTION statement:

```
begin transaction
    select price from titles where title_id = 'MC2222'
    update titles set price = $10.99 where title_id = 'MC2222'
    select price from titles where title_id = 'MC2222'
exec roll_them_back
select price from titles where title_id = 'MC2222'
commit transaction

price
--------
19.99
(1 row(s) affected)
```

```
(1 row(s) affected)

price
-----------
10.99

(1 row(s) affected)

Msg 266, Level 16, State 1
Transaction count after EXECUTE indicates that a COMMIT or
ROLLBACK TRAN is missing. Previous count = 1, Current count =
0.
price
-----------
19.99

(1 row(s) affected)

Msg 3902, Level 16, State 1
The commit transaction request has no corresponding BEGIN
TRANSACTION.
```

The ROLLBACK TRANSACTION statement in the stored procedure causes all the Transact-SQL statements between it and the first BEGIN TRANSACTION in the batch that called the stored procedure to be rolled back. This means that the ROLLBACK TRANSACTION statement in the stored procedure causes a rollback past the BEGIN TRANSACTION statement in the stored procedure. In other words, more than one nesting level is rolled back so an error message is displayed which specifies the change in nesting levels.

Note that as this has occurred, the last COMMIT TRANSACTION has no user transaction to commit and so another error message is also displayed.

The above is also true of triggers that contain a ROLLBACK TRANSACTION statement. However, there is a fundamental difference between triggers and stored procedures in this respect. While a ROLLBACK TRANSACTION statement in a stored procedure does not affect subsequent statements in the batch a ROLLBACK TRANSACTION statement in a trigger does. In fact all the subsequent Transact-SQL statements in the batch are canceled. In the above example the third SELECT statement in the batch executes. In the next example, which fires a trigger containing a rollback, the SELECT statement following the UPDATE does not execute:

```
create trigger roll_them_back_trigger on titles
for update
as
begin transaction
    print 'rolling back...'
rollback transaction

begin transaction
    select price from titles where title_id = 'MC2222'
    update titles set price = $10.99 where title_id = 'MC2222'
    select price from titles where title_id = 'MC2222'
commit transaction

price
-----------
19.99

(1 row(s) affected)

rolling back...
```

Note that any changes made by a remotely executed stored procedure cannot be undone by a ROLLBACK TRANSACTION statement in the user transaction that called it.

Within a user transaction a *savepoint* may be specified which flags a point in the transaction to which a rollback can undo changes. The transaction can then proceed to be ultimately committed or rolled back. A savepoint is specified with the SAVE TRANSACTION Transact-SQL statement which can be abbreviated to SAVE TRAN.

```
begin transaction
   select price from titles where title_id = 'MC2222'
   update titles set price = price + 9.01
      where title_id = 'MC2222'
   select avg(price) from titles
      save transaction a_savepoint_name
      update titles set price = price + 1000.00
         where title_id = 'MC2222'
      select avg(price) from titles
      rollback transaction a_savepoint_name
   select price from titles where title_id = 'MC2222'
commit transaction
```

```
price
-----------
19.99

(1 row(s) affected)

(1 row(s) affected)

-----------
15.33

(1 row(s) affected)

(1 row(s) affected)

-----------
77.83

(1 row(s) affected)

price
-----------
29.00
```

In any discussion of user transactions the subject of locking should be raised. Locking is discussed in detail in Chapter 8, however, it should be noted that certain classes of locks, particularly write locks, once placed on a table or database page will remain until the user transaction is committed or rolled back. This will have important ramifications when considering the multi-user aspects of an application. In general, user transactions should be kept as short as possible. This is discussed in Chapter 9.

7 Accessing Data

7.1 INTRODUCTION

We have previously discussed how data can be inserted into a table and retrieved from a table using Transact-SQL statements. As well as using Transact-SQL, many products are able to access SQL Server databases, often through the Microsoft ODBC interface which will be described in Chapter 12. Examples of such products from Microsoft would be Microsoft Access and Microsoft Visual Basic.

Also, workloads may be characterized as on-line transaction processing (OLTP) or decision support. OLTP transactions are usually short lived, access few tables and often result in writes to the database. Decision support transactions are usually long lived and complex, access many tables and rarely write to the database. Real life workloads are usually a mixture of the two.

Irrespective of the tool used or the workload type, the database designer will want to minimize the time and system resource needed to access the requested data. Although database performance is covered in Chapter 9, there are some fundamental areas that we will cover in this chapter concerning data access. These areas are as follows.

- Indexed Access
- The Query Optimizer
- The Database Cache

An understanding of these topics is essential if good database performance is to be realized through good database design.

7.2 INDEXED ACCESS

Suppose we executed the following Transact-SQL statement:

```
select * from publishers where pub_id = '0736'
```

How would SQL Server find the appropriate row? It could search the publishers table from the start of the table to the end of the table looking for rows which had a *pub_id* that contained the value 0736. This might be fine for small tables containing just a few rows but if the table contained millions of rows the above query would take a very long time to complete. This is like searching through a book page by page looking for the mention of a particular topic. You would have to start at page one and you would carry on searching until you reached the last page of the book.

What is needed is a fast and efficient way of finding the data that conforms to the query requirements. In the case of a book there is usually an index section whereby the required topic can be found in an alphabetically sorted list and the page numbers of the pages that feature that topic can then be obtained. The required pages can then be directly accessed in the book.

The method used to directly retrieve the required data from a table in SQL Server is not unlike that used with books. An object called an index may be created on a table which enables SQL Server to quickly look up the *database pages* that hold the supplied key value, in our example the value 0736 for the *pub_id* column.

Unlike a book which normally has one index, a table may have many indexes. These indexes are based on one or more columns from the table. If an index is based on a particular column or group of columns then a query which features the same columns in its WHERE clause may be able to retrieve the required data via the index. The ultimate decision as to whether an index is used or whether a complete scan of the table is performed is made by a component of SQL Server known as the *query optimizer* which we shall discuss later in this chapter.

If queries can be assisted by indexes, why not create lots of indexes on every table?

Unfortunately, like so many areas in database technology, there are swings and roundabouts concerning the use of indexes. On one hand indexes can speed up access to data, but on the other hand, they can slow down table insertions, updates and deletions. This is because SQL Server has more work to do maintaining all the indexes to ensure that they always truly reflect the current data in the table. Indexes also take up disk space.

Clearly, if disk space is plentiful and the database is predominantly read only there are good reasons to create many indexes. In reality most databases experience a mixture of read and write activity so the correct choice of indexes is critical to good performance. The choice of appropriate indexes should be a product of good up front design and transaction analysis which will be discussed in Chapter 9.

SQL Server supports two types of index that may be created on a table.

- Clustered
- Nonclustered

7.2.1 Clustered Indexes

One clustered index may be created per table. Creating a clustered index forces the data rows in the table to be re-ordered on disk such that they are in the same order as the index key. For example, if we were to create a clustered index on the *au_lname* column of the *authors* table the data rows would be sorted such that their physical order on the disk was in ascending order of the last name, that is, "Bennet" would appear in a database page that preceded the database page that held "White".

This order would be maintained as long as the clustered index was present. SQL Server would ensure that the insertion of a new data row would cause the row to be placed in the correct physical location. In the authors example, the insertion of an author "England" would cause the new row to be stored between the "Bennet" and "White" rows and the subsequent insertion of an author "Stanley" would cause the new row to be stored between the "England" and "White" rows.

Updates are important to consider also. In many instances updates are not done *in place*. This means that the update consists of two operations, a delete followed by an insert. The re-insert of the row may cause the row to change physical location if the key value has been updated to a new value. The affect of the UPDATE statement on performance is discussed in Chapter 9.

A clustered index, then, is tightly coupled with the underlying table rows. The order of the rows on disk is governed by the index. Also, if a clustered index is created on a segment, the table will migrate automatically away from the device it resides on to that segment.

To create a clustered index the CREATE INDEX statement is used:

```
create unique clustered index auth_id_index on authors
(au_id)
```

The above example creates a clustered index on the *au_id* column of the *authors* table. The *unique* clause ensures that more than one row cannot have the same key value, in this case *au_id*. Note that the table may or may not already contain data. If it does and there are duplicate values the above CREATE INDEX statement will fail:

```
create unique clustered index auth_id_index on authors
(au_id)

Msg 1505, Level 16, State 1
Create unique index aborted on duplicate key.  Primary key is
'998-72-3567'
```

Similarly, once the index has been successfully created an attempt to insert or update a row that would result in a duplicate key value will fail.

```
insert into authors (au_id, au_lname, au_fname, contract)
         values ('998-72-3567', 'England', 'Mike',1)

Msg 2601, Level 14, State 3
Attempt to insert duplicate key row in object 'authors' with
unique index 'auth_id_index'
Command has been aborted.
```

This is fine as we want the *au_id* column to contain no duplicate values as this is the way we uniquely identify an author. We may wish to index on the last name and first name of the author instead. In this case it is highly likely that more than one author may have the same name so we will want to create an index that does not enforce unique values.

```
create clustered index auth_name_index on authors
(au_lname,
 au_fname)
```

As the above example shows, we accomplish this by merely omitting the UNIQUE clause. The above example also shows that an index may be created consisting of more than one table column. This is sometimes known as a *multi-segment* index. An index can be created consisting of no greater that sixteen columns which in practical terms is a limit few people are likely to hit. Also, the sum of the column sizes in the index cannot be greater than 256 bytes.

As mentioned previously, only one clustered index can be created on a table which makes sense as data can only be physically sorted in one order. Any attempt to create a second clustered index will fail:

```
create unique clustered index auth_id_index on authors
(au_id)

Msg 1902, Level 16, State 1
Cannot create more than one clustered index on table 'authors'.
Drop the existing clustered index 'auth_name_index' before
creating another
```

Let us look at the structure of a clustered index in more detail. Figure 7-1 shows the structure of a simple clustered index.

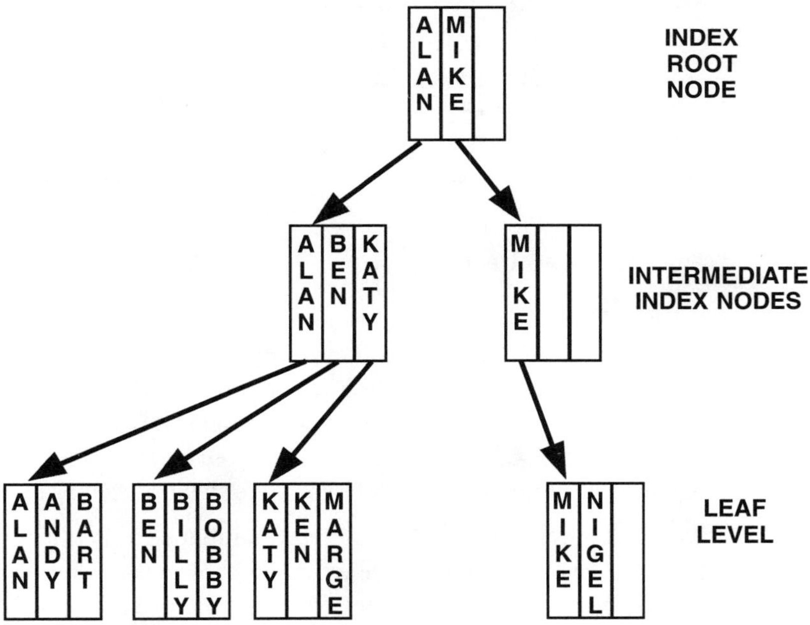

Figure 7-1 The Structure of a Clustered Index

The data pages contain rows from the table and in the above example we have chosen to show just the first name column in the rows. In a clustered index the leaf level is considered to be the data pages containing the table rows. Note that the data is in the same key sequence as the clustered index.

Above the data pages are *index pages* that contain entries that point to the data pages. Index pages are often referred to as *index nodes*. This is a traditional hierarchical index structure with a top level index node pointing to intermediate nodes which eventually point to the data page level.

Note that in a clustered index only the first table row in the data page is pointed to. Because the table rows are in key sequence, it is not necessary to point to every table row in the data page and in fact it would be a complete overkill to do so. In the above example, the first table row in one of the data pages, let's call it page 10, has a key value of *Katy*. The first table row in the next data page, let's call it page 11, has a key value of *Mary*. SQL Server knows that if a row is requested with a key value of *Ken* then it must be in page 10. For this reason, a clustered index is known as a *sparse* index.

How do the index entries in the index nodes point to the data pages? Figure 7-1 is oversimplified. Firstly, we have shown very few index nodes and very few entries per node and secondly we have omitted to show the pointers which are essentially page numbers. In our example, the index entry that points to Katy will consist of the key value of *Katy* and the page number of the data page where Katy is the first table row. Also, on any given index level the pages point to one another so SQL Server can scan along the index pages at that level.

7.2.2 Nonclustered Indexes

Unlike clustered indexes, many nonclustered indexes may be created per table. In fact up to 249 nonclustered indexes may be created. Creating a nonclustered index, unlike a clustered index, does not force the data rows in the table to be re-ordered on disk such that they are in the same order as the index key. For example, if we were to create a nonclustered index on the *au_lname* column of the authors table the data rows would not be moved.

Any order in the table rows would be maintained only if a clustered index was present; the nonclustered indexes on the table have no influence on the order at all. If only nonclustered indexes were present on a table, data that was inserted (or not updated in place) would be placed at the end of the existing data. This may create a hot-spot in the database and this will be discussed in Chapter 9.

A nonclustered index, then, is not tightly coupled with the underlying table rows and the order of the rows on disk is not governed by the index. Also, if a nonclustered index is created on a segment, the table will not migrate automatically away from the device it resides on to that segment as it would with a clustered index. If a clustered index is created or rebuilt on a table that already has nonclustered indexes created then all the nonclustered indexes will also be automatically rebuilt.

To create a nonclustered index the CREATE INDEX statement is used as it was for the clustered index only in this case NONCLUSTERED is specified.

```
create unique nonclustered index auth_id_index on authors
(au_id)
```

If neither CLUSTERED nor NONCLUSTERED is specified a nonclustered index is created.

Let us look at the structure of a nonclustered index in more detail. Figure 7-2 shows the structure of a simple nonclustered index.

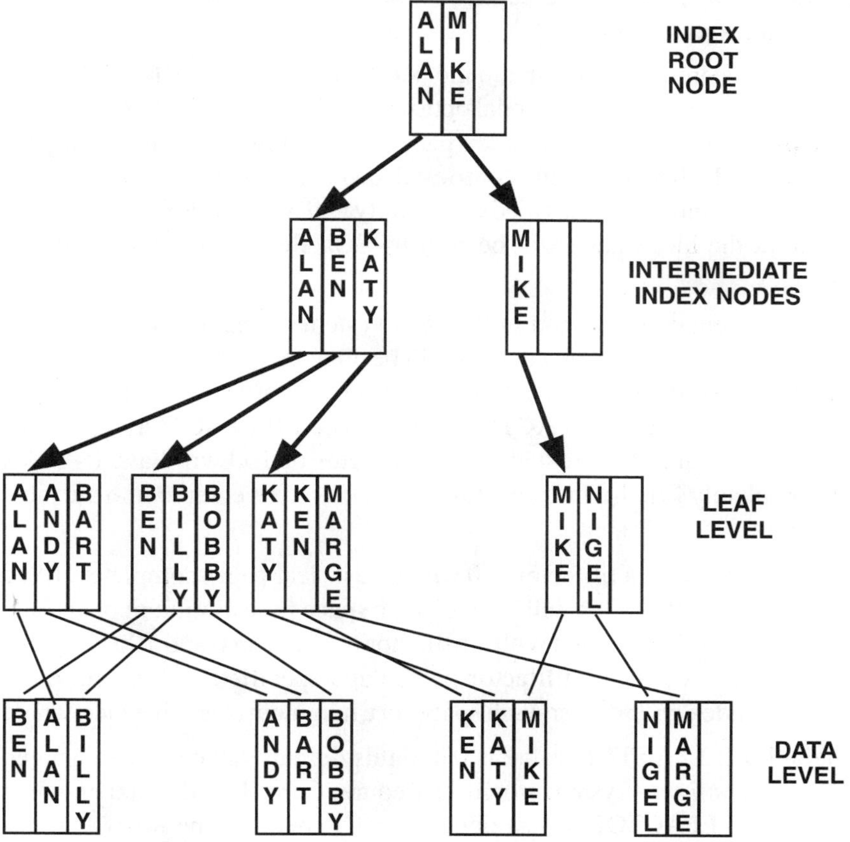

Figure 7- 2 The Structure of a Nonclustered Index

The data pages contain rows from the table and in the above example we have again chosen to show just the first name column in the rows. In a nonclustered index the leaf level is considered to be the level above the data pages containing the table rows. Note that the data is not in any key sequence as we do not have a clustered index present on this table.

Note that in a nonclustered index every table row in the data page is pointed to by an index entry. For this reason, a nonclustered index is known as a dense index.

How do the index entries in the index nodes point to the data pages in a nonclustered index? In our example, the index entry that points to Katy will consist of the key value of *Katy* and the page number of the data page where Katy is stored as in the clustered index case. However, the index entry now also contains a row number.

Whether a clustered or nonclustered index is being used, the CREATE INDEX statement can be used with additional options. The FILLFACTOR option specifies the packing density for an index page, that is, how much an index page should be filled when it has index entries placed in it by the CREATE INDEX statement. If an index page is filled completely and a new index entry must be placed in it, the index page will be split by SQL Server into two (or more) index pages.

This is an expensive operation in terms of system resource and so, if index page splitting can be minimized, it should be. One means of achieving this is to essentially reserve space in the index pages for future new entries and this can be done with the FILLFACTOR option. The FILLFACTOR is a value from 0 to 100. An index created with a fillfactor of 100 will have its index pages completely filled. This is useful if no data is to be entered into the table in the future.

An index created with a fillfactor of 0 will have its leaf pages completely filled but other levels in the index will have enough space for a minimum of another index entry. An index created with a fillfactor of between 0 and 100 will have its leaf pages filled to the fillfactor percentage specified and, again, other levels in the index will have enough space for a minimum of another index entry.

The default FILLFACTOR value is 0 and this default value can be changed with the *sp_configure* system stored procedure. Care should be taken when choosing a FILLFACTOR as its relevance will depend on the way the application uses the table data. For example, there is little point in reserving space throughout an index if the row inserted always has a key greater than the current maximum key value.

```
create clustered index auth_name_index on authors
(au_lname,
 au_fname)
 with fillfactor = 75
```

The above example creates an index with a FILLFACTOR of 75%. Note that over time, as rows are inserted into the table, the effectiveness of the fillfactor value will vanish and so a planned rebuilding of critical indexes at periodic intervals should be considered.

The ALLOW_DUP_ROW and IGNORE_DUP_ROW options are useful when a non-unique clustered index is to be created on a table that contains rows with identical values in their columns. Consider the following table and its data:

```
create table tab1 (f1 int, f2 int, f3 int)

select * from tab1

f1  f2   f3
--  --   --
1   1    1
2   2    2
3   3    3
4   4    4
4   4    4

(5 row(s) affected)
```

We can create a non-unique clustered index specifying that no options are to be used when dealing with duplicate rows or the ALLOW_DUP_ROW or IGNORE_DUP_ROW options are to be used. If we specify no options when creating a non-unique clustered index on the above table the index creation will fail:

```
create clustered index tab1_index on tab1
(f1, f2, f3)

Msg 1508, Level 16, State 1
Create index aborted on duplicate rows.  Primary key is '4'
```

If we specify the ALLOW_DUP_ROW option when creating a non-unique clustered index on the above table the index creation will succeed:

```
create clustered index tab1_index on tab1
(f1, f2, f3) with allow_dup_row
```

If we specify the IGNORE_DUP_ROW option when creating a non-unique clustered index on the above table the index creation will succeed, but any duplicate rows in the table will be eliminated and a warning will be output:

```
create clustered index tab1_index on tab1
(f1, f2, f3) with ignore_dup_row

Warning: deleted duplicate row.  Primary key is '4'

select * from tab1

f1  f2   f3
--  --   --
1   1    1
2   2    2
3   3    3
4   4    4

(4 row(s) affected)
```

The IGNORE_DUP_KEY option is useful when a unique clustered or nonclustered index is to be created on a table that might have rows with duplicate key values inserted into it. If the IGNORE_DUP_KEY option is set, rows containing duplicate key values are discarded but the statement will succeed whereas, if the IGNORE_DUP_KEY option is not set, the statement as a whole will be aborted.

The SORTED_DATA option is useful when a unique clustered or nonclustered index is to be created on a table that already has its rows placed in the same sorted order as the index to be created. This can save time as the sort data phase of the CREATE INDEX operation can be skipped, however, if the data is not found to be in order, the CREATE INDEX statement will fail:

```
select * from tab1

f1  f2   f3
--  --   --
4   4    4
1   1    1
2   2    2
3   3    3

(4 row(s) affected)
```

```
create unique clustered index tab1_index on tab1
(f1,f2,f3) with sorted_data

Msg 1530, Level 16, State 1
Create index with sorted_data was aborted because of row out
of order.  Primary key of first out of order row is '1'
```

Indexes can also be created and managed using the SQL Enterprise Manager. To do so click the required table name with the right mouse button. In the pop-up menu select Indexes. The Manage Indexes window is displayed and can be edited. This is shown in Figure 7-3.

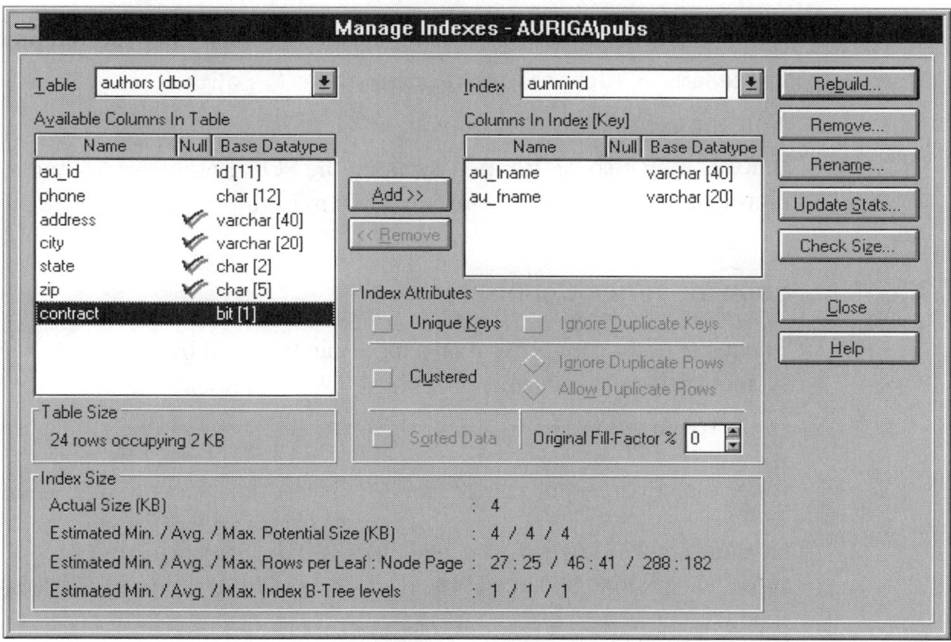

Figure 7- 3 Using the SQL Enterprise Manager to Manage Indexes

This window also provides the database administrator with useful index space usage information as well as the facility to update the distribution statistics. This may assist the query optimizer in choosing a good query strategy as discussed later in this chapter.

7.2.3 Dropping Indexes

Both clustered and nonclustered indexes can be dropped with the DROP INDEX Transact-SQL statement:

```
drop index authors.auth_name_index
```

Indexes may also be dropped by using the SQL Enterprise Manager. To do so merely click the Remove button shown in Figure 7-3.

7.2.4 Renaming Indexes

Indexes may be renamed by using the *sp_rename* system stored procedure:

```
sp_rename 'authors.auth_lname_index', auth_lname_idx
```

Note the use of the single quotes.

Indexes may also be dropped by using the SQL Enterprise Manager. To do so merely click the Rename button shown in Figure 7-3.

7.2.5 Showing Index Details

The indexes that are present on a table can be listed by using the *sp_helpindex* system stored procedure:

```
sp_helpindex authors

index_name index_description                    index_keys
---------- ------------------------------------ ----------
auidind    clustered, unique located on defaultau_id
aunmind    nonclustered located on default      au_lname,au_fname

(1 row(s) affected)
```

The catalog stored procedure *sp_statistics* can also be used to display a list of the indexes on a table.

Information about indexes may also be found in the SQL Enterprise Manager *Manage Indexes* window as shown in Figure 7-3.

7.3 THE QUERY OPTIMIZER

When we execute a query, whether by typing in a Transact-SQL statement or by using a tool such as Microsoft Access, it is highly likely we will be requiring that rows be read from one or more database tables. Suppose we require that SQL Server performs a join of two tables, table *A* containing a dozen rows and table *B* containing a million rows. How should SQL Server access the required data in the most efficient fashion? Should it access table *A* looking for rows that meet the selection criteria and then read matching rows from table *B* or should it access table *B* first? Should it use indexes if any are present or do a table scan? If indexes are present and there is a choice of index, which one should SQL Server choose?

The good news is that SQL Server contains a component known as the *query optimizer* which will automatically take a query passed to it and attempt to execute the query in the most efficient way. The bad news is that it is not magic and it does not always come up with the best solution. A database administrator should be aware of the factors that govern query optimization, what pitfalls there are and how the query optimizer can be assisted in its job. Database administrators who know their data well can often influence the optimizer with the judicious use of indexes to choose the most efficient solution.

What do we mean by efficient in the context of the query optimizer? Basically, the query optimizer is looking to minimize the number of I/Os required to fetch the required data. CPU and locking are not considered.

7.3.1 Tools for Investigating Query Strategy

There are a number of tools at our disposal for checking what the query optimizer is doing. In ISQL/w we can request the display of the query optimizer strategy for a query with the SET SHOWPLAN ON statement:

```
set showplan on

select * from publishers

STEP 1
The type of query is SELECT
FROM TABLE
publishers
Nested iteration
Table Scan
```

```
pub_id   pub_name             city          state
------   ---------------      -------------  -------
0736     New Moon Books       Boston        MA
0877     Binnet & Hardley     Washington    DC
1389     Algodata Infosystems Berkeley      CA

(3 row(s) affected)
```

The above example of a *showplan* shows that a SELECT statement has been executed against the publishers table and that the strategy chosen by the query optimizer is a table scan. We will look at a number of possible strategies in more detail later. Note that a query optimizer strategy will also be generated when statements other than SELECT are executed such as DELETE or UPDATE.

Sometimes the database administrator will wish to examine query optimizer strategies but not actually access the table data, that is, to terminate the query after the query optimizer has selected a strategy but before the execution of the query using that strategy takes place. To do this the SET NOEXEC ON statement can be used:

```
set showplan on
set noexec on
select * from publishers

STEP 1
The type of query is SELECT
FROM TABLE
publishers
Nested iteration
Table Scan
```

Hint: Take care with the use of the SET NOEXEC ON statement as it can drive you mad! Once you specify it, NO statement is executed until you specify SET NOEXEC OFF. This includes other SET statements. It is very easy to forget you have specified a SET NOEXEC ON statement and wonder why a query is taking an eternity or a SET statement seems to have stopped working.

Another SET statement that may be useful when investigating different query optimizer strategies is SET STATISTICS IO ON. This displays the count of table scans, logical and physical reads and database page writes for each Transact-SQL statement:

```
set statistics io on
select * from publishers

pub_id   pub_name              city          state
------   ---------------       -----------   -------
0736     New Moon Books        Boston        MA
0877     Binnet & Hardley      Washington    DC
1389     Algodata Infosystems  Berkeley      CA

(3 row(s) affected)

Table: publishers scan count 1, logical reads: 2, physical reads: 0
Total writes for this command: 0
```

Similarly, the SET STATISTICS TIME ON statement displays the time (in *timeclicks*) that SQL Server took to parse the command, compile the query optimizer strategy and execute the command:

```
Parse and Compile Time 0
SQL Server cpu time: 10 ms.

pub_id   pub_name              city          state
------   ---------------       -----------   -------
0736     New Moon Books        Boston        MA
0877     Binnet & Hardley      Washington    DC
1389     Algodata Infosystems  Berkeley      CA

Execution Time 0
SQL Server cpu time: 0 ms.  SQL Server elapsed time: 0 ms.
```

The ISQL/w window also contains the facility to view the query plan and resource usage for a query in a graphical fashion. Figure 7-4 shows a typical graphical showplan output.

The Transact-SQL that generated this output is shown below:

```
select title, au_lname from authors, titles, titleauthor
  where
    titles.title_id = titleauthor.title_id and
    authors.au_id = titleauthor.au_id and
    authors.au_id = '213-46-8915'
```

It can be seen that the authors table was accessed by its clustered index whereas the titles table and the titleauthor table have been accessed by a table scan.

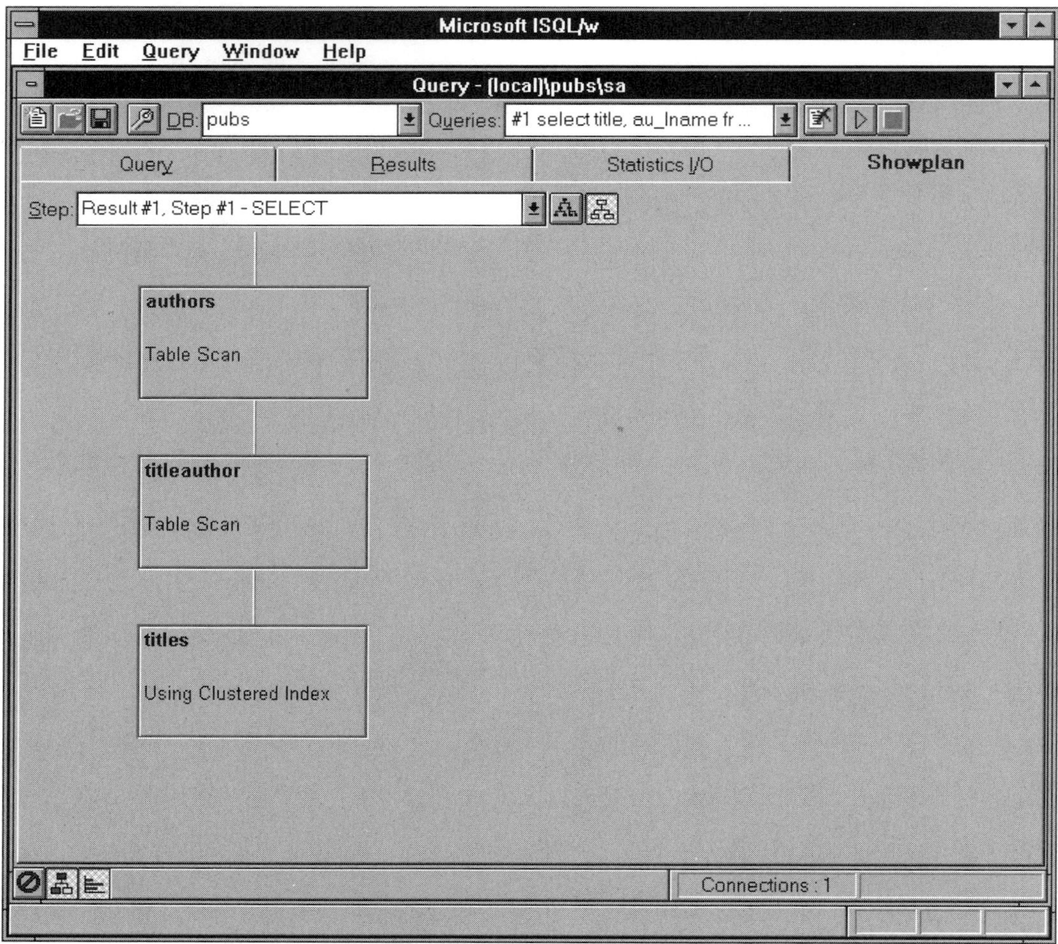

Figure 7-4 A Graphical Showplan Output

Figure 7-5 shows the statistics I/O output from the above query. The histogram shows the *scan count* which is the number of times the table was accessed, the *logical reads* which are the number of database pages needed from the table and its indexes to satisfy the query and the *physical reads* which are the number of database pages actually read from disk. This is usually less than the logical reads value as database pages will often be held in cache.

These graphical outputs can be very useful when analyzing queries to see if a different query design or index design can produce a better query strategy that results in less I/O.

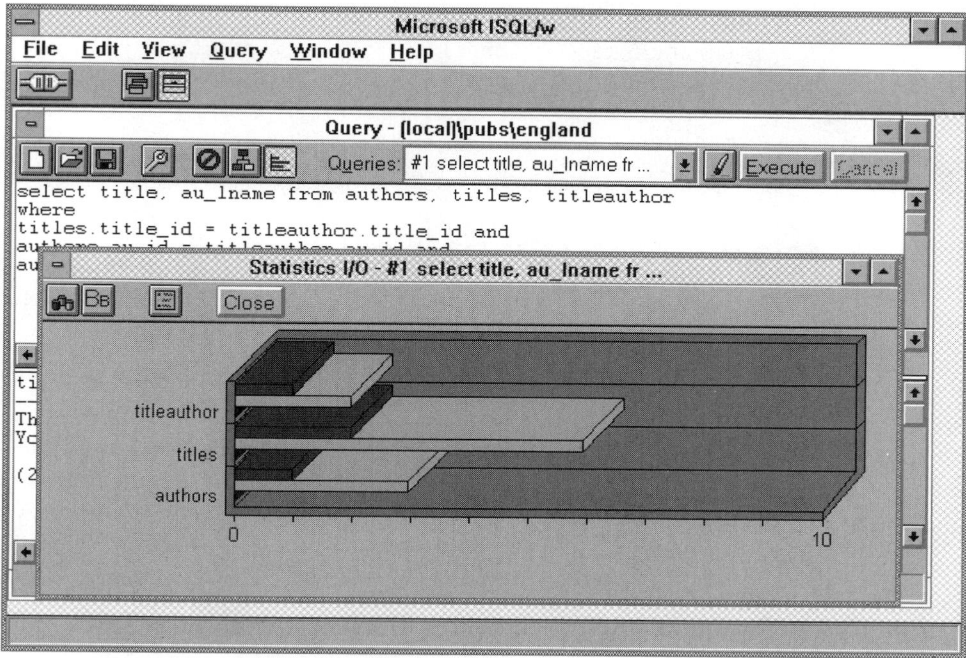

Figure 7-5 A Graphical Statistics I/O Output

7.3.2 Example Showplan Outputs

The following section will show some example showplans. We will use two tables that might be found in a database found in a bank. The first table holds information concerning customer accounts and the second table holds information concerning the bank branches where these accounts are held. We have chosen tables different from those found in the pubs database for these examples as we want to have a table with a large number of rows. The number of rows in a table is often known as its *cardinality*. In this case the accounts table has a cardinality of 10,000 rows whereas the branches table only has a cardinality of 11 rows. The definition of the tables is as follows:

```
create table accounts
    (account_no     char(10),
    customer_no     char(10),
    branch_code     char(4),
    balance         money)
```

```
create table branches
    (branch_code     char(4),
    branch_name      char(20),
    branch_address   char(120),
    managers_name    char(20))
```

We will also create some indexes on these tables:

```
create clustered index accounts_branch_no_idx on accounts
(branch_code)

create unique nonclustered index accounts_account_no_idx on accounts
(account_no)

create unique clustered index branches_branch_code_idx on branches
(branch_code)
```

Why did we choose these particular indexes? Perhaps, we know that the application has some frequently used transactions that query the accounts table by *account_no* and *branch_code*. The branches table only has 11 rows in it so its index is perhaps an overkill!

Query 1 – Find the balance of the customer with a customer_no of 159

```
select balance from accounts where customer_no = '159'

STEP 1
The type of query is SELECT
FROM TABLE
accounts
Nested iteration
Table Scan
balance
-----------------
7,390.36
5,026.09

(2 row(s) affected)

Table: accounts  scan count 1,  logical reads: 188,  physical reads: 0
Total writes for this command: 0
```

Let us investigate what has happened here. The first line of the showplan display is *STEP 1*. Every query is resolved in a number of steps, often just one as above. Some queries cannot be resolved in a single step and so *STEP* will appear a number of times. We shall see this later.

The type of query is SELECT shows that for this STEP a SELECT statement was issued. The type of query is often SELECT, INSERT, UPDATE or DELETE but other query types may also be seen. For example, a DROP TABLE statement would display *The type of query is TABDESTROY.*

FROM TABLE accounts shows that the query is retrieving rows from the table accounts. Sometimes the table name displayed is *worktable* indicating that SQL Server is retrieving data from a temporary worktable that it has created. The order that the *FROM TABLE* lines appear in the showplan output is important. It reflects the order in which the query optimizer has chosen to join the tables.

Nested iteration refers to the mechanism that SQL Server uses to return rows from a table or to join tables. It is usually not a useful line of display output.

The line displaying *Table Scan* is perhaps the most important line. It shows the table access strategy the query optimizer has chosen and it may not be what you expect. In our example a table scan has been chosen. This means that the query optimizer has chosen to read every page in the table in order to search for the rows that were requested. This might be fine for a small table but not a large one. Note that SQL Server must read *every* row in the table from the first to the last as it cannot know when it has retrieved the last row that satisfies the criteria.

Why was a table scan chosen? The query optimizer had no other choice as there was no index it could use. This underlines an important point. If there are no appropriate indexes, the query optimizer is forced to choose a table scan.

The statistics I/O display shows that 188 logical I/Os were needed to satisfy the query. Suppose that this query is frequently used. It might be worth creating a new index. Suppose that we replace the index *accounts_account_no_idx* with an index that contains *customer_no* as the second column:

```
create unique nonclustered index accounts_account_no_idx on
accounts
(account_no
 customer_no)
select balance from accounts where customer_no = '159'

STEP 1
The type of query is SELECT
FROM TABLE
accounts
```

```
Nested iteration
Table Scan
balance
------------------
7,390.36
5,026.09

(2 row(s) affected)

Table: accounts  scan count 1,  logical reads: 188,  physical reads: 0
Total writes for this command: 0
```

A table scan is still chosen by the query optimizer. This is because the *customer_no* column is the second column, sometimes known as *segment*, in the index definition. As we have not specified the first column *account_no* in the query to use this index the query optimizer would have to scan every leaf index node collecting the page numbers and row ids of the rows that satisfied the query and then read in those pages. If the query optimizer decides that it is less costly to choose a table scan it will do so.

Let us add an index *accounts_cust_no_idx* that contains *customer_no* as the only column:

```
create nonclustered index accounts_cust_no_idx on accounts
(customer_no)

select balance from accounts where customer_no = '159'

STEP 1
The type of query is SELECT
FROM TABLE
accounts
Nested iteration
Index : accounts_cust_no_idx
balance
--------------------
7,390.36
5,026.09

(2 row(s) affected)

Table: accounts  scan count 1,  logical reads: 5,  physical reads: 1
Total writes for this command: 0
```

Instead of seeing a table scan we now see the line *Index : accounts_cust_no_idx* displayed in the showplan output. This line shows that a nonclustered index, in this case *accounts_cust_no_idx*, has been used to satisfy the query. Note the reduction in logical I/Os. For retrieving accounts rows when only the *customer_no* is known this is clearly a very efficient access method using the *accounts_cust_no_idx*. However, remember that although indexes help operations that retrieve data from the database, they may hinder operations that write to the database. Adding this new index will slow down the insertion of new accounts and may exacerbate lock conflict. The addition of an index is often a balancing act!

Query 2 – Find the customers with accounts managed by branch 1009

```
select customer_no from accounts where branch_code = '1009'

STEP 1
The type of query is SELECT
FROM TABLE
accounts
Nested iteration
Using Clustered Index
customer_no
-----------------
50
504
  :
  :
4996
4997

(496 row(s) affected)

Table: accounts  scan count 1, logical reads: 13, physical reads: 0
Total writes for this command: 0
```

As there is a clustered index on *branch_code* the query *optimizer* has chosen to use it. The clustered index has sequenced the data on *branch_code* and so only 13 logical reads were needed to fetch all the 496 accounts rows that satisfied the query. The showplan output shows the fact that a clustered index is chosen by displaying the *Using Clustered Index* line.

Query 3 – Find the customers with accounts managed by branch 1009 or branch 1008

```
select customer_no from accounts where branch_code = '1009'
    or branch_code ='1008'
```

```
STEP 1
The type of query is SELECT
FROM TABLE
accounts
Nested iteration
Table Scan
customer_no
---------------
502
503
  :
  :
4997

(998 row(s) affected)

Table: accounts scan count 1, logical reads: 188, physical reads: 0
Total writes for this command: 0
```

In this example, even though there is a clustered index on *branch_code*, the query optimizer has determined that it is less costly to do the table scan. This may not be so but it is a choice we may have to live with. Beware the OR clause. It makes a query less *selective*, that is, more rows are likely to satisfy the query.

Query 4 – Find the customers with accounts at branch 1009 and a balance > 1000

```
select customer_no from accounts where branch_code = '1009'
         and balance > 1000

STEP 1
The type of query is SELECT
FROM TABLE
accounts
Nested iteration
Using Clustered Index
customer_no
-----------------
50
504
  :
  :
4996

(444 row(s) affected)

Table: accounts scan count 1, logical reads: 13, physical reads: 0
Total writes for this command: 0
```

In the above example the clustered index is again chosen. The AND clause makes the query more *selective*, that is, less rows are likely to satisfy the query and so the query *optimize*r is more likely to avoid a table scan.

Query 5 – Find the customers with accounts at branch 1009 that have a balance > 1000 and sort the result in ascending order of balance

```
select balance, customer_no from accounts where branch_code =
'1009' and balance > 1000 order by balance

STEP 1
The type of query is INSERT
The update mode is direct
Worktable created for ORDER BY
FROM TABLE
accounts
FROM TABLE
accounts
Nested iteration
Using Clustered Index
TO TABLE
Worktable
STEP 2
The type of query is SELECT
This step involves sorting
FROM TABLE
Worktable
Using GETSORTED
Table Scan
balance        customer_no
------------   -----------
1,012.60       846
1,033.97       4588
  :
  :
9,986.88       3579

(444 row(s) affected)

Table: accounts  scan count 1, logical reads: 13, physical reads: 0
Table: Worktable  scan count 0, logical reads: 453, physical reads: 0
Total writes for this command: 0
```

The simple act of adding an ORDER BY to this SELECT statement has added much more showplan output. This is because SQL Server must create a temporary worktable to hold the results of the query so that it can then sort the results at the end.

The query is executed it two steps represented by *STEP 1* and *STEP 2* in the showplan output above. The first step involves executing the query as shown previously, that is, using the clustered index. Instead of returning the rows to the user, however, they are inserted into a worktable. The worktable is then read and the results sorted before returning data to the user.

The type of query is INSERT shows that rows are to be inserted into a table rather than selected. *The update mode is direct* shows that the most efficient insertion method is being used by SQL Server. *Worktable created for ORDER BY* shows that a temporary worktable is being used, in this case to process an ORDER BY. Other reasons to use a worktable might be to process a SELECT with a DISTINCT clause, for example. It is this worktable that is being inserted into and hence the appearance of *The type of query is INSERT.*

The type of query is SELECT shows that a SELECT is being issued against the worktable. *This step involves sorting* shows that a sort is required and *Using GETSORTED* shows that the rows will be sorted using a sort routine. Note the *Table Scan* which shows that the rows from the worktable will be accessed by a table scan.

Query 6 – Find the total balance held at each branch

```
select branch_code, sum(balance) from accounts group by
branch_code

STEP 1
The type of query is SELECT (into a worktable)
GROUP BY
Vector Aggregate
FROM TABLE
accounts
Nested iteration
Table Scan
TO TABLE
Worktable
STEP 2
The type of query is SELECT
```

```
FROM TABLE
Worktable
Nested iteration
Table Scan
branch_code
-----------    ---------------
1000              2,624,919.21
1001              2,597,612.33
1002              2,478,104.36
1003              2,392,259.86
1004              2,667,447.94
1005              2,408,271.72
1006              2,534,309.82
1007              2,514,092.15
1008              2,541,700.86
1009              2,525,569.67
1234             25,085,229.33

(11 row(s) affected)

Table: accounts  scan count 1,  logical reads: 188,  physical reads: 0
Table: Worktable  scan count 1,  logical reads: 23,  physical reads: 0
Total writes for this command: 0
```

Adding a GROUP BY to this SELECT statement has also added more showplan output. Again, this is because SQL Server must create a temporary worktable to hold the results of the query so that it can then process the GROUP BY at the end.

The query is executed it two steps represented by *STEP 1* and *STEP 2* in the showplan output above. The first step involves executing the query and inserting the results into a worktable. The worktable is then read and the rows grouped as required by the GROUP BY before returning data to the user.

The *GROUP BY* line indicates that a GROUP BY has been used in the query. Because an aggregate function, in this case SUM(), is used in conjunction with a GROUP BY clause the line *Vector Aggregate* is displayed. If an aggregate function is used without a GROUP BY clause such that a single result is returned, for example a simple SUM() of all the balances in the database, a *Scalar Aggregate* line would be displayed.

The other lines of showplan output are as described previously.

Query 7 – Find the details of the branch that holds account number 1604

```
select branch_name, managers_name from branches, accounts
where accounts.account_no = '1604' and
branches.branch_code = accounts.branch_code

STEP 1
The type of query is SELECT
FROM TABLE
accounts
Nested iteration
Index : accounts_account_no_idx
FROM TABLE
branches
Nested iteration
Table Scan
branch_name    managers_name
------------   ----------------
Ropley         Ken England

(1 row(s) affected)

Table: branches  scan count 1, logical reads: 2, physical reads: 0
Table: accounts  scan count 1, logical reads: 4, physical reads: 0
Total writes for this command: 0
```

In the above example we have a join of two tables. We can see that the query optimizer has chosen to process the accounts table first and the line *Index : accounts_account_no_idx* shows that a nonclustered index has been used to access the table to retrieve the rows that satisfy the selection criteria, in this case, account_no = '1604'. The branches table is then accessed to retrieve the matching branches row. The query optimizer has taken this approach to reduce the number of accounts rows as much as possible before accessing the branches table. Note that the query optimizer has chosen to perform a table scan of the branches table, presumably as this is more cost effective than using the index.

Query 7 – Find the details of the branches that hold accounts with balances < $10

```
select branch_name, managers_name, account_no from branches,
accounts
where accounts.balance < $10 and
branches.branch_code = accounts.branch_code
```

```
STEP 1
The type of query is SELECT
FROM TABLE
branches
Nested iteration
Table Scan
FROM TABLE
accounts
Nested iteration
Using Clustered Index
branch_name    managers_name       account_no
-----------    ----------------    -----------
Reading        Keith Burns         4208
Reading        Keith Burns         7682
Hastings       Bill Burrows        2116
Beech          Margaret England    3032
Beech          Margaret England    7862
Urmston        Beryl England       3423
Urmston        Beryl England       3887
Urmston        Beryl England       3959
Urmston        Beryl England       5281
Urmston        Beryl England       5329
Urmston        Beryl England       8231
Urmston        Beryl England       8681
Urmston        Beryl England       9333

(13 row(s) affected)

Table: branches  scan count 1, logical reads: 2, physical reads: 0
Table: accounts  scan count 11, logical reads: 219, physical reads: 0
Total writes for this command: 0
```

This is slightly different from the previous example in that we cannot filter out the accounts rows we want using an index on balance as one does not exist. In this case the query optimizer has chosen to process the *branches* table first and then the *accounts* table. A table scan has been performed on the *branches* table and for every *branch_code* found the *accounts* table has been accessed using its clustered index on *branch_code*. Note that the *accounts* table has a scan count of 11 which is the number of rows in the *branches* table, so SQL Server has scanned (accessed) the *accounts* table once for every *branches* row.

The above seven examples give an overview of some of the showplan output that is commonly seen. Occasionally, other lines of showplan output may be seen and if this is found to be the case the Microsoft SQL Server documentation should be consulted to find the exact meaning of this output.

7.3.3 Influencing the Query Optimizer

The query optimizer works out a strategy for executing a query independent of the syntax of the query. By this we mean that the order of the tables in the query are ignored by the optimizer so the developer can avoid worrying about the order in which the tables are written in the query. Even so, it is worth experimenting with queries and showplan output to see if the addition or omission of columns and operators in the query might influence the query optimizer into choosing a less costly strategy.

It is possible to force the query optimizer to join tables in the order that they are written in the query with the SET FORCEPLAN ON statement. For example, consider Query 7. The *branches* table is processed before the *accounts* table. If we place the *accounts* table first in the query and use SET FORCEPLAN ON we can force the query optimizer to process the *accounts* table first.

```
set forceplan on

select branch_name, managers_name, account_no from accounts, branches
where accounts.balance < $10 and
branches.branch_code = accounts.branch_code

STEP 1
The type of query is SELECT
FROM TABLE
accounts
Nested iteration
Table Scan
FROM TABLE
branches
Nested iteration
Table Scan
branch_name    managers_name      account_no
------------   ----------------   ------------
Reading        Keith Burns        4208
Reading        Keith Burns        7682
  :
  :
Urmston        Beryl England      9333

(13 row(s) affected)
```

```
Table: accounts  scan count 1,  logical reads: 188,  physical reads: 0
Table: branches  scan count 13,  logical reads: 26,  physical reads: 0
Total writes for this command: 0
```

The above showplan output shows that the *accounts* table is processed first.

Another way of influencing the optimizer is to ensure that it has access to the latest statistics concerning the distribution of key values in the indexes. Information is accurate just after an index has been created or rebuilt but the statistics can diverge from reality over time and cause the query optimizer to make a less than optimum decision. To ensure that the statistics are recalculated the UPDATE STATISTICS statement can be executed.

```
update statistics accounts
```

The *Update Stats* button can also be clicked in the SQL Enterprise Manager *Manage Indexes* window, as shown in Figure 7-3.

6.0

SQL Server 6.0 has introduced additional ways in which to influence the query optimizer. It is now possible to specify which index should be used. Suppose we have the following query:

```
select branch_name from branches
      where managers_name = 'Andy James'

STEP 1
The type of query is SELECT
FROM TABLE
branches
Nested iteration
Table Scan
branch_name
---------
Poole

(1 row(s) affected)
```

The query optimizer has chosen to use a table scan to access the table. If there is an index on *managers_name* we can force the query optimizer to use it:

```
select branch_name from branches
(index=branches_managers_name_idx)
    where managers_name = 'Andy James'
```

The INDEX keyword allows us to specify an index name to be used by the query optimizer. If we specify a value 1 instead of an index name, the clustered index is used if there is one present:

```
select branch_name from branches (index=1)
    where managers_name = 'Douglas Adams'

STEP 1
The type of query is SELECT
FROM TABLE
branches
Nested iteration
Using Clustered Index
branch_name
--------------------
Gillingham

(1 row(s) affected)
```

Similarly, a value of 0 will tell the query optimizer to use a table scan:

```
select branch_name from branches (index=0)
    where managers_name = 'Graham Hunt'

STEP 1
The type of query is SELECT
FROM TABLE
branches
Nested iteration
Table Scan
branch_name
-----------------
Sandwich

(1 row(s) affected)
```

Another means of influencing the query optimizer that has been introduced with SQL Server 6.0 is that offered with the FASTFIRSTROW keyword. Usually, the query optimizer always attempts to optimize the total time taken to execute the whole query. If a large sort is to be performed there may be some delay before the first row is returned to the application. This is particularly noticeable when the query optimizer decides to choose a table scan rather than a nonclustered index which it may well do if it thinks that a table scan in conjunction with SQL Server 6.0's asynchronous read ahead capability will be a less costly strategy.

There are occasions, though, particularly with on-line, interactive queries when it is important to get information back to the application as soon as possible, even if this means that the total time to execute the query is increased. The FASTFIRSTROW keyword tells the query optimizer that it should use an appropriate nonclustered index, to return the first row as soon as possible:

```
select account_no from accounts (fastfirstrow) order by balance

STEP 1
The type of query is SELECT
FROM TABLE
accounts
Nested iteration
Index : accounts_balance_idx
account_no
-----------
8218
8675
7201
4767
3472
   :
   :
```

7.4 THE DATABASE CACHE

Before we finish this chapter on accessing data we should discuss the *database cache* often simply known as the *cache*. When SQL Server reads a database page from disk it places it in an area of memory known as a buffer. There are a number of these buffers and these are said to make up the cache. The cache can be thought of as existing in two parts:

- Procedure cache
- Data cache

The *procedure cache* is used to hold compiled stored procedures. If SQL Server needs to execute a stored procedure and it finds that it is already in the procedure cache it need not read it in from disk thus saving disk I/O. The *data cache* holds data and index pages. When a data or index page is required, SQL Server first checks to see if it is in the data cache. If it is, then disk I/O has been saved. If it isn't then the data or index page will be read into the cache.

How long will it stay in the cache for? SQL Server uses a *least recently used (LRU)* algorithm when looking for a free buffer to use. Assuming that all the buffers are being used, that is they all hold pages, SQL Server will have to overwrite a buffer to read in a new page.

A buffer that holds a page that has not been used for a while will be chosen in preference to a buffer that holds a page that has just been read in. If the buffer that is to be flushed has not been modified in any way, it can just be discarded. If the buffer has been modified it is said to be *dirty* and it must be written back to disk.

In versions of SQL Server prior to 4.21 each process that needed to find a free buffer would look for one in the data cache and if it could not find one a buffer that had been modified would be written to disk thus freeing up the buffer. SQL Server Version 4.21 made this activity more efficient by implementing a *Lazywriter* process. If the number of free buffers in the data cache drops below a predefined threshold the Lazywriter process writes dirty buffers out to disk until the number of free buffers grows above the threshold. This means that when a process needs to find a free buffer in the data cache it should find one and not have to wait while it writes out a dirty buffer to free one up.

SQL Server also writes dirty buffers back out to disk when a *checkpoint* occurs. A checkpoint can be an automatic or a manual event. SQL Server works out how often to issue an automatic checkpoint based on the *recovery interval* configuration option and how busy the system is. When a checkpoint occurs, dirty pages are written out to the relevant databases on disk and this then minimizes recovery time in the event of a failure.

The data cache, then, can reduce disk I/O by holding frequently used data and index pages in memory. The larger the cache the larger the number of data and index pages that can be held and the more likely that a request for a page will not result in a physical disk I/O. However, the size of the cache is limited by the memory that can be allocated to SQL Server. If more memory is allocated to SQL Server then a larger cache may be created. Care should be taken not to allocate large amounts of memory to SQL Server such that increased *page faulting* occurs which then degrades overall system performance.

8 Database Concurrency

8.1 INTRODUCTION

This chapter introduces the concepts of transactions and locking, perhaps two of the most important features provided by a modern database management system and, perhaps, also two of the features whose correct implementation by a database designer are most critical to database performance. SQL Server does not rely on the underlying Windows NT operating system to provide lock management, instead it manages its own locking protocol which will now be described in this chapter.

8.2 WHY A LOCKING PROTOCOL?

If the only requirement of a database management system is to provide single user access to a database at any one time, a locking protocol would not be required. Database management systems in reality must support more than one user concurrently accessing a database and it is this multi-user access than requires the database management system to provide a protocol to ensure that the changes being made to the database data by one user are not corrupted by another. Locking is not a luxury in a multi-user environment, it is a necessity. Of course, in a database environment where users only retrieve data and do not change it, locking is not necessary. However, as soon as there is a requirement to allow one user to change data then a locking protocol must be adopted.

Locking protocols are not all or nothing. Some protocols are more stringent than others with different database management systems adopting their own unique approaches. Locking is the natural enemy of performance and so a more stringent locking protocol is more likely to adversely affect performance than a less stringent one. However, a more stringent locking protocol is also likely to provide a more consistent view of the data.

To provide a taste as to why a locking protocol is necessary let us consider some multi-user scenarios:

Scenario 1

In this scenario Mike modifies a stock level by subtracting one thousand from it, leaving 100 items. Katy reads the stock level and sees that there are only 100 items in stock. Immediately after Katy has read this value and acted upon it, Mike's transaction fails and is rolled back returning the stock level to its original value of 1100.

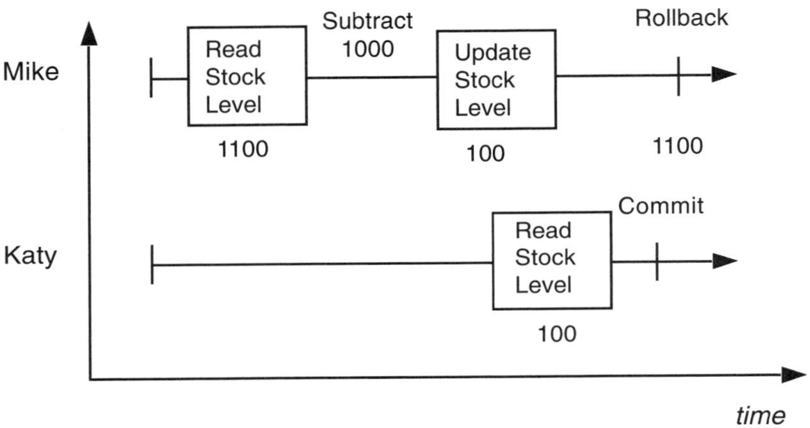

Figure 8-1 Reading Uncommitted Changes

This scenario highlights a problem whereby Katy has been allowed to read changes made by Mike before Mike has committed the changes, in other words, before Mike has irrevocably changed the data by ending the transaction with a commit. Until the transaction ends, Mike can choose to rollback the transaction, change the value again or commit the transaction. In our example, Mike's transaction actually fails before it completes causing the database management system to rollback the change. Katy is said to have read *uncommitted* or *dirty* data.

Scenario 2

In this scenario Mike's transaction sums a list of debts in a table and checks it against a total debt value held elsewhere in the database. While Mike's transaction is summing the values in the list, Katy's transaction inserts a new row into the debt table after Mike's transaction has passed by and updates the total debt value. When Mike finishes summing the list and compares the calculated sum with the total debt value it reports a discrepancy where in fact there is no discrepancy at all. This is called a *phantom* phenomenon.

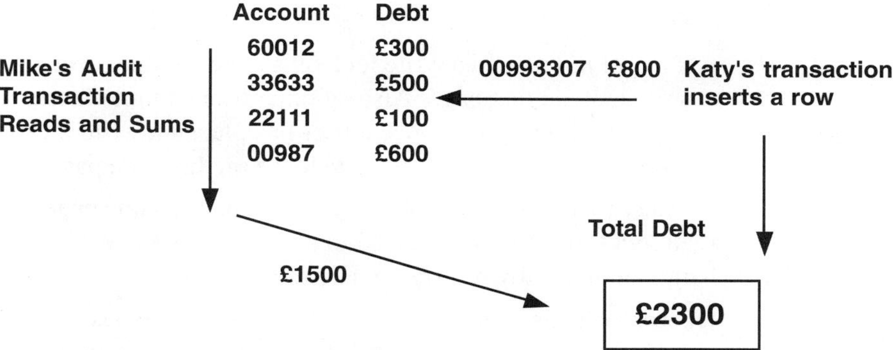

Figure 8-2 The Phantom Phenomenon

These are only two of a number of possible results that can occur if locking protocols are not used or the locking protocol used is not stringent enough and we shall revisit some of these scenarios later. We have said that SQL Server uses a locking protocol so let us now investigate how this works.

8.3 THE SQL SERVER LOCKING PROTOCOL

The locking protocol adopted by SQL Server consists of placing different types of lock on database pages. A SQL Server database page is 2Kb (2 kilobytes) in size and any object resident within this 2Kb is locked implicitly when the database page is locked. There is no row level locking so that, if a database page is locked, every row held on that page is effectively locked. Typically a database page will be a data page or an index page.

8.3.1 Shared and Exclusive Locks

At its simplest level, SQL Server applies a write lock when it writes information onto a page or a read lock when it reads information off a page. Writing information usually refers to inserting, updating or deleting rows whereas reading information usually refers to retrieving rows with, for example, a SELECT verb. There are some simple rules that we can make at this point.

- If a user has placed a read lock on a page, another user can also place a read lock on that page. In other words, both users can read the same page simultaneously. In fact any number of users can place a read lock on a page at the same time.
- If a user has placed a write lock on a page, another user cannot also place a write lock on that page. Also, another user cannot place a read lock on that page. In other words, once a user has placed a write lock on a page, other users cannot place read or write locks on the same page simultaneously.

Because many users can place read locks on the same page concurrently these read locks are usually referred to as *shared* locks. Write locks, on the other hand, are normally referred to as *exclusive* locks.

Once a lock has been placed on a database page it has a lifetime. The default situation is that shared locks live for the time it takes for the SQL statement to complete whereas exclusive locks live for the length of the transaction. This behavior can be overridden with the use of the HOLDLOCK keyword as we shall see shortly.

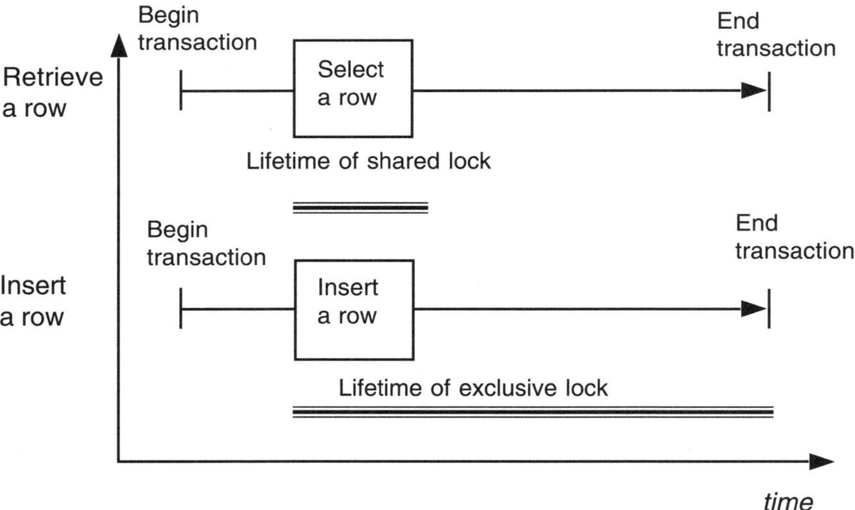

Figure 8-3 The Default Lifetime of SQL Server Locks

8.3.2 Page and Table Locks

So far, only locking at the database page level has been discussed. SQL Server can and will lock at the table level in certain situations. If SQL Server decides that a SQL statement is likely to process the majority of the rows in a table it will lock at the table level. While locking at the page level, if SQL Server decides that it is holding many page locks it will also attempt to lock at the table level. This occurs when SQL Server finds it is holding more than 200 page locks. This attempt may or may not succeed depending on the locks held by other users in the table. If it does succeed, the page locks will be released and the table lock acquired.

The advantage to holding a single table lock is down to system resource. Managing a single table lock is less resource intensive than managing multiple page locks and a lock will typically require 32 bytes of memory. However, locking at the table level may reduce concurrency. An exclusive lock held at the table level will block all other users from accessing rows within that table whether they wish to acquire shared or exclusive locks.

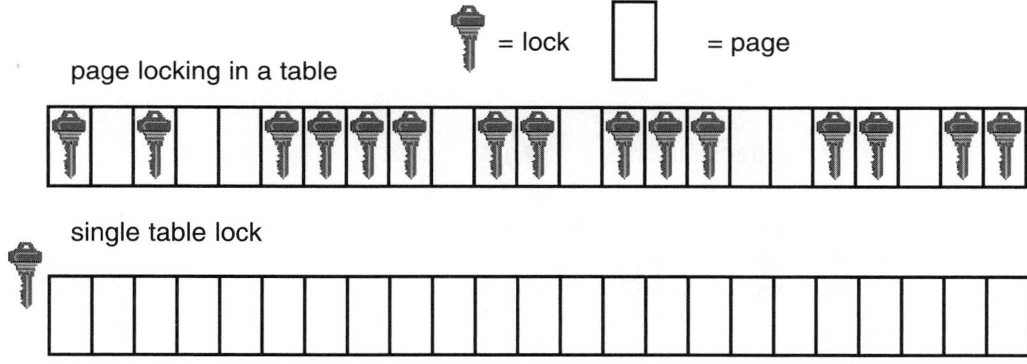

Figure 8- 4 Page Locking Versus Table Locking

It is also possible to observe SQL Server using extent locks. A table or index is allocated disk space in units of eight 2Kb pages known as an extent. While the table or index is being allocated the extent an extent lock is placed upon it.

Prior to SQL Server 6.0, the database administrator had no control over when SQL Server escalated page locks to table locks. At the point when greater than 200 page locks were acquired, SQL Server would attempt to replace the page locks with a table lock. The value of 200 was hard-wired into SQL Server.

SQL Server 6.0 now allows the database administrator to specify when lock escalation occurs. Using *sp_configure*, three configuration options pertaining to lock escalation may be set:

- LE threshold percent
- LE threshold minimum
- LE threshold maximum

The LE threshold percent option allows the database administrator to choose the percentage of pages locked in the table before SQL Server attempts to acquire a table lock. A value of 10, for example, means that once 10% of the pages in the table have page locks, SQL Server attempts to acquire a table lock.

Obviously, this percentage will equate to very different numbers of pages depending on the table size. For this reason the two other options are provided. The LE threshold minimum option places a minimum value on the number of pages locked before SQL Server attempts to acquire a table lock. For example, if the LE threshold percent is set to 10% and the LE threshold minimum is set to 50, SQL Server would not attempt to acquire a table lock if 10% of the pages in a 100 page table were locked. SQL Server, however, would attempt to acquire a table lock if 10% of the pages in a 1000 page table were locked as 10% of the pages is greater than the LE threshold minimum of 50 pages.

The LE threshold maximum option is used in a similar way and it places a maximum value on the number of pages locked before SQL Server attempts to acquire a table lock. If, for example, a table consists of 10,000 pages and the LE threshold percent is set to 10%, SQL Server will attempt to acquire a table lock when 1000 pages are locked. If, however, the LE threshold maximum is set to 500, SQL Server would attempt to acquire a table lock when 500 pages are locked.

The LE threshold minimum option is in place to minimize frequent lock escalation in small tables and the LE threshold maximum option is in place to allow the database administrator to keep the number of locks below a reasonable limit for large tables. If LE threshold percent is set to 0 then a table lock is acquired only when the number of locked pages reaches LE threshold maximum. This is the default value.

So we have introduced shared and exclusive locks and page and table level locking. We need to introduce some more types of lock before we can give some examples of the SQL Server locking protocol in action.

8.3.3 Update Locks

As well as placing shared and exclusive locks on database pages SQL Server also makes use of a type of lock known as an update lock. These locks are associated with SQL statements that perform update and delete operations which need to initially read in database pages. These pages have update locks placed on them which are compatible with shared read locks but are not compatible with other update locks or exclusive locks. If the data on the page must subsequently be updated or deleted SQL Server attempts to promote the update locks to exclusive locks. If other shared locks are associated with the database page SQL Server will not be able to promote the update locks until these are released. In reality the update lock is not promoted but a second lock is taken out which is in fact an exclusive lock.

8.3.4 Intent Locks

As well as placing shared and exclusive locks on database tables SQL Server also makes use of a type of lock known as an *intent* lock. Intent locks are placed on the table when a user locks pages in the table and stay in place for the life of the page locks. These locks are used primarily to ensure that a user cannot take out locks on a table that would conflict with another user's page locks. For example, if SQL Server decided that a user was holding many page locks and an escalation to a table lock was desirable, the page locks held by others users would not be overlooked when attempting the escalation.

8.3.5 Demand Locks

SQL Server uses *demand* locks to ensure that a situation does not arise where an exclusive lock cannot be granted because there are always shared locks present on a database page. Suppose Mike has placed a shared lock on a database page and Katy wishes to place an exclusive lock on that page. Katy will be blocked and forced to wait as an exclusive lock is incompatible with a shared lock. Suppose now that Margaret attempts to place a shared lock on the page. Her request will be granted as her shared lock is compatible with Mike's shared lock. Katy will still be forced to wait. Mike could release his shared lock and another user's shared lock request could be granted. Katy, requesting the exclusive lock, will still be blocked. This situation could go on ad infinitum and is shown graphically in Figure 8-5.

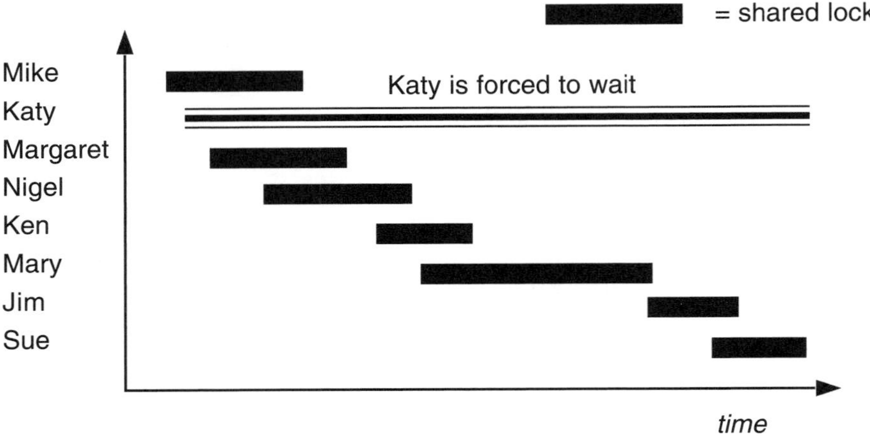

Figure 8-5 The Demand Lock Mechanism

This situation is known as a *livelock*. SQL Server deals with livelocks by allowing the user requesting an exclusive lock to be granted a demand lock when four shared read requests from other users have been granted. Once the user has the demand lock, no other shared lock request is granted and users requesting these are blocked. Once the previously granted shared locks are released the user holding the demand lock will be granted their exclusive lock.

8.3.6 Deadlocks

Another situation can occur in SQL Server whereby a user holds a lock on a resource needed by fellow user who holds a lock on a resource needed by the first user. This is a deadly embrace and the users would wait for ever if SQL Server did not intervene.

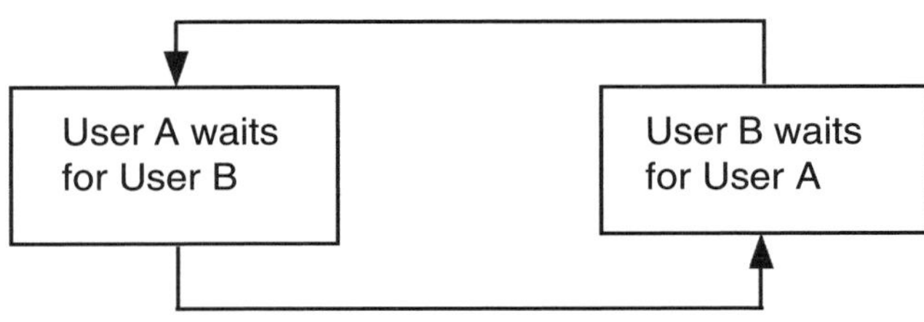

Figure 8-6 A Deadlock Between Two Users

SQL Server chooses one of the deadlocked users as a victim and issues a rollback for their transaction. They will receive an error message similar to the one below:

```
Msg 1205, Level 13, State 2
Your server command (process id 4) was deadlocked with another
process and has been chosen as deadlock victim. Re-run your
command
```

In the application code, this error should be trapped and dealt with cleanly. The application might retry a number of times before giving up and informing the user that there is a problem.

8.3.7 Modifying Default Locking Behavior

There are two ways in which to modify SQL Server's default locking behavior. Individual SQL statements can be qualified with a keyword to modify the locking behavior for that particular statement or a default environment can be set with the SET TRANSACTION ISOLATION LEVEL statement. Apart from the HOLDLOCK keyword, all the keywords mentioned in this section and the SET TRANSACTION ISOLATION LEVEL statement are newly introduced with SQL Server 6.0. The keywords used to modify the locking behavior for a particular SELECT statement are classified in SQL Server 6.0 as *optimizer hints.*

Optimizer Hints

The keywords available as optimizer hints for modifying locking behavior are:

- HOLDLOCK
- NOLOCK
- PAGLOCK
- TABLOCK
- TABLOCKX
- UPDLOCK

They are used on a SELECT statement, for example:

```
select * from titles holdlock

select price from titles (nolock) where title_id = 'MC2222'
```

The affect of these optimizer hints is described below:

Holdlock

The HOLDLOCK keyword forces a shared lock on a table to stay until the transaction completes. This will increase data integrity as it will enforce *repeatable reads*. This means that a data value that is read on more than one occasion within a transaction is guaranteed to be the same value, that is, it cannot have been changed by any *other* transaction.

Using the HOLDLOCK keyword may, and usually will, degrade performance as lock contention may increase. An example of using the HOLDLOCK keyword is given later in this chapter.

Nolock

The NOLOCK keyword allows a *dirty read* to take place, that is, a transaction can read the uncommitted changes made by another transaction.

Paglock

The PAGLOCK keyword forces shared page locks to be taken where otherwise SQL Server may have used a table lock. This keyword essentially overrides the *LE threshold* configuration options for the specific SELECT statement.

Tablock

The TABLOCK keyword forces a shared table lock to be taken where otherwise SQL Server may have used page locks. This keyword essentially overrides the *LE threshold* configuration options for the specific SELECT statement.

Tablockx

The TABLOCKX keyword forces an exclusive table lock to be taken.

Updlock

The UPDLOCK keyword forces an SQL Server to take update locks where otherwise SQL Server would have used shared locks.

Transaction Isolation Level

SQL Server allows the *transaction isolation level* to be set for a connection which sets a default locking behavior.

Levels of transaction isolation are specified by the ANSI standard with each one defining the type of phenomenon not permitted while concurrent transactions are running. The higher the isolation level number, the more stringent the locking protocol with the higher levels being a superset of the lower levels. The transaction isolation levels that can be set in SQL Server 6.0 are:

- Read Uncommitted
- Read Committed
- Repeatable Read
- Serializable

The locking behavior that corresponds with *read uncommitted* provides the least integrity but potentially the best performance. The *read committed* isolation level provides more integrity than *read uncommitted* and the *repeatable read* isolation level more so still. The greatest integrity is provided by the *serializable* isolation level. We have already met repeatable reads and the phantom phenomena. Table 4 shows whether the repeatable read and the phantom phenomena are allowed by the various isolation levels.

Isolation Level	Dirty Reads	Nonrepeatable Reads Allowed	Phantoms Allowed
Serializable	No	No	No
Repeatable Read	No	No	Yes (see below)
Read Committed	No	Yes	Yes
Read Uncommitted	Yes	Yes	Yes

Table 4 Isolation Levels and Allowed Locking Phenomena

It can be seen that only the *serializable* isolation level prevents all these phenomena from occurring. However, in SQL Server 6.0 the *serializable* and *repeatable read* isolation levels are identical in that they prevent all the phenomena, hence, the *repeatable read* isolation level also prevents phantoms.

By default, SQL Server runs at *transaction isolation level read committed.*

The transaction isolation level is set for the connection with the following syntax:

```
set transaction isolation level read uncommitted

set transaction isolation level read committed

set transaction isolation level repeatable read

set transaction isolation level serializable
```

The DBCC utility with the USEROPTIONS parameter can be used to check the current isolation level of the connection.

8.3.8 Monitoring Locks

Finally, we need to introduce the means by which we can observe SQL Server lock management in action and then we can look at some examples of the SQL Server locking protocol. There are a number of ways to find information about the locking that is happening within SQL Server.

- Use the *sp_lock* system stored procedure
- Use the *SQL Enterprise Manager*
- Use the *Performance Monitor*
- Interrogate the system table *syslocks* directly

Additionally, the *sp_who* system stored procedure is useful in finding blocked and blocking processes and the DBCC utility can be used to set trace flags to record lock and deadlock information.

Using sp_lock

The *sp_lock* system stored procedure displays information about the locks held by processes using the server. It can be entered as a standalone statement in which case it will display all locks managed by the server or can take a SQL Server process identifier (spid) as a parameter. Some example output from the *sp_lock* system stored procedure is shown below:

```
sp_lock
```

```
spid    locktype     table_id     page   dbname
----    -----------  ---------    -----  --------
4       Sh_intent    496004798    0      master
4       Ex_extent    0            40     tempdb
6       Sh_intent    3            0      pubs
6       Sh_intent    176003658    0      pubs
6       Sh_page      176003658    368    pubs
7       Sh_intent    3            0      pubs
7       Sh_table     48003202     0      pubs
9       Ex_intent    16003088     0      pubs
9       Ex_page      16003088     136    pubs
9       Update_page  16003088     136    pubs

(1 row(s) affected)
```

Hint: To translate the table_id to a table name use the built-in system function OBJECT_NAME. For example:

```
select object_name(176003658)

-----------
titles

(1 row(s) affected)
```

The above output from *sp_lock* shows a number of locks held on various objects. SQL Server process identification number (spid) 6 has requested and been granted a shared intent lock on the titles table and a shared page lock on database page number 368 allocated to the titles table.

```
6       Sh_intent    176003658    0      pubs
6       Sh_page      176003658    368    pubs
```

Spid 7 has requested and been granted a shared table lock on the publishers table.

```
7       Sh_table     48003202     0      pubs
```

Note that spid 6 had performed an indexed access on the table to retrieve the row whereas spid 7 had performed a table scan of the table.

Spid 9 has requested and been granted an exclusive intent lock on the table authors and an exclusive page and update page lock on database page number 136 allocated to the authors table.

```
9       Ex_intent    16003088     0      pubs
9       Ex_page      16003088     136    pubs
9       Update_page  16003088     136    pubs
```

Note that shared intent locks can be seen held on table id 3. This table is the *syscolumns* table and is locked because we are seeing processes reading metadata.

Using the SQL Enterprise Manager

The SQL Enterprise Manager allows the database administrator to monitor current locking activity in a graphical fashion. If *Server...Current Activity* is selected from the menu the *current activity* window is displayed as shown in Figure 8-7 with the *user activity* tab in the foreground.

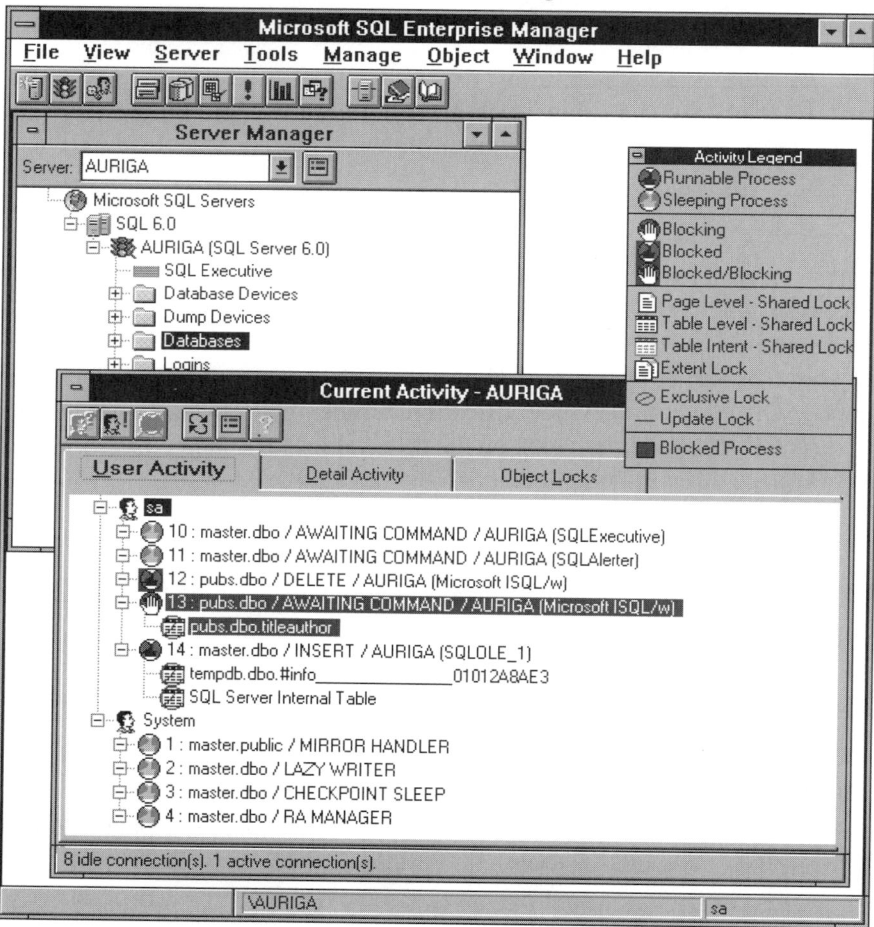

Figure 8-7 The SQL Enterprise Manager User Activity Tab

The current active users are shown and, as the legend shows, some processes are *sleeping*, and some processes are *runnable*. The process with spid 12 is blocked by the process with spid 13. This blocking can be seen more clearly in Figure 8-8 if the *Detail Activity* tab is selected.

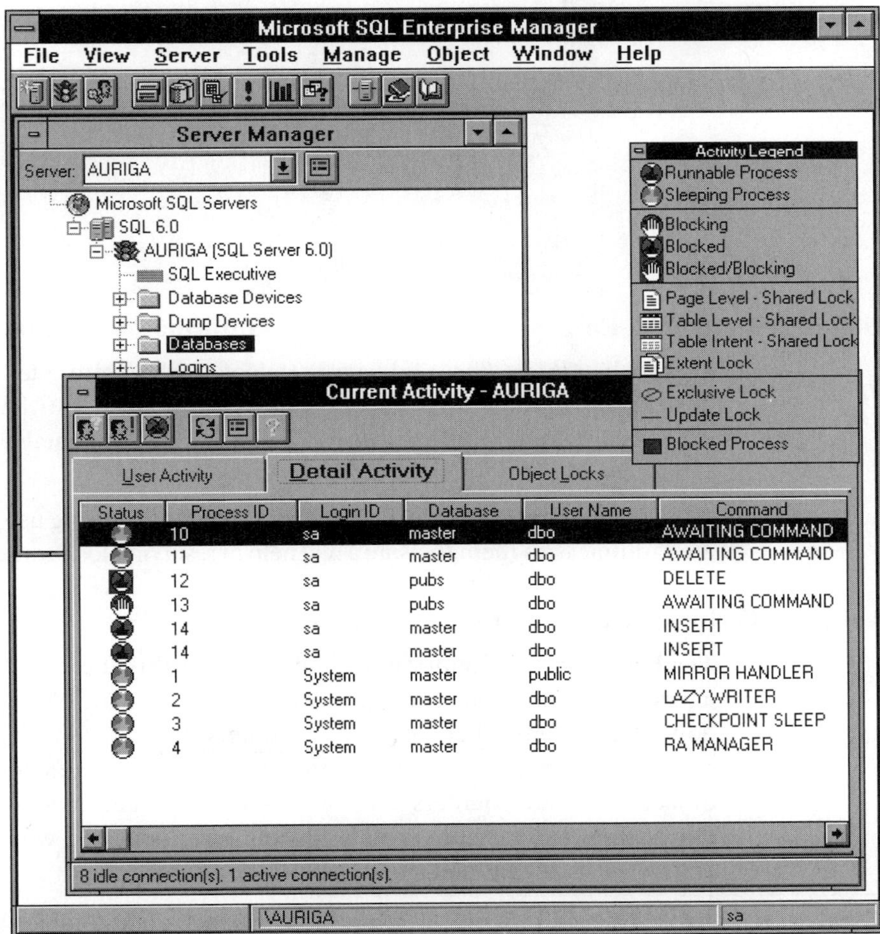

Figure 8-8 The SQL Enterprise Manager Detail Activity Tab

To see more information about what a processes is doing the entry in the list can be double-clicked which displays the *process information* window as shown in Figure 8-9. As can be seen, the last Transact-SQL statement executed can be observed.

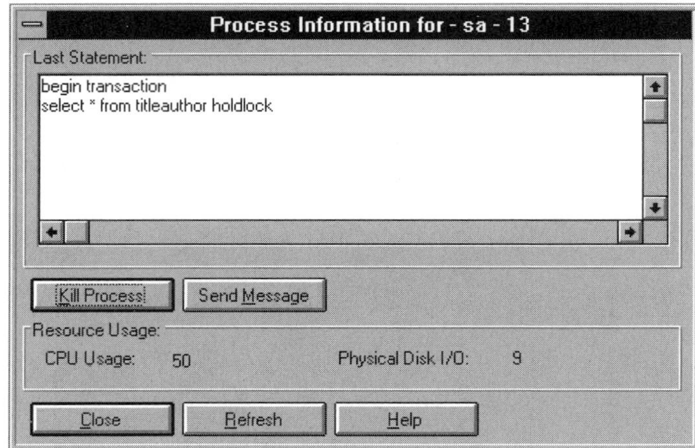

Figure 8-9 The SQL Enterprise Manager Process Information Window

Lastly, the *Object Locks* tab can be selected which provides information on the objects a process has locked. For example, spid 13 (the blocker) has a shared table lock on the titleauthor table in the pubs database, as shown in Figure 8-10.

The SQL Enterprise Manager displays take a little getting use to but once you are familiar with them they are a real help in resolving lock contention problems.

Using the Performance Monitor

The Performance Monitor is a Windows NT utility that enables system managers and database administrators to monitor the many objects within a Windows NT system. There are many counters that can be monitored for many objects but here we are interested in those counters specific to the SQL Server object. There are counters associated with I/O, cache and the network but, in this chapter, our concern is with the counters associated with locking. These counters can be grouped under the following categories:

Total	total exclusive, shared, blocking and demand locks and total for server
Table	total exclusive table locks, shared table locks and total table locks
Extent	total exclusive extent locks, shared extent locks and total extent locks
Intent	total exclusive intent locks, shared intent locks and total intent locks
Page	total exclusive page locks, shared page locks and total page locks

Table 5 Data Values Monitored for the SQL Server Object

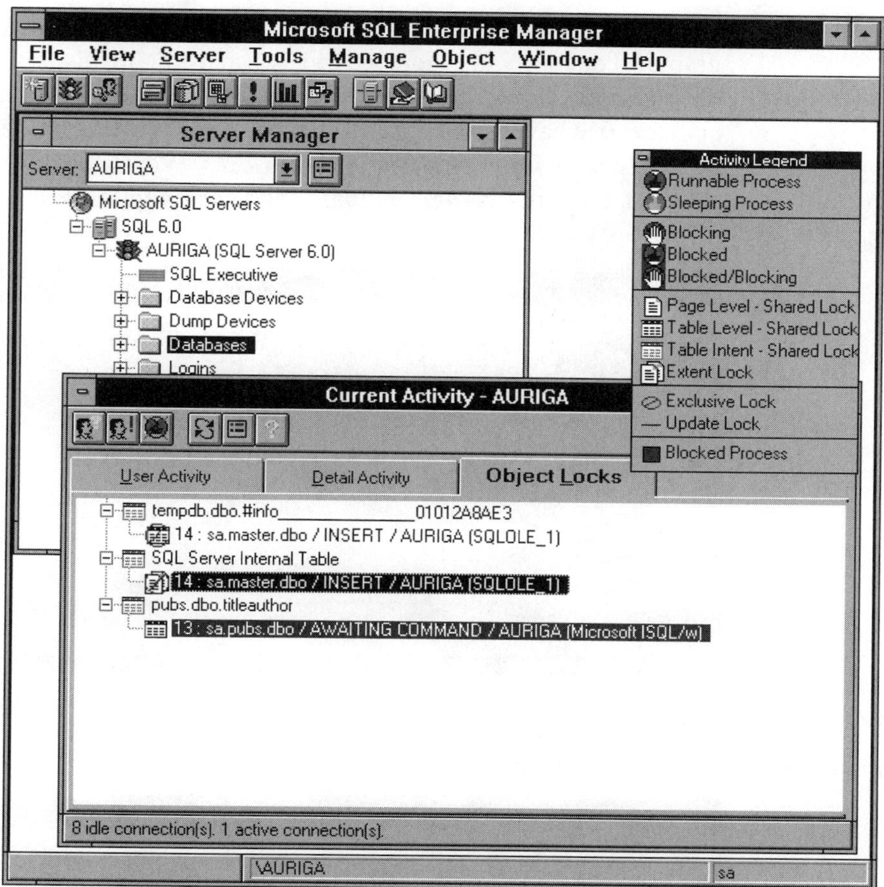

Figure 8-10 The SQL Enterprise Manager Object Locks Tab

There are many ways in which data can be displayed with the Performance Monitor. Data can be displayed in a customizable chart from which lock activity can be continuously monitored or data can be collected to a log file and then later replayed. An alert window can be used to display information about counters whose values have exceeded a user definable maximum and optionally a program can be executed when this happens. The values of counters can also be displayed in a simple, but easy to read, report format. The best mode of display is down to user preference and the actual monitoring task that is being performed.

Figure 8-11 and Figure 8-12 show two chart displays. Figure 8-11 shows a graphical display and Figure 8-12 shows a histogram display. The top half of each display shows the chosen chart format and the bottom half shows the counters that have been chosen as targets for monitoring. For example, one of the counters being monitored is *Total Locks*. When one of these counters is selected, the *last, average, minimum* and *maximum* values for that counter is displayed.

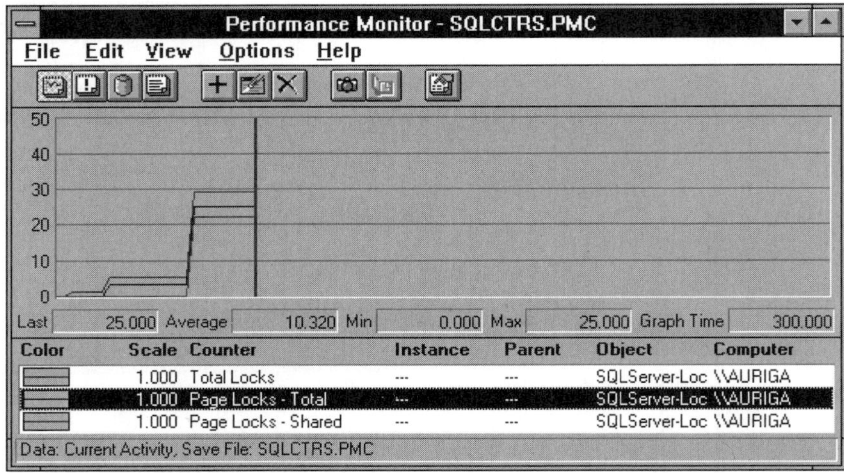

Figure 8-11 Example Performance Monitor Output Using a Graphical Display

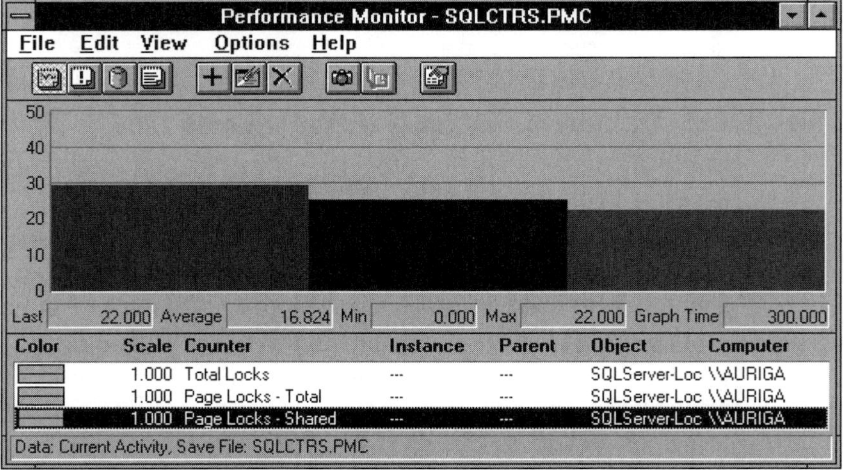

Figure 8-12 Example Performance Monitor Output Using a Histogram Display

The Performance Monitor is an invaluable monitoring tool and any would be SQL Server database administrator would be well advised to study the chapter describing it in the Windows NT documentation.

Interrogating the Syslocks Table

The *syslocks* system table can be interrogated in the same way that any other system table can be interrogated. It is only found in the master database where it holds information concerning the locks held in the SQL Server. Unlike other system tables it is materialized when a query is executed that accesses it, otherwise it does not exist physically. A query issued against the *syslocks* table produces output such as that shown below:

```
select * from syslocks

id     dbid    page    type    spid
---    ----    ----    ----    ----
3      1       0       4       4
0      2       128     8       4

(2 row(s) affected)
```

The *id* and *dbid* columns are the id of the table and the database respectively. The *page* column is the page number and the *spid* is the SQL Server process identifier of the process holding the lock. Perhaps the most interesting column is the lock *type* column. This column holds a value (which may be additive) that refers to the kind of lock as shown in the following table:

Value	Lock Type
1	table lock (exclusive)
2	table lock (shared)
3	intent lock (exclusive)
4	intent lock (shared)
5	page lock (exclusive)
6	page lock (shared)
7	update page lock
8	extent lock (exclusive)
9	extent lock (shared)
256	Lock is causing a process to be blocked
512	demand lock

Table 6 The Meaning of Lock Type Values in Syslocks

Using sp_who

The system procedure *sp_who* can be used to obtain information on the users and processes active within a SQL Server. It can be entered as a standalone statement in which case it will display information on all users and processes or it can take a SQL Server process identifier (spid) or alternatively a SQL Server login name as a parameter. Some example output from the *sp_who* system stored procedure is shown below:

```
spid status   loginame hostname blk dbname cmd
---  ------   -------  -------- --- ------ ------------------
1    sleeping sa                0   master MIRROR HANDLER
2    sleeping sa                0   master CHECKPOINT SLEEP
3    sleeping sa                0   master LAZY WRITER
4    runnable england  AURIGA   0   master SELECT
5    sleeping england  AURIGA   0   pubs   AWAITING COMMAND
6    sleeping stanley  AURIGA   5   pubs   SELECT
```

Note that the process with spid 6 has a 5 in the *blk* column whereas other processes have 0. This is because the process with spid 6 is being blocked by another user – in fact the user with spid 5. If we were to issue an *sp_lock* as shown below we would see an entry for spid 5. In this case we can see that spid 5 is holding an exclusive table lock. The fact that it is blocking another process can be seen from the -blk suffix.

```
spid  locktype      table_id   page     dbname
---   ------------  ---------- ----     ------
5     Ex_table-blk  16003088   0        pubs
```

Note that using *sp_lock* alone does not provide information on which process is being blocked, the database administrator must also use *sp_who*.

Using Trace Flags with DBCC

The SQL Server documentation states that *trace flags are not part of the supported feature set*. It is worth mentioning them here though as they can be used to provide some lock trace information. The database consistency checker, more usually referred to as DBCC, can be used to set trace flags or they can be set if SQL Server is started at the command line. Trace information can be sent to destinations such as the errorlog (using trace flag 3605) or the client (using trace flag 3604). Locking information can be generated by setting the trace flags to 1200 or 1204 for deadlock information. Some example trace output is shown below:

```
dbcc traceon (3604)
dbcc traceon (1200)
use pubs
begin transaction
select * from titles where title_id = 'BU1111'

Process 8 requesting table lock of type SH_INT on 4 3
Process 8, lock SH_INT not needed
Process 8 requesting page lock of type SH_PAGE on 4 50
chaining lock onto PSS chain
Process 8 releasing page lock of type SH_PAGE on 4 50
Process 8 requesting page lock of type SH_PAGE on 4 52
chaining lock onto PSS chain
Process 8 releasing page lock of type SH_PAGE on 4 52
Process 8 requesting page lock of type SH_PAGE on 4 25
chaining lock onto PSS chain
Process 8 releasing page lock of type SH_PAGE on 4 25
Process 8 requesting page lock of type SH_PAGE on 4 25
chaining lock onto PSS chain
Process 8 releasing page lock of type SH_PAGE on 4 25
DBCC execution completed. If DBCC printed error messages, see your System
Administrator.
DBCC execution completed. If DBCC printed error messages, see your System
Administrator.
Process 8 requesting table lock of type SH_INT on 4 176003658
chaining lock onto PSS chain
Process 8 requesting page lock of type SH_PAGE on 4 368
chaining lock onto PSS chain
title_id   title
type    pub_id   price advance    royalty    ytd_sales  notes       pubdate
------- ----------------------------------------    -------    ---------
------- -----    -------    --------------------------------------------
-------------------- -------------

BU1111  Cooking with Computers: Surreptitious Balance Sheets business  1389
11.95   5,000.00 10    3876 Hints on how to use electronic resources to the
best advantage. 9 Jun 1985  0:00

(1 row(s) affected)

Process 8 releasing page lock of type SH_PAGE on 4 368
Process 8 releasing table lock of type SH_INT on 4 176003658
```

The output can be somewhat cryptic but with a little effort a database administrator can follow what is happening.

8.4 SQL SERVER LOCKING IN ACTION

Now that we understand how SQL Server uses its locking protocol we can look at some examples. Our examples will all follow the same format, that of the 'T' graph. Some folk believe it is called a 'T' graph because it looks like a 'T', others believe it is because the vertical axis represents time! Whatever the reason, it is a useful method of representing the interaction of locks in a multi-user scenario. In order to keep the output as clear as possible, the actual results of the SELECT statements are not shown.

Our first set of examples will use the titles table in the pubs database. In these examples, all indexes have been removed from this table.

Mike	Katy
select * from titles	select * from titles
*** OK ***	*** OK ***

In the above example, Mike retrieves all the rows in the titles table. Katy attempts to concurrently retrieve all the rows in the titles table and is successful. This is because Mike places a shared lock on the titles table. Katy also attempts to place a shared lock on the titles table and, as shared locks are compatible, her attempt is also successful.

The reason that table level locks are used is that no indexes are present. Even if there were, the fact that the query optimizer uses a table scan instead of an index to retrieve the data dictates that page level locks will not be used.

In the next example, Mike updates all the rows in the titles table. He performs this operation within a transaction which he does not end. Katy attempts to retrieve rows from the titles table.

Mike	Katy
begin transaction update titles set advance = 0	
	select * from titles
*** OK ***	
	*** wait ***

In this example, Katy again attempts to place a shared lock on the titles table. This time, however, the shared table lock she attempts to place on the titles table is incompatible with Mike's exclusive table lock and so her attempt is unsuccessful. She will be forced to wait until Mike finishes his transaction.

This example serves to illustrate a very important point, which is, transactions should be kept as short as possible. If they are not, then they could block another transaction for an unacceptable length of time.

If we were to issue an *sp_lock* at this point we would see the following fragment of output:

```
spid  locktype      table_id    page   dbname
----  ------------  ---------   ----   ------
6     Ex_table-blk  176003658   0      pubs
```

Mike, spid 6, is holding an exclusive table lock with a -blk suffix that denotes that this lock is blocking another. An *sp_who* issued at this point would show:

```
spid status   loginame hostname blk dbname cmd
--- ------    -------  -------- --- ------ -----------------
5    sleeping katy     AURIGA   6   pubs   SELECT
6    sleeping mike     AURIGA   5   pubs   AWAITING COMMAND
```

In the next example, Mike again updates all the rows in the titles table. Again, he performs this operation within a transaction which he does not end. This time Katy attempts to delete the rows in the titles table.

Mike	Katy
begin transaction update titles set advance = 0 *** OK ***	begin transaction delete titles *** wait ***

In this example, Katy attempts to place an exclusive lock on the titles table. The exclusive table lock she attempts to place on the titles table is incompatible with Mike's exclusive table lock and so her attempt is unsuccessful. Again, she will be forced to wait until Mike finishes his transaction.

In the next example Mike will again update rows in the titles table and Katy will retrieve them. This is the same as the second example except that now

Katy will issue her SELECT statement first. We will use BEGIN TRANSACTION for both users.

Mike	Katy
	begin transaction select * from titles
	*** OK ***
begin transaction update titles set advance = 0	
*** OK ***	

In this example, Katy attempts to place a shared lock on the titles table. She is successful as Mike has not issued his update yet. Mike then issues his update which is also successful. Mike's exclusive table lock is not blocked by Katy's shared table lock because SQL Server only holds a shared lock for the duration of the select operation. Katy's lock has been and gone before Mike issues his update. The fact that Katy issues her SELECT statement within a transaction is irrelevant.

We can now introduce a *holdlock* example. As previously mentioned, the HOLDLOCK keyword forces a shared lock on a table to stay until the transaction completes. This will increase data integrity (it will provide repeatable reads as we shall see shortly) but possibly at the expense of concurrency. The last example is repeated below but Katy now uses the HOLDLOCK keyword.

Mike	Katy
	begin transaction select * from titles holdlock
	*** OK ***
begin transaction update titles set advance = 0	
*** wait ***	

Now Mike is forced to wait. Katy's shared table lock blocks Mike's exclusive table lock. If we were to issue an *sp_lock* at this point we would see the following fragment of output:

```
spid  locktype      table_id    page    dbname
----  ------------  ---------   ----    ------
5     Sh_intent     3           0       pubs
5     Sh_table-blk  176003658   0       pubs
```

Katy, spid 5, is holding an shared table lock and the -blk suffix can be seen that denotes that this lock is blocking another.

In the next example, Mike and Katy both attempt to update different rows.

Mike	Katy
begin transaction update titles set advance = 0 where titlesid = 'BU1032' *** OK ***	begin transaction update titles set advance = 0 where title_id = 'TC7777' *** wait ***

Even though both Mike and Katy are updating different rows, because there is no index defined on the title_id column resulting in a table scan, table locks will be used. Concurrency is therefore low and Katy must wait for Mike to complete his transaction before her update can execute.

Let us now replace the indexes on the titles table. There are two indexes - titleidind and titleind. The definitions can be found using *sp_helpindex*:

```
sp_helpindex titles

index_name  index_description                       index_keys
----------  -----------------------------------     ----------
titleidind  clustered, unique located on default    title_id
titleind    nonclustered located on default         title

(1 row(s) affected)
```

If we repeat the last example we see a different result. Now Katy is not blocked.

Mike	Katy
begin transaction update titles set advance = 0 where titlesid = 'BU1032' *** OK ***	begin transaction update titles set advance = 0 where title_id = 'TC7777' *** OK ***

This is because indexed access can now be used and consequently page level locks can be taken out.

If we were to issue an *sp_lock* at this point we would see the following fragment of output:

```
spid  locktype      table_id   page  dbname
----  ----------    ---------  ----  ------
5     Ex_intent     176003658  0     pubs
5     Ex_page       176003658  304   pubs
5     Update_page   176003658  304   pubs
6     Ex_intent     176003658  0     pubs
6     Ex_page       176003658  305   pubs
6     Update_page   176003658  305   pubs
```

Katy has placed an update and an exclusive page level lock on page 304 and Mike has placed an update and an exclusive page level lock on page 305. Note that they have both placed exclusive intent locks. The update transactions have not locked any index pages as the column updated (advance) is not involved in either index.

Suppose Mike had issued the following update statement:

```
update titles set title = 'Tales from an Indian Restaurant'
      where title_id = 'BU1032'
```

If we were to issue an *sp_lock* at this point we would now see the following fragment of output:

```
spid  locktype      table_id   page  dbname
----  ----------    ---------  ----  ------
5     Ex_intent     176003658  0     pubs
5     Ex_page       176003658  304   pubs
6     Ex_page       176003658  320   pubs
5     Update_page   176003658  304   pubs
6     Ex_intent     176003658  0     pubs
6     Ex_page       176003658  305   pubs
6     Update_page   176003658  305   pubs
```

We can see that an exclusive page lock is now also held on page 320. This is because an index page is now being written to as the title column is part of the titleind index.

8.5 UNCOMMITTED DATA, NON-REPEATABLE READS & PHANTOMS

With our new found knowledge of locking protocols we can now investigate how SQL Server deals with the reading of uncommitted data, non-repeatable reads and phantoms.

8.5.1 Reading Uncommitted Data

Figure 8-1 illustrated the problems with reading uncommitted data. As should already be clear, SQL Server forbids this by virtue of the fact that any row that has been changed cannot be read by another user as an exclusive page or table level lock will prevent the row being retrieved until the write transaction ends.

SQL Server 6.0, however, allows the default behavior to be overridden. A query is allowed to read uncommitted data with the use of the NOLOCK keyword, introduced in Section 8.3.7. For example, the following SELECT statement would read the row from the titles table regardless of whether another transaction had the page or table locked with an exclusive lock:

```
select price from titles (nolock) where title_id = 'MC2222'
```

Suppose Mike updates a row in the titles table. He performs this operation within a transaction which he does not end. Katy attempts to retrieve rows from the titles table.

Mike	Katy
begin transaction update titles set price = 50.00 where titlesid = 'MC2222'	
	select price from titles (nolock) where title_id = 'MC2222'
*** OK ***	
	*** OK ***

In this example, Katy does not attempt to place a shared lock and she can read the row that Mike has updated. She will read a value of $50.00 for the price of this book, however, Mike may well ultimately choose to rollback his change leaving Katy with incorrect pricing information.

8.5.2 Non-Repeatable Reads

In the case of a non-repeatable read, a transaction is allowed to read a data item on more than one occasion and retrieve different values each time. This is shown graphically in Figure 8-13. By default, SQL Server allows non-repeatable reads. It is sometimes desirable, however, to guarantee repeatable reads, that is, each read of the same data item while in the same transaction returns the same value. The means of guaranteeing repeatable reads in SQL Server is by the use of the HOLDLOCK keyword.

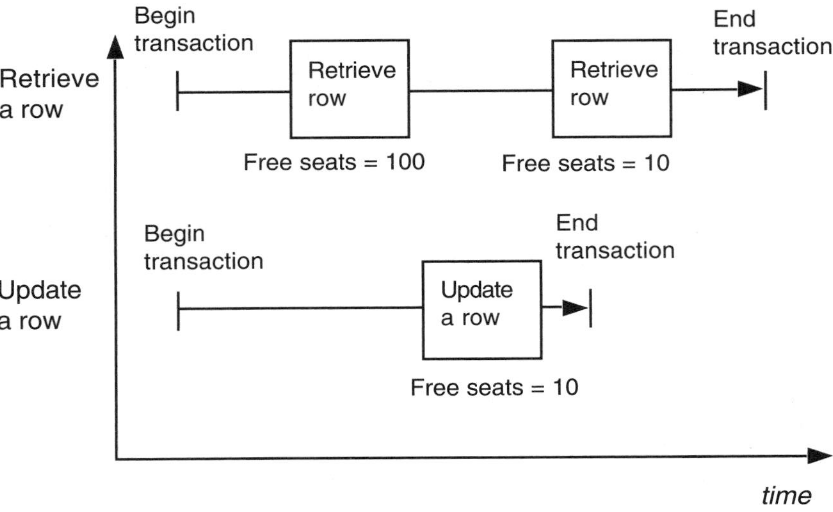

Figure 8-13 Non-Repeatable Reads

When the data item is read the first time, a shared lock is used which remains until the end of the transaction. This blocks any other transaction from changing the data item.

Mike	Katy
	begin transaction select price from titles holdlock where title_id = 'MC2222' *** OK ***
begin transaction update titles set price = 50.00 where titlesid = 'MC2222' **** wait ****	
	select price from titles holdlock where title_id = 'MC2222' *** OK ***

Now Mike is forced to wait. Katy's shared table lock blocks Mike's exclusive table lock and when Katy repeats her read she will receive the same value, hence, the use of the HOLDLOCK keyword has provided repeatable reads. Again, this is at the expense of concurrency.

With SQL Server 6.0 setting the isolation level to repeatable read (or serializable) will also provide repeatable reads.

Mike	Katy
	set transaction isolation level repeatable read begin transaction select price from titles where title_id = 'MC2222' *** OK ***
begin transaction update titles set price = 50.00 where titlesid = 'MC2222' **** wait ****	
	select price from titles where title_id = 'MC2222' *** OK ***

Again, Mike is forced to wait. Katy's shared table lock blocks Mike's exclusive table lock and when Katy repeats her read she will receive the same value. The use of the HOLDLOCK keyword is not required as the *set transaction isolation level repeatable read* statement has provided repeatable reads.

8.5.3 Phantoms

The phantom problem was illustrated in Figure 8-2. By default, SQL Server does not forbid phantoms but the use of the HOLDLOCK keyword will prevent them as the following examples show:

Mike	Katy
begin transaction select sum(qty) from sales 493 **** OK ****	
	insert into sales values ('7896','TQ2323','10 Dec 1994', 200,'Net 60','MC2222') *** OK ***
select sum(qty) from sales 693 **** OK ****	

In the example above, phantoms are allowed to occur. The two sums of the same list of values give different results. In the next example, Katy's transaction is blocked and the phantom phenomenon is not allowed to occur.

Mike	Katy
begin transaction select sum(qty) from sales holdlock 493 **** OK ****	
	insert into sales values ('7896','TQ2323','10 Dec 1994', 200,'Net 60','MC2222') *** wait ***
select sum(qty) from sales 493 **** OK ****	

The use of the HOLDLOCK keyword is not required if the *set transaction isolation level serializable* (or repeatable read statement - see Section 8.3.7) is used.

Mike	Katy
set transaction isolation level serializable begin transaction select sum(qty) from sales 493 **** OK ****	
	insert into sales values ('7896','TQ2323','10 Dec 1994', 200,'Net 60','MC2222') *** wait ***
select sum(qty) from sales 493 **** OK ****	

8.5.4 More Modified Locking Behavior

While showing examples of how the HOLDLOCK keyword and transaction isolation levels can modify the default locking behavior, its also worth looking at examples of some more of the keywords introduced in 8.3.7. We have already seen an example of NOLOCK so let us look at TABLOCKX, for example. The TABLOCKX keyword forces an exclusive table lock to be taken on a table which means that no other user, regardless of their Transact-SQL statement, can access rows in the table.

Mike	Katy
begin transaction select qty from sales (tablockx holdlock) **** OK ****	
	begin transaction select sum(qty) from sales *** wait ***

Even though the two transaction are only reading the table, Katy is must wait.

The PAGLOCK keyword forces shared page locks to be taken where otherwise SQL Server may have used a table lock.

Suppose we execute the following SELECT statement within a transaction:

```
select price from titles holdlock where pub_id = '0736'
```

We would see the following output from *sp_lock*:

```
spid  locktype     table_id    page   dbname
----  ---------    ---------   ----   ------
11    Sh_table     192003715   0      pubs
12    Sh_intent    544004969   0      master
12    Ex_extent    0           352    tempdb
```

However, suppose we execute the SELECT statement within a transaction using the PAGLOCK keyword:

```
select price from titles (paglock holdlock) where pub_id ='0736'
```

We would see the following output from *sp_lock*:

```
spid  locktype     table_id    page   dbname
----  ---------    ---------   ----   ------
11    Sh_intent    192003715   0      pubs
11    Sh_page      192003715   408    pubs
11    Sh_page      192003715   409    pubs
11    Sh_page      192003715   410    pubs
12    Sh_intent    544004969   0      master
12    Ex_extent    0           352    tempdb
```

As can be seen, the first SELECT statement uses a single shared table lock whereas the second SELECT statement uses three shared page locks.

8.6 A SUMMARY OF LOCK COMPATIBILITY

We have seen a number of scenarios involving locks and it is worth now summarizing the compatibility between different locks. Page level locks are either shared, exclusive or update, and these interact as shown in Table 7 below:

Mode of Currently Granted Lock	Mode of Requested Lock		
	exclusive	shared	update
exclusive	✘	✘	✘
shared	✘	✔	✔
update	✘	✔	✘

Table 7 Page Level Lock Compatibility

A cross denotes incompatibility, that is, one lock will block the other. A tick denotes compatibility, that is, the locks can happily exist with each other.

Table locks are a little more involved as intent locks must also be considered as shown in Table 8 below:

Mode of Currently Granted Lock	Mode of Requested Lock			
	exclusive	shared	exclusive intent	shared intent
exclusive	✘	✘	✘	✘
shared	✘	✔	✘	✔
exclusive intent	✘	✘	✔	✔
shared intent	✘	✔	✔	✔

Table 8 Table Level Lock Compatibility

As discussed in Section 8.3.4, intent locks are used to flag the fact that page locks are being held in a table. If Mike is holding shared page locks on a table, SQL Server will place a shared intent lock on the table and, if Katy is holding exclusive page locks on the table, SQL Server will place an exclusive intent lock on the table. From Table 8 it can be seen that these intent locks are compatible. However, if an attempt is made to escalate the page locks, belonging to either Mike or Katy, to a table lock, it will not be allowed as incompatibility between the intent locks and the requested table locks will forbid it.

What about the locks that are placed when an index is created on a table? If we consider what is actually happening, in a non-clustered index the index leaf level is stored on separate pages from the actual data. This means that the leaf level index pages that are being written to during the non-clustered index creation are not the same pages as those holding the data rows. Therefore the pages holding the data rows need only be read by SQL Server in order to create the index and only a shared lock needs to be placed on the table.

The index leaf level of a clustered index, on the other hand, is essentially the data itself. This means that the leaf level index pages that are being written to during the clustered index creation are the same pages as those holding the data rows. Therefore the pages holding the data rows must be written to by SQL Server in order to create the index and an exclusive lock needs to be placed on the table.

Because locking is a very important topic and can be crucial to transaction throughput, this chapter has looked at locking in some detail and locking will also be revisited in Chapter 9 in the context of performance.

9 Performance Monitoring and Tuning

9.1 INTRODUCTION

This chapter introduces the performance monitoring tools available with SQL Server and the facilities available to tune the server and associated databases for increased performance. It also discusses the physical database design process.

9.2 THE PHYSICAL DATABASE DESIGN PROCESS

Once the database logical design has been satisfactorily completed it can be turned into a database physical design. In the physical design process the database designer will be considering such issues as the placement of data and the choice of indexes and, as such, the resulting physical design will be crucial to good database performance. Two important points should be made here:

- A bad logical design means that a good physical design cannot be performed. Good logical design is crucial to good database performance and a bad logical design will result in a physical design that attempts to cover up the weaknesses in it. A bad logical design is hard to change and once the system is implemented it will be almost impossible to do so.
- The physical design process is a key phase in the overall design process. It is too often ignored until the last minute in the vain hope that performance will be satisfactory. Without a good physical design, performance is rarely satisfactory and throwing hardware at the problem is only occasionally completely effective. There is no substitute for a good physical design and the time and effort spent in the physical design process will be rewarded with an efficient and well tuned database, not to mention happy users!

Before embarking on the physical design of the database it is worth stepping back and considering a number of points:

- What kind of system are we trying to design? Is it a fast *On-line Transaction Processing (OLTP)* system perhaps comprising of hundreds of users with a throughput of hundreds of transactions per second (TPS) with an average transaction response time that must not exceed two seconds? Is it a multi-gigabyte *data warehouse* that must support few on-line users but must be able to process very complex ad-hoc queries in a reasonable time or is it a combination of the two?
- The type of system will strongly influence the physical database design decisions that must be made. If the system is to support OLTP and complex decision support then maybe more than one database should be considered - one for the operational OLTP system and one, fed by extracts from the operational OLTP system, to support complex decision support.
- What are our hardware and budget constraints? The most efficient physical database design will still have a maximum performance capability on any given hardware platform. It is no use spending weeks trying to squeeze the last few CPU cycles out of a CPU bound database when, for a small outlay, another processor can be purchased. Similarly, there is little point purchasing another CPU for a system that is disk I/O bound.
- Has the database design been approached from a textbook normalization standpoint? Normalizing the database design is the correct approach and has many benefits but there may be areas where some denormalization might be a good idea. This might upset a few purists but if a very short response time is needed for a specific query it might be the best approach.
- How important is data consistency? For example, is it important that if a transaction re-reads a piece of data it is guaranteed that it will not have changed? Data consistency and performance are enemies of one another and therefore, if consistency requirements can be relaxed, performance may be increased.

How does a database designer move from the logical design phase to a good physical database design? There is no single correct method, however, certain information should be captured and used as input to the physical design process. Such information includes data volumes, data growth and transaction profiles.

9.2.1 Data Volume Analysis

It is very important to capture information on current data volumes and expected data volumes. Without this information it is not even possible to estimate the number and size of the disk devices that will be required by the database. Recording the information is often a case of using a simple spreadsheet as shown in Figure 9-1.

Table Name	# of Rows	Row Size	Space Needed	% Annual Growth	Space Needed in 12 Months
Accounts	10,000	100	1,000,000	10	1,100,000
Branches	100	200	20,000	5	21,000
Customers	5,000	200	1,000,000	20	1,200,000
Transactions	400,000	50	20,000,000	25	25,000,000

Figure 9-1 Capturing Simple Data Volume Information

This may appear a trivial operation but it is surprising how few database designers do it and it is also interesting to find the different views from the business users on what the figures should be! Another column that could be added might represent how volatile the data in a particular table is. The percentage annual growth of a table might be zero but this may be because a large amount of data is continually being removed as well as being added.

Simple addition of these figures gives the data size requirements but this is only part of the calculation. The database designer must take into account the space required by indexes, the transaction log, the dump devices and no experienced database designer would ask for the disk space that came out of the sum from Figure 9-1. They would, of course, add a percentage on for safety. Users typically do not phone you to complain that you oversized the database by 20%, however, they do phone you to complain that the system just stopped because the database was full!

So how are the sizes of indexes calculated? The Microsoft SQL Server documentation gives sample calculations to assist in the sizing of clustered and non-clustered indexes for tables with both fixed and variable length columns. It is highly recommended that these calculations are performed and so it is worth using a spreadsheet such as Microsoft Excel to perform the calculations to save time and effort. There are also stored procedures in circulation that do these calculations.

A rule of thumb is to double the size of the user data to estimate the size of the database. Crude though this appears, by the time indexes have been added and some space for expansion, double the size is not far off!

What about the size of the transaction log? This is difficult to size as it depends on the write activity to the database, frequency of transaction dumps and transaction profiles. Microsoft suggest that about 10% to 25% of the database size should be chosen. This is not a bad start but once the system testing phase of the development has started the database designer can start monitoring the space usage in the transaction log with dbcc (checktable) and dbcc sqlperf (logspace). The transaction log space is a critical resource and running out of it should be avoided.

Remember that, in an operational system, if a transaction log dump fails for some reason the transaction log will continue to fill until the next successful transaction log dump. It may be desirable to have a transaction log large enough such that it can accommodate the failure of one transaction log dump.

Lastly, do not forget that, as a database designer/administrator, you will need lots of disk space to hold at least one copy of the production database for performance tuning testing. Not having a copy of the production database can really hinder you.

So we now have documented information on data volumes and growth. This in itself will determine a minimum disk configuration, however, it is only a minimum as transaction analysis may determine that the minimum disk configuration will not provide enough disk I/O bandwith.

If data volume analysis is concerned with the amount of data in the database and the space it needs, transaction analysis is concerned with the way in which that data is manipulated and at what frequency.

9.2.2 Transaction Analysis

The data in the database may be manipulated by 3GL code such as Visual Basic or a tool such as Microsoft Access or a third party product accessing SQL Server though Microsoft ODBC. Whichever way the data is accessed, it will presumably be as a result of a business transaction of some kind. Transaction analysis is about capturing information on these business transactions and investigating how they access data in the database and in which mode. For example, Figure 9-2 shows some attributes of a business transaction it might be useful to record:

Attribute	Explanation
Name	a name assigned to the transaction
Average frequency	average number of times executed per hour
Peak frequency	peak number of times executed per hour
Priority	a relative priority assigned to each transaction
Mode	whether the transaction only reads or also writes to the database
Tables accessed	tables accessed by the transaction and in which mode
Table keys	keys used to access the table

Figure 9-2 Capturing Transaction Attributes

Clearly, by their very nature, it is not possible to capture the above information for ad-hoc transactions nor is it practical to capture this information for every business transaction in anything other than a very simple system. However, this information should be captured for at least the most important business transactions. By most important we mean those transactions that must provide the fastest response times and/or are frequently executed. A business transaction that runs every three months and can be run at a weekend probably does not appear in the most important transaction list!

It is important to prioritize transactions as it is virtually impossible to be able to optimize every transaction in the system. Indexes that will speed up queries will almost certainly slow down inserts.

An example of the attributes captured for a transaction might appear as shown in Figure 9-3.

Attribute	Value
Name	Order Creation
Average frequency	10,000 per hour
Peak frequency	15,000 per hour
Priority	a1 (high)
Mode	Write
Tables accessed	Orders (w), Order Items (w), Customers (r), Parts (r)
Table keys	Orders (order_number), Order Items (order_number), Customers (cust_number), Parts (part_number)

Figure 9-3 Example Transaction Attributes

There are various ways to document the transaction analysis process and some modeling tools will automate some of this documentation. The secret is to document the important transactions and their attributes such that the database designer can decide which indexes should be defined on which tables. Again, it is often a case of using simple spreadsheets as shown in Figure 9-4.

Transactions/Tables	orders	order_items	parts	customers
Customer inquiry				R
Order inquiry	R	R		
Order entry	I	I	R	R

Transactions/Tables	orders	order_items	parts	customers
Customer inquiry				cust_number
Order inquiry	order_number	order_number		
Order entry	order_number	order_number	part_number	cust_number

Figure 9-4 Capturing Simple Transaction Analysis Information

The first spreadsheet maps the transactions to the mode in which they access tables with the modes being 'I' for insert, 'R' for read, 'U' for update and 'D' for delete. The second spreadsheet maps the transactions to the key with which they access tables. Again, there is nothing complex about this but it really pays to do it. Depending on how the system has been implemented a business transaction may be modeled as a number of stored procedures and, if desired, one may wish to use these instead of transaction names.

It is also important when considering the key business transactions, not to forget triggers. The trigger accesses tables in various modes just as the application code does.

With SQL Server 6.0 foreign key constraints have been introduced which will cause other tables in the database to be accessed.

Once the transaction analysis has been performed the database designer should have a good understanding of the tables that are accessed the most, in which mode and with which key. From this one can begin to derive the following:

- Which tables are accessed the most and therefore experience most disk I/O.
- Which tables are written to frequently by many transactions and therefore might experience the most lock contention.

- For a given table, which columns are used to access the required rows, i.e, which common column combinations form the search arguments in the queries.

In other words *where are the hot spots in the database?*

The database designer, armed with this information, should now be able to make informed decisions about the estimated disk I/O rates to tables, the type of indexes required on those tables and the columns used in the indexes.

Relational databases, and SQL Server is no exception, are reasonably easy to prototype so there is no excuse for not testing out the physical design that you are considering. Load data into your tables, add your indexes and stress your database with some representative Transact-SQL. See how many transactions a second you can perform on a given server or, to look at it another way, how much disk I/O does a named transaction generate? What resource - CPU or disk do you run out of first?

Here is some simple Transact-SQL that can help you populate tables with test data. We want to populate the table accounts with 1000 rows.

```
create table accounts
    (account_no      char(10),
    customer_no      char(10),
    branch_code      char(4),
    balance          money)

declare   @count int
select    @count=0
while     @count<1000
    begin
      select @count=@count+1
      insert accounts values(convert(char(30),@count),
                    convert(char(30),@count),
                    '1234',
                    20000 )
    end
```

Depending on how representative you want the data to be, you could replace the constant values in the INSERT statement above with expressions containing functions such as:

```
round(rand() * 10000,2))

((datepart (millisecond, getdate())/100)+1000))
```

These kind of expressions would generate a range of random values.

Do not forget multi-user testing! Lock contention cannot be tested unless some kind of multi-user testing is performed. In its simplest form this might involve persuading a number of potential users to use the test system concurrently by following set scripts while performance statistics are monitored. In its more sophisticated form this might involve the use of a multi-user testing product that can simulate multiple users while running automated scripts.

Transaction analysis and performance testing can be approached in a much more sophisticated way than has been described above. The important point, however, is that it should be done, the level of sophistication being determined by the available resource be it time or money.

Another important point is that physical design and performance testing is an on-going activity not a one-off activity. Systems are usually in a constant state of flux because business requirements are usually in a constant state of flux. Therefore performance should be regularly monitored and, if necessary, the database tuned.

9.2.3 Hardware Environment Considerations

The previous section described pre-production performance testing. This should have given the database designer a feel for the hardware requirements of the production system. Obviously there is a hardware budget for any project but it is clearly critical to have sufficient hardware to support the workload of the system. It is also critical to have the correct balance and type of hardware.

For example, there is no point in spending a small fortune on CPU power if only a small amount of money is spent on the disk subsystem. Similarly, there is no point in spending a small fortune on the disk subsystem if only a small amount of money is spent on memory. Would the application benefit from a multiprocessor configuration or a single powerful processor?

If the application's main component is a single report that runs through the night but must be finished before 9:00 a.m., a single powerful processor might be a better choice. On the other hand, if the application consists of a large number of users in an OLTP system, a more cost-effective solution would probably be a multiprocessor configuration.

Take a step back and look at the application and its hardware as a whole. Make sure the system resource is not unbalanced and do not forget the network!

9.3 OPTIMIZING SYSTEM RESOURCE USAGE

Given a hardware configuration the challenge for the database designer is to then optimize the resource available. This resource is typically in the form of disk, CPU and memory which are all closely linked. Creating a large memory cache, for example, can reduce the need to perform physical disk I/O although this may increase CPU usage. The secret is to get this balance right and to not waste the resource available. In this section will look at a number of ways to do this. Be warned, there is one way to dramatically reduce disk I/O and CPU usage – increase locking contention through bad database design such that only one user is performing useful work while the others are forced to wait!

9.3.1 Inefficient Query Strategies

Perhaps one of the areas where the most dramatic improvements to performance can be made is where a query strategy that is inefficient is replaced by a much more efficient one that saves many disk I/Os. A classic example of this is where a table scan is replaced by an indexed access. It should be noted, however, that with SQL Server 6.0 sort performance has been enhanced by the new asynchronous read ahead capability and if a query specifies an ORDER BY the optimizer may choose to perform a table scan and sort instead of using a nonclustered index as it believes that the query will run faster.

However, in many instances, apart from small tables consisting of a few rows, an indexed access will be faster than a table scan and will usually not have as detrimental an effect on concurrency.

We have already met the optimizer in Chapter 7 and have an understanding of its operation and how to check the strategy it uses with SHOWPLAN. Let us investigate this further using our accounts table and branches table. To remind ourselves, the structure of these tables is as follows:

```
create table accounts
    (account_no         char(10),
    customer_no         char(10),
    branch_code         char(4),
    balance             money)

create table branches
    (branch_code        char(4),
    branch_name         char(20),
    branch_address      char(120),
    managers_name       char(20))
```

They also have the following indexes:

```
create clustered index accounts_branch_no_idx on accounts
(branch_code)

create unique nonclustered index accounts_account_no_idx on
accounts
(account_no)

create unique clustered index branches_branch_code_idx on
branches
(branch_code)
```

The accounts table has a cardinality of 10,000 rows whereas the branches table only has a cardinality of 11 rows.

Given the indexes on the accounts table we can guess that fast indexed access will likely occur if the *account_no* or *branch_code* columns are specified in the selection criteria whereas a table scan is likely to occur if neither are. This is only a guess as the query optimizer may decide that a table scan is more efficient even if an indexed column is specified. To make sure we must examine the showplan output. Let us suppose that transaction analysis has highlighted the following important transactions:

- Find an account's balance given the account number.
- Find the sum of the account balances for a given branch code.
- Find the sum of the account balances for a given customer.

As a database designer we should ensure that the query plans generated by the query optimizer are going to be efficient and there are no nasty surprises! Let us check the query plans for the above three important queries:

Find an account's balance given the account number

```
select balance from accounts where account_no = '2323'

STEP 1
The type of query is SELECT
FROM TABLE
accounts
Nested iteration
Index : accounts_account_no_idx
```

```
balance
----------------
2,885.83

(1 row(s) affected)

Table: accounts scan count 1, logical reads: 3, physical reads: 1
```

As expected, this query uses the *accounts_account_no_idx* and returns the row with little logical or physical I/O. With a reasonably sized cache we might hope to keep the index pages in memory but would probably expect that the data page holding an account would need to be read in from disk.

Find the sum of the account balances for a given branch code

```
select sum(balance) from accounts where branch_code = '1002'

STEP 1
The type of query is SELECT
Scalar Aggregate
FROM TABLE
accounts
Nested iteration
Using Clustered Index
STEP 2
The type of query is SELECT

----------------
5,183,277.42

(1 row(s) affected)

Table: accounts scan count 1, logical reads: 21, physical reads: 0
```

As expected, this query uses the clustered index on *branch_code* and sums the balances for the accounts rows with 21 logical I/Os. There are in fact 1000 accounts that belong to branch 1002 so this seems an efficient strategy.

Find the sum of the account balances for a given customer

```
select sum(balance) from accounts where customer_no = '700'

STEP 1
The type of query is SELECT
Scalar Aggregate
FROM TABLE
accounts
Nested iteration
Table Scan
STEP 2
The type of query is SELECT

----------------
15,699.63

(1 row(s) affected)

Table: accounts scan count 1, logical reads: 188, physical reads: 0
```

This is not so good. The query optimizer has chosen a table scan and has needed 188 logical I/Os to satisfy the query. As there is no index on the customer number the optimizer has no choice but to scan the table. All the rows in the table must be scanned as SQL Server will not know until the last row has been processed that all accounts for the customer have been included in the sum.

As this is an important on-line query it is probably a good idea to create an index on *customer_no*:

```
create nonclustered index accounts_customer_no_idx on accounts
(customer_no)
```

The query should now use this new index.

```
select sum(balance) from accounts where customer_no = '700'

STEP 1
The type of query is SELECT
Scalar Aggregate
FROM TABLE
accounts
Nested iteration
Index : accounts_customer_no_idx
```

```
STEP 2
The type of query is SELECT

----------------
15,699.63

(1 row(s) affected)

Table: accounts scan count 1, logical reads: 4, physical reads: 1
```

As expected, the *accounts_customer_no_idx* has been used and the logical I/O value has dropped to 4. Of course, the addition of this new index will use up more disk space and will slow down inserts, updates and deletes executed against the accounts table but if this query is executed frequently and only the *customer_no* column is present in the selection criteria it is difficult to find a better option.

9.3.2 Other Query Optimizer Considerations

There are a number of facts to keep in the back of one's head when writing Transact-SQL queries – facts that are often forgotten.

Omitting the First Index Column

Suppose an index is composed of more than one column, for example:

```
account_no, customer_no
```

It is important to ensure that the query specifies the leftmost column or SQL Server is *unlikely* to use the index. For example, suppose the following index exists on the accounts table:

```
create nonclustered index accounts_account_cust_no_idx on
accounts
(account_no, customer_no)
```

If we specify the leftmost column of the index the query optimizer can use the index and will return the data efficiently:

```
select balance from accounts where account_no = '6399' and
customer_no = '3200'
```

```
STEP 1
The type of query is SELECT
FROM TABLE
accounts
Nested iteration
Index : accounts_account_no_idx
balance
----------------
6,100.96

(1 row(s) affected)

Table: accounts scan count 1, logical reads: 3, physical reads: 2
```

However, if by mistake we omit the leftmost column of the index the query optimizer uses a table scan and returns the data less efficiently:

```
select balance from accounts where customer_no = '3200'

STEP 1
The type of query is SELECT
FROM TABLE
accounts
Nested iteration
Table Scan
balance
----------------
6,100.96

(1 row(s) affected)

Table: accounts scan count 1, logical reads: 188, physical reads: 0
```

Of course, omitting a selection criteria may also result in an unexpected answer, but we are interested in showing query optimizer behavior here!

Note that the query optimizer may still choose to use the index and perform an index scan if it determines that this would be a less costly option.

Query Selection Criteria

If the selection criteria in a query is complex, the query optimizer is more likely to choose a table scan. This often occurs when there are many OR clauses in a query. The OR clause tends to broaden the result set and may therefore cause the query optimizer to decide that the result set will be large and so a table scan may be the best strategy.

```
select customer_no from accounts
    where
         customer_no = '1630' or
         customer_no = '1780' or
         balance = 1000  or
         balance = 1500

STEP 1
The type of query is SELECT
FROM TABLE
accounts
Nested iteration
Table Scan
customer_no
------
1630
1630
1780
1780

(4 row(s) affected)

Table: accounts scan count 1, logical reads: 188, physical reads: 0
```

The query optimizer has chosen to use a table scan for the above query. At first sight this may seem inefficient, but the query optimizer has no choice as there is no index on balance and every row must therefore be examined to see if the balance satisfies the selection criteria.

Note that the AND clause tends to narrow the result set.

Complex Table Joins

Is it really a good idea to do, say, a 9-way join on a group of large tables in one Transact-SQL statement? Perhaps it might be better to break the join into a number of discrete steps with the use of temporary tables to store intermediate results. Sure, SQL Server will handle a 9-way join but it may take a fair chunk of CPU to decide the best query plan and any less than optimal strategy will be *magnified* by the number of joins in the query and the size of the tables involved.

This also holds true where complex queries contain many subqueries. SQL Server 6.0, however, does now optimize subqueries along with the main query instead of optimizing them separately.

If performing complex join queries is a frequent operation then consider running the queries against a report database in which some denormalization has been performed and more indexes added.

Calculations in Selection Criteria

Suppose we have created an index on the balance column in the accounts table.

```
create nonclustered index accounts_balance_idx on accounts
(balance)
```

We would expect the following query to use the index which in fact it does:

```
select account_no, balance from accounts
    where
         balance > 1000 and
         balance < 1002

STEP 1
The type of query is SELECT
FROM TABLE
accounts
Nested iteration
Index : accounts_balance_idx
account_no     balance
951            1,000.70
2905           1,001.01
4437           1,001.01
8560           1,001.01
7212           1,001.92

(5 row(s) affected)

Table: accounts scan count 1, logical reads: 7, physical reads: 0
```

However, consider the following query:

```
select account_no, balance from accounts
    where
         balance*1.175 > 1000 and
         balance*1.175 < 1002
```

We have introduced a calculation in the selection criteria and this causes the query optimizer to adopt the following strategy:

```
STEP 1
The type of query is SELECT
FROM TABLE
accounts
Nested iteration
Table Scan
account_no       balance
7883             852.69
6497             852.69
98               852.69
2207             852.38

(4 row(s) affected)

Table: accounts scan count 1, logical reads: 188, physical reads: 0
```

As we can see, the query optimizer has decided to do a table scan. Be very careful about performing calculations in selection criteria!

Stored Procedures and the Query Optimizer

The query optimizer must create a plan for any stored procedures in the same way that it would for stand-alone Transact-SQL statements. This occurs on the first execution of the stored procedure. The stored procedure is read into the cache from disk and the query optimizer determines a query plan and stores this in cache also.

As we have seen previously, the query optimizer will consider the Transact-SQL statements in the stored procedure when determining the query plan and it will also consider table sizes and available indexes. It will also consider the values of the parameters that may be passed to the stored procedure on this first execution. The Transact-SQL statements and the tables sizes and available indexes may be fairly static but it is possible that the values of the parameters may vary widely between different executions of the stored procedure and so the query plan created by the query optimizer may be different depending on which parameter values were used on the first execution.

If one user is executing a stored procedure and a second user also executes the same stored procedure, SQL Server cannot use the same instance of the query plan in the cache and it will create a second query plan based on the second user's parameters. The cache will then contain two instances of the query plan for the stored procedure that can be used subsequently by other users.

Here lies a potential problem. If the second user's parameters to the stored procedure are different from the first user's, the second user's query plan might be different. Depending on which plan subsequent users of the stored procedure are given, different users may experience different performance characteristics. This is also true if, for example, UPDATE STATISTICS had been performed between the two executions of the stored procedure. The second stored procedure might be given a different query plan as the query optimizer would use the most recent statistics.

There is no perfect solution to this situation. If the problem is occurring and causing serious performance issues the database administrator can drop and re-create the stored procedure which will flush all the instances of it from cache. An alternative approach would be to specify the WITH RECOMPILATION clause when the stored procedure is created or executed. This means that the stored procedure is recompiled every time it is executed which, unfortunately, means that the performance benefits of using a stored procedure are lost!

9.3.3 Clustered Versus Nonclustered Indexes

We have already seen that it is extremely important to create appropriate indexes otherwise the query optimizer may determine that a scan of the table is required in order to fetch the required rows. We have also mentioned that many indexes will have a detrimental effect on insert, update and delete performance as SQL Server will have more work to do maintaining the entries in the index. We have not discussed, however, when it is more appropriate to use a clustered index and when it is more appropriate to use a nonclustered index.

To remind ourselves, only one clustered index is allowed on a table whereas up to 249 nonclustered indexes are allowed, so the database designer must choose the clustered index carefully. The clustered index determines the physical order of the data on disk, for example, if a clustered index is created on a last name column then the row containing "England" is physically stored before the row containing "Stanley". If a row containing "Phillips" is then inserted it would be stored on a data page physically between "England" and "Stanley" and this might result in new pages being added into the chain if there is not enough room for the "Phillips" row.

The important point here is that a clustered index determines *where* new rows are inserted in the table.

A nonclustered index does not determine the physical order of the data on disk and, in the absence of a clustered index on the table, new rows are stored in the order in which they are inserted. In effect, they are *appended* to the table.

This brings us to a major reason for using a clustered index. If many users are inserting rows then, without a clustered index, SQL Server will insert these rows at the end of the table and consequently there will be great contention for the last page allocated to the table. By using a clustered index on an appropriate key the inserts can be spread across the pages allocated to the table, thus avoiding a hot spot.

Another advantage to using a clustered index is that, because the rows are stored and maintained in the clustered index key order, range retrievals based on that key will be very efficient as the range of rows required will be stored in consecutive database pages.

Given that a clustered index has been chosen, in most cases the database designer, will then choose appropriate nonclustered indexes.

Sometimes it is useful to create a nonclustered index that contains all the columns in the key that are required by an important query. This will save SQL Server the overhead of going to the table itself. This is called a *covered* query. As a general rule, though, the smaller the index key the better. This is because SQL Server can hold more index key entries in a smaller space which means a smaller index, perhaps with fewer levels.

To summarize then, it is likely that for all but the smallest of tables the database designer will need to define indexes. These will probably consist of a clustered index with a number of nonclustered indexes.

Consider using a *clustered* index when:

- It is desired to avoid hot spots caused by insertions into the last page of the table.
- The physical ordering supports the range retrievals of important queries.
- The clustered index key is used in the ORDER BY clause of critical queries.
- The clustered index key is used in important joins to relate the tables.

Consider using a *nonclustered* index when:

- A single or few rows will be retrieved.
- The nonclustered index key is used in the ORDER BY clause of critical queries.
- The nonclustered index key is used in important joins to relate the tables.
- A covered query is required.

Also consider that many applications will require the selection of a row by its primary key. This is a single row selection and therefore would normally benefit from the creation of an index containing the same columns as the primary key. As it is not common to request ranges of primary keys a nonclustered index is probably the best option. Also, rows are often inserted in ascending primary key order, especially if the primary key value is system generated, such as an invoice number or sales number. In this case, a clustered index would not eliminate the hot spot on the last page as rows would be added to the *end* of the index.

The choice of index and index columns is often a compromise, however, in the authors' experience, regardless of the database product, this choice is perhaps the most critical one the database designer must face as incorrect indexes will result in potentially much greater disk I/O, CPU, locking contention and a lower caching efficiency.

9.3.4 Table Updates

Updating a row or set of rows in a table is not quite as simple as one might imagine and there are performance implications. SQL Server essentially performs an update as a DELETE followed by an INSERT and, depending on certain conditions, the update of the row may or may not occur *in-place*. By in-place we mean that the insert will insert the row in the place from which it has just been removed.

In older versions of SQL Server, such as SQL Server version 4.2 for OS/2, if an UPDATE statement was executed against a table that changed columns that contained variable-length data or nulls, it could not be done in-place and, potentially, the inserted row generated by the update operation would find itself on a new page, often the last one.

Microsoft SQL Server for Windows NT performs all updates that do not change the physical length of the row in-place irrespective of the datatypes of the columns affected.

There are, however, some restrictions to performing an in-place update, including:

- A unique index must be present such that SQL Server can determine that zero rows or one row qualify for the update.
- There must be no update trigger on the table.

There is obviously a large overhead when an in-place update cannot be done. There will be more index key maintenance resulting in more disk I/O and CPU usage and more lock contention. Where possible, therefore, the database designer should try and ensure that in-place updating occurs.

9.3.5 Non-Logged Operations

Most operations such as insert, update and delete are logged in the transaction log. This is necessary for recovery purposes but it does impose an overhead and will cause the transaction log to grow. It is possible to execute certain operations that do not log changes into the transaction log with a corresponding improvement in performance. These operations are:

- TRUNCATE TABLE
- SELECT INTO

TRUNCATE TABLE will delete all the rows in a table and is equivalent to executing DELETE FROM tablename with no WHERE clause. However, TRUNCATE TABLE writes much less information to the transaction log than a DELETE and is consequently much faster.

SELECT INTO can be used to create a new table and populate it based on the selection criteria. Again, transactions are not logged and the operation is consequently much faster than using the INSERT statement. However, to use SELECT INTO the database administrator must have turned the *select into/bulkcopy* database option on which has ramifications for recovery.

9.3.6 Memory and the Database Cache

As mentioned in Chapter 7, a disk I/O to a database device results when a database or index page cannot be found in the database cache and must be read in from disk. If a page in cache must be written to disk then this too will result in a physical I/O. Similarly, the transaction log on disk must be written to when a transaction commits.

To reduce disk I/O, the cache should be of a size such that often used data and index pages are held in memory. From this it follows that the hardware should be configured with plenty of physical memory – the more memory on the server, the more memory that can be allocated to SQL Server's cache.

The memory is in fact used for a data cache to hold data and index pages and a procedure cache to hold compiled stored procedures. Other objects use memory as well as the SQL Server code itself which needs about 2 Mb. There are also various other structures that account for about 5% of the memory.

To allocate memory to SQL Server the *sp_configure* system stored procedure can be used:

```
sp_configure 'memory', 8192
```

This allocates SQL Server 8,192 2Kb pages or 16Mb. Alternatively, the SQL Enterprise Manager can be used as shown in Figure 9-5.

The other objects that also need memory include user connections, open databases, open objects, locks and devices. User connections need about 37 Kb each, open databases need about 1 Kb each, open objects need about 70 bytes each and locks need about 32 bytes each. If the *sp_configure* default of each object just mentioned (for example, user connections is 20) is multiplied by their memory requirement the value obtained is less than 1 Mb.

If we have 16 Mb allocated to SQL Server we can immediately subtract the memory requirement for the above objects (say 1 Mb) plus the memory requirement for the server (2 Mb), leaving us with 13 Mb for the cache.

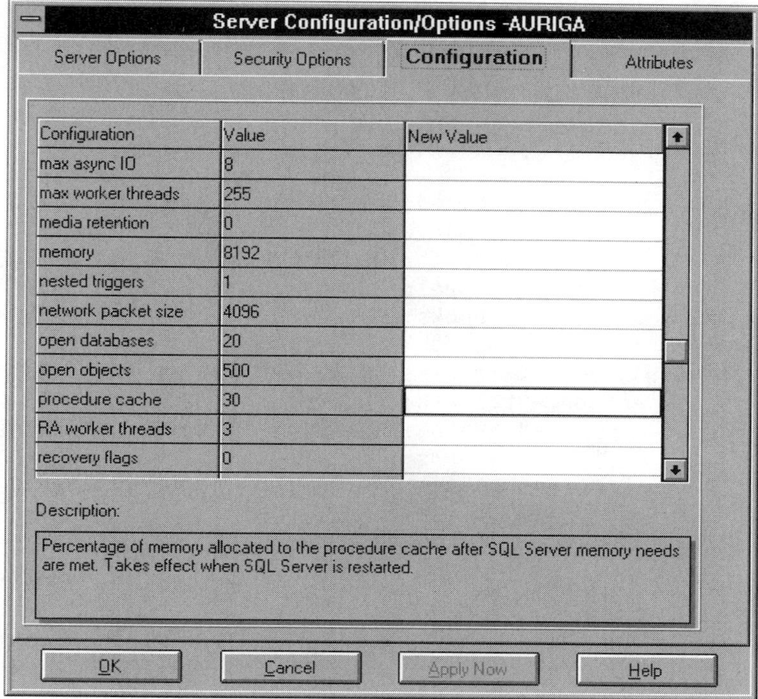

Figure 9-5 Using the SQL Enterprise Manager to Allocate Memory

To specify a value for the size of the data cache and procedure cache a value for the procedure cache is in fact specified, the size of the data cache being then the difference between the memory left from the above calculation (13 Mb) and the procedure cache.

By default 30% of the cache goes to procedure cache, so the cache will be apportioned as follows:

- procedure cache will be 13 * 0.3 = 3.9 Mb
- data cache will be 13 * 0.7 = 9.1 Mb

Note that the 5% overhead for other data structures mentioned above is actually added to the procedure cache value so it will in reality be allocated a little more memory and the data cache a little less. Therefore, our data cache will be allocated about 9 Mb and our procedure cache about 4Mb.

A database administrator will typically want to fine tune the cache. One useful tool is DBCC MEMUSAGE:

```
dbcc memusage

Memory Usage:
                              Megs    2K Blks       Bytes
           Configured: 16.0000       8192    16777216
               Memory:
            Code size:  1.7166        879     1800000
    Static Structures:  0.2489        128      261040
                Locks:  0.2480        127      260000
         Open Objects:  0.1068         55      112000
        Open Databases  0.0031          2        3220
   User Context Areas:  0.7447        382      780912
           Page Cache:  8.9682       4592     9403792
         Proc Headers:  0.2161        111      226554
       Proc Cache Bufs:  3.6289       1858     3805184

Buffer Cache, Top 20:

  DB Id   Object Id    Index Id   2K Buffers
      5           5           0           27
      1           5           0           25
      1           1           0           13
      1    54404969           0           11
      1          36           0            8
      1          99           0            8
      1           1           2            5
      1           2           0            5
      1           3           0            5
      1           5           1            3
      5           2           0            3
      1           6           0            2
      1           6           1            2
      1          45         255            2
      2           2           0            2
      2          99           0            2
      3           2           0            2
      4           2           0            2
      5           1           0            2
      5           3           0            2
```

```
Procedure Cache, Top 3:
Procedure Name: sp_helpdistributor
Database Id: 1
Object Id: 1856009643
Version: 1
Uid: 1
Type: stored procedure
Number of trees: 0
Size of trees: 0.000000 Mb, 0.000000 bytes, 0 pages
Number of plans: 1
Size of plans: 0.019249 Mb, 20184.000000 bytes, 10 pages

Procedure Name: sp_helptask
Database Id: 5
Object Id: 272004000
Version: 1
Uid: 1
Type: stored procedure
Number of trees: 0
Size of trees: 0.000000 Mb, 0.000000 bytes, 0 pages
Number of plans: 1
Size of plans: 0.018894 Mb, 19812.000000 bytes, 10 pages

Procedure Name: sp_server_info
Database Id: 1
Object Id: 1436532151
Version: 1
Uid: 1
Type: stored procedure
Number of trees: 0
Size of trees: 0.000000 Mb, 0.000000 bytes, 0 pages
Number of plans: 2
Size of plans: 0.005947 Mb, 6236.000000 bytes, 4 pages
DBCC execution completed. If DBCC printed error messages, see
your System Administrator.
```

The first section shows the allocation of the memory. In this example the *configured memory* is 16 Mb. Within this 16 Mb, *locks* use 0.2489 Mb and the SQL Server *code size* takes 1.7166 Mb. The data cache, represented as the *page cache* is configured to have 8.9682 Mb. The procedure cache is configured to have 3.6289 Mb.

The second section displays information about the data cache and shows the number of 2 Kb buffers allocated to the top twenty objects in it.

The third section displays information about the procedure cache and shows the cache usage of the top three compiled objects in it.

To calculate the size of the procedure cache needed, try taking the size of the largest plan in your server, as shown by DBCC MEMUSAGE, and multiply it by the maximum number of concurrent users on the system. Now multiply this figure by a fudge factor, say 1.3, and you will have a first cut procedure cache sizing.

Memory is a fairly straightforward resource to plan. Assuming that there is enough memory for Windows NT to perform well, the remaining memory can be used for SQL Server. This remaining memory can be used for data and procedure cache. A big data cache means that more data and index pages can be held in memory and then logical disk I/Os will not have to become physical disk I/Os. This will manifest itself as a good cache hit ratio which can be observed with the SQL Performance Monitor.

A big procedure cache means that there will be plenty of room for compiled stored procedures. If the procedure cache is too small then there may not be enough room to load a stored procedure in and the user may be forced to wait.

The simple way to increase the data and procedure cache is simply to purchase more memory!

9.3.7 Increasing Disk I/O Throughput to Tables and Indexes

Suppose that your transaction analysis points to a table or index in a database you are designing that will be a potential hot spot. It is a critical table and you have calculated that the disk I/O to the table could be large. How can you ensure that the table will not cause a disk bottleneck?

If we assume that there is a limit to how much of the table can be held in cache so we will be generating physical disk I/O, then we must look at ways of handling the disk I/O load. There are a number of possibilities but probably the two main ones are:

- Using segments
- Using RAID

Both of these topics have been described earlier in the book but they can be very effective approaches to dealing with disk I/O bottlenecks so we will revisit them here.

Tables and indexes can be placed on segments and segments can be created on multiple devices which can be created on multiple physical disks. In this way a table and its clustered index, for example, can be spread over multiple physical disks. If each physical disk can perform on average 100 I/Os per second then the application can generate 200 I/Os per second to a table and its clustered index before a bottleneck occurs. Of course, there may be other bottlenecks such as the disk controller if the disks share the same one but the approach is basically sound. Note that nonclustered indexes can be placed on different segments to their table.

Managing segments, however, is not always simple and in a large database with many tables and indexes it can become complex. The use of segments can also complicate recovery from media failures. A more straightforward approach and one that more and more SQL Server users are adopting is the use of RAID.

Microsoft Windows NT provides RAID 0 and RAID 5 support. RAID 0 is known as *striping* and RAID 5 is known as *striping with parity*. By using the RAID capabilities of Windows NT the database designer can ensure that database devices are spread over multiple disks without SQL Server needing to know that this is the case. In other words, the definition of the multiple device support is at the operating system level not the database level.

RAID 5 is more resilient than RAID 0 as the loss of a disk can be tolerated, however, both approaches essentially spread the blocks of the database device evenly across a number of disks. The effect is that of having multiple disk heads accessing the device, and therefore greater disk I/O throughput is possible. By letting Windows NT deal with the multiple device support the management of segments can be avoided which simplifies database administration.

For recovery and for performance purposes it is highly recommended that the transaction log resides on its own device. The transaction log can be placed on a database device that resides on its own disk or set of RAID disks if required.

The *tempdb* database is used for the creation of temporary tables if the query optimizer chooses strategies that require them. It is also used for sort workspace. The database designer can specify that tempdb should be held in memory which can increase performance considerably if temporary tables and sort workspace are used frequently. Of course there is a trade off as this increases the memory requirement of SQL Server which must come from somewhere and if it cannot be taken from outside SQL Server it must be found at the expense of the existing database cache. The *sp_configure* system stored procedure is used to specify that the tempdb should be held in memory using the *tempdb in ram* option.

9.3.8 Factoring in Data Integrity

As we have seen in Chapter 6, there are many features available in SQL Server to help the database administrator ensure that database integrity is maintained. The more sophisticated features include triggers and the primary and foreign key constraints that are newly provided with SQL Server 6.0.

However, these integrity features come with a performance price tag. If other tables are to be checked to see if a key value exists whereas otherwise they would not have been accessed, it is obvious that extra system resource, especially disk I/O, will be used.

Therefore, factor in database integrity constraints and triggers when performing transaction analysis and remember to add them to the database when performance testing starts. Do not forget that any table access must be performed as a table scan if no suitable indexes are present. There is nothing magic in the way database integrity constraints and triggers access tables. Treat them like any other query.

9.3.9 Choosing a Recovery Interval

When a transaction commits, its changes are written to the transaction log. More specifically, database and index pages in the cache that have been modified are written to the database's transaction log. If these modified pages were not written to the database device and a failure occurred, SQL Server would have to spend a long time processing transaction logs to ensure that the changes made by committed transactions were applied correctly to its databases. To minimize this *recovery* time an automatic checkpoint event occurs at intervals which flushes modified pages to the database devices.

The desired recovery time is set using *sp_configure* and has a default value of 5 minutes. If SQL Server detects that the workload running against a database would mean that recovery might take longer than 5 minutes it issues a checkpoint that flushes all the modified pages to the database. The checkpoint process may not use a lot of resource but it will use some and so the recovery interval should not be set too low or normal runtime performance may be adversely affected.

9.3.10 Balancing Workload

An obvious thing to do perhaps? Look at the workload as a whole across the day, week and even month and do not forget weekends.

There will be times of high activity and times of low activity. Try and run large reports and table loads in the times of low activity. Users will often demand their reports as soon as possible but with a little cajoling many will accept that the report can be run in the early hours of the morning to be ready for their arrival in the office the next day. Being a database administrator often means being a diplomat.

Being a database administrator also often means that 0900-1700 office hours rarely apply. Database administration tasks usually get done at the weekend so make sure that you make full use of SQL Server's task scheduling capabilities and the remote dial-in capabilities of Windows NT!

Remember that, although dumping the database is an on-line activity, it is not recommended in peak time.

9.3.11 The Evils of Lock Contention

No matter how well the database is tuned to minimize disk I/O, all the database designer's efforts will be wasted if lock contention is prevalent in the database. It's a bit like having a fast sports car only to find that you cannot drive past another car parked in a narrow road! SQL Server's locking mechanisms were described in Chapter 8 and we will now look at some general guidelines that should be followed when designing a database.

Rule 1: Keep transactions as short as possible.

If a transaction has placed an exclusive lock on a page or table it will keep that lock until it ends with a commit or rollback. This is also true if the HOLDLOCK keyword is used. Do not perform work inside a transaction that can be performed outside of it.

Rule 2: Do not hold locks across user interactions.

This follows from Rule 1. Unless special considerations apply, you have a real need to and you know what you are doing, this rule that should be adhered to at all costs in a multi-user environment. What does this mean? It means that transactions should be completed before control is passed back to the user and the transaction should not be *active* while the user is staring at the screen.

The reasons are obvious. The computer may process a transaction's workload in less than a second and if that transaction then completes another transaction will only have waited a fraction of a second before it acquired its locks. If, however, a transaction places locks on pages or tables and the transaction is left active while the application returns to the user, it will keep its locks while the user stares at the screen, scratches his or her head, chats to a colleague, or worse still, goes to lunch!

This could, and usually is, disastrous for system throughput and it is more commonplace that one might imagine! The authors know of instances where businesses have stopped trading for critical periods of time because a user went to lunch with a screen prompt sat on their workstation. This is not the user's fault. Blame resides with the application designer.

If it becomes necessary to browse data in the database it is usually far better to choose an option whereby locks are not held on database objects and an *optimistic locking* approach is taken, that is, the retrieved rows are not locked and, when updates are eventually performed, a check is made in the application to see if another user has changed the data since it was read. SQL Server provides various means of doing this.

Rule 3: Try to update the database in a separate transaction.

Suppose data is to be read from different tables, calculations made and then tables updated. It is sometimes better to perform lengthy reads and calculations in one transaction then the updates in a short second transaction. If this is not possible, save all of the updates until the end of the transaction and then issue then in one short burst. This minimizes the length of time that exclusive locks are held.

Rule 4: Help the query optimizer to choose indexed access.

The query optimizer chooses whether a table scan or index is used to retrieve data. Judicious use of indexes and care when writing Transact-SQL statements will help the query optimizer to choose an indexed access. From a locking contention viewpoint this is preferable to a table scan as a table scan will lock at the table level.

Rule 5: Choose indexes carefully.

We have already seen how clustered indexes can help to remove hot spots in a database table when multiple users are inserting rows. Also consider the columns chosen when creating nonclustered indexes. If, for example, a chronological key is used for the index key such as an order date and for any given day that order date will be the same for all users entering orders, contention in the index is likely to occur. This is also true if, for example, the application generates a monotonically increasing key for the order number and there is an index defined on order number.

Rule 6: Only lock as strictly as is necessary to meet your integrity requirements.

For example, only use HOLDLOCK if you require that the row you have read must not be changed by anyone else before your transaction ends.

Rule 7: Update tables in the same order throughout the application.

If one program updates table *A* and then updates table *B* and another program updates table *B* and then updates table *A* there is potential for deadlock. It is better to settle on some simple application development standard such as always updating tables in alphabetic order wherever possible.

In this case, the first program will cause the second program to wait cleanly and avoid the potential deadlock scenario.

Rule 8: Perform multi-user testing before the application goes live.

This is often forgotten or left to the last minute. Whether you use sophisticated multi-user testing products or you persuade your users to stay late in the evening – do it!

We could add more rules but we have found that, if the above eight are adhered to, lock contention should be minimized.

There will always be hot spots in a database and in these cases the individual hot spots should be analyzed and removed. This may involve changing indexes or the application and there is usually a trade off. For example, as we have stated, SQL Server will lock at the page or table level. If a table contains small rows there will be many in a database page and so many will be locked when the page is locked.

To minimize the number of rows locked they can be padded out to increase their size. This will reduce the number of rows locked when a page is locked as there are now fewer resident on a page. There will be a corresponding increase in disk space requirements and potentially disk I/O requirements but this may be an acceptable price to pay to remove a hot spot.

9.3.12 Archiving Data

This is a requirement that usually gets left until the last minute to specify, if at all. The fact remains, however, that the larger a database gets, the more performance is likely to degrade. Many database administration tasks will also take longer such as database dumps, the update of statistics, DBCC checks and index builds.

The reasons that performance degrades include the following:

- Larger tables mean longer table scans.
- Larger tables mean deeper indexes hence more I/O to reach the table row.
- Longer table scans and index traversals means locks may be held for longer.

Ensure that there is an archiving strategy in place before the database gets too large.

9.3.13 Read Only Report Databases

If we consider a typical OLTP production system perhaps comprising of many users we would probably expect to find that the system comprised of many short transactions that updated the tables in the database in real time. In reality, we would also find that there was a requirement to run long and perhaps complex reports against portions of the database. The fast response time requirements of the lightweight on-line transactions and the data hungry requirements of the heavyweight report transactions often do not mix well. The report transactions may often severely impact the response times of the on-line transactions in the production system and in the worst case may cause lock conflict.

One option is to separate these two different workloads into their own databases on their own server. This can never, in reality, be completely done as there is usually no clear break between the requirements of the two systems, but there is a case for off-loading as much reporting work as possible to another database. This also means that there will be a natural *frozen* cut-off point. If the report database is only updated overnight then it will hold the close of day position all the following day which can be a useful asset.

A separate report database can also have extra indexes added to it that would have been unacceptable in the production database for performance reasons.

Updating information in the report database could be a simple matter of loading the database from last night's dump of the OLTP database or the replication capabilities introduced with SQL Server 6.0 could be used. Whatever the method, consider the approach of separating the different workloads as it can greatly help performance and increase flexibility.

9.3.14 Network

The detailed tuning of networks is outside the scope of this book but don't forget that, in a client/server system, network performance is very important. The server may be highly tuned but, if data cannot be passed swiftly between it and the clients, the overall system performance will be poor.

9.4 MONITORING PERFORMANCE

Physical database design is not a static one-off process. Once the database has gone live the users will typically have changing requirements. Even if they do not the database data is likely to be volatile and tables are likely to grow. Figure 9-6 shows the typical monitoring and tuning cycle.

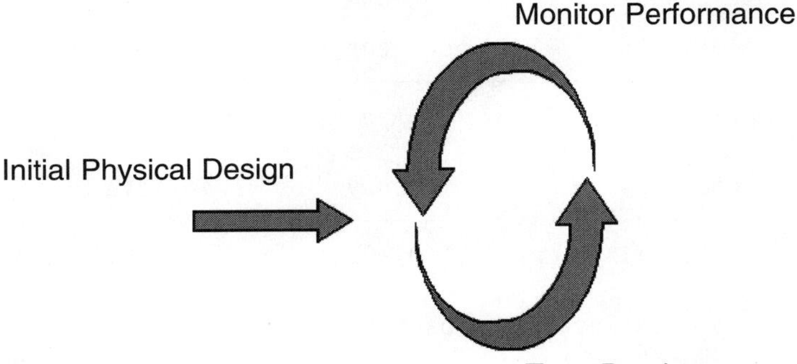

Figure 9-6 The Monitoring and Tuning Cycle

As can be seen, there is a continuous cycle of monitoring performance and then tuning the database. Database administrators can think of themselves as sailors navigating a vessel across a lake and making continuous adjustments to keep a constant course in the face of changing wind and tides.

To help them keep a constant course, SQL Server provides performance monitoring tools in the form of system stored procedures, DBCC reports, the Windows NT Performance Monitor and the SQL Enterprise Manager.

9.4.1 System Stored Procedures

There are a number of system stored procedures that can assist in performance monitoring, including:

- *sp_lock*
- *sp_who*
- *sp_monitor*
- *sp_configure*

The system stored procedures *sp_lock* and *sp_who* provide information on locks and on blocked processes. Both these system stored procedures are described in Chapter 8 and so we will concentrate on *sp_monitor* here.

SQL Server writes resource usage information into a number global variables and *sp_monitor* then formats and displays this information. In fact it displays the current values of the global variables and the difference between these current values and the values last time *sp_monitor* was run.

```
sp_monitor

last_run          current_run       seconds
----------------- ----------------- -------
27 Apr 1995 13:57 27 Apr 1995 14:09 669

cpu_busy          io_busy           idle
----------        --------          ---------------
11(10)-1%         1(0)-0%           17514(636)-95%

packets_received  packets_sent      packet_errors
----------------  ------------      -------------
36(13)            234(213)          0(0)
```

```
total_read          total_write          total_errors     connections
----------          ------------         -------------    -----------
343(136)            826(707)             0(0)             3(0)
```

The *cpu_busy*, *io_busy* and *idle* values are measured in seconds. The value 11(10)-1% is decoded as 11 seconds of CPU use since SQL Server was started and (10) is decoded as 10 seconds of CPU use since *sp_monitor* was last executed. The CPU has been busy 1% of the time since *sp_monitor* was last executed. Similarly, for *total_write* the value 826(707) can be decoded as 826 writes since SQL Server was started and (707) is decoded as 707 writes since *sp_monitor* was last executed.

These global variables are available to be read by Transact-SQL statements if the database administrator prefers their own format. The *sp_monitor* Transact-SQL definition can easily be examined using the SQL Enterprise Manager.

The *sp_configure* system stored procedures has been mentioned on many occasions throughout this book. It is worth mentioning again here as it is used to display or change configuration options. Alternatively, the SQL Enterprise Manager can be used as shown in Figure 9-5.

9.4.2 DBCC Reports

There are a number of DBCC reports that have been already mentioned in this and previous chapters that are useful for performance tuning, such as DBCC MEMUSAGE. Various performance statistics can also be obtained through the use of DBCC SQLPERF which takes a number of options:

- IOSTATS
- LRUSTATS
- NETSTATS
- THREADS
- LOGSPACE

These options can be used to obtain I/O, cache and network statistics since the server was started and also information on Windows NT threads and transaction log space.

```
dbcc sqlperf (iostats)

Statistic                 Value
--------------------      --------
Log Flush Requests        204.0
Log Logical Page IO       1033.0
Log Physical IO           232.0
Log Flush Average         0.87931
Log Logical IO Average    4.45259
Batch Writes              457.0
Batch Average Size        28.5625
Batch Max Size            8.0
Page Reads                390.0
Single Page Writes        263.0
Reads Outstanding         0.0
Writes Outstanding        0.0
Transactions              93.0
Transactions/Log Write    0.400862

DBCC execution completed. If DBCC printed error messages, see
your System Administrator.

dbcc sqlperf (lrustats)

Statistic                 Value
--------------------      --------
Cache Hit Ratio           99.7137
Cache Flushes             0.0
Free Page Scan (Avg)      0.0
Free Page Scan (Max)      0.0
Min Free Buffers          409.0
Cache Size                4419.0
Free Buffers              2787.0

DBCC execution completed. If DBCC printed error messages, see
your System Administrator.

dbcc sqlperf (netstats)

Statistic                 Value
--------------------      --------
Network Reads             0.0
Network Writes            397.0
Command Queue Length      0.0
Max Command Queue Length  0.0
Worker Threads            3.0
Max Worker Threads        3.0
```

```
Network Threads           0.0
Max Network Threads       0.0

DBCC execution completed. If DBCC printed error messages, see
your System Administrator.
```

Hint: Display all the above three classes of statistics easily with dbcc perform.

```
dbcc sqlperf(threads)

Spid Thread ID  Status   LoginName IO   CPU MemUsage
---- ---------  -------- --------- ---- --- -------
1               sleeping (null)    0    0   1
2               sleeping (null)    0    0   0
3               sleeping (null)    71   0   0
4               sleeping (null)    5    0   0
5               sleeping (null)    0    0   0
6               sleeping (null)    0    0   0
7               sleeping (null)    0    0   0
8               sleeping (null)    0    0   0
9               sleeping (null)    0    0   0
10   161(0xa1)  sleeping sa        14   10  1
11   191(0xbf)  sleeping sa        10   40  1
12   191(0xbf)  sleeping sa        7    60  1
13   136(0x88)  sleeping sa        43   80  1
14   186(0xba)  runnable sa        2    50  1

DBCC execution completed. If DBCC printed error messages, see
your System Administrator.
```

The Windows NT system thread ID can be related to a SQL Server spid from the information provided by *sqlperf(threads)*. The Windows NT Performance Monitor can then be used to observe a SQL Server user by checking their corresponding thread on the system.

```
dbcc sqlperf(logspace)

Database Name   Log Size (MB)  Log Space Used (%)   Status
-------------   -------------  ------------------   ------
pubtest1        5.0            1.52344              0
banking         10.0           0.0585938            0
distribution    15.0           9.34896              0
msdb            2.0            0.78125              0
pubs            0.0            0.0                  1
tempdb          0.0            0.0                  1
model           0.0            0.0                  1
master          0.0            0.0                  1
```

```
DBCC execution completed. If DBCC printed error messages, see
your System Administrator.
```

As long as the transaction log is on a separate device from the database, sqlperf(logspace) will display the percentage of the log used. In the display above, the banking database has its transaction log on a separate device but the pubs database does not.

The values of many of the statistics are self explanatory and they are all documented in the Microsoft SQL Server documentation. If it is required to reset the statistics, the *clear* option can be used:

```
dbcc sqlperf (lrustats,clear)

LRU statistics have been cleared.

DBCC execution completed. If DBCC printed error messages, see
your System Administrator.
```

9.4.3 The Windows NT Performance Monitor

The Windows NT Performance Monitor is a tool provided with Windows NT to facilitate performance monitoring through a graphical interface. There are many *objects* that can be monitored for Windows NT, such as the *processor* object and the *memory* object and for each object *counters* can be monitored. The processor object has counters such as *%Processor Time*.

There are special objects for SQL Server such as *SQLServer*, *SQLServer-Locks*, *SQLServer-Log*, *SQLServer-Users*. There are also objects to assist in monitoring replication. The *SQLServer* object has associated counters such as *Cache Hit Ratio*, the *SQLServer-Locks* object has associated counters such as *Total Locks*, the *SQLServer-Log* object has associated counters such as *Log Space Used (%)* and the *SQLServer-Users* object has associated counters such as each user's *Physical I/O*. A typical display, showing *Cache Hit Ratio* and four other counters, is shown in Figure 9-7.

Many counters can be displayed simultaneously and the display can be changed to be a histogram or a report. Alerts can also be set as shown in Figure 9-8. In this case when a counter reaches or drops below a value set by the database administrator an alert is recorded.

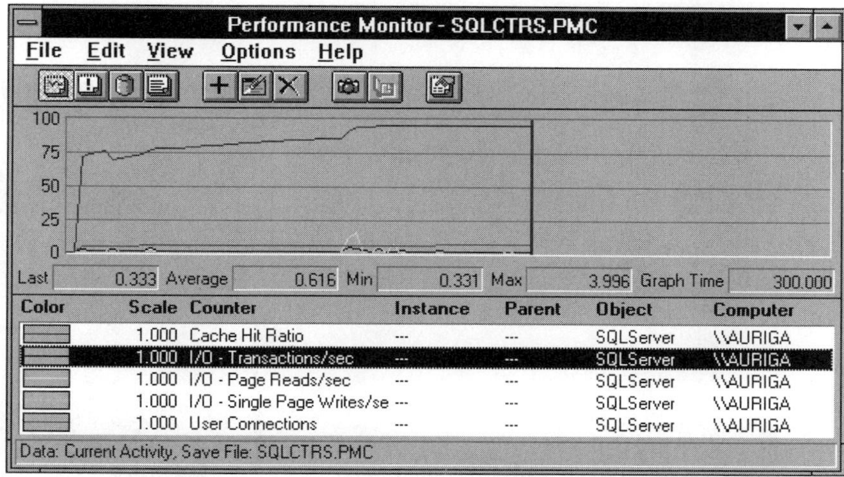

Figure 9-7 The Performance Monitor Showing Cache Hit Ratio

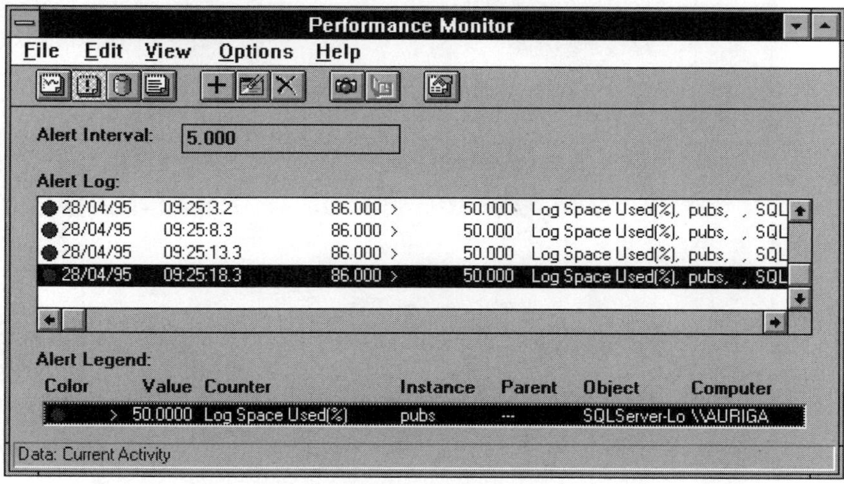

Figure 9-8 The Alert Log Showing a Log Space Alert

The Windows NT Performance Monitor can be an invaluable tool in researching SQL Server performance problems.

9.4.4 The SQL Enterprise Manager

The SQL Enterprise Manager can be used to assist in performance monitoring. Figure 9-9 shows the *current activity* display which can be used to, for example, display locking activity.

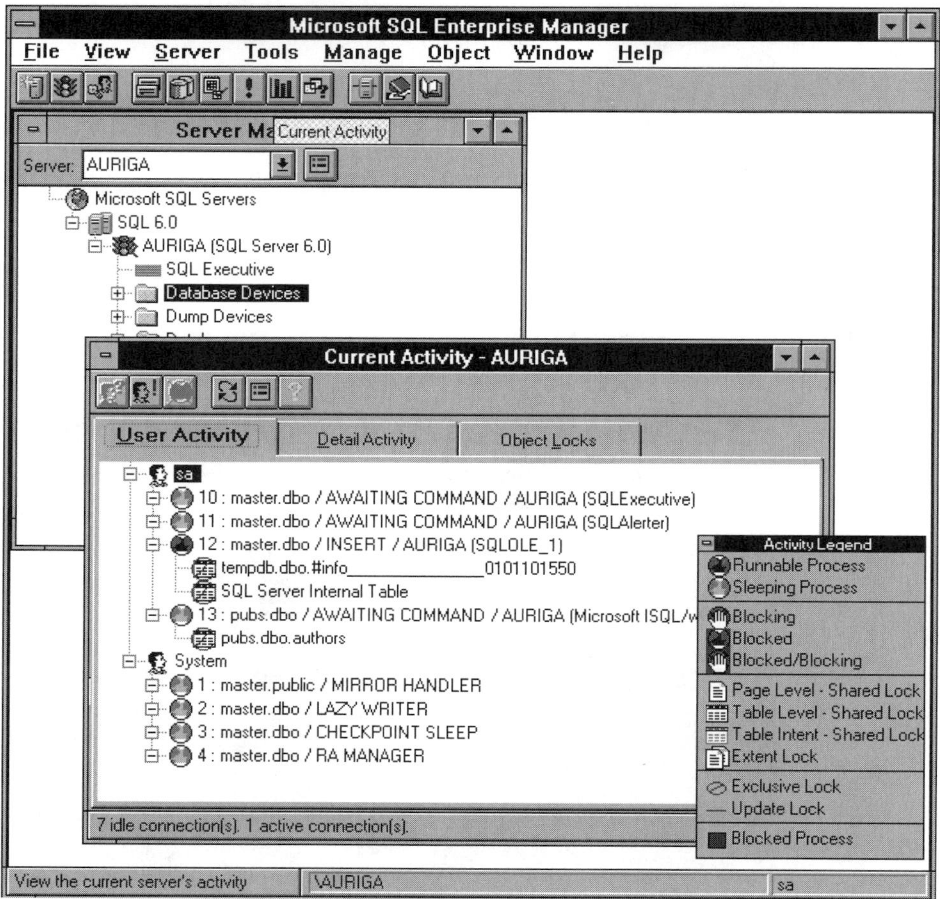

Figure 9-9 Monitoring Current Activity in the SQL Enterprise Manager

This chapter has covered many aspects of performance from physical design through to monitoring and tuning tools. Good performance normally comes with good design and testing, in other words, it is rare to achieve good performance without some hard work. For that reason, do not just hope that the performance of your database will be satisfactory, make sure it is.

10 Database Administration

10.1 INTRODUCTION

Database administration, the act of housekeeping within the database, is critical to the successful operation of any SQL Server system. This chapter will give readers and potential database administrators a good overview of general administration tasks including:

- User management
- Database mirroring
- Backup
- Recovery
- Import and export of data

By the end of the chapter the reader should feel comfortable with carrying out these tasks.

10.2 TOOLS OF THE TRADE

SQL Server offers the database administrator, sometimes known as the system administrator (SA), two ways of managing a database.

- Transact-SQL
- Graphical administration tools

This chapter will cover both methods as it is felt to be important to understand what happens when each of the tools are used, and in some instances the database administrator will be obliged to use ISQL (interactive command line SQL) when performing a recovery of SQL Server.

We have met some of the graphical tools in Chapter 3. Here is a more complete list of the SQL Server graphical administration tools that a database administrator may need:

SQL Enterprise Manager

The base tool for the database administrator, the SQL Enterprise Manager provides graphical set up of user accounts and management of existing users and logons. Multiple SQL Servers can be administered across the network with this tool, whether they are Windows NT or OS/2 servers.

SQL Transfer Manager

This copy management tool enables the wholesale movement of databases or individual objects between servers in a single step. The long process of duplicating databases, rebuilding indexes and unloading/loading tables can be reduced with this tool. SQL Transfer Manager can support a Sybase SQL Server as a source server.

SQL Security Manager

This tool gives the database administrator a graphical interface for security related management tasks.

Client Network Configuration

This tool enables the changing of the clients default NET-Library from named pipes, IPX/SPX or Banyan Vines IP.

SQL Service Manager

The *traffic light* control dialogue to start, stop or pause a server to prevent users logging on prior to maintenance. In SQL Server 6.0 the server has been renamed *MSSQLServer* to differentiate it from other brands of SQL Server. This is shown in Figure 10-1.

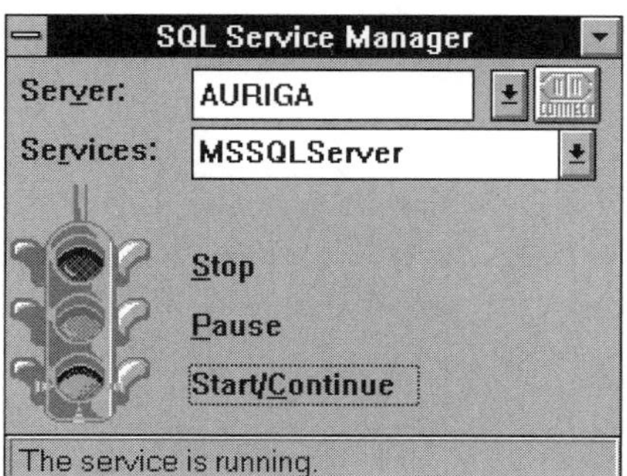

Figure 10-1 The SQL Service Manager

ISQL/w

The interactive SQL window interface exists as a stand-alone tool as well as a component of the SQL Enterprise Manager. An interactive query tool, this gives the database administrator a graphical representation of the SHOWPLAN output.

ISQL

ISQL is an operating system command line utility which accepts SQL statements and passes them straight to the SQL Server. Results are formatted and displayed on the screen.

SQL Performance Monitor

Integrated with the Windows NT performance monitor this tool enables the performance characteristics of a SQL Server installation to be observed.

SQL Object Manager

The SQL Object Manager was used in versions of SQL Server prior to SQL Server 6.0. It can, if desired, still be used with SQL Server 6.0 although its functionality has now been integrated into the SQL Enterprise Manager. SQL Server objects, such as tables and indexes, can be created from this tool.

SQL Administrator

Like the SQL Object Manager, the SQL Administrator was used in versions of SQL Server prior to SQL Server 6.0. It also, if desired, can still be used with SQL Server 6.0 although its functionality has now been integrated into the SQL Enterprise Manager. SQL Server administration tasks such as granting object permissions and database backup, can be managed from this tool.

SQL Distributed Management Objects

SQL Distributed Management Objects (DMO) is an OLE automation layer that connects the SQL Server tools to the database engine. It is a component of *the Distributed Management Framework* (DMF) which allows cross enterprise management of servers. As it is based upon OLE, clients such as Visual Basic can interact with the management capabilities of SQL Server automatically via OLE automation. For further details see Chapter 13.

10.3 SQL SERVER SECURITY

Once SQL Server has been installed the next step is for the system administrator to set up accounts and security access rights for the system users. SQL Server allows users to be established with one of three different login security types on SQL Server for Windows NT:

- Standard
- Integrated
- Mixed

Using *standard security*, users log in to SQL Server by specifying a login name and password.

With *integrated security*, if the default named pipes protocol is used, users are automatically logged into SQL Server using the Windows NT username and login. This has the added benefit of not sending the login name and password across the network to the SQL Server.

Mixed Security is a mixture of standard and integrated security. If the SQL Server is using protocols other than named pipes then mixed security will enable any user, with either standard or integrated security, to login with a valid SQL Server login ID and password.

If integrated or mixed security is being used, the SQL Security Manager can be used to map Windows NT users and groups to SQL Server.

10.3.1 Types of SQL Server Users

There are a number of types of SQL Server user who are recognized as having different needs and privileges in the SQL Server. At the top of the hierarchy are the people who must administer the system, typically the database administrators. At the lower levels of the hierarchy are the users of the database. These types of SQL Server user are listed below:

System Administrator

The system administrator (SA) is the SQL Server name for a database administrator (DBA). The system administrator is responsible for all the database housekeeping activities unrelated to specific applications. Typical activities can include installation of the SQL Server, managing memory usage and the

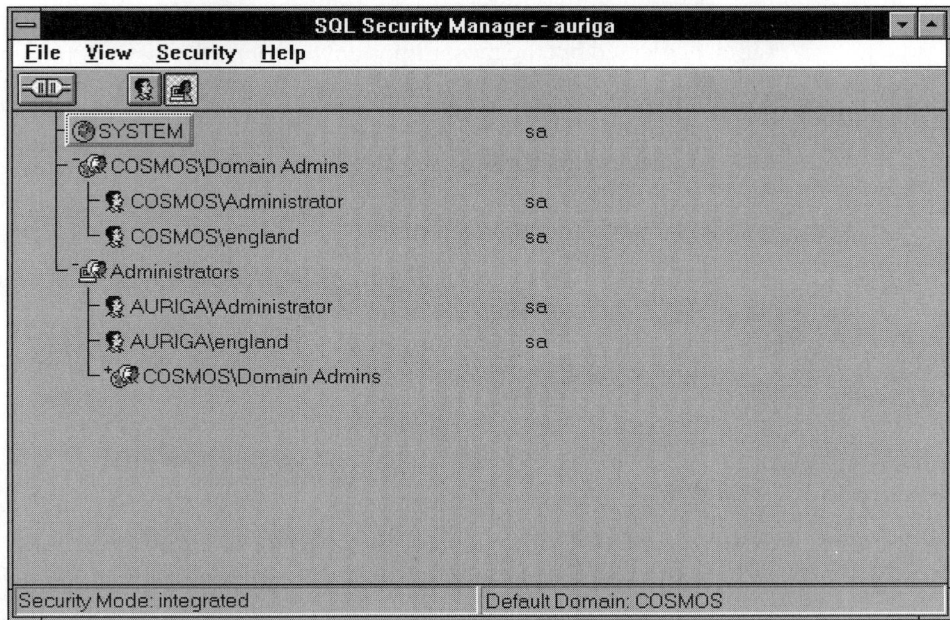

Figure 10-2 The SQL Security Manager

creation of devices and databases. Object management may also be part of system administration, such as the creation of stored procedures, views and triggers. The master database is owned by the system administrator. In this chapter we will use the term system administrator, not only in the sense of a database administrator, but as a person who uses the SQL Server login ID of SA.

Database Owner (DBO)

The DBO is the creator of a database, and within that database the DBO has full privileges and can allow user access, grant permissions on objects, set up user groups and assign users to groups

Database Object Owner

The DBO can grant permission for any user to create indexes, tables, views, defaults, triggers and stored procedures within the database that they have ownership of. The creator of a database object automatically has full permissions on it and explicit permission must be granted for other users to access objects such as tables.

User

Often neglected but the most important *customer* for the system administrator!

Guest or Visitor

Guest accounts can be used for users with no established system username, so they logon with the guest user ID. Visitors are often people with SQL Server or Windows NT login names and passwords that need ad hoc system access.

The Guest or Visitor is the bottom of the tree within SQL Server as far as access rights and privileges are concerned.

Probe Login

The probe login is used by administration applications to connect to servers set up in standard security mode. Users should not login to a SQL Server using this ID.

SQL Server 6.0 has also added a user *repl_subscriber*. This user is automatically created on some databases when a replication publishing server is created. It should not be modified or deleted as it is used by subscription servers to connect to the publishing server. For further details see Chapter 11 on SQL Server replication.

10.3.2 Creating Accounts

New login IDs can be added to SQL Server by using Transact-SQL or SQL Enterprise Manager if standard security has been implemented, otherwise the SQL Security Manager can be used.

To determine the current security model running on a SQL Server use the extended system stored procedure *xp_loginconfig* or the SQL Server setup program:

```
xp_loginconfig

name              config_value
--------------    ------------
login mode        standard
default login     (null)
default domain    (null)
audit level       none
set hostname      false
```

```
map _           domain separator
map $           space
map #           -
```

The server in this example uses standard security. Out of interest, *map _* determines the Windows NT character assigned to the SQL Server character underscore(_), the default is the domain separator (\), *map $* determines the character mapping to the dollar sign and *map #* does the same for the hash (or pound) sign. *Audit level* determines whether security auditing is enabled, giving the administrator a history of unsuccessful logins. *Set hostname* determines whether the client login host name is replaced with the Windows NT network username.

If mixed or integrated security has been enabled then the Windows NT user manager must be used to setup SQL Server users, but as we have standard security set up we can go straight to the system procedures that establish our users on the SQL Server. Note that when we refer to users here we are in fact referring to login IDs on the SQL Server. These are not necessarily database users although, in reality, these users will be given permissions on various databases as we shall see shortly.

The system procedures concerned with managing users are:

- *sp_addlogin*
- *sp_addgroup*
- *sp_adduser*

These system stored procedures are used to add a new user to a SQL Server, add a group to a database and add a user to a database or group respectively. They are explained below.

10.3.3 Creating a New SQL Server User

The *sp_addlogin* system stored procedure allows the system administrator to add a new login ID to the SQL Server:

```
sp_addlogin ken, margaret, pubs
```

This will add the user *ken*, with a password of *margaret* and a default database of *pubs*. If no default database is specified then the master database is used for the user's default database and, whilst this is fine for the system administrator, it is not a good idea for users to be accessing the master database!

The users default language can be appended to the statement if the system administrator wished to change it.

This will add a user with no password, which is replaced by the *null* value:

```
sp_addlogin nigel, null, pubs
```

SQL Server login IDs can also be created using the SQL Enterprise Manager. To do so double click the *Logins* folder for the database in which you want to create the login ID. In the *Manage Logins* window add the login ID and password as required. The *Manage Logins* window is shown in Figure 10-3.

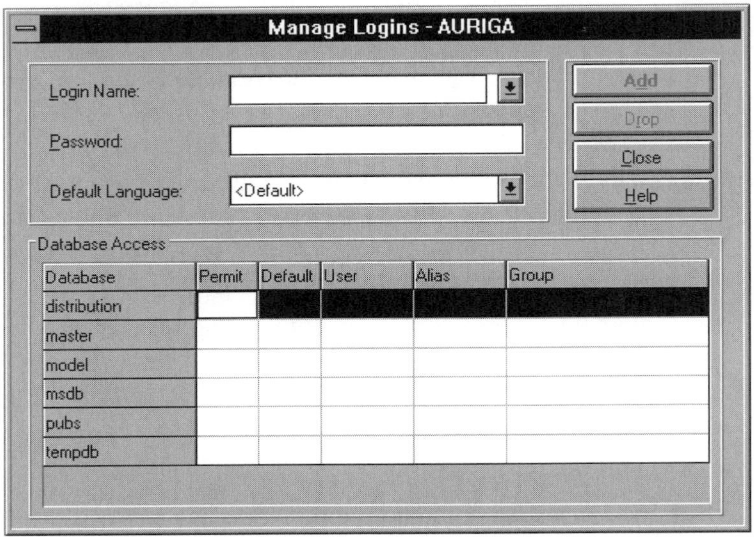

Figure 10-3 Adding a Login ID with the SQL Enterprise Manager

Once *sp_addlogin* has been successfully executed a row will be added to *master.dbo.syslogins* system table with the login information. The *syslogins* system table contains one row for every SQL Server login ID and comprises of columns such as the login ID of the user and the password. Only the system administrator can execute a SELECT statement on the password column of the *syslogins* table.

10.3.4 Adding a Group to a Database

The system administrator's time is valuable, and it would be extremely time consuming (and tedious!) to manage individual permissions for everyone in sales, accounts, marketing and so on. To overcome this problem the system administrator can use the *sp_addgroup* system stored procedure:

```
use pubs
sp_addgroup sales
```

This will create a group called *sales* which can be assigned permissions as a whole. Once successfully executed a row will be added to the *sysusers* table with the group information. Users are then added to that group with *sp_adduser*.

So, for example, the system administrator could create the sales group in a database and add the organizations fifty sales personnel to it. The sales group could then be given access to, for example, tables and views as a single entity. All the members of the sales group would then possess those access rights.

10.3.5 Adding a User to a Database or Group

Similarly, to add a user to a database or group the *sp_adduser* system stored procedure can be used:

```
use pubs
sp_adduser nstanley, nigel
```

The above example adds the login ID *nstanley* to the pubs database. He will be known as *nigel* in the database. This capability allows different databases to know different login IDs as *nigel*. For example, the pubs database knows *nstanley* as *nigel* whereas the public_houses database knows *nsmith* as *nigel*.

Note that, by default, *nigel* has become a member of the *public* group as no group name was mentioned in the *sp_adduser* system stored procedure. A user may not be a member of more than one group.

The following example adds the login ID *kengland* to the pubs database. He will be known as *ken* in the database. In this example, the sales group is named in the *sp_adduser* system stored procedure and so *kengland* becomes a member of it.

```
use pubs
sp_adduser kengland, ken, sales
```

The above operations may also be performed by the SQL Enterprise Manager. Figure 10-3 shows the *Manage Logins* window. It can be seen that the lower half of the window allows a default database to be set for a login ID as well as a username for that login ID in the database and group membership.

10.3.6 Managing Aliases

Aliases are useful tools if you have a number of individual users who you wish to deal with inside a database as if they were one user. A system administrator could allow all these individuals to login to a SQL Server using one login ID, however, that would not be very useful from an accountability standpoint. Instead, the system administrator can use aliases whereby a number of login IDs can be mapped to one username. This is useful if you want a number of login IDs to be treated as the database owner. To create aliases the *sp_addalias* system stored procedure is used:

```
sp_addalias Ken, accts

sp_addalias Rue, accts
```

This will give both Ken and Rue access to the current database with the alias *accts*, using their own login ID.

Figure 10-3 shows that the *Manage Logins* window also contains a column for each database so that aliases may be set up for the login ID.

10.3.7 Dropping Users, Logins, Aliases and Groups

Now that the system administrator has done all the hard work of creating users and groups, the time inevitably comes when users need to be removed or dropped from the system. Dropping users, groups and aliases is as straightforward as creating them. Again, we use a few simple Transact-SQL system procedures:

```
sp_dropuser ken
```

This will drop the user ken from the current database. The only users with enough privilege to drop users are the system administrator and database owner, however, if the user is an object owner in the database, for example has created a table, that user cannot be dropped unless the objects are dropped. If dropping the objects is not practical, the username must be kept in the database and its password changed to stop the user gaining access to that database. This is because ownership of objects cannot be transferred.

```
sp_password bond, solo, agent
```

In the above example the login ID *agent* has their password changed from *bond* to *solo* by the system administrator.

The system stored procedures *sp_droplogin* is used to drop a users login id. Unlike *sp_dropuser*, the *sp_droplogin* system stored procedure will happily remove a login ID that owns objects in a database, so take care!

The *sp_droplogin* system stored procedure has been enhanced so it is not possible to drop the login ID of a user who is still an object owner.

To drop an alias the *sp_dropalias* system stored procedures can be used:

```
use pubs
sp_dropalias  figaro
```

In this case *figaro* is the login ID mapped to an alias in the database. Once the alias is dropped, figaro will not be able to access the database pubs unless he is associated with another alias in pubs or the username figaro is added to pubs.

Groups can be dropped in the same way, but before it is dropped the group must be empty. If is not, SQL Server will error and list out the members of the group:

```
sp_dropgroup clerks

Msg 15144, Level 16, State 1
Group has members.  It must be empty before it can be dropped.
name
------------------
fred
jane

(1 row(s) affected)
```

Group members can be dropped using the *sp_changegroup* system stored procedure.

10.3.8 Miscellaneous System Stored Procedures

There are a number of system stored procedures that we will mention here that are concerned in some way with user management in some way:

- *sp_defaultdb*
- *sp_changedbowner*
- *sp_defaultlanguage*

The *sp_defaultdb* system stored procedure is used to change the default database:

```
sp_defaultdb rue, pubs
```

The above example changes the default database of the login ID *rue* to *pubs*.

The *sp_changedbowner* system stored procedures is used to change the ownership of a database:

```
use pubs
sp_changedbowner margaret
```

The above changes the database ownership of *pubs* to the login ID *margaret*.

The *sp_defaultlanguage* system stored procedures is used to change the default language:

```
sp_defaultlanguage mike, us_english
```

The above example changes the default language of the login ID *mike* to *us_english*.

10.3.9 User Permissions

As one would expect not all users in a SQL Server system would want or require the same access rights or privileges to all the objects. As discussed earlier SQL Server has four main types of users - system administrator, database owner, database object owner and other users.

System administrators have full permissions to do anything to a SQL Server database, and there are additional statements which are exclusive to system administrators as shown in Table 9.

Statement	Description
DISK INIT	Formats physical storage for a database device
DISK REFIT	Restores a damaged master database
DISK REINIT	Used with DISK REFIT to restore a damaged master database
DISK MIRROR	Creates a software mirror (copy) of a database device
DISK UNMIRROR	Suspends software mirroring
DISK REMIRROR	Restarts software mirroring
KILL	Terminates a specified process
RECONFIGURE	Used to reset system options
SHUTDOWN	Closes down the SQL Server system

Table 9 Transact-SQL Statements Exclusive to System Administrators

Database owners have the ability to undertake any activity in *their* database, and additionally have the permissions shown in Table 10 available to themselves which cannot be transferred to other users.

CHECKPOINT	Forces dirty pages to be written from cache to disk
DBCC	Database Consistency Checker
DROP DATABASE	Removes a database from SQL Server
GRANT and REVOKE	Add or Remove user privileges
LOAD DATABASE	Loads a backup copy of a database
LOAD TRANSACTION	Loads a backup copy of a transaction log
SETUSER	Used by a DBO to impersonate another user

Table 10 Non-Transferable DBO Permissions

In SQL Server 6.0 SETUSER has now been changed so that, when system administrators use SETUSER to impersonate another user, they immediately lose all of their global administration privileges which can only be regained by issuing another SETUSER to change back to the system administrator.

DBOs can also explicitly grant permissions to other users to undertake a number of tasks including:

- CREATE TABLE
- DUMP DATABASE
- DUMP TRANSACTION.

Database object owners have all permissions on objects that they have created by default.

10.3.10 Assigning Permissions to Users

Assigning permissions to users is remarkably straightforward, using the GRANT and REVOKE statements. The system table *sysprotects* lists the permissions granted or revoked for each user. Here is a simple example of using the GRANT statement:

```
grant create table, create view
to ken, margaret, rue
```

This example will grant statement permissions to create tables and views for the users ken, margaret and rue.

To grant permissions for insertion and deletion of data similar syntax is used:

```
grant insert, delete
on authors
to rue
```

This example will give the user rue the ability to insert and delete data in the authors table. Reversing this granting of access is a simple matter of using the REVOKE statement:

```
revoke insert, delete
on authors
from rue
```

Note that you GRANT TO and REVOKE FROM with these statements.

To see which permissions have been added use the system procedure *sp_helprotect*. Here is an example using the authors table:

```
use pubs
go
sp_helprotect authors

type     action    user     column
-----    ------    ------   ------
Grant    Delete    guest    All
Grant    Insert    guest    All
Grant    Select    guest    All
Grant    Select    public   All
Grant    Update    guest    All

(1 row(s) affected)
```

The additional syntax of *use pubs* and *go* was used as the *master* database was the current database at the time of the query. From the results we can see the user and the type of privileges given.

By REVOKING the DELETE privilege from guest we can see how the output of *sp_helprotect* has been changed:

```
type     action    user     column
-----    ------    ------   ------
Grant    Insert    guest    All
Grant    Select    guest    All
Grant    Select    public   All
Grant    Update    guest    All
Revoke   Delete    guest    All

(1 row(s) affected)
```

Hint: If most of your users will be luxuriating in the majority of the privileges, then the easiest way of managing permissions is to GRANT to an entire group and then REVOKE permissions on the few users who need reduced privileges.

User permissions can also be managed using the SQL Enterprise Manager. The approach depends on whether the system administrator wishes to base the permission management around a user or an object. The system administrator can either click the username name with the right mouse button or the object name with the right mouse button. In the pop-up menu select *Permission...* should be selected. The *Object Permissions* window is displayed which comprises of two tabs which are labeled *By Object* or *By User*. The tab in the foreground is determined by whether a username or object name was mouse clicked. Either tab can then be selected. Figure 10-4 shows an example of managing permissions by user, in this case *ken*.

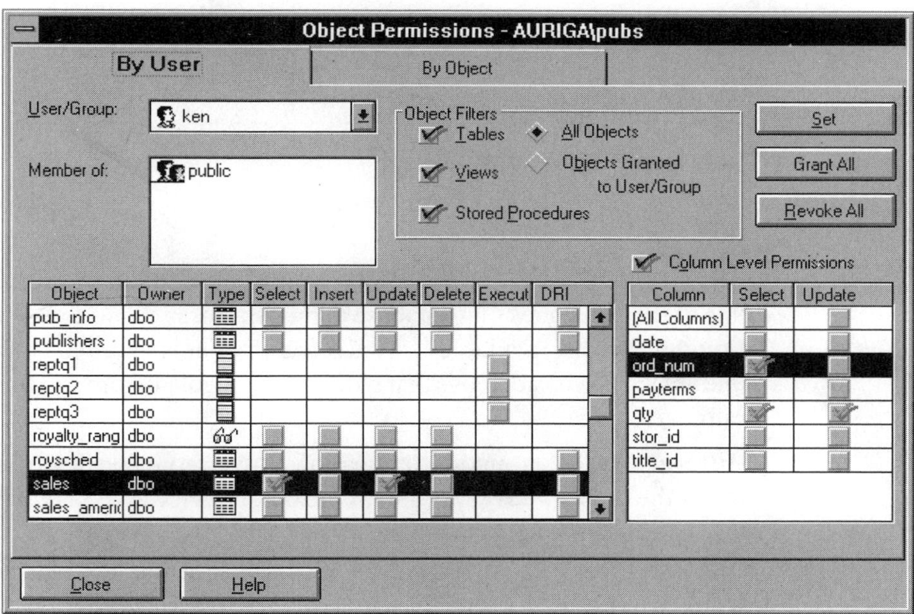

Figure 10-4 Managing Permissions by User

Figure 10-5 shows an example of managing permissions by object, in this case the authors table.

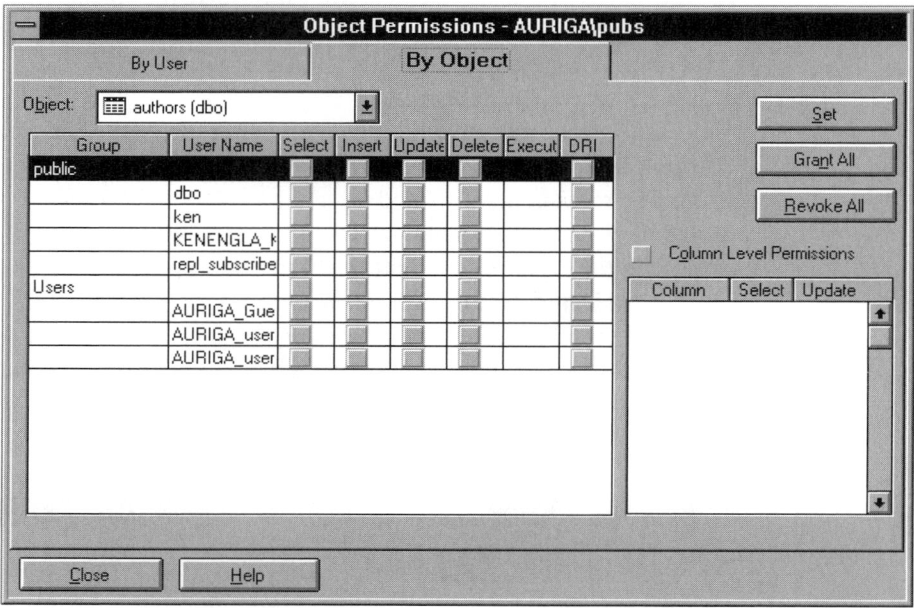

Figure 10-5 Managing Permissions by User

10.4 DEVICE MIRRORING

One of the key duties of a database administrator is ensuring that the database provides a highly available service if that is what is required by the company. One area to be considered is that of tolerating media failure and this is achieved with *mirroring*.

Mirroring is the continuous duplication of data from one device to another. If one of the devices develops a fault the other device automatically takes over and the system remains available.

10.4.1 RAID Technology

As well as SQL Server device mirroring, described shortly, Windows NT Server provides support for RAID 5. RAID (Redundant Array of Inexpensive Disks) is an accepted way of ensuring system data security in event of a media failure. Although not directly related to SQL Server the authors believe that it is important to have an understanding of this technology as it is the way forward for database system security.

There are 5 versions of RAID:

- RAID 0 implements striping of data with no drive redundancy. This has the advantage of speed but offers no fault tolerance and limited system reliability.
- RAID 1 is disk mirroring where data is written to two or more disks simultaneously. This provides good fault tolerance but only utilizes half of the available disk space due to data duplication and may adversely affect system performance, which some manufacturers are overcoming with duplexing which involves giving each drive its own host adapter.
- RAID 2 is best used when large amounts of data are read at high transfer rates. This is because it uses several check disks which have striped bits and the data contains an interleaving hamming code to detect single or double bit errors. In any operation a large number of disks may need to be read thereby imposing an overhead. RAID 2 is generally seen to be best for large systems and may not always be suitable for Windows NT.
- RAID 3 uses a single parity or check disk for each set of drives, which receives the exclusive OR (XOR) of the written data.
- RAID 4 uses a single dedicated disk for check data. Entire blocks or sectors are striped, as opposed to the single bits in RAID 3, which allows many different sectors to be read simultaneously. This lends itself very well to reading smaller amounts of data, although write operations have to occur serially.
- RAID 5 has an equivalent dedicated check disk as RAID 4 but this check data is spread over all of the drives in the array.

RAID 3,4 and 5 data recovery is achieved by using the exclusive OR (XOR) of the remaining data values and the check disk data.

10.4.2 Which Mirroring System to Use?

Every SQL Server system is different and there is no hard and fast rule which determines the best way to ensure system integrity. The systems administrator must examine each system individually and determine the best model to use.

Here are some examples of mirroring scenarios:

- The most straight forward model is the mirroring of a user database transaction logs on a separate device. This uses minimum disk space, but as it does not back up the master or other user databases it does not provide non-stop recovery. To recover, it is necessary to reload the transaction logs.
- The second model is to mirror the user databases, transaction log and master database on another device. Although using additional disk space, it does provide non-stop recovery, with the overhead of slower write operations.
- The third model is to mirror the master database and transaction log on one device with the user database mirrored on a second device. This provides a high level of redundancy but ensures full non-stop recovery. Increased write times will be found but the read time should be quicker as the transaction log is on a different device to the user database, reducing disk head travel time.

10.4.3 Creating a Mirror

To mirror a device, the syntax used is fairly straightforward:

```
disk mirror
name = 'publishers'
mirror = 'c:\publish.dat'
```

This will mirror the logically named publishers device, using its physical data stored on the path c:\publish.dat. The *sysdevices* table will be updated with the mirrorname of the device to be mirrored. SQL Server for Windows NT always uses SERIAL mirroring, meaning that writes to the primary disk must finish before the mirror disk is written to. It is possible to come across NOSERIAL mirroring which is retained for backwards compatibility with older versions of SQL Server.

Probably the most important device to mirror is the master database. If the system should fail then special steps need to be taken to restart SQL Server so that it uses the secondary mirrored device rather than the primary device. The following switches must be used in conjunction with the SQLSERVR utility:

-d	Path of the primary device for the master database
-c	Starts SQL Server without using the Windows NT Service Control Manager
-e	The error log path
-r	Path of the mirroring device to be used to mirror the master database.

For example:

```
sqlservr   -de:\sql\data\master.dat -ee:\sql\data\log\error.log
-rp:\sql\mirror\mstrmir.dat
```

In this example the mirror device was the *p* drive, as the *d* drive had failed. SQLSERVR will always try the primary device before resorting to the mirror device and it cannot be forced to use the mirror device if the original primary device is still working. The system administrator must always use care with mirrored devices, as it may not come to his or her attention that the mirror device is being used following a failure. The consequences of this do not bare thinking about!

Further information on recovery is contained in the Database Recovery section, later in this chapter.

10.4.4 UNMIRROR and REMIRROR

Mirroring can be removed on a permanent or temporary basis:

```
disk unmirror
name = 'publishers',
side = primary,
mode = retain
```

This will UNMIRROR our publishers device on a temporary basis as we used the RETAIN statement. Replacing RETAIN with REMOVE will make the UNMIRROR permanent. Primary means that the device is listed in the name column of *sysdevices*, secondary means that the device is listed in the mirrorname column in *sysdevices*. If RETAIN is used then to reinitialize mirroring the REMIRROR statement can be used:

```
disk remirror
name = 'publishers'
```

10.5 DATABASE CONSISTENCY CHECKER (DBCC)

Like any complex database software, SQL Server requires a mechanism to check the integrity of the database or elements of the database when required. The Database Consistency Checker (DBCC) is a utility which will check both the logical and physical status of a SQL Server installation.

The system administrator will normally DBCC following an error message which has a severity level between 20 and 23, but in most companies it is usually run periodically to check the database status. It is quite a useful tool to show the I/O statistics of a particular SQL Server, as well as information regarding cache usage and networking statistics.

DBCC can be used via ISQL/w with a variety of extensions depending on the task you wish to complete.

10.5.1 DBCC CHECKDB and CHECKTABLE

CHECKDB will check each table in the specified database to ensure that the table's index pages and data pages are correctly linked. Indexes will be checked to ensure that they are in the correct sort order, all the pointers are correct and that the page data and offsets are within limits. Here is an example using our pubs database:

```
dbcc checkdb (pubs)

Checking pubs
Checking 1
The total number of data pages in this table is 2.
Table has 37 data rows.
Checking 2
The total number of data pages in this table is 3.
Table has 34 data rows.

    :
    :
    :

Checking 768005767
The total number of data pages in this table is 2.
The total number of TEXT/IMAGE pages in this table is 210.
Table has 15 data rows.

DBCC execution completed. If DBCC printed error messages, see
your System Administrator.
```

Hint: Note the use of the brackets around the database name in the Transact-SQL.

The output we get is self explanatory. If need be individual tables can be checked using the CHECKTABLE extension:

```
dbcc checktable authors

Checking authors
The total number of data pages in this table is 1.
Table has 23 data rows.

DBCC execution completed. If DBCC printed error messages, see
your System Administrator.
```

10.5.2 DBCC CHECKALLOC, NEWALLOC, TEXTALLOC, TEXTALL

CHECKALLOC will check to see if all of the database pages have been allocated correctly and ensure that unused pages are not deemed to be allocated. To do this CHECKALLOC will report on the amount of space used and the amount of space allocated:

```
dbcc checkalloc

Checking pubs
Database 'pubs' is not in single user mode - may find spurious
allocation problems due to transactions in progress.
Alloc page 0 (# of extent=32 used pages=65 ref pages=63)
Alloc page 256 (# of extent=31 used pages=152 ref pages=152)
Alloc page 512 (# of extent=20 used pages=147 ref pages=147)
Alloc page 768 (# of extent=18 used pages=144 ref pages=141)
Total (# of extent=101 used pages=508 ref pages=503) in this
database

DBCC execution completed. If DBCC printed error messages, see
your System Administrator.
```

Hint: A quick rule of thumb calculation to establish the database size is to multiply the total number of used pages by 2K.

In this example there are 4 allocation units which can contain up to 32 extents, which are the internal storage structures of SQL Server. These tell you if it is possible to create more objects in the database. Each extent can have up to 8 associated pages.

NEWALLOC provides a more detailed report than CHECKALLOC which it now replaces, CHECKALLOC merely being retained for compatibility. The next example is a sample of the DBCC NEWALLOC consistency check run on the same database as above. It's actually the analysis of the famed authors table:

```
***************************************************
TABLE: authors      OBJID = 16003088
INDID=1    FIRST=136     ROOT=352     DPAGES=1     SORT=1
     Data level: 1.  1 Data  Pages in 1 extents.
     Indid   : 1.  2 Index Pages in 1 extents.
INDID=2    FIRST=128     ROOT=128     DPAGES=1     SORT=1
     Indid   : 2.  2 Index Pages in 1 extents.
TOTAL # of extents = 3
****************************************************
```

TEXTALLOC will check the allocation of text fields for a specified table. By using the options FULL or FAST you can determine if you get a report where all of the allocation pages are checked or just a check of the linkages of the text chains. TEXTALL can be used to select all tables in a database that contain text fields and run TEXTALLOC against them.

```
dbcc textall (pubs)

Checking pubs
****************************************************
TABLE: sysarticles                      OBJID = 16
INDID=255  FIRST=288     ROOT=288     DPAGES=0     SORT=0
     Data level: 1.  1 Data  Pages in 0 extents.
     Indid   : 255.  0 Index Pages in 0 extents.
****************************************************
TABLE: pub_info                         OBJID = 864006109
INDID=255  FIRST=568     ROOT=608     DPAGES=0     SORT=0
    Data level: 1.  1 Data  Pages in 0 extents.
    Indid   : 255.  16 Index Pages in 0 extents.

DBCC execution completed. If DBCC printed error messages, see
your System Administrator.
```

10.5.3 DBCC CHECKCATALOG

DBCC CHECKCATALOG is used to check the consistency of system tables and to ensure that the system tables contain the appropriate values. For example, every table and view in *sysobjects* contains a minimum of one column in *syscolumns*:

```
dbcc checkcatalog (pubs)

Checking pubs
The following segments have been defined for database 4
(database name pubs).
virtualstartaddr    size    segments
----------------    ----    --------
            6148    1024    0
                            1
                            2

DBCC execution completed. If DBCC printed error messages, see
your System Administrator.
```

10.5.4 DBREPAIR

With SQL Server versions earlier than SQL Server 6.0, it is not possible to DROP a damaged database so DBREPAIR is used instead. The following DBCC statement will drop our pubs database if it is damaged:

```
dbcc dbrepair(pubs,dropdb)
```

In SQL Server 6.0, the DROP DATABASE Transact-SQL statement can now drop damaged databases.

10.5.5 DBCC MEMUSAGE

MEMUSAGE is fairly straightforward, giving the system administrator a view of the SQL Server memory use, including memory allocated at startup, memory used by the 12 biggest procedures in the procedure cache and the memory used by the top 20 biggest objects in the data buffer cache. The use of DBCC MEMUSAGE is described in more detail in Chapter 9. The following shows an example of DBCC MEMUSAGE (the output has been edited for brevity):

```
Memory Usage:
                          Meg.        2K Blks    Bytes

  Configured Memory:     16.0000     8192       16777216
          Code size:     1.7166      879        1800000
  Static Structures:     0.2489      128        261040
              Locks:     0.2480      127        260000
       Open Objects:     0.1068      55         112000
     Open Databases:     0.0031      2          3220
 User Context Areas:     0.7447      382        780912
         Page Cache:     8.9682      4592       9403792
       Proc Headers:     0.2161      111        226554
    Proc Cache Bufs:     3.6289      1858       3805184

Buffer Cache, Top 20:

DB Id     Object Id  Index Id   2K Buffers
5         5          0          27
1         5          0          25
1         1          0          13
          :
          :
Procedure Cache, Top 3:

 Procedure Name: sp_helpdistributor
Database Id: 1
Object Id: 1856009643
Version: 1
Uid: 1
Type: stored procedure
Number of trees: 0
Size of trees: 0.000000 Mb, 0.000000 bytes, 0 pages
Number of plans: 1
Size of plans: 0.019249 Mb, 20184.000000 bytes, 10 pages
          :
          :

DBCC execution completed. If DBCC printed error messages, see
your System Administrator.
```

10.5.6 DBCC SQLPERF, IOSTATS, LRUSTATS, NETSTATS, LOGSPACE

DBCC SQLPERF provides system performance statistics. I/O statistics since the server was started can be obtained using IOSTATS, cache usage is obtained using LRUSTATS and NETSTATS provides network usage information. DBCC SQLPERF is described in more detail in Chapter 9. Here is an example of using DBCC SQLPERF to find I/O statistics:

```
dbcc sqlperf (iostats)

Statistic                    Value
-------------------------    ---------
Log Flush Requests           204.0
Log Logical Page IO          1033.0
Log Physical IO              232.0
Log Flush Average            0.87931
Log Logical IO Average       4.45259
Batch Writes                 457.0
Batch Average Size           28.5625
Batch Max Size               8.0
Page Reads                   390.0
Single Page Writes           263.0
Reads Outstanding            0.0
Writes Outstanding           0.0
Transactions                 93.0
Transactions/Log Write       0.400862

DBCC execution completed. If DBCC printed error messages, see
your System Administrator.
```

DBCC SQLPERF(LOGSPACE) monitors the percentage of log space used at the time it is executed:

```
dbcc sqlperf(logspace)

Database Name  Log Size (MB) Log Space Used (%)  Status
-------------  ------------  ------------------  -------
pubtest1       5.0           1.52344             0
banking        10.0          0.0585938           0
distribution   15.0          9.34896             0
msdb           2.0           0.78125             0
pubs           0.0           0.0                 1
tempdb         0.0           0.0                 1
model          0.0           0.0                 1
master         0.0           0.0                 1
```

```
DBCC execution completed. If DBCC printed error messages, see
your System Administrator.
```

The status in our example shows 1, indicating that the log is not on a separate segment so we cannot obtain space usage. A status of 0 indicates no problems, 2 that the *sysindexes* row for *syslogs* could not be found, 4 indicates that the object descriptor could not be found and 8 and 16 indicate log space underflow and overflow respectively, probably due to database statistics becoming inaccurate.

10.5.7 Enhancements to DBCC

The following extra options are available for the DBCC Utility in SQL Server version 6.0:

- INPUTBUFFER can be executed by the system administrator to view the last query sent from a client.
- NEWALLOC details all table information as well as information supplied by the SQL Server version 4.x CHECKALLOC command but will not stop processing if an error is encountered.
- OPENTRAN is used to determine if an open transaction exists within the log which may prevent proper truncation of the transaction log during DUMP TRANSACTION.
- OUTPUTBUFFER returns the current output buffer and therefore displays the results that have been sent to a specific client.
- PERFMON views all three SQLPERF statistics - IOSTATS, LRUSTATS and NETSTATS.
- SHOW_STATISTICS displays statistical information on the distribution page for an index on a specified table.
- SHRINKDB returns the minimum size to which a database can shrink, highlighting the objects that are preventing the shrink to go any further.
- SHOWCONTIG determines the fragmentation of a given index or data page.
- TRACESTATUS displays the status of a specified trace flag.
- UPDATEUSAGE reports and corrects any inaccuracies in sysindexes which may result in incorrect space usage returned from *sp_spaceused*.

- USEROPTIONS returns the list of SET options currently active.
- WITH NO_INFOMSG prevents the printing of informational messages.
- SQLPERF(THREADS) provides a means of relating the Windows NT system thread ID to a SQL Server spid.

The following options have been enhanced:

- CHECKALLOC
- CHECKDB
- CHECKTABLE

10.6 BACKING UP AND RESTORING A DATABASE

Backing up and subsequently restoring a SQL Server are the two operations that a systems administrator will need to do on a regular basis if they are not going to incur the wrath of both their users and managers alike once a system fails. SQL Server offers two types of database backup:

- Automatic Recovery
- Non-automatic Recovery

10.6.1 Automatic Recovery

Automatic recovery occurs every time a SQL Server is started. All post failure/shutdown uncommitted transactions are rolled back and any committed transactions between the last checkpoint and failure or shutdown are rolled forward. The system databases are recovered initially, starting with the master database and going through model, tempdb and finally the user databases. Users are able to logon to the system once the system databases have been fully recovered.

Of interest here is the recovery interval. This is an option which can be fine tuned to set the maximum number of minutes per database that SQL Server uses to complete its recovery tasks. The default is 5 minutes, and this may need to be changed depending upon database and disk activity. SQL Server uses this value to decide the best moment to perform a checkpoint on the database and write any *dirty pages* (pages which contain changed data but have not yet been written to the disk) to disk. The recovery flag determines the amount of information displayed during recovery. The default is 0, a value of 1 will display each individual transaction and say if it was canceled or committed.

Transaction Logs

A transaction log will record changes made to a SQL Server database, there being one transaction log per database. SQL Server uses the write-ahead log method, with the data modifications being written to the transaction log prior to the data change being executed on the database. A *begin transaction* event is recorded in the log every time a transaction begins, and SQL Server will use this statement during automated recovery. User defined transactions were discussed in Chapter 6.

10.6.2 Checkpoints

A checkpoint is used to force dirty pages to be written to disk. The checkpoint may be initiated by SQL Server or it can be forced to occur by the system administrator or user. By using checkpoint, recovery time is reduced as all completed transactions are securely written to disk. The automated use of checkpoint is determined by the recovery interval, as discussed above.

The checkpoint statement is generally used to flush dirty pages prior to system restart for maintenance so that the system has little to recover, forcing changes to any database option to take effect, for example after using *sp_dboption*, or to force a rollback following the cancellation of a user transaction containing a modification to a database option.

Here is an example of using checkpoint to force the pubs database to be read only:

```
use master
go
sp_dboption pubs, read, true
use pubs
go
checkpoint
go
```

10.6.3 Non-Automatic Recovery - Database Backups and Restores

The routine of database backups is one that the system administrator will soon accept as one of the chores that need to be completed on a regular basis. The question that always occurs is how often should a database be backed up? The database should ALWAYS be backed up after:

- Creating a database – a database must always be loaded prior to loading the associated transaction log. With a newly created database which is corrupt this is naturally impossible as no transaction log would have been built.
- Creating an index – any pages created with the CREATE INDEX statement are not recorded in the log, so a failure at this stage will necessitate a rebuilding of the index and, whilst not catastrophic, can certainly be time consuming.
- Undertaking any task which is not recorded in the transaction log. Fast bulk copy, SELECT INTO, WRITE TEXT and DUMP TRANSACTION WITH NO_LOG all bypass the transaction log.

Generally it is advisable to back up the transaction log every day, with the back up held for 2 weeks in secure storage, and back up the database and transaction log every week with the back up held securely for two months. This is, of course, a guide and each SQL Server system will differ. Highly volatile systems may need their transaction logs and databases backed up much more frequently to speed up recovery and limit the growth of the transaction logs.

As well as backing up databases the system administrator would normally be responsible for monitoring the size of the transaction log and using the DUMP TRANSACTION command if the log grows too big.

It is always strongly recommended that integrity checks such as DBCC CHECKDB, CHECKALLOC/NEWALLOC and CHECKCATALOG be run either just before or immediately after a database dump. This will ensure that the database is physically intact as any errors in the database will naturally be carried over in the dump process. For this reason, and the fact that transactions can occur during or after DBCC has been used, it is usual to run DBCC after the database has been dumped. In some cases it is possible for a database to fail during loading if there are problems with its integrity.

Backing Up a Database

The process of backing up a database using Transact-SQL is quite straightforward, for example:

```
dump database pubs to diskette
```

This will backup the pubs database to the diskette dump device we created in Chapter 2.

Further options on this command may be used to assist with tape devices:

- UNLOAD – this will automatically rewind the tape and unload it when the dump is complete
- NOUNLOAD – this is the default and prevents the tape from being unloaded.
- INIT – ensures that the dump is the first file on the tape and overwrites any existing files
- NOINIT – appends the file to the current tape.

The SQL Enterprise Manager can be used to manage database backup and restore. Figure 10-6 shows the *Database Backup/Restore* window with the *Backup* tab in the foreground. The SQL Enterprise Manager can be used to choose a dump device and define a schedule of backups.

Enhancements to the DUMP Statement

SQL Server 6.0 has introduced a number of enhancements to the DUMP statement which reduce the amount of time needed for database maintenance. Enhancements include:

- Parallel DUMPS to multiple devices.
- Ability to specify a DUMP device without previously defining it.
- Use of named pipe DUMP devices.
- Ability to DUMP to devices using the Universal Naming Convention (UNC).
- Use of compression on tape devices.
- Ability to find out information about a DUMP file.

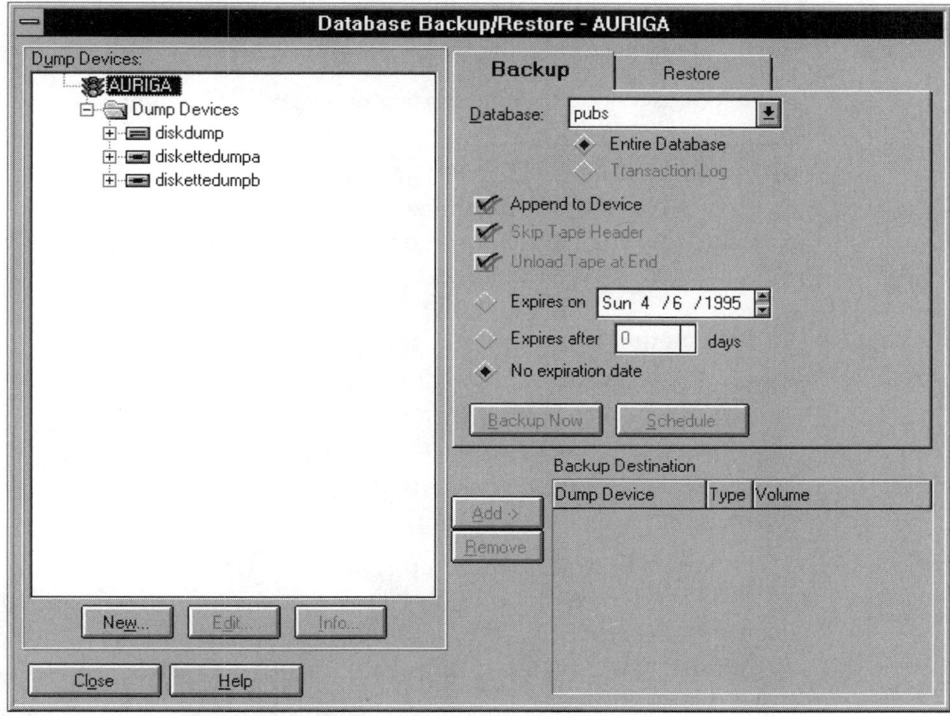

Figure 10-6 Database Backup and Restore with the SQL Enterprise Manager

To support these changes the following extensions have been added to the Transact-SQL DUMP command:

- The dump device name DISK/TAPE/PIPE do not have to exist. The full pathname of the device is needed as they are temporary DUMP devices and do not have an entry in *sysdevices*. The named pipe must be given if PIPE is used.
- VOLUME specifies the DUMP volume id which defaults to SQ0001 for SQL Server and is the name of the ANSI VOL1 label for a new tape. Used to validate the volume name of a DUMP device.
- SKIP/NOSKIP tells SQL Server whether or not to read the ANSI TAPE device headers.
- EXPIREDATE sets the date when the DUMP media can be overwritten.

- RETAINDAYS specifies the number of days that must elapse before the DUMP media can be overwritten.
- STATS used to determine the percentage of pages dumped to a device.

Hint: As a database DUMP is an on-line operation it may at times adversely affect the performance of a SQL Server. It may be advisable to schedule the DUMP for times when the server is not busy.

Backing Up the Transaction Log

The transaction log can only be backed up separately if it exists on a different device to its associated database which is probably the wisest method of working in the event of device failure anyway. Backing up a transaction log will use less media space than the associated database and will generally be achieved quicker than a database backup.

The transaction log is backed up using the DUMP TRANSACTION statement. This removes any committed transactions from the log once they have been written to the dump device. There are optional extensions to the DUMP TRANSACTION syntax. These are TRUNCATE_ONLY and NO_LOG.

- TRUNCATE_ONLY can be used if the transaction log is not to be used for recovery purposes. The inactive part of the log is removed, thereby saving media space.
- NO_LOG is used when media space has been exhausted and the TRUNCATE_ONLY option cannot be used to recover any space from the log. NO_LOG does not write a log record to the transaction log detailing the transaction dump and so does not require space in it.

It is important to remember that DUMP TRANSACTION used with either option above will not enable you to recover data from anywhere other than the point when the last DUMP TRANSACTION or DUMP DATABASE was executed. Always use the DUMP DATABASE statement after using these commands to ensure that you can recover back to this point.

Hint: If DUMP DATABASE is used exclusively rather than using DUMP TRANSACTION the transaction log will never be cleared out, and will grow larger and larger. To clear the transaction log use the DUMP TRANSACTION WITH TRUNCATE_ONLY option after the database has been dumped.

Here is an example of using the DUMP TRANSACTION syntax:

```
dump transaction pubs to pubdump
```

This will dump the transaction log from the *pubs* database to the dump device *pubdump*.

There is a further option, NO_TRUNCATE, which will dump the entire transaction log without purging the database of committed transactions. This is useful when the database has become inaccessible after a media failure. If the media failure occurred at 16:00 and the last transaction dump executed at 08:00, the day's work from between 08:00 and 16:00 is not resident in any transaction dump. To save this work the system administrator must execute a DUMP TRANSACTION statement with NO_TRUNCATE which will produce a final transaction dump that can be used to recover the database in conjunction with the other transaction dumps.

Like the database backup the system administrator has the options of using syntax to control the tape device such as UNLOAD, NOUNLOAD, INIT and NOINIT.

Hint: Use the DBCC command DBCC SQLPERF(LOGSPACE) to monitor space used by the transaction log.

It is worth mentioning here the option *trunc.log on chkpt*. Switching this option on will save media space as each time a checkpoint is initiated the transaction log will be truncated. By default, for all databases other than master, this option is off, so that the transaction log is not truncated following a checkpoint. The master database has this option set on by default to save filling up the transaction log, and as the master database transaction log cannot be dumped separately to the database, the option is best left alone.

There are many possible backup and restore strategies, and probably just as many pitfalls! It is outside the scope of this book to go into the detail on all of these but the process of backup, restore and managing transaction log space is vital to the smooth running of any SQL Server site and so any database backup/ restore strategy should be tested exhaustively.

Loading the Database following Media Failure

Once you have composed yourself following media failure the database needs to be reloaded. After system restart, if SQL Server is unable to access a database an error is generated and the database locked and marked as suspect. The damaged database must then be dropped either using DROP DATABASE or DBCC DBREPAIR if necessary.

The database dump can then be reloaded using the LOAD DATABASE command, during which the recovering database is not accessible by other users, but they can use the other unaffected databases normally. Once loaded SQL Server will assess the page utilization of the database and re-initialize any unused pages.

Hint: Use the SQL Enterprise Manager for loading the database. This prevents you from having to use the console utility and ISQL when restoring from diskette and tape which can save considerable time.

The Transact-SQL for loading a database is fairly self explanatory:

```
load database pubs from pubdump1
```

In the above example *pubdump1* is the dump device. If you are restoring from tape then it is possible to specify the file number on the tape with the FILE= extension. Similarly UNLOAD and NOUNLOAD can be used to control the tape device as discussed earlier.

Loading the Transaction Log following Media Failure

Loading a transaction log follows the same routine as database recovery. Transaction log back ups must be restored in the same order as they were backed up as the logs are time stamped to ensure correct order of loading. The changes recorded in the transaction log are automatically re-executed and any uncommitted transactions at the time of back up will be rolled back. LOAD TRANSACTION can only be used once the associated database has been restored, having been backed up with the DUMP DATABASE command.

The Transact-SQL is just like the LOAD DATABASE commands:

```
load transaction pubs from pubdump2
```

Note the use of a different dump device from the database example given previously. Similarly it is possible to use tape device controls such as FILE=, UNLOAD and NOUNLOAD.

Enhancements to the LOAD Statement

In a similar fashion to DUMP, the LOAD statement has been extended and enhanced in SQL Server 6.0 with the following options:

- DISK/TAPE/PIPE enable the loading of a database from temporary devices not contained in *sysdevices*.
- VOLUME to specify the DUMP volume being used.
- STATS to return the percentage of pages loaded.
- LOAD HEADERONLY to load volume and header information about a specific database DUMP.

10.6.4 Restoring the Master Database

The system administrator will recognize a damaged master database as the SQL Server may become unusable, input/output errors may be generated or segmentation faults become apparent.

Due to the importance of the master database it should be backed up each time it is changed. Changes occur to the master database when any of these statements or system stored procedures are executed:

- DISK INIT
- CREATE/ALTER DATABASE
- DISK MIRROR, UNMIRROR, REMIRROR
- *sp_droppremotelogin*
- *sp_addumpdevice*
- *sp_dropdevice*
- *sp_addlogin*
- *sp_droplogin*

- *sp_addserver*
- *sp_dropserver*
- *sp_addremotelogin*

Note: no user defined objects should ever be created in the master database.

The steps to rebuild the master database:

All of the SQL Server configuration values must be restored to the default values by using the *bldmastr* utility:

```
bldmastr /d c:\sql\data\master.dat /r
```

The /d option specifies the physical pathname to the master database device, the /r option will rewrite the default configuration settings to the configuration block which contains the system startup parameters. With this option the master database is not rebuilt.

To rebuild the master database the /m option is used to rewrite the master database without changing the configuration block. Typically this is used if the physical operating system file is intact. Both of these options can be used together resulting in a rewriting of the configuration block and the master database together.

If the media failure is such that it is unusable, a new master.dat file needs to be created. The following example will rebuild master.dat with a size of 30MB:

```
bldmastr /d c:\sql\data\master.dat /s 15360
```

The size is specified in 2Kb pages, with a default of 6144 or 12MB.

The SQL Server now needs to be started in single user mode:

```
sqlservr /c /d c:\sql\data\master.dat /m
```

Using the /c option will ensure that SQL Server bypasses the Windows NT Service Control Manager which speeds up the time to load the server, but disables the SQL Service Manager. Using the /m option specifies single user mode startup which prevents more than one user logging on and disables the checkpoint mechanism.

The install master batch file now needs to be run. This is a piece of Transact-SQL that contains the SQL to install the master database:

```
isql /Usa /P /i c:\sql\install\instmstr.sql
```

/U is the user login id, /P the associated password, /i indicates the file to be used which contains the SQL statements.

The next stage is to add a dump device using *sp_addumpdevice* before performing the load if the master backup was to hard disk or tape. Again, ISQL needs to be used:

```
isql /Usa /P
sp_addumpdevice 'disk', 'diskdump', 'c:\dump\dump1.dat',2
```

Where *diskdump* is the logical name, followed by the physical name and *2* specifies the controller to be a hard disk.

The LOAD DATABASE command can now be used to load the latest dump of the database. Once complete the server will automatically shutdown. If there have been no changes to the master database since the dump was made the server can be restarted in multi-user mode and the task is now complete!

If not then some further remedial action may be needed:

- Altered login ID or devices must be reapplied either manually or using stored SQL batches.
- Databases which have been added or changed must be re-created and the data re-entered from batch files or dumps.

Hint: The authors strongly recommend that scripts are kept of changes made to databases. This will facilitate the recovery of the system if the master is lost.

DISK REINIT

DISK REINIT is used to recreate rows in the *sysdevices* table in the MASTER database for devices which were added following the latest MASTER database dump. The underlying disk file is not formatted so any existing data is preserved. Care must be taken with the DISK REINIT command as incorrect information about device names or sizes can result in permanent corruption of the database.

DISK REFIT

DISK REFIT is used to recreate rows in *sysusages* and *sysdatabases* for any ALTER DATABASE and CREATE DATABASE command that may have been executed following the last database dump. As with DISK REINIT great care must be taken with this command as data may be permanently corrupted if misused.

10.7 TRANSFERRING DATA TO AND FROM SQL SERVER

Almost inevitably, at some stage, the system administrator will be expected to import or export data to or from the SQL Server. There are a number of ways of achieving this, and this next section will deal with the most straightforward method using the SQL Server Transfer Manager.

No discussion of data import and export with SQL Server can avoid the mention of the bcp or bulk copy program utility. This is, in the opinion of the authors, a dreadful utility that does nothing to enhance the ease of use of SQL Server and is probably best avoided. Therefore we will not be discussing it further.

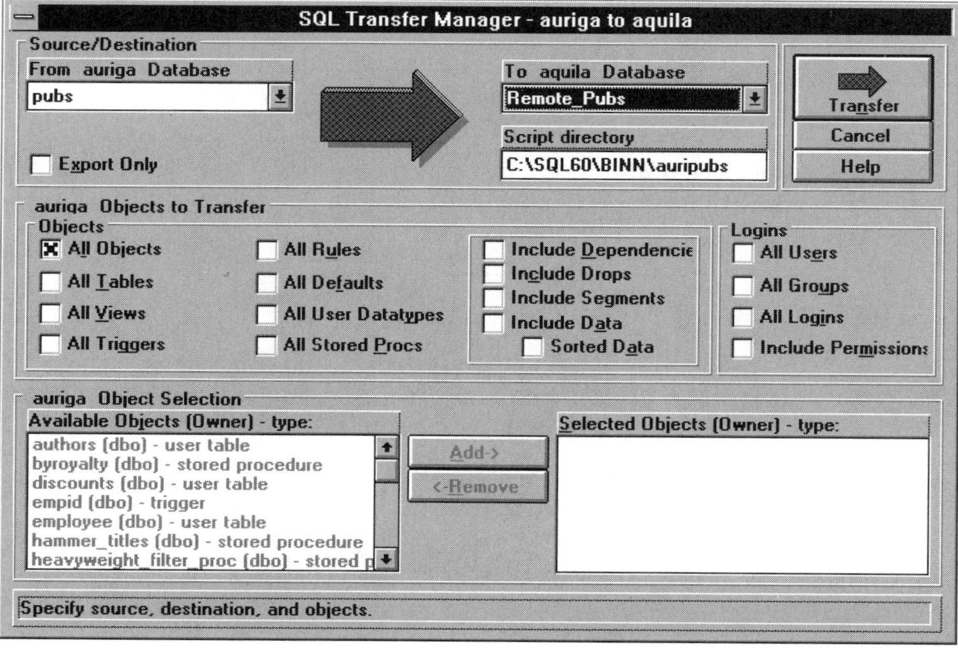

Figure 10-7 The SQL Transfer Manager

The SQL Transfer Manager, shown in Figure 10-7, is a comprehensive tool enabling data to be transferred between different SQL Servers. The SQL Servers do not both need to be version 6.0, indeed data can be taken from a version 4.2x SQL Server and transferred using this tool. This tool is also useful for transferring data between SQL Servers on different hardware architectures such as DEC Alpha and Intel based Windows NT systems. Care has to be taken with differing sort orders and character sets that may be encountered between different servers and in some instances a version 4.2x server may make references to object names which are now reserved words for SQL Server version 6.0.

10.8 SCHEDULED AND UNATTENDED OPERATIONS

One of the key features of SQL Server 6.0 is the ability to schedule operations to be executed with out the intervention of an operator and the ability to send alerts when certain events occur within the server.

The integration of SQLMAIL via the MAPI interface enables these alerts to be sent as mail messages or pager messages, expanding the scope of the more traditional alert systems.

The schedules are created by using the SQL Enterprise Manager. If the right mouse button is clicked on the SQL Executive symbol and *Edit Tasks* selected the *Task Scheduling* window appears as shown in Figure 10-8.

If the *New Task* button is now selected the *New Task* window appears as shown in Figure 10-9. The new task is named and a *Task Type* selected which can be one of the following:

- CmdExec
- Distribution
- LogReader
- Sync
- TSQL

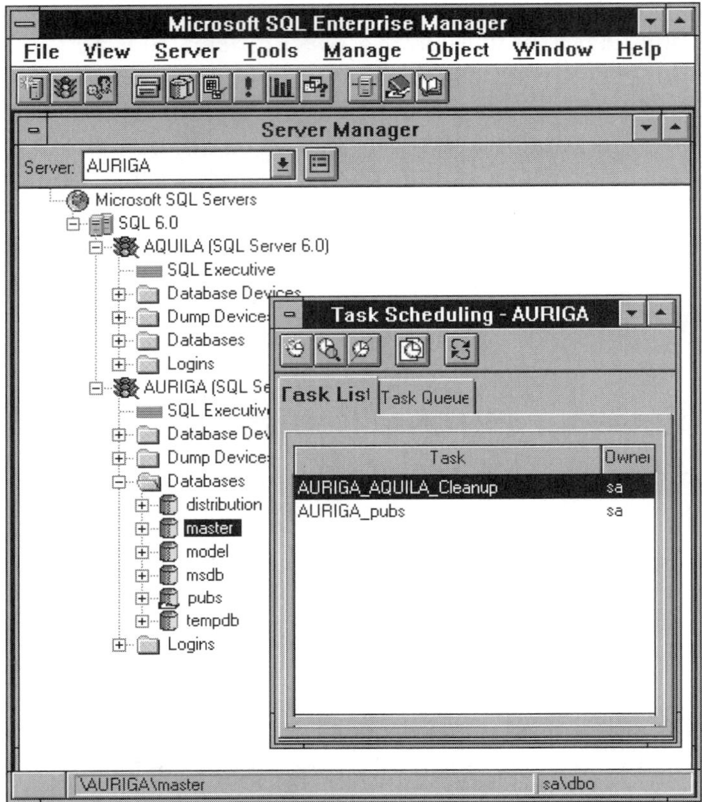

Figure 10-8 Scheduling Tasks with the SQL Enterprise Manager

A *CmdExec* task type is an operating system command or .EXE file. *Distribution*, *LogReader* and *Sync* are a concerned with replication and *TSQL* is a Transact-SQL statement.

The schedule options are used to specify whether the task is a one-time event or will recur at fixed intervals.

Recurring tasks can be scheduled at frequent intervals – daily, weekly or monthly. The date of the task can be pre-set or left to be unending with no specified start and finish date. Parameters can be set for the tasks which include Email on event success or failure, Windows NT log entries on success or failure and retry parameters to try and force through an execution.

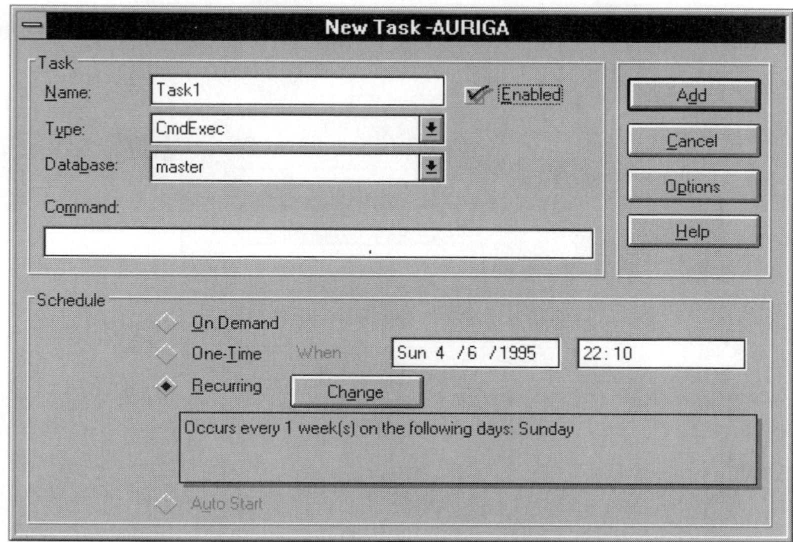

Figure 10-9 The New Task Dialogue Box

10.9 ALERTS

SQL Server events can be trapped by the Windows NT event log which in turn is monitored by the SQL Executive. If an event occurs which has been set up as requiring an alert to be executed, the SQL Executive ensures a mail message, pager alert or executable event is initiated to inform the appropriate person.

The following events will be trapped by the Windows NT event viewer and are therefore most suitable for initiating an alert:

- *sysmessages* with a severity greater than 19
- Non sysmessages and errors with severity between 120 and 130
- Any RAISERROR invoked by the WITHLOG syntax
- Any event logged by *xp_logevent*
- *sysmessage* errors modified with *sp_altermessage*

To create an alert the *Manage Alerts* window is invoked from the *Server...Alerts* menu item in the SQL Enterprise Manager. The *New Alert* button is clicked displaying the *New Alert* window as shown in Figure 10-10.

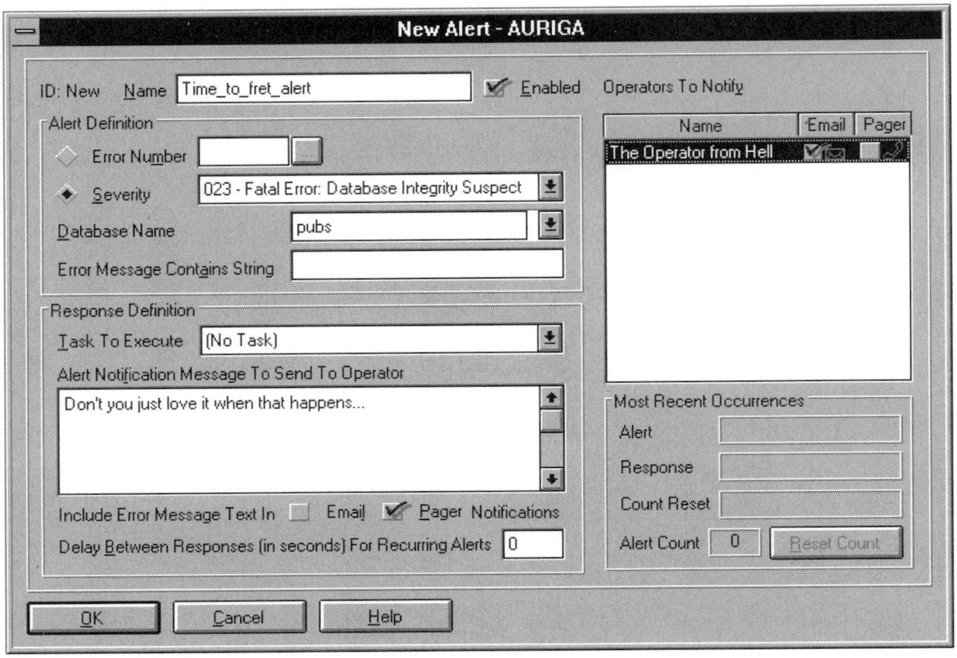

Figure 10-10 The New Alert Window in the SQL Enterprise Manager

There is a tremendous amount of flexibility available to the system administrator to specify alerts based on error messages. The SQL Server error message repository can be searched for messages containing a particular string to facilitate the setting up of the new alert. Operators can be Emailed or paged in response to the alert.

This chapter has covered some major database administration topics. It is critical to understand the processes of database backup and restore, data integrity checking and transaction log management. Ensure that your site has set database administration policies and that these are tested regularly. You don't want to be testing them at 3:00 a.m. in the morning with the company databases falling down around you or at 3:00 p.m. in the afternoon with your boss breathing down your neck!

11 Data Replication

11.1 INTRODUCTION

For some years now, there has been a move away from centralized systems towards more distributed systems. There are a number of reasons why this trend is growing and these are highlighted in the next section. To support the distribution of data it is necessary for database management systems to provide more and more distributed functionality but without a corresponding massive increase in management or implementation complexity. Microsoft SQL Server has always provided a number of useful distributed capabilities such as remote stored procedures but SQL Server 6.0 adds the capability of data replication. This chapter will focus on this new data replication capability.

11.2 WHY DISTRIBUTE DATA?

For some companies, distributing their data around the network makes no sense whatsoever. Their organizational structure is based around a centralized model and the way they do business works best with a central database running on a large minicomputer or mainframe. However, for some companies this centralized approach is not suitable and they have decided to place pieces of their database around their network. Some, reasons why more and more companies may wish to distribute their databases are:

- Organizational Mapping
- Growth Flexibility
- Cost of Ownership
- Availability
- Performance

Many companies have a distributed organization and wish to model their data along similar lines. As their company expands (or contracts) they may wish to incrementally grow or shrink their computer resource and not have to knock down the computer room wall to completely replace the mainframe! Mainframes are expensive whereas, at least from a hardware perspective, more price performance can be obtained from multiple small servers.

If a company's data is spread over multiple servers there is a greater chance that, at a given point in time, a server will not be functioning correctly. However, this will result in a small reduction in the overall system availability whereas if a centralized database fails, it is likely that the overall system availability will be severely compromised.

If data is moved close to the users who need it most, then communication overheads will be reduced and performance will be increased. There may also be a cost benefit resulting from reduced network usage.

Let us look at the above reasons to distribute data from the perspective of a fictitious company. This company might have a number of distribution outlets around the country. It makes sense to place the data that is manipulated by the respective outlets at those outlets instead of in one centralized database. This has a number of advantages. As 80% of the data needed by each outlet is local to that outlet, the communication overhead of accessing a centralized database is largely removed with a corresponding increase in performance.

As communication lines are usually one of the least reliable components in a system, reducing the reliance on them should increase overall system availability. If the company adds a new outlet it merely adds a new server and local database. Unexpected company growth can be accommodated more easily.

However, we have made an important assumption which is that data sharing is *low* between the outlets. Once the requirement to share data becomes *high*, the advantages that we have seen of the distributed approach are quickly eroded and a centralized approach becomes attractive again.

This highlights an important phenomenon concerning distributed systems, which is, they are more attractive for systems which do not have a need to share most of the data in the database. This can be taken a step further. Distributed systems are more attractive for systems which do not have a requirement to share and update most of the data in the database.

To demonstrate this fact with our fictitious company, suppose that 80% of each outlet's data was frequently read by the other outlets. The communication overhead would rapidly increase as each server would be in constant communication with every other server. With this constant intercommunication, a communications failure or server failure would result in a severely degraded system. Incremental growth would not be as simple as before because the addition of a new server would have a greater affect on existing servers.

The above only demonstrates the negative affect of increased data sharing. We could make the distributed approach attractive again by keeping multiple copies of data at the outlets. When an outlet needed to look at another outlet's data it would find it locally. This is fine so long as we rarely wished to update the data. In reality, this is often not the case. Most key data is constantly updated to reflect the state of a business at any given point in time. If we keep more than one copy of a piece of data on the network we are faced with the problem of synchronizing updates to the multiple copies.

What point are we trying to make here? Quite simply, distributing data around the network may not be the best approach for your company. There again, it may be the perfect solution to all your data access problems. Either way, you will have to think through the ramifications of data distribution extremely carefully. Do not just consider initial set up for, once your distributed system is ticking along smoothly, some user somewhere will want you to change it!

If more than one copy of a piece of data must be held on the network, as a database designer, you will also have to decide whether the copies are *loosely coupled* or *tightly coupled*.

11.3 LOOSELY COUPLED DATA VERSUS TIGHTLY COUPLED DATA

This can simply be described as whether all the copies of the data are updated at the same time, that is, synchronously or all the copies of the data are updated at different times, that is, asynchronously.

If the data copies are tightly coupled, the *tight consistency model*, when one piece of data is updated all the other copies are also updated. They enjoy a peer to peer relationship as there is no primary copy of the data and no secondary copies, that is, no master copy and no slave copies. All the copies are updated in a single distributed transaction which cannot complete successfully until all the copies have been updated irrespective of where they are on the network and how many copies are present.

If the data copies are loosely coupled, the *loose consistency model*, one piece of data is updated and then the other copies are updated at some later point in time which may be seconds or hours after the first copy is updated. The copies do not enjoy a peer to peer relationship as there is now a designated primary copy and a set of secondary copies. Also, the copies are not now updated in a single distributed transaction.

There are advantages and disadvantages to both approaches. The advantage of the tight consistency model is that each copy of the data is always up to date. There is no *latency* involved with using tightly coupled data copies. This may be important as it might be highly desirable that changes in the price of gold, for example, are made to each server database at the same instant in time.

There are a number of disadvantages to this approach. As previously stated, all the copies are updated in a single distributed transaction which cannot complete successfully until all the copies have been updated. Each copy must, therefore, be available if the distributed transaction is to complete successfully which means that each server must be available which also means that the network must be available. This might not be always the case. Another consideration is that the duration of the distributed transaction is a function of the time it takes to update each copy. This means that the response time, as perceived by the user who issued the update, is unlikely to be good.

The more copies involved in the distributed transaction the higher the chance a server will be unavailable and the greater the transaction duration. This is why it is often stated that the tight consistency model is not scaleable. This does not mean that this approach is not practical, rather it has its place, which is likely to be updating a low number of copies on a fast local area network rather than a large number of copies on a slow wide area network.

It is worth mentioning that to implement the tight consistency model requires the provision of a two-phase commit protocol (2PC). SQL Server provides a two-phase commit service special library to support update co-ordination between multiple SQL Servers.

The advantage of the tight consistency model is that each copy of the data is always up to date. The disadvantage of the loose consistency model is that each copy of the data is not always up to date. Indeed there is usually some delay in updating all the copies. In the loose consistency model, a designated primary copy of the data is updated and at some later point in time the secondary copies are updated. The transaction that updates the primary copy, which is invariably local, completes the instant the copy is updated successfully.

This means that the response time, as perceived by the user who issued the update, is likely to be good. It also means that there is no requirement for all of the copies to be available. As long as some component of the system *remembers* the changes made to the primary copy, these can be propagated to an unavailable copy at some later time when the copy becomes available again. The loose consistency model is therefore tolerant of network or server failure. As the updating of the multiple secondary copies is an asynchronous operation, tolerant of failures, the loose consistency model is much more scaleable than the tight consistency model and better able to function in a wide area network environment.

However, the loose consistency model can become complex and hard to manage if the designation of what is a primary copy and what is a secondary copy becomes blurred. In other words, if certain data on the network is designated as being updatable by applications (the primary copy) and if certain data on the network is designated as not being updatable by applications (the secondary copies), then the management of the distributed data should not be overly complex. However, if the applications are allowed to update any copy, then anarchy will usually reign and the management of the distributed data will become a nightmare.

It is this loose consistency model that has become popularly known as *replication* and at the time of writing is a hot marketing topic amongst many database vendors. It is likely to remain so for some time. It is the replication capabilities of SQL Server 6.0 that we will now describe.

11.4 INTRODUCTION TO SQL SERVER REPLICATION

SQL Server 6.0 provides replication functionality based on the loose consistency model. Essentially, data is copied from a primary table or set of tables to secondary tables distributed around the network. It can copy changes to the data that occur in the primary tables to the secondary tables continuously or it can refresh the secondary tables at periodic intervals. It is worth mentioning at this point that replication is an integral part of the SQL Server 6.0 product and is not an additional cost bolt on extra.

Although the above description is correct it does not reflect the sophistication present in the replication capabilities of SQL Server 6.0. We will be examining these features in some detail shortly. First, though, let us circle SQL Server 6.0 replication at a high altitude.

SQL Server 6.0 replication is designed to support a number of replication scenarios. For example, tables on a production server can be replicated to databases on servers used for decision support work that host complex and resource hungry queries. This eliminates the degradation that would occur on the production server if the complex decision support queries were hosted on it.

To do this, SQL Server uses the *publisher/subscriber* model. We have referred to a primary or source database in previous paragraphs and, in SQL Server vernacular, the server that holds a primary database is known as a *publication server*. Data that is available to be replicated is said to be *published*. When data is published, other servers on the network can *subscribe* to all or part of it and these servers are then known as *subscription servers* or *subscribers*.

What is actually replicated? The fundamental unit of replication is known as an *article*. An article can be thought of as a table or part of a table. These articles may be grouped together into a *publication* and an article must always be part of a publication. This is important to database integrity in the same way that transactions are. Tables have integrity rules that relate them and so replication must be concerned with copying data in a fashion that adheres to these rules. It is not acceptable to copy the sales table at noon and the titles table eight hours later if the copy of the sales table is going to contain a row for eight hours that refers to a non existent title.

A very confusing scenario would occur if we replicated changes to a destination table on a server to find that the row to which the changes referred had been previously deleted by a user on that subscription server. This is known as a *collision* and SQL Server avoids this unpalatable scenario by specifying that replication is a one way flow, that is, from the publication server to the subscription server. In essence, the tables on the publication server are allowed to be written to but they must be read only on the subscription server. This is no bad thing as managing databases around the network and replication in general is often quite a tricky feat and to have data replicated in every possible direction would be an unmanageable nightmare!

Hint: A subscription server can also be a publication server so some quite complex scenarios are still possible. Also multiple publishers can publish to the same table on a subscription server, however, as any experienced database administrator knows, simple is often best!

So how does all this work? Basically, the database administrator specifies that certain tables and subsets of tables are to be published. Any committed changes to database tables always end up in the transaction log as normal but now they are marked for replication. A special replication component, known as the *log reader process* copies these marked transactions into another replication component known as the *distribution database*. This can be thought of as a *queue* or *half-way house* as this is the stopover where transactions stay until they continue their journey to the subscription servers where changes are eventually applied to the target tables. The movement of transactions from the distribution database to the subscription servers is managed by the *distribution process*.

Typically, the log reader process, the distribution process and the distribution database reside on the publication server with the databases that are being replicated as shown in Figure 11-1.

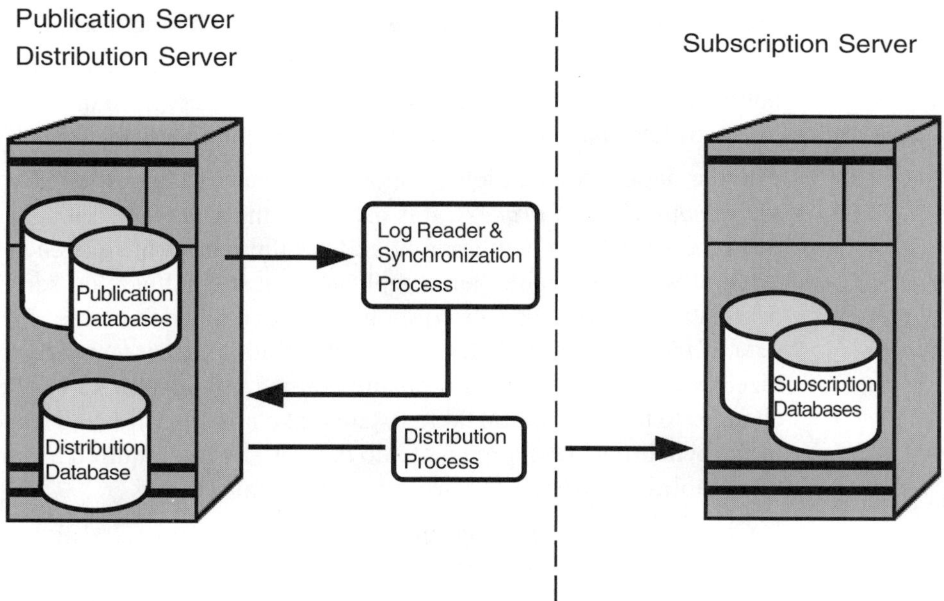

Figure 11- 1 A Typical Replication Configuration

However, this need not be the only possible configuration. Another option is shown in Figure 11-2.

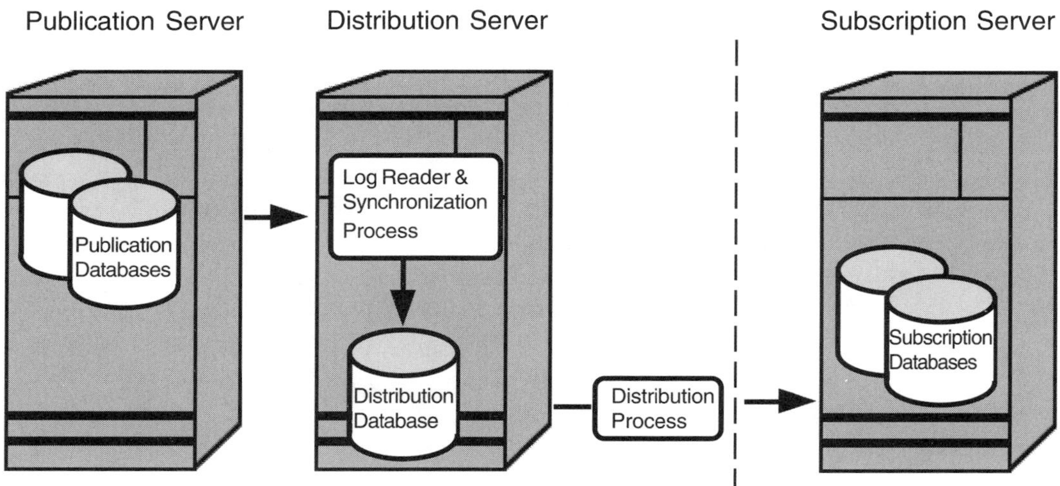

Figure 11-2 A Replication Configuration to Support High Throughput

The configuration shown in Figure 11-2 has separated the distribution database and the replication processes on to another server. In this configuration the distribution database could support other publication servers if required.

There is another replication component we have so far not mentioned called the *synchronization process*. It is natural to think of replication as a continuous process with no beginning or end but there must have been some initial point at which the table being replicated on the publication server and the destination table on the subscription server contained the same version of the data. If the destination tables on the subscription server were never synchronized with the tables being replicated on the publication server, replicating changes to the destination table would make no sense. It is the responsibility of the synchronization process to do the initial work required to synchronize these tables and we will discuss how it does this shortly.

In Chapter 1 we looked at the architecture of SQL Server and also the Distributed Management Framework (DMF). One of the components in this architecture is the SQL Executive service and it is this component that looks after the log reader, synchronization and distribution processes.

An important point to consider is whether the action of publishing a table imposes an extra overhead on any processes that change the data in the table. It should not, and this is because replication is centered around the transaction logs of any publication databases. Any processes that change data in tables will ultimately instigate writes to the transaction log and the database itself. As the log reader process reads the transaction logs looking for transactions marked for replication, user processes that are changing data in publication databases will not need to perform any extra disk I/O over and above what they would do normally. Of course, replication will use system resource and so in a sense it may degrade the performance of applications on the server if system resource is at a premium. In this situation the database administrator may consider placing the distribution database on a separate server.

11.5 SETTING UP SQL SERVER REPLICATION

There are two methods of setting up replication:

- The SQL Enterprise Manager
- System Stored Procedures

We will concentrate on the former method as it is much easier and more pleasant to use the graphical interfaces than a host of system stored procedures. It is also the method we expect most database administrators to use. We will, however, introduce some of the informational system stored procedures later.

11.5.1 First Steps

Before the database administrator sets up replication there are some rules that must be followed. From a hardware perspective, replication consumes system resource and this must be taken into account. Microsoft suggest that, any server that acts in a distribution server role whether as a standalone distribution server or a server that is performing both publications and distributions, should be configured with at least 32 Mb of memory and 16 Mb of this should be given to SQL Server. The distribution database will also take up extra disk space.

The security model can be standard, mixed or integrated, however, Microsoft recommend integrated security. Character sets and sort orders must be consistent across the publication, distribution and subscription servers.

Transaction log space is an important consideration. If a transaction that is marked for replication cannot proceed to the distribution database it will stay in the transaction log and, as such, the transaction log cannot be truncated passed this transaction. For this reason, it is a good idea to be somewhat more generous with transaction log space when considering a publication database. In SQL Server 6.0, a new DBCC option OPENTRAN can be used to output statistics on the oldest active transaction and the oldest distributed and non-distributed replicated transactions in a transaction log.

Another feature new in SQL Server 6.0 that is needed in order to set up replication is the primary key constraint. Any table that is to be published must contain a primary key constraint. A primary key constraint can be added when the table is created or at a later time using the ALTER TABLE Transact-SQL statement. Primary key constraints are discussed in Chapter 6.

11.5.2 Installing Publishing

Once the first steps have been accomplished the Install Publishing step should be performed. This is the step where a decision must be made as to whether the distribution server and the publication server are to be one and the same. The server is selected in the SQL Enterprise Manager Server Manager window, in our case *Auriga*. From the *Server* menu *Replication Configuration* is chosen. The *Install Replication Publishing* option is then selected which displays the Install Replication Publishing dialog box as shown in Figure 11-3.

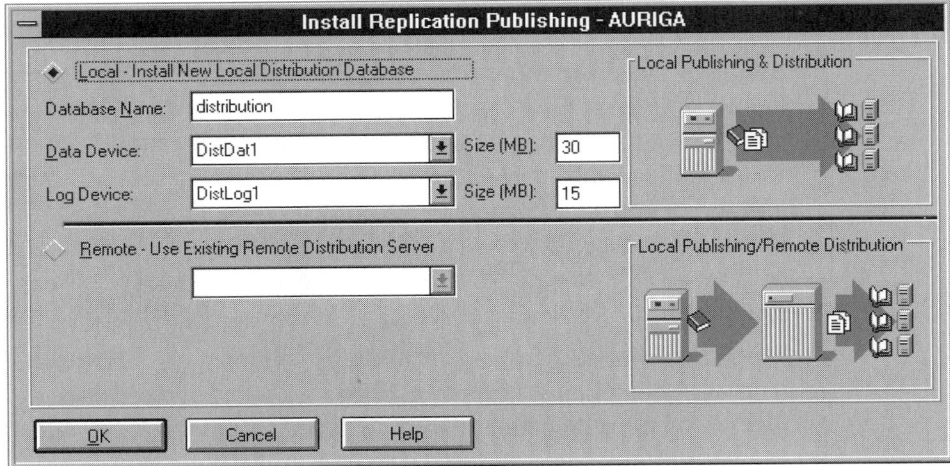

Figure 11-3 The Install Replication Publishing Dialog Box

If the *Local* option is selected then the distribution server and the publication server are to be one and the same. If the *Remote* option is selected then the distribution server will be separate from the publication server. In Figure 11-3 the Local option has been selected. SQL Server then requires the name of the database device and log device where the distribution database will reside. If *<New>* is selected for the device name a further dialog box enables a new database and log device to be created. SQL Server then creates the distribution database. At this point SQL Server will ask whether you wish to continue. You can choose to continue or carry on where you left off later.

11.5.3 Setting the Server Publication Preferences

The next step is to select the various publishing options for the server. From the *Server* menu *Replication Configuration* is chosen. The *Publishing* option is then selected which then displays the *Replication - Publishing* dialog box as shown in Figure 11-4.

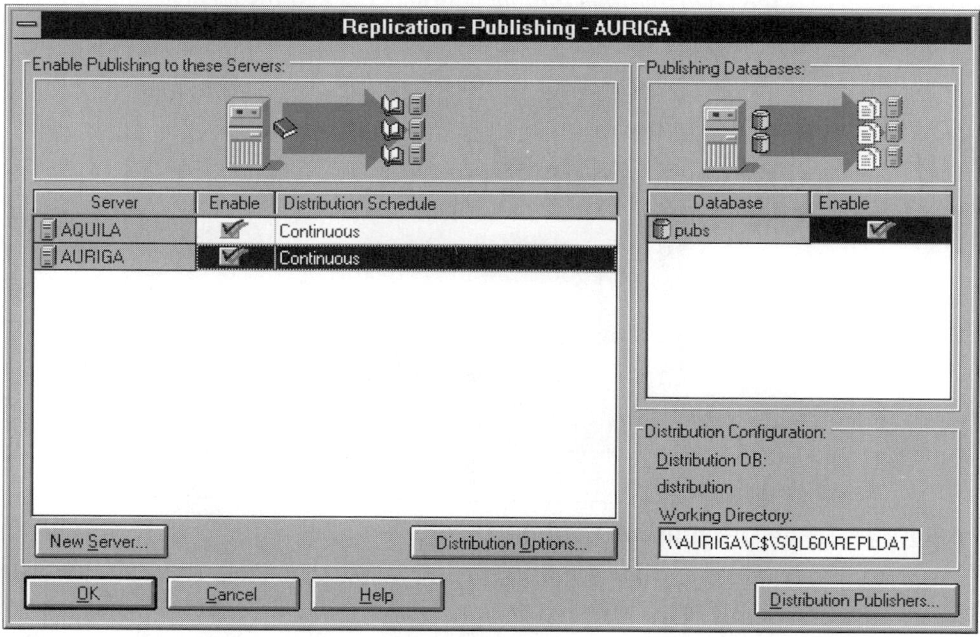

Figure 11-4 The Replication - Publishing Dialog Box

As can be seen, this dialog box allows a number of options to be selected. On the left hand side of the dialog box there is a list of servers displayed. By selecting a server, publishing is enabled to it. This means that a server is now authorized to subscribe to the publications from this server. In our example, *Aquila* has been authorized to subscribe to the publications from this server, that is, *Auriga*.

On the right hand side of the dialog box there is a list of databases displayed. This lists the databases residing at the server and these can be enabled which means that they are then authorized to publish data. In our example, *pubs* is the only database which we can choose to enable for publishing.

Near the bottom right hand corner of the dialog box is a section concerned with the configuration of the distribution database. Its name is specified, which in the example here is *distribution*, and so is its working directory – \\AURIGA\C$\SQL60\REPLDATA. The working directory may be changed if desired.

If the *Distribution Options* button is clicked the *Distribution Options* dialog box appears as shown in Figure 11-5.

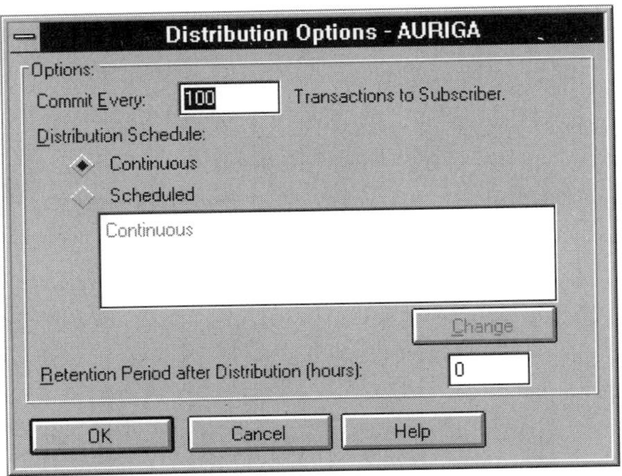

Figure 11-5 The Distribution Options Dialog Box

This allows the database administrator to change some of the distribution options. The option *Commit Every 100 Transactions to Subscriber* is the maximum number of transactions that will be sent to a subscription server as a single element, in our example 100. If the number of transactions marked for replication is greater than this value they will be sent as a number of elements which may have an affect on performance. The *Distribution Schedule* option specifies the interval at which transactions will be sent to the subscription servers.

For example, the *Continuous* option means that transactions are sent to the subscription servers on a continuous basis. This means that the changes made to the source tables are *trickled* through to the destination tables which are thus out of date for the minimum amount of time. The *Scheduled* option means that the transactions are sent to the subscription servers based on a schedule. This is sometimes known as *time-based replication*. It might be useful, perhaps, when data at a subscription server used for decision support needs to be updated every night with production data. The schedule that can be set is very flexible as Figure 11-6 shows.

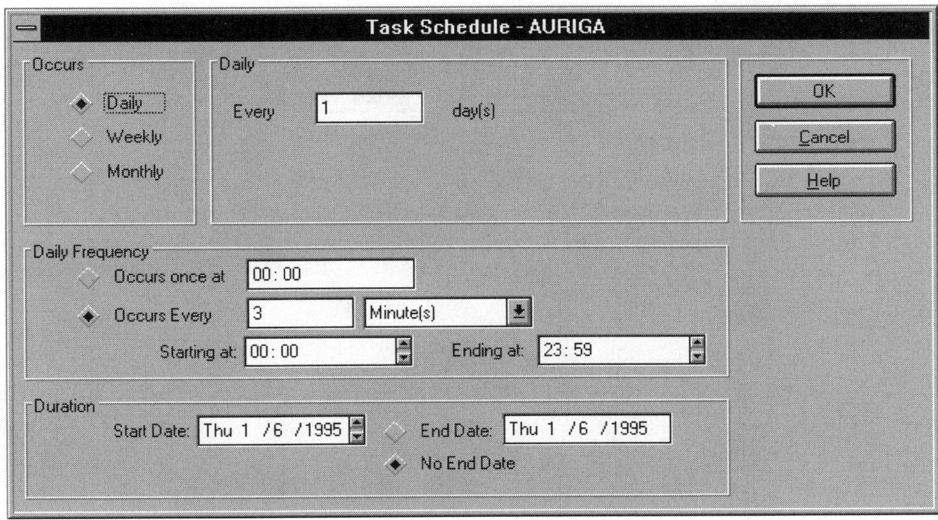

Figure 11-6 Scheduling a Replication

Lastly, the *Retention Period After Distribution* option sets how long the transaction information is retained in the distribution database after it is sent to the subscriber.

At the bottom right hand corner of the dialog box is a button labeled *Distribution Publishers*. This allows the database administrator to choose any remote servers that are able to use this local server as their remote distribution server. The dialog box that is displayed is shown in Figure 11-7.

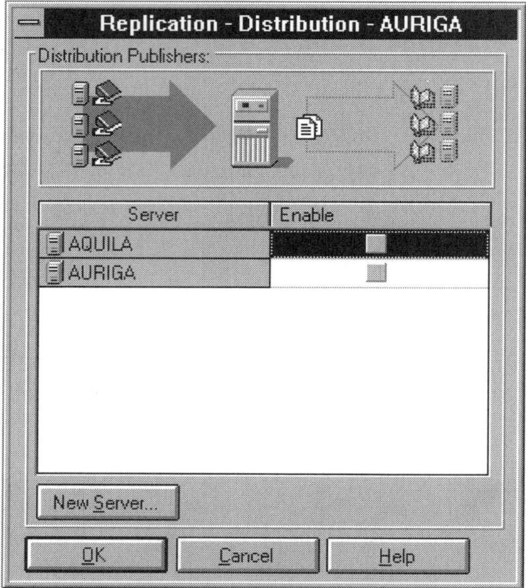

Figure 11-7 The Distribution Publishers Dialog Box

The server publication preferences have now been set. Next, the database administrator will set the server subscription preferences.

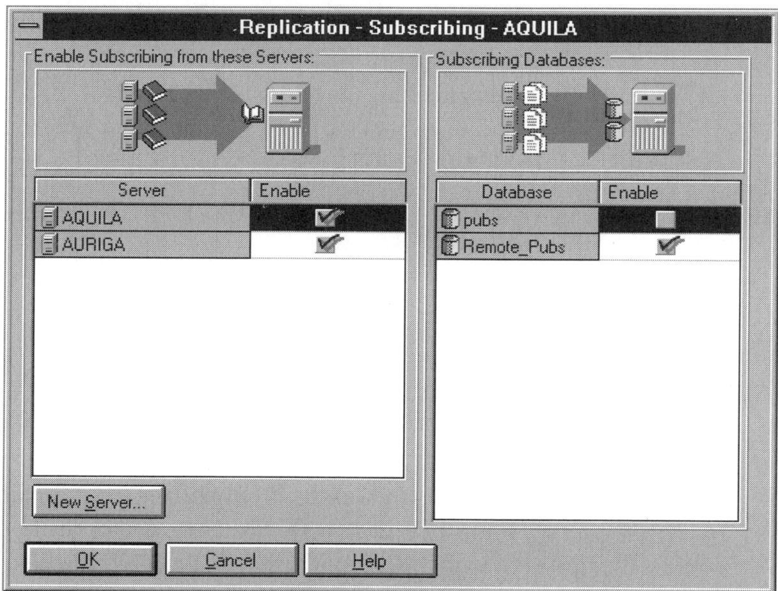

Figure 11-8 The Replication - Subscribing Dialog Box

11.5.4 Setting the Server Subscription Preferences

From the *Server* menu *Replication Configuration* is chosen. The *Subscribing* option is then selected which then displays the *Replication - Subscribing* dialog box as shown in Figure 11-8.

This dialog box enables the database administrator to specify which servers are allowed to send replicated data to this server and which databases on this server are allowed to receive replicated data. Note that before we activated this dialog box we selected the server *Aquila*. We did this because we currently only want the server *Auriga* to be a publisher and the server *Aquila* to be a subscriber.

11.5.5 Publishing Tables and Articles

Now that the publication and subscription servers and databases have been specified the database administrator can define the data that is to be published. As previously mentioned, a publication can consist of one or more tables and a table is known as an *article*. Once the publication server is selected in the *Server Manager* window, in this example *Auriga*, the *Replication - Publishing* button can be clicked. The *Manage - Publications* dialog box is then displayed as shown in Figure 11-9.

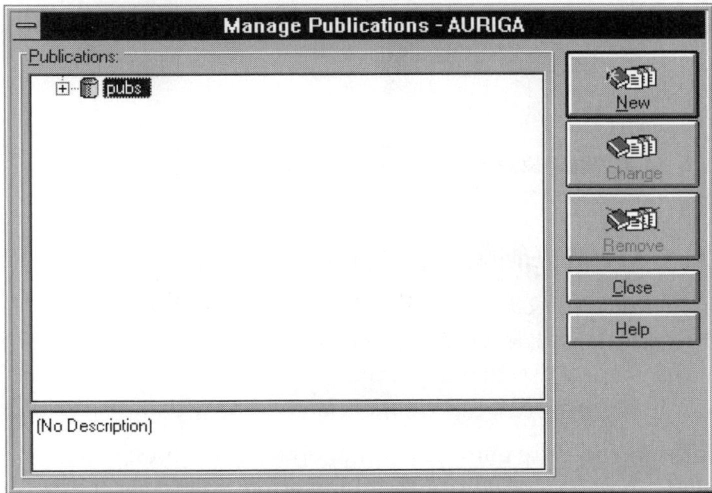

Figure 11-9 Manage - Publications Dialog Box

Note that the *Replication - Publishing* button is the middle button in a group of three buttons associated with replication. These are shown in Figure 11-10. To the right of it is the *Replication - Subscribing* button and to the left of it is the *Replication - Topology* button. We shall see these buttons being used shortly.

Figure 11-10 Three Useful Replication Buttons

We can see that in the *Manage - Publications* dialog box we only have the one publication database which is our pubs database. By selecting it and clicking on the *New* button, the *Edit Publications* dialog box appears as shown in Figure 11-11.

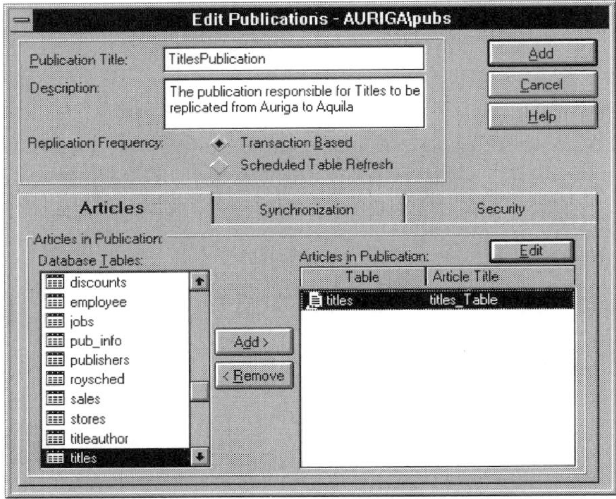

Figure 11-11 The Edit Publications Dialog Box

In the *Edit Publications* dialog box in Figure 11-11 we have given the publication a title and description and we have added the titles table to the *Articles in Publication* list. In our example, this will be the only article in the publication. In other words, this publication will only contain the titles table.

Note that there are number of other options we can specify. We can specify the *Replication Frequency* for the publication, whether it is *Transaction Based* or a *Scheduled Table Refresh*. We can specify the *Synchronization* method and we can specify *Security* options.

The *Synchronization* tab is shown in Figure 11-12. This specifies the means by which a new subscription will be synchronized. The *Bulk Data Copy* method is chosen as is the *Schedule*.

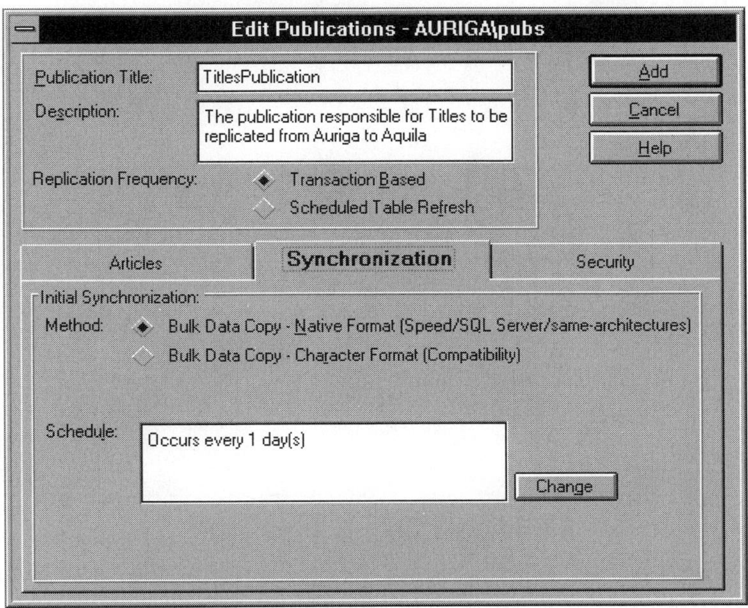

Figure 11-12 The Synchronization Tab

The *Bulk Data Copy* method depends on whether the subscription server is the same architecture as the publication server. If the architectures are the same, for example both Intel or both Digital AXP, the native data format can be used which is the fastest method as data conversion need not be performed. If mixed architectures are to be used, character format should be specified. The *Schedule* is the frequency that SQL Server will carry out synchronizations for new subscriptions. Replicated data cannot be sent to new subscribers until synchronization has occurred, however, synchronization is often an activity that uses high amounts of system resource. This is to be expected as whole tables and their metadata must be sent to any new subscribers. For this reason, carrying out synchronization should not occur too frequently nor should it occur when the system is busy or it may degrade performance.

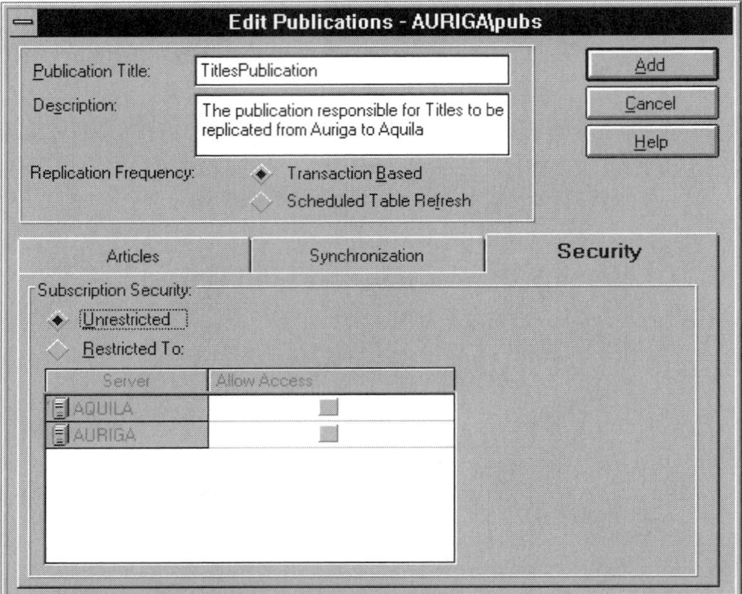

Figure 11-13 The Security Tab

The *Security* tab is shown in Figure 11-13. This allows the database administrator to specify whether a subscription server can receive a publication. In our example, *Subscription Security* is set to *Unrestricted* which means that our publication is visible to any subscription server and can be subscribed to by any subscription server.

The *Edit* button is selected in order to modify the article, for example, to specify a subset of the columns in the table. This will be described later.

The publication has now been defined so we can click the *Add* button and the *Manage Publications* dialog will now appear as shown in Figure 11-14.

11.5.6 Subscribing to Publications

Now we have defined a publication we can define subscriptions, that is, we can select which databases are going to be destination databases to receive the replicated data from the publication. There are two approaches to doing this:

- Pull Subscriptions
- Push Subscriptions

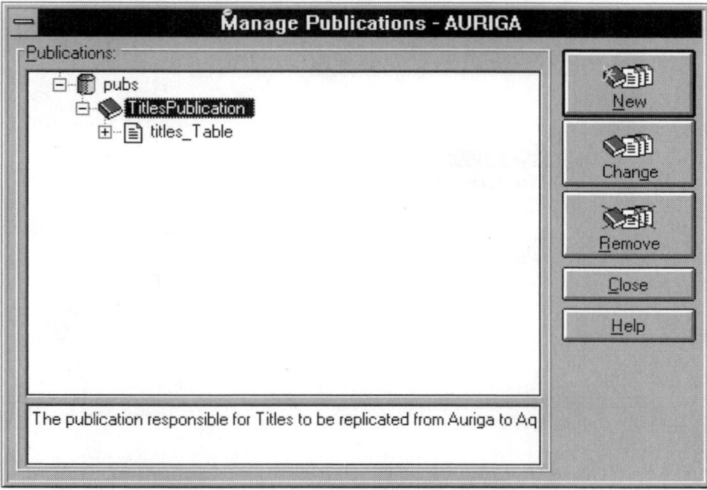

Figure 11-14 The Updated Manage Publications Dialog Box

The approach that is used depends very much on the administrative models adopted by the company setting up replication. If the remote sites enjoy high site autonomy, that is, administration is managed by the individual remote sites, then the *pull subscription* approach is likely to be favored. If, on the other hand, the remote sites are centrally managed then the *push subscription* approach is likely to be the one chosen.

Defining Pull Subscriptions

Pull subscriptions are typically defined at the subscription server by the database administrator responsible for managing it. The database administrator can see a set of publication servers located around the network and he or she can then select which publications their server should subscribe to. This process is not dissimilar to browsing through the available magazines in a shop and deciding to sign up for the ones that interest you while ignoring any others.

To define a pull subscription the subscription server should be selected in the *Server Manager* window of the SQL Enterprise Manager and the right button of the group of three replication buttons, the *Replication - Subscribing* button, clicked.

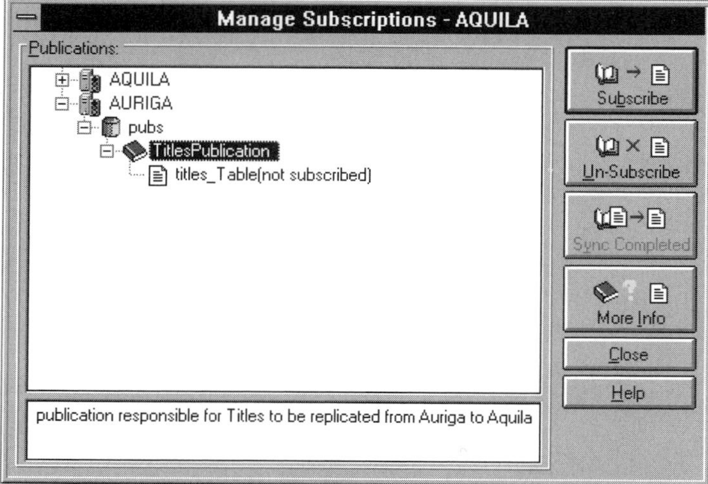

Figure 11-15 The Manage Subscriptions Dialog Box

The *Manage Subscriptions* dialog box appears as shown in Figure 11-15. Note that the server is *Aquila*, our subscription server. Note also that we have expanded the *Auriga* server tree to display our publication and selected it. Any articles belonging to the publication are shown along with status information, in this case *not subscribed*. The *Subscribe* button can now be clicked and the *Subscription Options* dialog box displayed as shown in Figure 11-16.

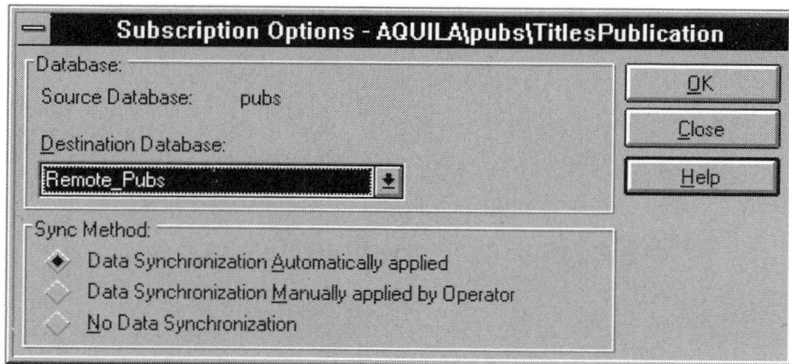

Figure 11-16 The Subscription Options Dialog Box

This dialog box allows the database administrator to specify a destination database to receive replicated data and the synchronization option favored by him or her. The *OK* button can be clicked and the *Manage Subscriptions* dialog box appears again. Notice that, as shown in Figure 11-17, the status information has now changed.

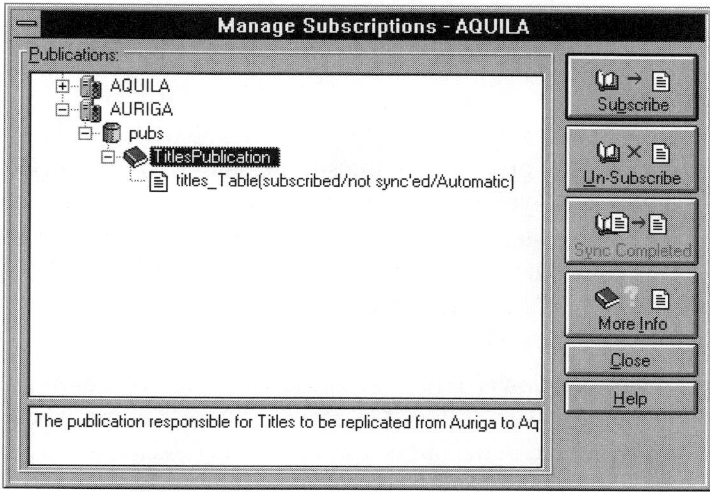

Figure 11-17 Manage Subscriptions - Status Information

If the publication server is selected in the *Server Manager* window of the SQL Enterprise Manager and the middle button of the group of three replication buttons, the *Replication - Publishing* button is clicked, the *Manage Publications* dialog box appears. If the publications tree is expanded, as shown in Figure 11-18, the subscribers to the publication can be easily seen.

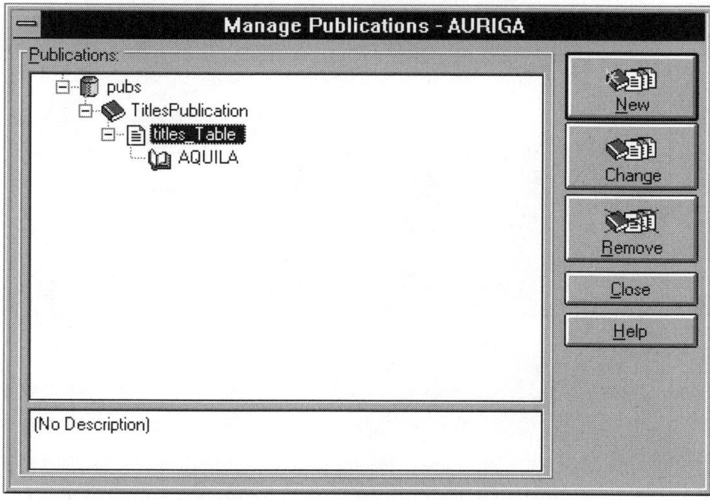

Figure 11-18 Finding the Subscribers to a Publication

Defining Push Subscriptions

Push subscriptions are typically defined at the publication server by a central database administration function responsible for managing the publication and subscription servers. The database administrator will need System Administrator (SA) privilege on the subscription server as well as the publication server, however, if the subscription servers are being centrally administered this will be the case anyway. To continue the analogy of the magazine shop, the subscriber is no longer browsing through the available magazines in a shop and deciding to sign up for some. Instead, his or her manager is selecting appropriate magazines for them to read!

A push subscription is defined at the publication server and can be done when a publication is being created or at a later time. As described previously, to create a publication, the publication server is selected in the *Server Manager* window and the *Replication - Publishing* button clicked. The *Manage - Publications* dialog box is then displayed as shown in Figure 11-18. If the desired publication is selected and the *Change* button clicked the *Edit Publications* dialog box is displayed as was shown in Figure 11-11.

However, the *Edit* button can now be clicked to display the *Manage - Article* dialog box as shown in Figure 11-19. We shall look at this in more detail later.

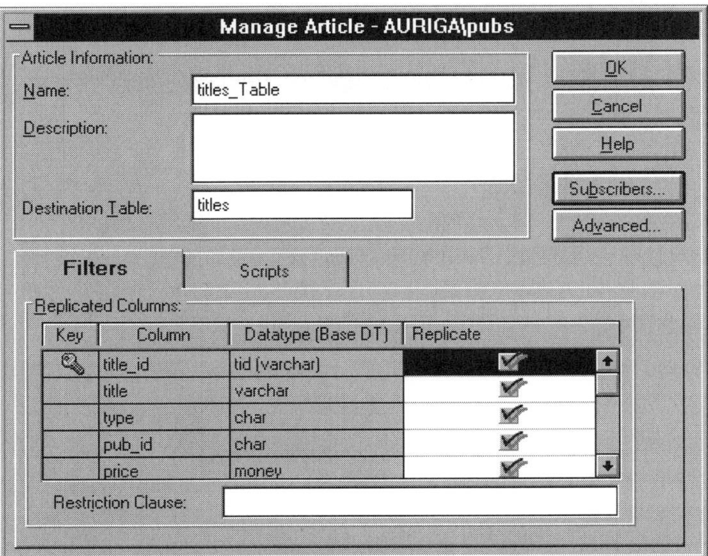

Figure 11-19 The Manage Articles Dialog Box

If the *Subscribers* button is now clicked the *Publication Subscribers* dialog box is displayed as shown in Figure 11-20.

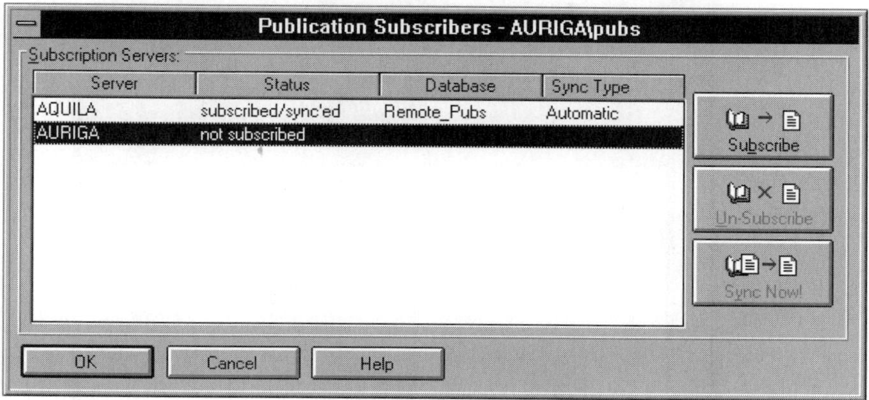

Figure 11-20 The Publication Subscribers Dialog Box

The desired subscription server can be selected and the *Subscribe* button clicked. This will then display a *Subscription Options* dialog box as was shown in Figure 11-16 which will allow the database administrator to choose appropriate options. The push subscription is now defined.

11.5.7 The Replication Topology Window

We have been clicking the middle and right replication buttons, *Replication - Publishing* and *Replication - Subscribing* on many occasions, but what about the left button? This is the *Replication Topology* button and database administrators will find that they click this button a lot too. This will display the *Replication Topology* window as shown in Figure 11-21.

OK, we admit it, two servers are a bit pathetic! Have you not heard of the Great Subscription Server Famine in this part of Great Britain? Just imagine, though, how useful this window would be in managing many publication and subscription servers. A database administrator can drag a server from the server window and drop it into the *Replication Topology* window. Depending on which servers he or she has System Administrator (SA) privilege, the new server is automatically configured as a subscription server to the *central* server.

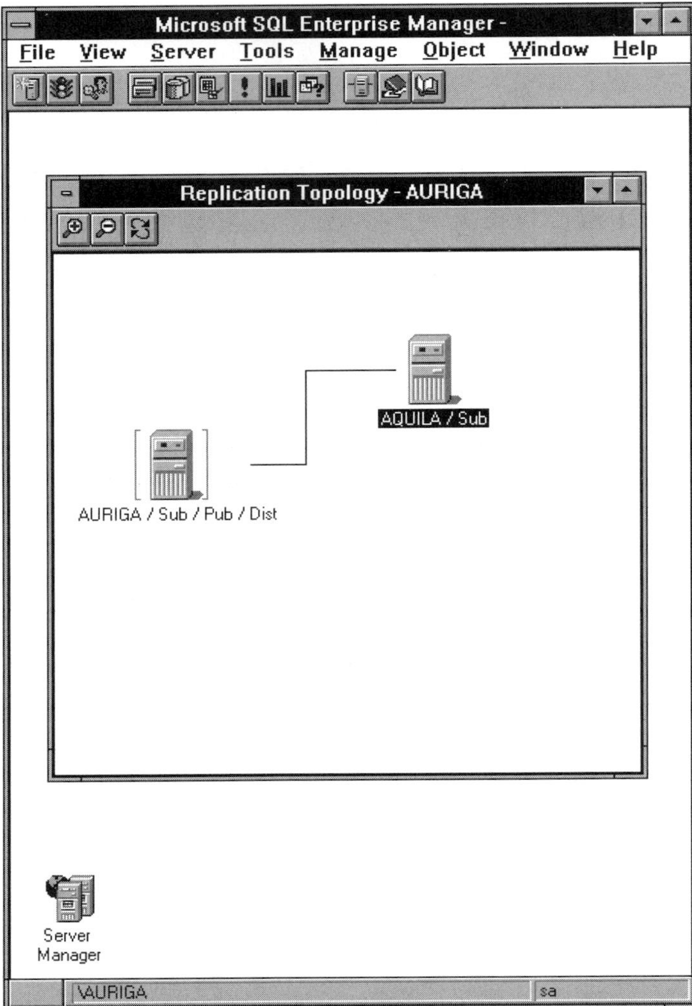

Figure 11-21 The Replication Topology Window

Note that the bracketed [] server is the server that was selected in the SQL Enterprise Manager server window before the *Replication Topology* window was displayed. This is considered to be the *central* server. Underneath each server icon is a line of information pertaining to the server with respect to the topology. In Figure 11-21 *Auriga* has the line of information *Sub/Pub/Dist* and *Aquila* has the line of information *Sub* as it is subscriber to *Auriga*.

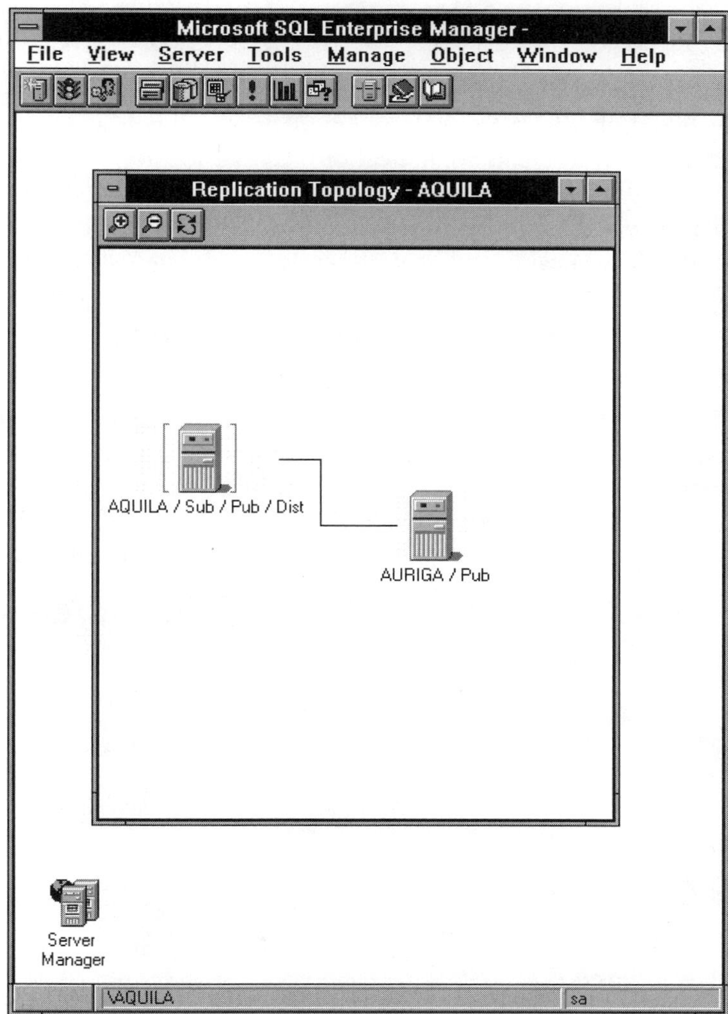

Figure 11-22 The Replication Topology Window with Aquila Selected

Note the *Replication Topology* window in Figure 11-22. The server *Aquila* was selected before it was displayed. Now *Aquila* is bracketed. The information lines show that, as far as *Aquila* is concerned, *Auriga* is a publisher to it.

The *Replication Topology* window can be zoomed in and out and, if the right mouse button is clicked, publications and subscriptions can be managed from pop up menus.

11.5.8 Editing Articles

So far we have only created an article that is identical to the table on which it is based, that is, it has the same number of columns and rows. As described previously, to create a publication, the publication server is selected in the *Server Manager* window and the *Replication - Publishing* button clicked. The *Manage - Publications* dialog box is then displayed as shown in Figure 11-18. If the desired publication is selected and the *Change* button clicked the *Edit Publications* dialog box is displayed as was shown in Figure 11-11.

However, the *Edit* button can now be clicked which displays the *Manage - Article* dialog box as shown in Figure 11-23.

This dialog box enables the database administrator to horizontally and vertically partition the table data. By entering a WHERE clause in the *Restriction Clause* box the employee table is partitioned horizontally and by not ticking each column it is vertically partitioned. The name of the article can also be changed.

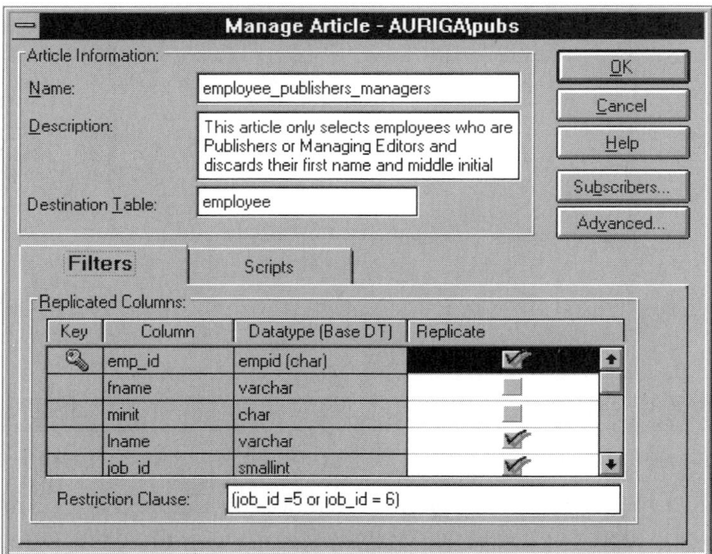

Figure 11-23 Editing an Article

This partitioning capability will probably be sufficient for many database administrators but SQL Server provides a lot more capability if it is required. If we select the *Scripts* tab, more options appear as shown in Figure 11-24.

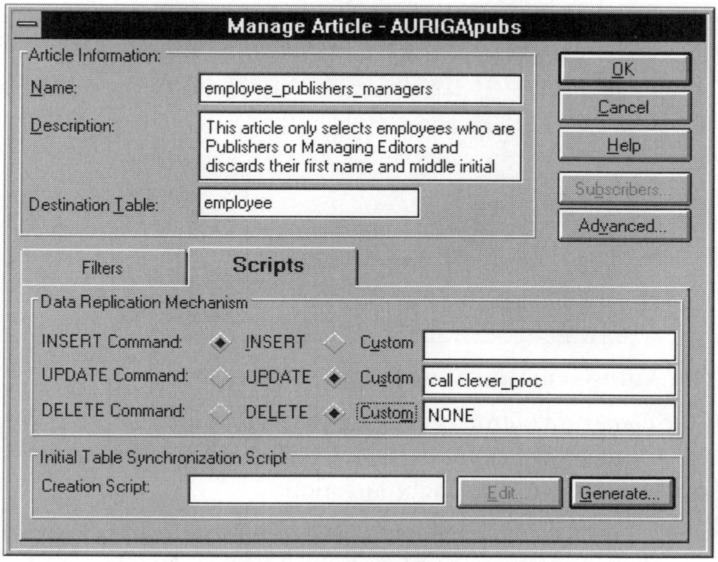

Figure 11-24 The Manage Articles Scripts Tab

There are two facilities provided on this tab. These are the ability to change the *Data Replication Mechanism* and to change the *Initial Table Synchronization Script*. The Data Replication Mechanism specifies what action SQL Server takes when it encounters an INSERT, UPDATE or DELETE. By default these statements are *passed through* to the subscription database so the action on the destination table is the same as the action on the source table. This behavior can be modified in two ways.

First the *Custom* button can be clicked next to the INSERT, UPDATE or DELETE, whichever is required, and NONE entered into the box. This means that the action will not be replicated. In 11-24 the database administrator specifies that the DELETE is not replicated.

Second a stored procedure name can be entered in the box. The stored procedure, which must reside in the publication database, will be called and the column values passed to it.

The Initial Table Synchronization Script facility enables a database administrator to change the initial synchronization script in order to modify the behavior of the initial synchronization.

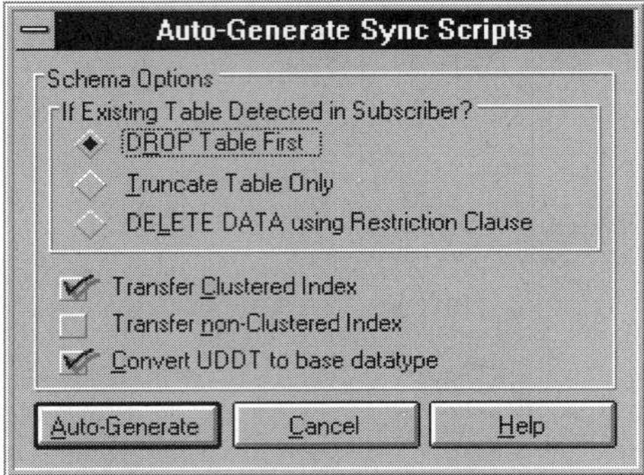

Figure 11-25 The Auto-Generate Sync Scripts Dialog Box

If the *Generate* button is clicked, the *Auto-Generate Sync Scripts* dialog box appears, as shown in Figure 11-25, giving an idea of what modifications might be made to the initial synchronization.

Another button that appears in the *Manage Article* dialog box is labeled *Advanced*. If this button is clicked, the *Manage Article - Advanced* dialog box appears, as shown in Figure 11-26.

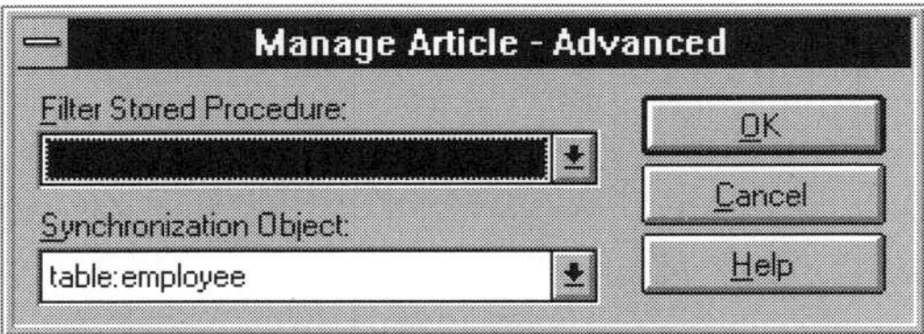

Figure 11-26 The Manage Article - Advanced Dialog Box

This enables a database administrator to add a custom filter stored procedure to execute more complex filter processing.

11.5.9 Halting Replications

The database administrator can halt a replication from the publishing or the subscription server. If a remote distribution server is being used the database administrator can also halt replication from there. To halt a replication from a subscription server, select the subscription server from the SQL Enterprise Manager *Server Manager* window, click the *Replication - Subscribing* button and expand the required publishing database tree in the *Manage Subscriptions* window. Click the *Un-Subscribe* button as shown in Figure 11-27.

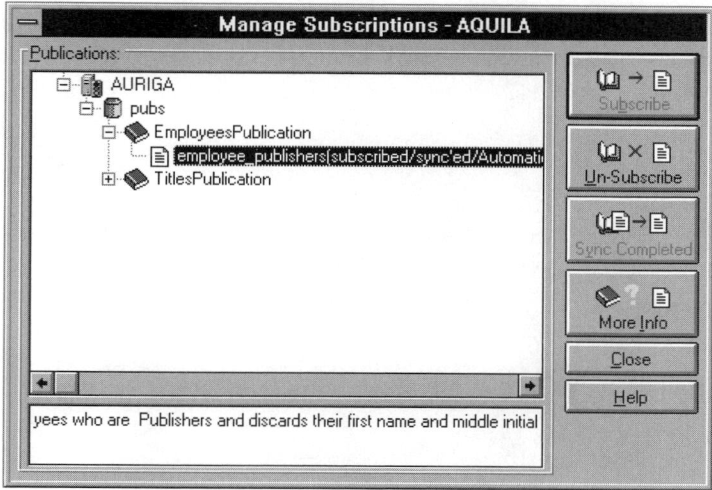

Figure 11-27 Halting Replication from a Subscriber

To halt a replication from a publishing server, select the publishing server from the SQL Enterprise Manager *Server Manager* window, click the *Replication - Publishing* button and expand the required publishing database tree in the *Manage Publications* window. Click *Change* which displays the *Edit Publications* dialog box and then Click *Edit* which displays the *Manage Article* dialog box. Next click *Subscribers*, select the subscription to halt and click *Un-Subscribe*.

To delete a publication, select the publishing server from the SQL Enterprise Manager *Server Manager* window, click the *Replication - Publishing* button and expand the required publishing database tree in the *Manage Publications* window. Select the publication to remove and click the *Remove* button.

11.5.10 Do-It-Yourself Synchronization

We have already mentioned synchronization in that, before data can be replicated to a destination table, the destination table must be synchronized with the source table. Usually a database administrator will let SQL Server take care of this automatically. However, it is possible to perform synchronizations manually. Perhaps the source and destination databases are connected by a slow line or the source table is very large. In this case it may be more practical to perform a *manual synchronization*.

A manual synchronization may be requested, for example, when a subscription is being defined, as was shown in Figure 11-16. In this case, SQL Server will still create its *synchronization* files. There are two of these files:

- Schema script file (.DAT)
- Data file (.TMP)

The database administrator must then apply the files and, when completed, inform SQL Server that this has been done. SQL Server creates these files in a default location and in our examples the files are created in:

```
\\AURIGA\C$\SQL60\REPLDATA
```

An example .SCH file might contain:

```
if not exists (select * from sysobjects where id =
object_id('employee') and sysstat & 0xf = 3)
create table employee
(
    emp_id     char (9)        not null,
    lname      varchar (30)    not null,
    job_id     smallint        not null,
    job_lvl    tinyint         not null,
    pub_id     char (4)        not null,
    hire_date  datetime        not null
)
go

create  clustered  index employee_ind on employee
    (lname, fname, minit)
go
```

A .TMP filename may resemble something like *emp3D.tmp*. The filename can be linked in with the synchronization task by looking at its *Task History* as shown in Figure 11-28.

To tell SQL Server that a manual synchronization has completed, the *Synch Completed* button can be clicked in the *Manage Subscriptions* dialog box. This can be seen in Figure 11-17.

11.5.11 Monitoring Replication Activity

Once replication is underway, and the publishers are publishing, and the subscribers subscribing, it becomes increasingly important to know exactly what's going on in the system.

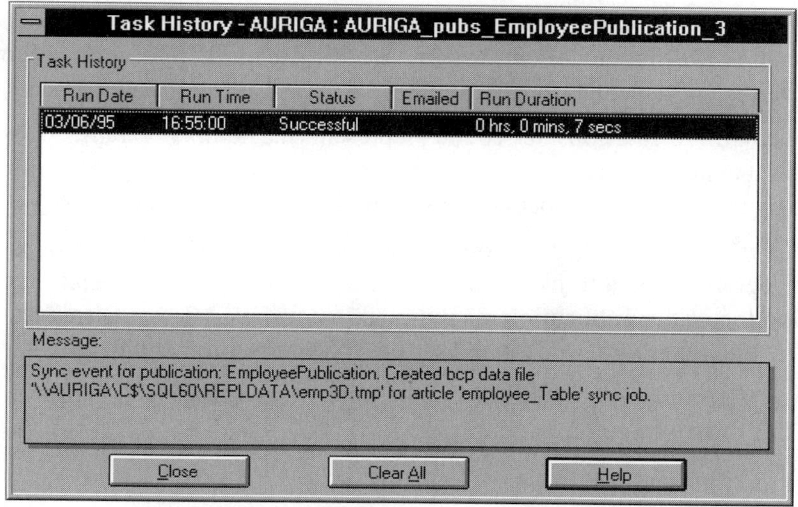

Figure 11-28 A Synch Event in the Task History List

There are a number of tools at our disposal, including:

- Performance Monitor
- Tasks
- Alerts
- System Stored Procedures
- Database Consistency Checker (DBCC)

Performance Monitor

Our old friend the Windows NT Performance Monitor comes to our rescue again, at least up to a point. There are two replication oriented objects:

- SQL Server Replication - Published DB
- SQL Server Replication - Subscriber

SQL Server Replication - Published DB is the object concerned with publication and has the following three counters:

- Replicated Transactions
- Replicated Transactions/sec
- Replication Latency (msec)

The *Replicated Transactions* counter represents the number of transactions in the transaction log of the publication database that are marked for replication but have not yet been sent to the distribution database by the log reader process.

The *Replicated Transactions/sec* counter represents the number of transactions per second that have been retrieved from the transaction log of the publication database by the log reader process and sent to the distribution database.

The *Replication Latency (msec)* counter represents the number of milliseconds between the time a transaction marked for replication is written to the transaction log of the publication database and is retrieved from the transaction log by the log reader process and sent to the distribution database.

SQL Server Replication - Subscriber is the object concerned with subscription and has the following four counters:

- Delivered Transactions
- Delivered Transactions/sec
- Delivered Latency (sec)
- Undelivered Transactions

The *Delivered Transactions* counter represents the delivered transactions in the distribution database. By delivered we mean a transaction that has already *completed* at the destination database, however, it has not yet been removed from the distribution database.

The *Delivered Transactions*/sec counter represents the number of transactions delivered per second.

The *Delivered Latency (sec)* counter represents the number of seconds a transaction is held in the distribution database before release to the subscription server. This is a measure of the time between insertion into the distribution database and completion at the destination database.

The *Undelivered Transactions* counter represents the undelivered transactions in the distribution database. By undelivered we mean a transaction that has not been *completed* at the destination database.

Figure 11-29 below shows the Windows NT Performance Monitor monitoring a subset of the replication counters in a chart display.

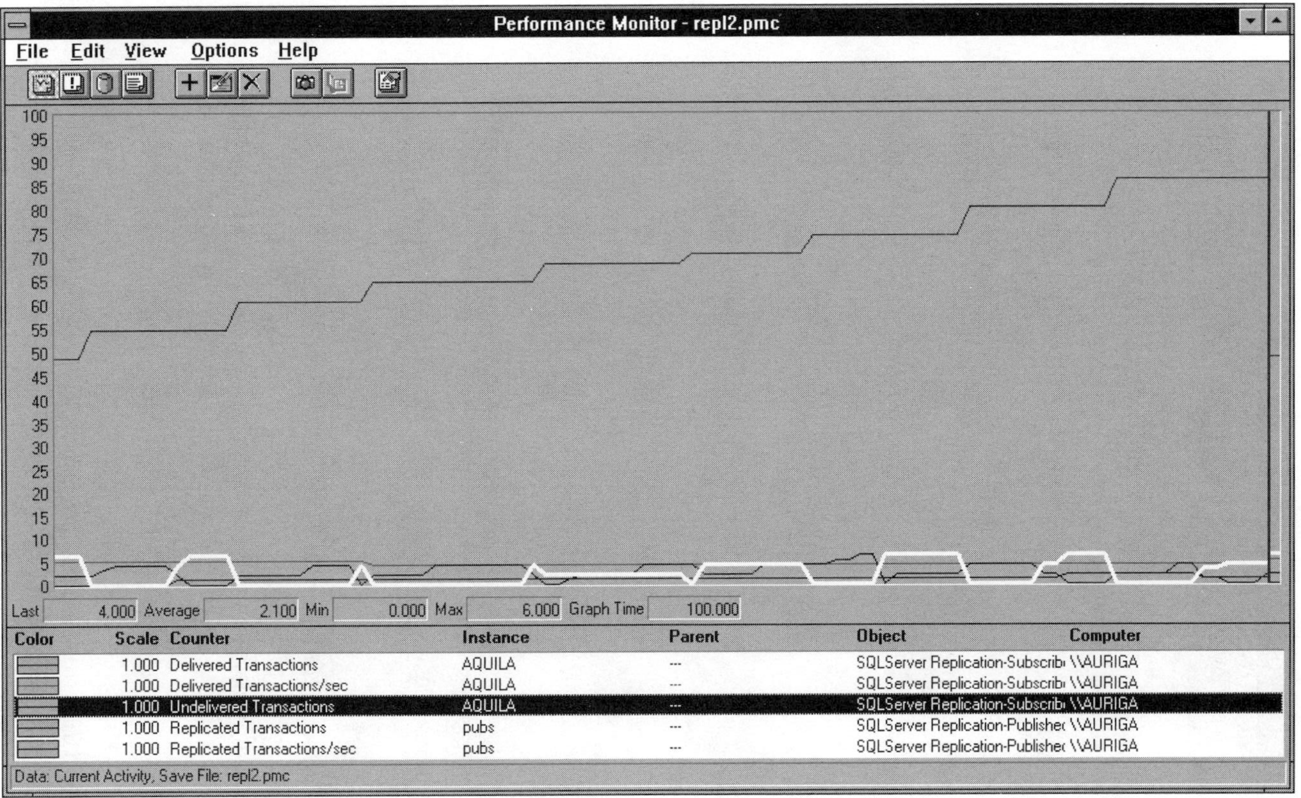

Figure 11-29 The Performance Monitor Displaying Replication Counters

The highlighted white line is undelivered transactions. Sometimes a report display is clearer as can be seen in Figure 11-30.

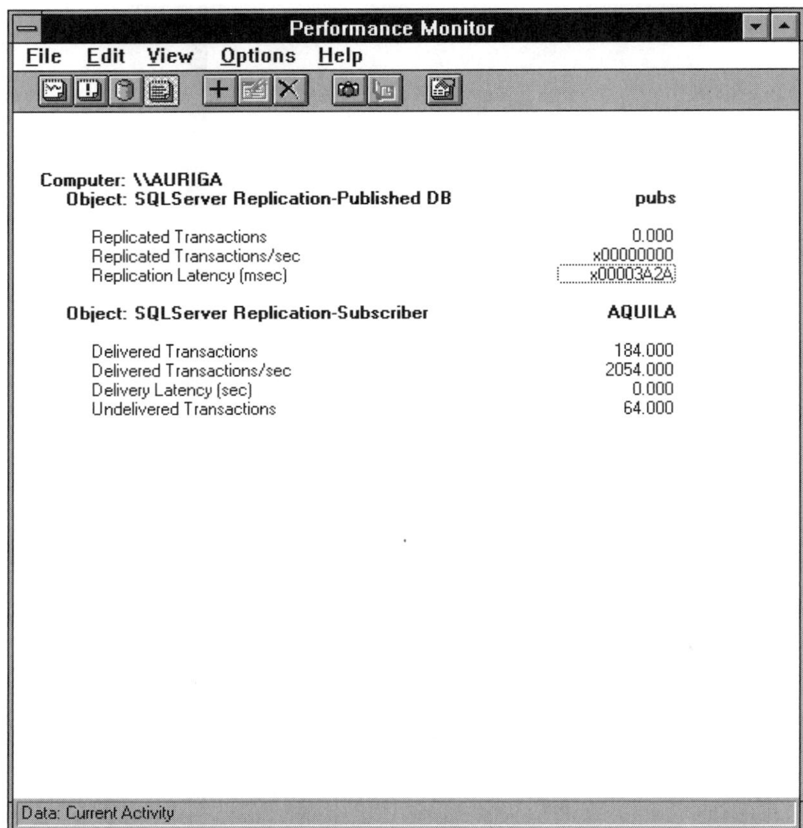

Figure 11-30 The Performance Monitor Reporting Replication Counters

Tasks

We have already come across *Tasks* in Chapter 10 but we shall now look at them with replication in mind. Looking at the *Task History* can be useful to find out what replication tasks are happening and have already happened. It can also be a useful place to look when tracking down problems. There are various routes that can be taken to display the *Task Scheduling* window. One way is to double click the SQL Executive icon in the selected server. Another way is to make sure that the required server is selected in the *Server Manager* window and then from the *Tools* menu choose *Task Scheduling*. Alternatively, the *Task Scheduling* button can be clicked. Whichever way is chosen, the *Task Scheduling* window appears as shown in Figure 11-31.

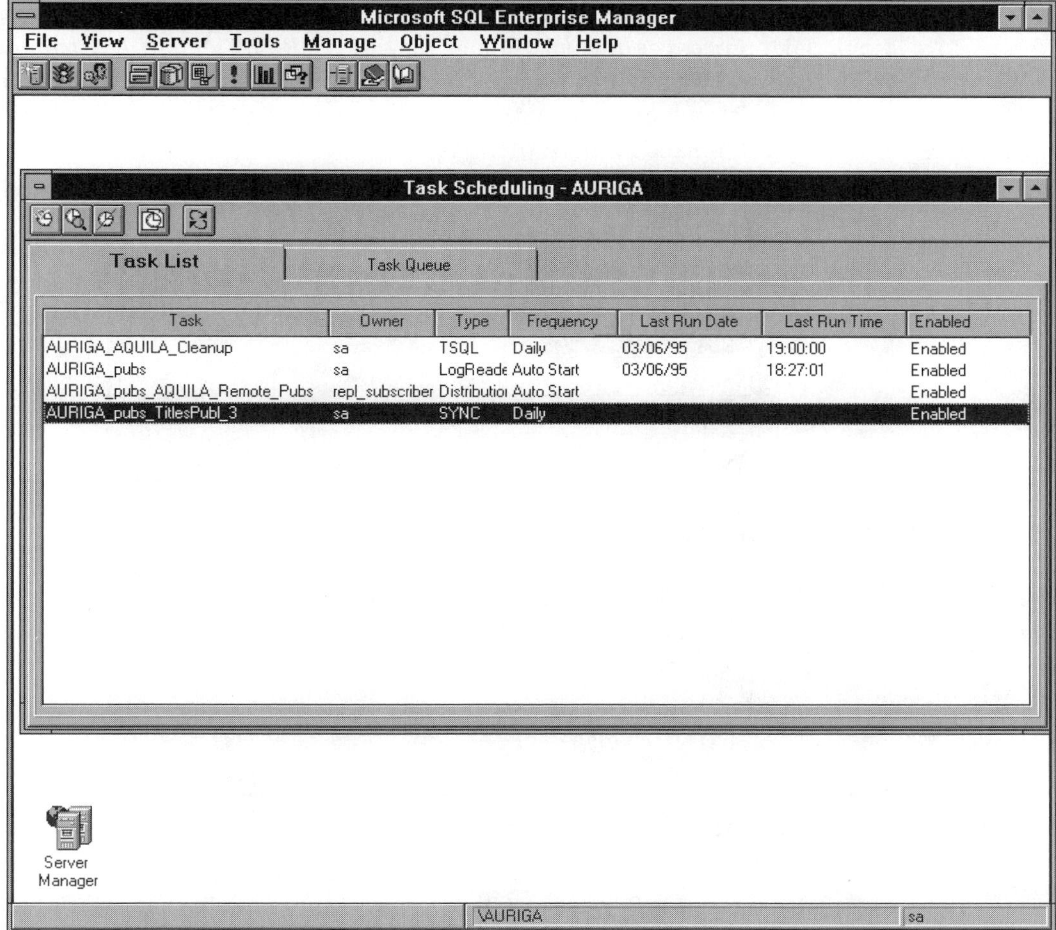

Figure 11-31 The Task Scheduling Window

The Task Scheduling window consists of two tabs which are the *Task List* and *Task Queue*. The *Task List* is the list of tasks that are scheduled for the server and the *Task Queue* is the queue of tasks running or waiting to run.

In the *Task List* in Figure 11-31 a number of tasks can be seen. One of these is the task *AURIGA_pubs_titlesPubl_3* which has a *Type* of SYNC which means it is a replication synchronization process command. The next task in the list is *AURIGA_pubs_AQUILA_Remote_Pubs* has a *Type* of Distribution which means it is a replication distribution process command. The task,

AURIGA_pubs has a *Type* of LogReader which means it is a replication LogReader process command. Finally, the task *AURIGA_AQUILA_Cleanup* has a *Type* of TSQL which means it is a Transact-SQL statement. One other task *Type* exists which is the type CmdExec which is a Windows NT operating system command or .EXE file.

Let us look at the replication synchronization task. If we double click the task the *Edit Task* window appears as shown in Figure 11-32.

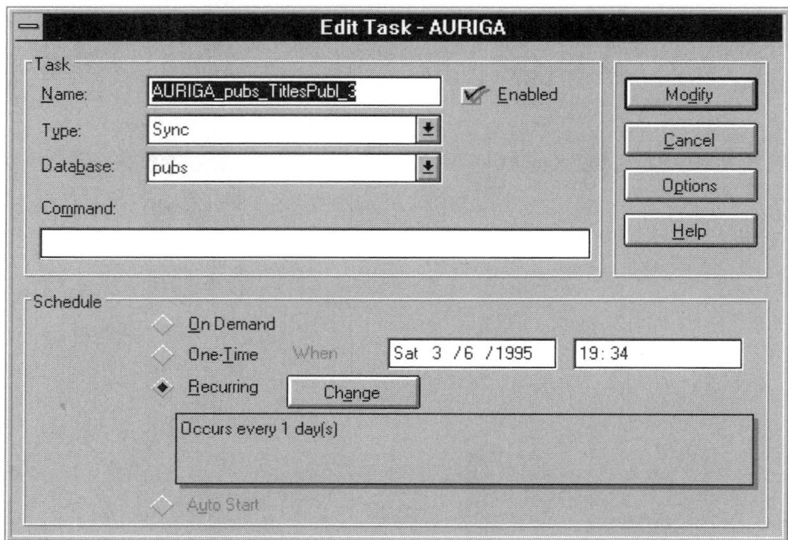

Figure 11-32 Examining the Synchronization Task

In this particular example, there are no *Command* qualifiers. The *Schedule* shows that the task is *Recurring*. Clicking on *Change* will display more information on the schedule for this task as shown in Figure 11-33.

It can be seen that this replication synchronization task executes every 5 minutes, essentially looking for new subscription servers. As a database administrator you may not want this to happen at this frequency.

While this task is selected we can click on the *Task History* button. A display will appear as shown previously in Figure 11-28.

Let us look at the replication LogReader task. If we double click the task the *Edit Task* window appears as shown in Figure 11-34. For this task there is a parameter *-b*. This specifies the size of the transaction batch, in this case 100, which means 100 transactions will be read out of the log in each access.

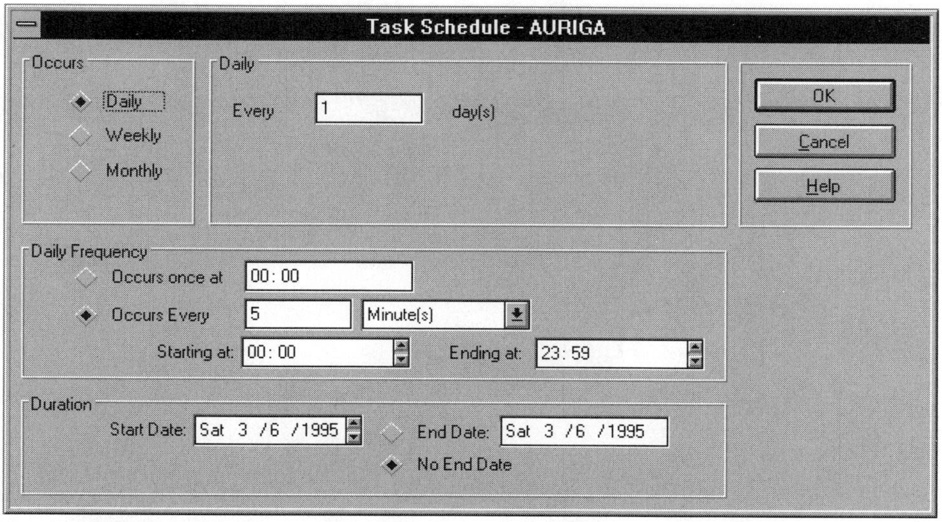

Figure 11-33 Examining a Task Schedule

Note that the *Schedule* specifies *Auto Start* which means that the LogReader task is started when the SQL Executive service starts.

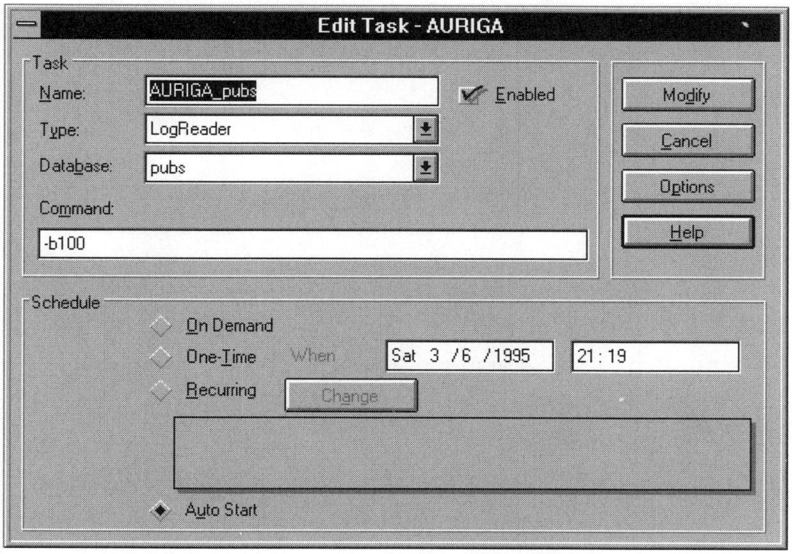

Figure 11-34 Examining the LogReader Task

If the *Task History* button is clicked, a display will appear as shown in Figure 11-35 showing the LogReader *Task History*.

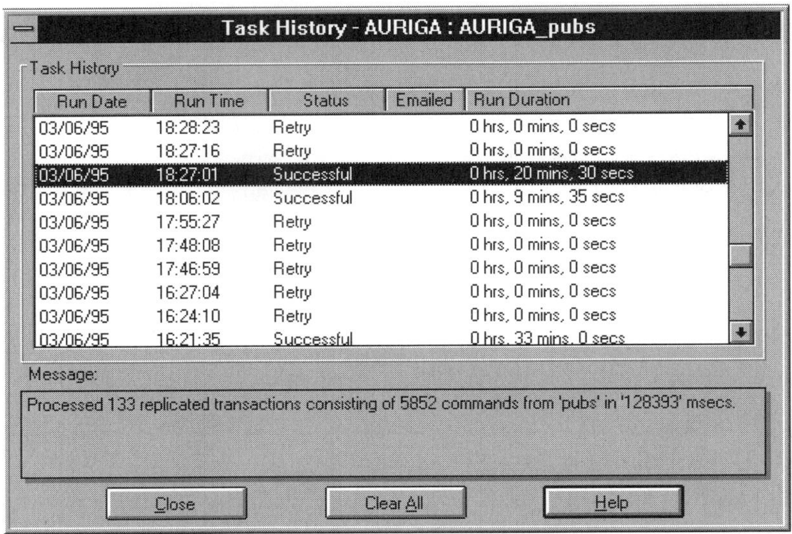

Figure 11-35 The LogReader Task History

Tasks can provide useful assistance when tracking down problems and, as such, should be one of the first areas to check.

Alerts

We have already met alerts in Chapter 10. Alerts play an important role in SQL Server replication and are closely tied in with tasks. Most tasks are set up to post a notification in the Windows NT Event Log if they fail. Alerts can be created to detect specific messages posted to the Event Log and to then Email and/or Page an operator. This is a very powerful means of receiving notification as soon as a problem arises.

System Stored Procedures

Underneath the nice graphical interface of SQL Server replication lie a number of system stored procedures. Some of these can be executed to quickly obtain information about the replication environment. Here are a few examples:

```
sp_helpdistributor
```

```
distributor    distribution database  directory                   account
-----------    ---------------------  --------------------------  -------------
AURIGA         distribution           \\AURIGA\C$\SQL60\REPLDATA  COSMOS\england
```

This system stored procedure provides information about the distribution server.

```
sp_helpsubscriberinfo aquila

publisher subscriber type login  password commit_batch_size
--------- ---------- ---- ------ -------- ------------------
AURIGA    AQUILA     0    (null) (null)   100
```

This system stored procedure displays information about the named subscription server. Note this is only a subset of the information actually returned.

```
sp_helpreplicationdb

name
------------------
pubs
```

This system stored procedure displays a list of all the published databases on a server.

```
sp_distcounters

subscriber  delivered_jobs  undelivered_jobs  delivery_rate  delivery_latency
---------   -------------   ----------------  -------------  ---------------
AQUILA      0               0                 0              0
```

This system stored procedure displays performance information about subscribers.

```
sp_replcounters

database replicated transactions replication rate trans/sec replication latency(sec)
-------  ----------------------  -------------------------  ----------------------
pubs     0                       1.75131                    8020.0
```

This system stored procedure displays performance information about published databases.

Database Consistency Checker (DBCC)

We have met DBCC on a number of occasions. A DBCC option that was introduced with SQL Server 6.0 can be useful when used in a replication environment.

DBCC OPENTRAN assists the database administrator in finding whether or not an unfinished transaction exists within the transaction log for a particular database. This will help to quickly find any transactions that are causing a DUMP TRANSACTION not to truncate the transaction log completely.

11.5.12 Some Replication Options

We have looked at replication in some depth in this chapter. Let us finish by looking at just some of the possible replication scenarios that are possible with SQL Server 6.0.

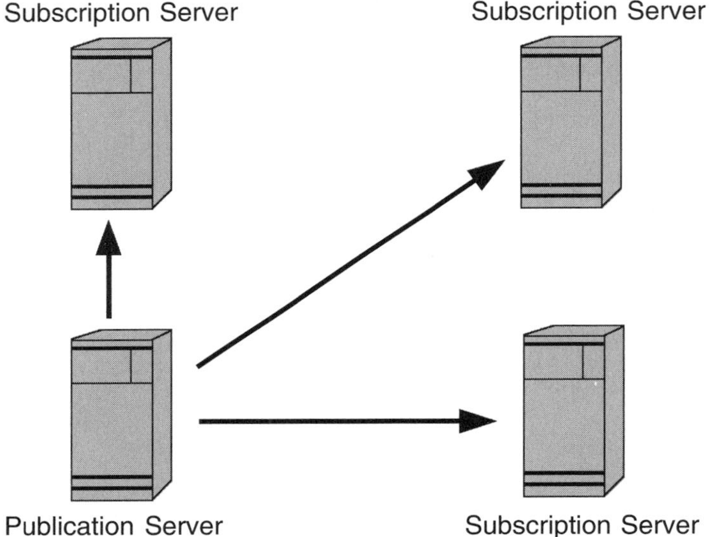

Figure 11-36 Primary Publisher to Satellite Subscribers

This is likely to be a common scenario as it is quite straightforward. The subscription servers could be decision support servers or just servers that are geographically located next to their users.

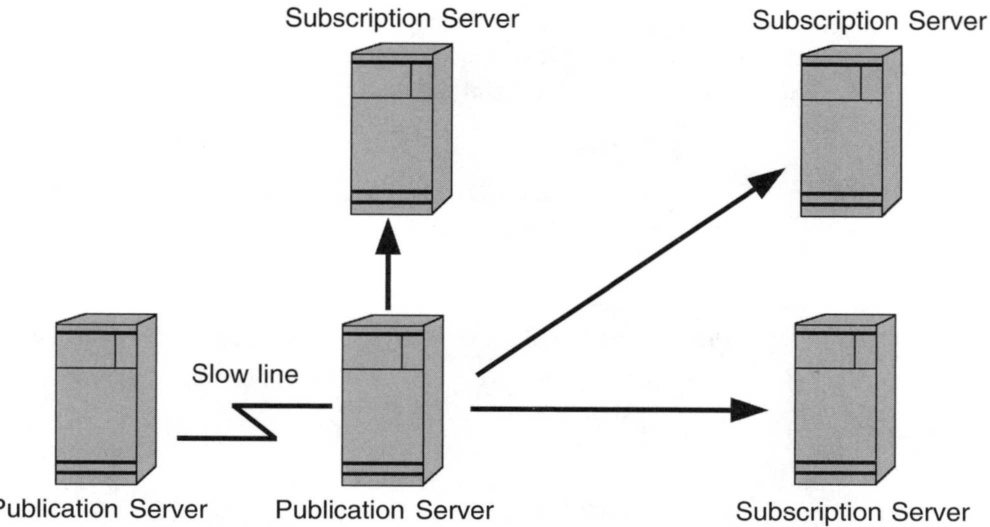

Figure 11-37 Secondary Publisher

This is also likely to be a common scenario. A publication server, perhaps in the United States, replicates data down a slow communications line to a subscription server in the United Kingdom. This then re-publishes the data to neighboring subscription servers over a fast communications link.

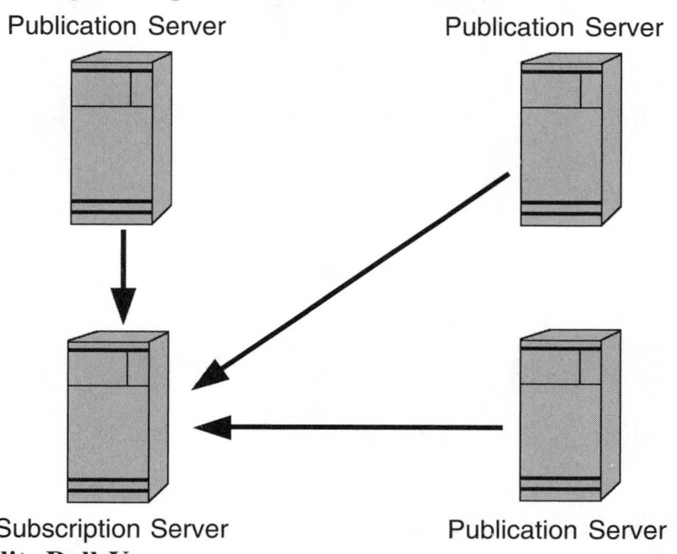

Figure 11-38 Satellite Roll-Up

In the above scenario, a number of publication servers publish to a central subscription server. This scenario might be used for rolling up regional sales figures to headquarters for analysis.

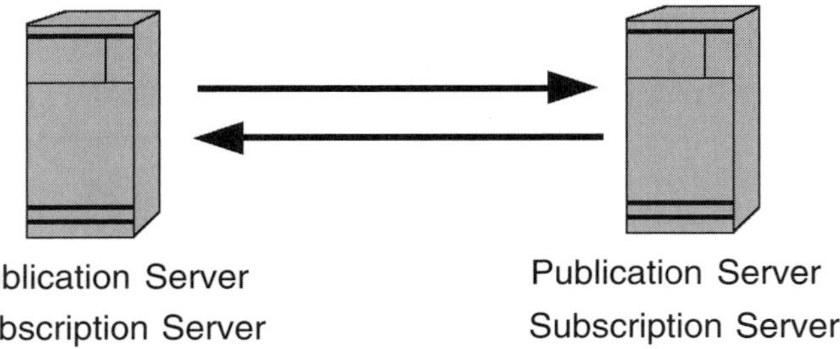

Figure 11-39 Multiple Publishers

In this scenario each server is responsible for its section of a table. Each server, therefore, publishes changes from the section it manages to its neighbor. This might be useful if two or more outlets have their own data stored locally but they need to be able to read each others. Note, however, this can quickly become unmanageable with multiple servers.

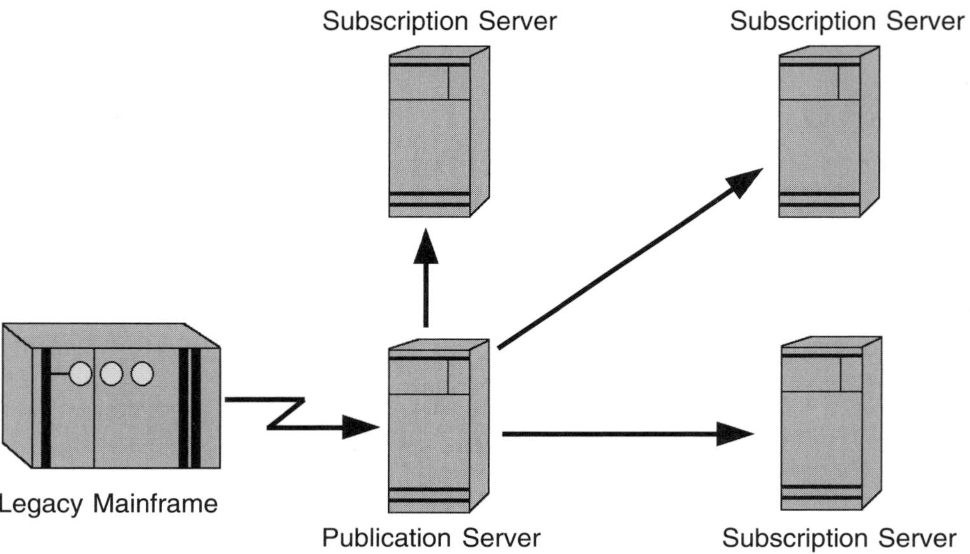

Figure 11-40 Replication of Legacy Data

This is similar to the first scenario except the publication server is fed from a legacy mainframe. This is an ideal scenario when multiple users around the network need read access to the mainframe data.

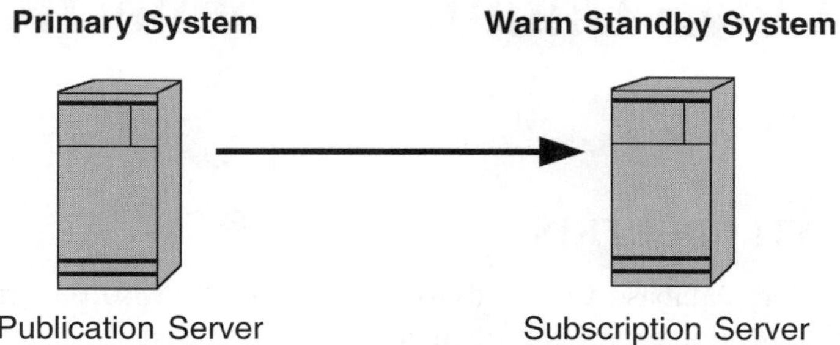

Figure 11-41 Replication to a Warm Standby

Although not really designed for this scenario, a warm standby system can be built using replication. However, note that the primary can fail before transactions are replicated to the warm standby so data could be lost.

12 Open Database Connectivity

12.1 INTRODUCTION

Open Database Connectivity (ODBC) is Microsoft's strategic data access application programming interface (API). Based upon an open standard generated by the SQL Access Group (SAG) it has had good acceptance in the market place since its inception. This chapter is designed to give the reader a broad understanding of ODBC and how it can be used to create database solutions. If a reader requires a more in-depth understanding of ODBC then it is suggested that they read the ODBC version 2.0 Software Developers Toolkit published by Microsoft Press.

12.2 DATABASE CONNECTIVITY - A BRIEF HISTORY

The proliferation of the Personal Computer during the late 1980's lead to unprecedented demands from users to access data across the enterprise. Constantly frustrated by large IT departments seen to be obstructing the throughput of simple reports and requests for data and wooed by the easy to use graphical user interface of the new Windows environment users began to demand better and easier data access.

The myriad of solutions from the computing industry brought confusion to users and IT professionals alike. The use of a common protocol such as IBM's DRDA (Distributed Relational Database Architecture) was expensive, both in terms of money and local PC memory requirements. Common interface solutions abounded, for example, SQL-Link from Borland, DataLens from Lotus and Data Access Language from Apple gave a confusing choice. Common gateway technologies again proved expensive.

Vendors soon realized that the customer base demanded a consistent solution, easy to use and supported by a majority of software companies.

The SQL Access Group was formed in 1988 from a group of vendors with a variety of backgrounds - diverse companies from the world of mainframe, mini and PC computing. The SAG produced a Call Level Interface which is the basis for Open Database Connectivity – the ODBC SQL syntax is based on X/Open and the SAG SQL CAE specification (1992). In 1995 the SQL Access Group moved to become a working group of X/Open.

ODBC from Microsoft is only implemented on the Windows and Apple Mac platforms, although other vendors are creating similar programming interfaces for other operating systems. ODBC is the data access component of Microsoft's WOSA (Windows Open Services Architecture) architecture.

12.3 INTRODUCTION TO OPEN DATABASE CONNECTIVITY

The architecture of ODBC is, from a high level, surprisingly straight forward and comprises of four separate layers:

- The application. This must have an ODBC compliant interface to the ODBC driver manager. Examples of ODBC client applications include Microsoft Access or Forest and Trees.
- ODBC Driver Manager. The driver manager maintains the latest information as to which data sources the application can talk to, loads individual drivers when required and generally looks after the ODBC connectivity interface.
- ODBC Driver. An appropriate driver has to be installed for each database that is to be connected. The driver undertakes some initial processing of the ODBC call from the application, will match datatypes with the underlying server database and return any results to the application.
- Database server or data source. This is the data repository that is storing data to be accessed by ODBC.

All of the ODBC specific software remains on the client PC, and no extra software needs to be loaded onto the server. The architecture is shown in Figure 12-1.

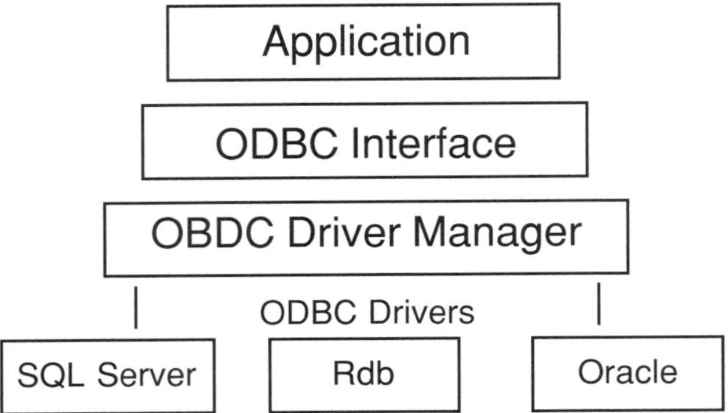

Figure 12-1 The ODBC Architecture

12.3.1 ODBC Conformance Levels

ODBC specifies two areas of conformance – the ODBC API level and ODBC SQL syntax level. An agreed conformance level gives the developer a guarantee of standard sets of data access functionality for use within applications.

12.3.2 API Conformance

The ODBC core level API functions map onto the SAG call level interface specifications. ODBC has two further supersets of this, levels one and two respectively. The developer is not prevented from incorporating the different levels of function calls into an application, but driver vendors are advised to incorporate as many functions as possible.

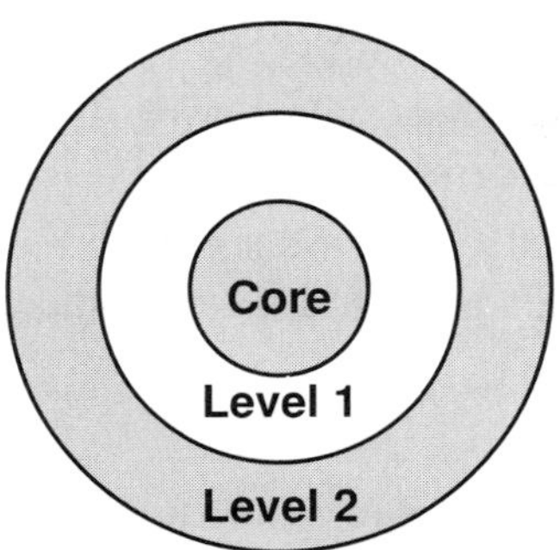

Figure 12-2 ODBC API Levels Are Supersets Of One Another

Core API calls give basic database functionality:

- Allocation and freeing of environment space, data source connection and handles for statements.
- Preparation and execution of SQL statements and immediate SQL statement execution.
- Result column and statement parameter storage.
- Data retrieval and result set information.
- Commit or roll back of transactions.
- Error message handling.
- Data source disconnection.

The Level 1 API permits additional functionality:

- All Core level functionality.
- The connection to data sources using dialog boxes which are driver specific.
- Control and inquiry about the values of statements.
- Manipulation of long data values.
- Manipulation of large result sets.
- Retrieval of metadata (database statistics and tables).
- Retrieval of information about data source and driver functionality.

The Level 2 API permits even more functionality:

- All Core and Level 1 API functionality.
- List available data sources and browse through connection information.
- Send and receive arrays of parameter values and result columns.
- Use of scrollable cursors.
- Native SQL statement retrieval.
- Retrieve catalogue information.
- Call translation DLL's.

12.3.3 SQL Conformance Levels

Minimum SQL Grammar corresponds to SAG CAE specification 1992:

- CREATETABLE
- DROPTABLE
- SELECT
- INSERT
- UPDATE SEARCHED
- DELETE SEARCHED
- Simple expressions and data types CHAR, VARCHAR and LONGCHAR

Core grammar:

- All minimum SQL grammar and data types plus:
- ALTERTABLE
- CREATEINDEX
- DROPINDEX
- CREATEVIEW
- DROPVIEW
- GRANT
- REVOKE
- full SELECT
- Subquery and other functions such as SUM, MAX, MIN
- Datatypes INTEGER, SMALLINT, NUMERIC, DECIMAL, REAL, FLOAT, DOUBLE PRECISION

Extended grammar:

- All minimum and core SQL grammar and data types plus:
- Outer joins, unions and positioned UPDATE, DELETE, SELECT FOR UPDATE

- Scalar functions such as ABS, date, time and literals
- Data types: TIMESTAMP, TIME, LONG VARBINARY, DATE, VARBINARY, BINARY, BIGINT, TINY INT, BIT
- Procedure calls and batch SQL statements

12.4 ODBC COMPONENTS IN DETAIL

12.4.1 The Application

The client application needs to specify the datasource and any another information required for the connection to take place. The SQL string that it receives from the user is then placed into a text string and any parameter values set. If the SQL statement is row returning then a cursor name is allocated and the application passes the string on for execution.

The application can establish from the data source the attributes of any data about to be returned, including the number, name and type of column. Storage is allocated for each of the columns and the results fetched from the server.

Any errors returned from the server are processed by the application and the appropriate action taken.

Any transactions are then terminated and the connection closed.

ODBC functions called to connect to a data source, process SQL statements and disconnect from the data source are listed below:

- SQLAllocEnv – allocates memory for the environment handle.
- SQLAllocConnect – allocates memory for the connection handle.
- SQLConnect – loads the required driver and establishes connection to the specified datasource.
- SQLAllocStmt – allocates memory for the statement handle.

Process SQL Statements and Results

- SQLFreeStmt – stops processing of a statement handle and closes any open cursors.

- SQLDisconnect – closes the connection to a specified datasource.
- SQLFreeConnect – releases connection handle and frees associated memory.
- SQLFreeEnv – frees the environment handle.

12.4.2 ODBC Driver Manager

The Driver Manager is a Dynamic Link Library (DLL) responsible for the loading of individual data source drivers when required. The Driver Manager will also map the data source name to a specific driver using the ODBC.INI file in Windows 3.11 or the Registry in Windows NT, process the ODBC initialization calls, provide the entry points for ODBC functions for each driver and provide parameter and sequence validation for ODBC calls.

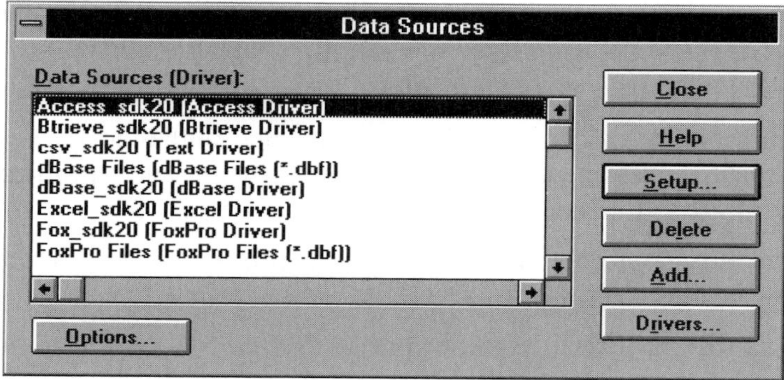

Figure 12-3 Data Source Setup

12.4.3 ODBC Driver

The appropriate ODBC driver is loaded when required by the ODBC Driver Manager following an application calling the functions SQLBrowserConnect, SQLConnect or SQLDriverConnect. The driver can then carry out the following functions when required:

- Establish the data source connection.
- Send requests to the data source.
- Undertake data type matching – the translation of data from or to differing formats.

- Return any results to the application.
- Format error messages and codes.
- Cursor creation and manipulation.
- Initiate transactions if required by the datasource.

Types of Driver

Within ODBC there are three different types of ODBC driver and architecture:

- **Single Tier** drivers include those used to access ISAM based data such as dBASE and Paradox. Due to the nature of ISAM data, extra functionality has to be included in these drivers to translate SQL set orientated language into appropriate language that the ISAM data understands. These drivers are often said to contain an *engine in the box* to undertake this translation.
- **Two Tier** drivers are the standard client to server architecture, used with RDBMS data sources such as Microsoft SQL Server.
- **Three Tier** is used to describe the use of gateway servers to access remote data such as DB2 on MVS or Rochester Software Showcase gateway, built upon APIs including Microsoft Open Data Services.

12.4.4 The Data Source

The data source can be any collection of data resident in any format – if the ODBC driver has been correctly implemented then the data can be accessed. An example of different data sources that might be accessed include local dBASE data on a PC or remote LAN based data on an ORACLE server.

12.5 ODBC OR NATIVE API?

The developer of any client server solution is now faced with the question of whether to use the native API of the data source, for example DB-Library with SQL Server, or to create an application based upon ODBC.

Much has been written and discussed around these points, most notably around applications such as Microsoft Access and Visual Basic. Both of these utilize Microsoft Jet as a common data engine (see Chapter 14). The functionality of Jet is exceptional but an overhead is imposed upon data access via Jet/ODBC, and in some cases the performance of the system may be reduced significantly. These problems were significant in earlier release of the Jet engine, but at the time of writing the current version (Jet 2.5) has a number of features to assist the developer in overcoming performance problems. Most importantly the *pass through* feature of Jet 2.5 enables the by-passing of the Jet engine and direct interfacing with the individual data source. This enables the use of stored procedures and other data source specific tasks.

From the author's experience the choice of direct access via the native API or use of ODBC generally revolves around the following questions:

Is the current server architecture based upon a single standardized RDBMS? Many organizations have undergone some rationalization of their chosen RDBMS, and many have standardized upon a single database server such as Microsoft SQL Server or Oracle. In this case the developer would generally be recommended to use the native API of the selected server, with the caveat that any change in the standard server may impose a rewrite of the majority of the existing solutions, not a happy prospect.

Does the organization's IT strategy demand an open standard when implementing a solution? In this case it would be far better to use a generic solution such as ODBC, which would provide a good basis for an open data access strategy.

Is the proposed solution required to perform some rather abstract functionality on the back end server? If so it would generally be better to use the native RDBMS API, simply as it would be easier to implement this type of functionality.

12.6 INTRODUCTION TO THE ODBC SOFTWARE DEVELOPERS KIT

The Microsoft ODBC Software Developers Kit (SDK) is designed for developers who wish to construct ODBC drivers or ODBC enabled applications. Version 2.0 of the SDK enables developers to create drivers with enhanced functionality over ODBC Version 1.0.

Key enhancements in ODBC version 2.0 include:

- The ability to create 16 or 32 bit applications and drivers.
- The provision of a driver independent cursor library to support scrollable cursors.
- Improved installation for ODBC drivers.

The ODBC SDK also includes some tools which ease the process of creating ODBC applications and drivers.

- **ODBC Test** is an ODBC enabled application that can be used to test drivers. The tests can be completed on a function by function basis or by using an automated testing DLL. Figure 12-4 shows some example ODBC Test output.

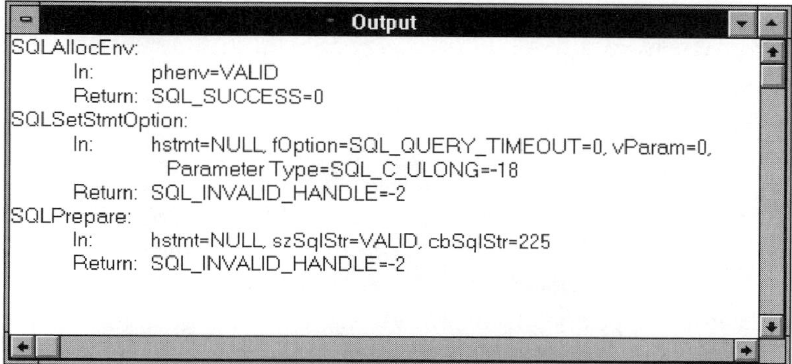

Figure 12-4 An Example Output Window from ODBC Test

- **ODBC Spy** is a debugging tool which can be used to intercept and trace ODBC commands being sent from an application to a driver, or emulate an ODBC driver or application.

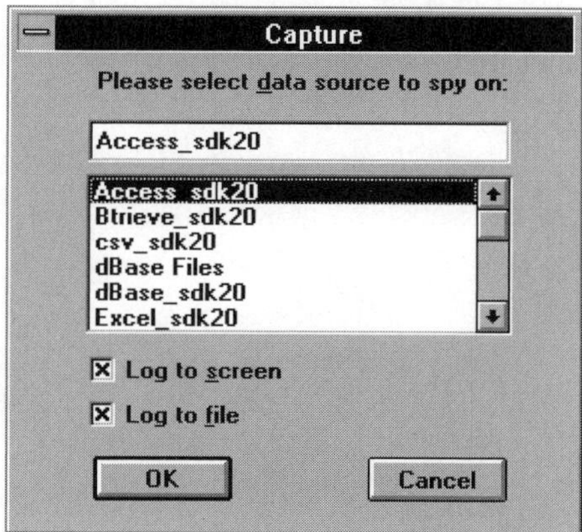

Figure 12-5 ODBC Spy Prompts the User to Select a Datasource for Logging

12.7 ODBC – THE FUTURE

At the time of writing Microsoft have just announced ODBC Version 3.0. Objectives for the release of Version 3.0 include a more extensible model for setting column attributes and establishing client side buffers, with the use of the SQL '92 model for reporting errors. It is proposed to release the 3.0 software development kit in the first quarter of 1996.

Prior to Version 3.0 Microsoft have announced that there will be a release of ODBC, Version 2.5, to take advantage of features within Windows 95.

Alongside discussions for the future of ODBC are some questions on the role of OLE for database access.

There is no doubt that databases and data storage mechanisms are becoming more complex and distant from the standard relational database technologies of the 1980s and evolving into component or object repositories. Data is now stored in a variety of formats including spreadsheets, word processors and cardfile type applets. SQL and ODBC are designed for relational data access, where they do a good job, but when non-relational data is accessed with SQL, performance can be rather poor.

Microsoft are working at extending the OLE interface to manage these objects in a COM environment. This technology will probably not be available until 1996, but users of OLE and ODBC have been guaranteed a migration path if they require it.

13 Microsoft OLE

13.1 INTRODUCTION

OLE 2, pronounced *Oh-lay*, is probably one of the key Microsoft technologies. It is a set of object components that can be used to implement features within an application, for example data sharing. This chapter introduces some concepts behind Object Orientation and OLE 2 but a full discussion of the OLE 2 architecture is out of the scope of this book, further detailed information can be found in a number of other publications, including *Inside OLE 2* by Kraig Brockschmidt, published by Microsoft Press.

13.2 THE OBJECT ORIENTED PARADIGM

At the moment Object Orientation (OO) appears to be one of the fashionable areas of computing. Despite its current vogue, OO techniques have been around since the mid-sixties. Probably the earliest accepted OO programming language was the Scandinavian designed SIMULA or SIMUlated LAnguage, which was the basis for the now successful Smalltalk language.

There is currently a heated debate underway between the Object Oriented Programming (OOP) purists, who believe that an OO language must contain a specific set of features, and those who are happy with an object oriented environment.

Generally to be accepted as an object oriented programming language the following features need to be present:

- User definable classes
- Object class hierarchies
- Instantiation

- Inheritance
- Polymorphism
- Messaging
- Encapsulation

13.2.1 Classes, Objects and Instances

Objects are very much abstract data types – the internal configuration and characteristics of an individual object need not be known by the developer. The internal data elements (data abstraction) and processes (process abstraction) can, in theory, therefore be ignored and the developer can focus on the object interfaces.

A good example of this is the telephone receiver where a user does not need to know its internal workings, only the ability to interface with the telephone by using the handset. This also demonstrates abstraction, the fact that the characteristics of an object differ according to the viewer. A secretary sees the telephone as a box with which conversations can take place but an engineer may see the telephone as a complex assortment of electro-mechanical components, all interacting with each other.

A class is a special object containing data and procedural abstraction. It is a concept only, but this concept is delivered as an object. This class represents a set of objects that share a common structure and behavior, for example, all telephones enable communication to take place but the design of the telephone may be upright, squat, wall mounted or a hands-free mobile in a car! Instantiation is the process of having multiple instances of an object which can be manipulated independently without affecting each one's functionality or attributes.

13.2.2 Containment and Inheritance

Containment is literally the containment of objects within each other. For example, a telephone object may contain a bell object which in turn may contain a plunger object. Inheritance allows these objects to acquire some properties of other objects. Single inheritance or multiple inheritance indicates the number of parent objects that a child object can have.

13.2.3 Polymorphism, Messaging And Encapsulation

Polymorphism is the ability for the system to determine the best way of executing code at runtime. The same or similar messages may be sent to different objects to achieve abstract results. For example the word OPEN is polymorphic. OPEN applied to a door will be interpreted differently to OPEN applied to an MS-DOS file.

Message passing is key to OO programming. It can be thought of as the application of methods to an object following a pre-determined format which in turn are handled in a very specific manner. For example, the message may change an object's data and therefore its behavior.

Encapsulation is the containment of the properties (or data) and the methods (or code) of an object. Objects that contain the same properties and methods are said to be of the same type. Objects have unique properties which are not shared with other objects, although other objects may have identical properties. In some languages, such as Smalltalk, the encapsulation happens at a physical level, using the syntax of the programming language. Smalltalk also offers the developer the ability to encapsulate methods, operations and features to create a logical class. Using the telephone analogy again, the outer plastic casing of the phone encapsulates the internal implementation of the phone or object, effectively hiding its complexities.

13.3 OLE COMPONENTS

13.3.1 Component Object Model

The *Component Object Model* (COM) is a binary standard specification for building code modules. Primarily aimed at C++ developers it is increasingly used by programmers using other languages or tools.

COM provides a consistent memory structure and programming interface.

The memory structures exist as tables of function pointers with COM treating each table as an interface, with a name prefaced by the letter "**I**". Once the interface has been implemented the object agrees a *contract* with it so that any object user will know what to expect from function calls to the interface.

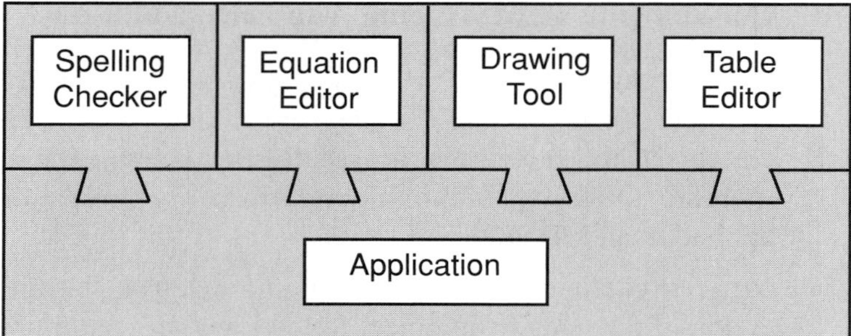

Figure 13-1 OLE Components all use a Common Interface Like a Jigsaw

13.4 KEY OLE ELEMENTS

13.4.1 Monikers

Monikers are component objects that contain references to the location of a set of data. A compound document needs to understand the location of embedded data as soon as the user double clicks on the embedded object. This is the job of the moniker, establishing connections between a data source and the data consumer.

13.4.2 Compound Files

OLE 2 specifies a format for the structured storage of information, based upon a hierarchical structure of storage objects. The benefit of this model is that small data changes can be made with out affecting the overall compound file and re-writing large amounts of data.

13.4.3 Uniform Data Transfer

Using data objects, uniform data transfer provides a very efficient and powerful way of exchanging data, for example drag and drop, between applications. Used in conjunction with monikers the user will be given an environment where they do not need to manage any links from a compound document to its underlying data.

13.4.4 Drag and Drop

Drag and drop is very similar to a cut and paste. Dragging an object will cut it and dropping an object will paste it. Any application that has utilized the

Windows Clipboard in a cut and paste function is able to utilize the Drag and Drop feature of OLE 2 and the code for using data objects in the clipboard is mostly reusable for implementing Drag and Drop.

13.4.5 Automation

Sometimes called OLE Automation, automation is a way to expose the attributes and functionality of an application. These properties and methods use the IDispatch interface to expose their automation objects. Once exposed the application becomes an automation server and, with information about the application stored in a type library, users can examine an application without needing to load and run it.

13.4.6 Linking and Embedding

Embedded data is actually contained within the compound document but at times this may prove to be inefficient. In these circumstances it is better to link to the data which is stored in another location. Once a linked object is activated the user can edit the data as if it was embedded.

13.4.7 In-Place Activation

Normally when an embedded or linked object is activated the data server will generate another window with a set of separate toolbars and menus for the user to manipulate the object. In-Place Activation places its toolbars and menus within the compound document, removing the need to generate a separate window. This produces a better document-centric as opposed to an application-centric solution where the user is concerned about the application underlying the data.

13.4.8 Distributed Capabilities of OLE 2

OLE 2 implements a local lightweight remote procedure call (LRPC) mechanism to transfer data and operations between objects on a single computer. A newer version of OLE 2 will enable the inter-process communication between computers on a network using Microsoft RPC as opposed to LRPC. Microsoft RPC is compatible with the Open Software Foundation (OSF) Distributed Computing Environment (DCE) specification enabling exchange of information with other DCE systems such as OpenVMS from Digital and AS/400 from IBM.

Typically, creating a distributed object system is fraught with problems as the multitude of interfaces each need a unique name. Traditional naming conventions for modules, objects, classes and methods is bound to produce problems of duplicated names within any reasonably large system. Any such duplication will cause failure of the software-despite the actual components being valid. To overcome this, OLE uses a set of global unique identifiers based upon 128-bit integers which are virtually guaranteed to be unique, even in systems with millions of objects. Traditional names may be applied to these components; scoped locally they will not impact the overall naming convention.

As well as the network RPC functionality Microsoft RPC will also have a tool set capable of automatically packaging data for transmission across the network. This will enable developers to create new object interfaces to work outside of the single process.

13.5 COMMON OBJECT MODEL

The Common Object Model is an architecture developed by Microsoft and the Digital Equipment Corporation (DEC) based upon the component object model allowing interoperation between OLE and ObjectBroker. With this architecture it is possible for Objects on a Windows NT Server to connect to objects on a host of other platforms including OSF/1, OpenVMS and IBM AIX.

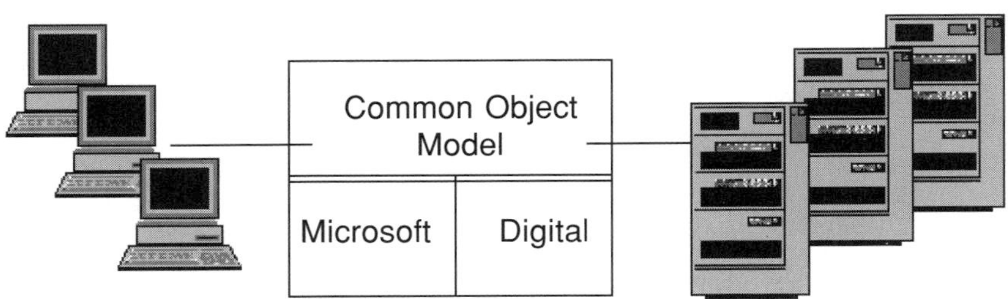

Figure 13- 2 The Common Object Model

The impact on users of this technology should not be underestimated. The ability to manipulate objects across the enterprise, on multiple platforms and multiple locations is a very powerful prospect.

14 Microsoft Jet

14.1 INTRODUCTION

This chapter will introduce the reader to the *Jet database engine* and explain how a user or developer can make the most out of this technology. The features covered will be the following:

- Architecture of the Jet database engine
- Jet datatypes
- Jet concurrency architecture
- Query optimization
- Connecting to external data sources
- Jet security model
- Data access objects

Any reader wishing to base a client/server development project on SQL Server and Access or SQL Server and Visual Basic is recommended to read this chapter so that they can fully exploit the Jet integration with SQL Server. It is also recommended that this chapter be read in conjunction with Chapter 15 as that details Microsoft Access, the prime *customer* of Jet in further detail.

14.2 JET ARCHITECTURE

Jet is the database engine underlying Microsoft Access and Microsoft Visual Basic Professional Edition (VB). Jet is the result of many years work at Microsoft by a number of leading database engineers, and the resulting database engine is a powerful relational database product.

Jet comprises of a number of key elements as shown in Figure 14-1.

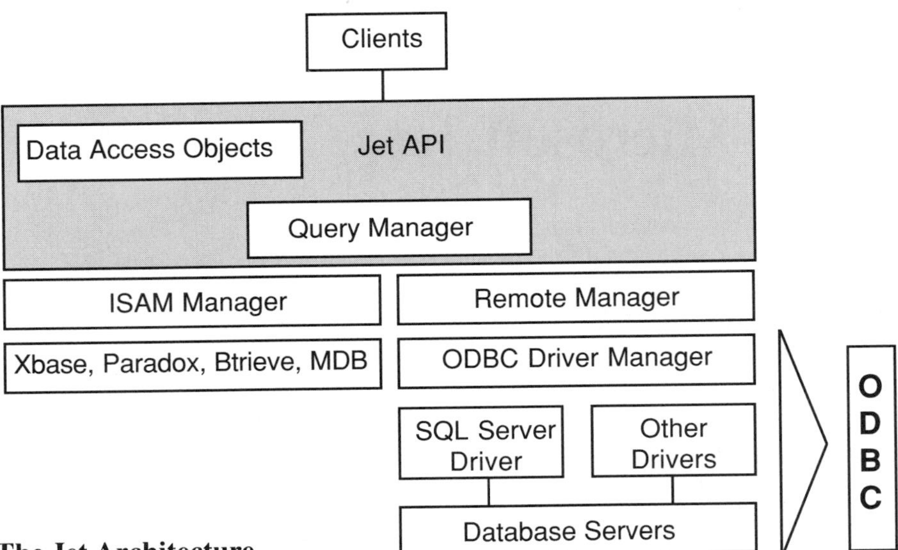

Figure 14-1 The Jet Architecture

14.2.1 Data Access Objects

The Data Access Objects (DAO) dynamic link library provides a high level object oriented Jet interface for data manipulation language (DML) and data definition language (DDL), the languages needed to create a database and then manipulate its data. These objects are shared by both Visual Basic and Access and, for example, allow the developer programmatic access to table relationships and the security model.

14.2.2 Query Manager

The Query Manager is the mechanism that allows the creation and optimization of complex queries, ranging from single table scans through to cross format heterogeneous (different format) queries via the ISAM manager and ODBC driver manager. From Version 2, Jet contains the *Rushmore* query optimization technology that was initially developed for the Microsoft FoxPro product.

14.2.3 ISAM Manager

The ISAM (Indexed Sequential Access Method) Manager provides an interface to external PC database formats. It contains a dispatch layer which effectively makes the external datasource look like a Jet table.

Jet supports 3 types of ISAM interface:

- Paradox
- xBASE
- Btrieve

All have a specific Dynamic Link Library (DLL) which is loaded when access to these formats is required.

14.2.4 Remote Manager

The Remote Manager is responsible for the external datasource connections via ODBC. Effectively making the datasource look like a native Jet table, it performs a similar task to the ISAM Manager.

14.3 JET SUPPORTED DATATYPES

All data and metadata (data about data, such as table and column names) in a Jet database is stored within a single MS-DOS file with the extension .MDB. This architecture frees the developer from standard MS-DOS 8+3 naming conventions for all database objects. Table 11 shows the supported datatypes.

Datatype	Storage Size	Information Stored
Text	Maximum 255Bytes	Variable length text
Memo	Maximum 1.2Gb*	Large variable length text
Numeric Byte	1 byte	0 - 255
Numeric Integer	2 bytes	-32,768 to + 32,767
Numeric Long Integer	4 bytes	-2,147,483,648 to + 2,147,483,647
Numeric Double	8 bytes	-1.8x10E308 to +1.8x10E308
Numeric Single	4 bytes	-3.4x10E38 to +3.4x10E38
Currency	8 bytes	Any number up to 15 digits to the left and 4 to the right of the decimal point
Counter	4 bytes	Automatically incremented long integer
Yes/No	1 bit	Boolean data
Date/Time	8 bytes	Dates and time values
OLE	Maximum 1.2Gb *	OLE objects
Binary	Maximum 1.2Gb *	Variable length binary data

** maximum database file size*

Table 11 Jet Supported Datatypes

14.4 JET CONCURRENCY ARCHITECTURE

The Jet database engine has been designed from the outset to function within a multiuser environment. As with any multiuser database, decisions have to be made at the beginning of the design process about appropriate record locking strategies.

Due to the variable length nature of Jet rows it was determined that 2Kb page level locking would give the user better performance than row level locking. A record cannot span more than a single page, but any OLE objects or memo fields can be stored on pages separate from the rest of the record.

The .LDB file contains locking information when Jet is used in a multiuser environment. Each user will have an entry in this file which is used by Jet to determine who has which records locked and prevents any possible data corruption. This file can be deleted (if the linked .MDB file is not being used) and the .MDB file moved as the .LDB file will automatically be recreated if the original cannot be found.

Locking a 2Kb set of pages may present some developers with a problem within their application, such as conflicts between users. To overcome this, there are two choices of locking that a developer can select.

14.4.1 Optimistic Locking

With optimistic locking the 2Kb page is available to other users for read or write activities during the period of row editing. The 2Kb page is only locked for the duration of the commit, that is, when the user hits the return key, and for that instance only. If there is a conflict between users with identical rows having been updated prior to the commit the user is warned and given the choice of storing the changed data to the Windows clipboard and thus preserving their data changes as shown in Figure 14-2.

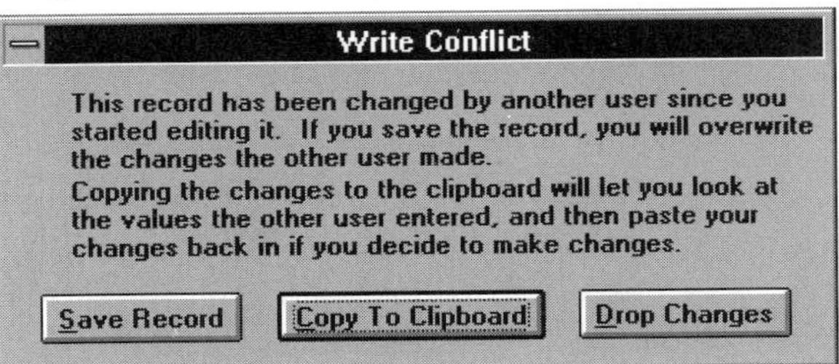

Figure 14- 2 The Lock Conflict Dialog

Optimistic locking is the default mode of operation for Jet. Figure 14-3 shows the Microsoft Access window that is used to specify locking options.

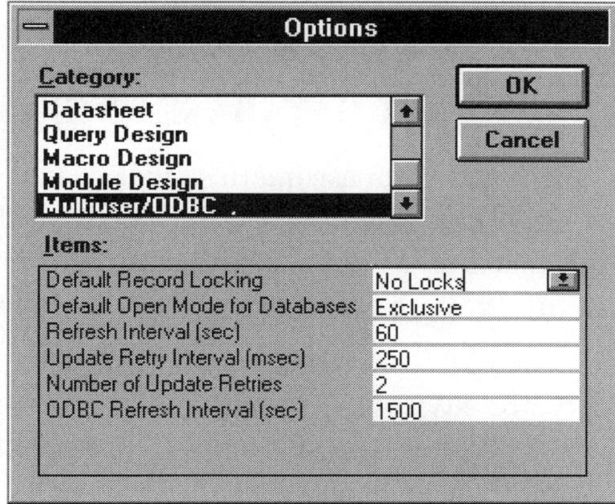

Figure 14-3 Setting Optimistic or Pessimistic Locking within Microsoft Access

14.4.2 Pessimistic Locking

With *pessimistic locking* the entire 2Kb page is locked for the duration of the edit. Other users may read data but will be prevented from writing to any rows within the 2Kb page.

Naturally it will be dependent upon the developer to select the best locking mechanism for the particular application.

It is interesting to note that Microsoft SQL Server also locks at the 2Kb page level.

14.4.3 Transaction Processing in Jet

Jet supports basic transactions within the Access Basic language:

- BeginTrans – initiates a transaction.
- CommitTrans – commits any changes required by the transaction.
- RollBack – terminates the transaction

The use of transactions can considerably speed up any batch processing that an application based on Jet is required to do, as only one disk write is used to commit a set of data. If used with a non-Jet data format then that data format or engine must also support transactions.

14.5 QUERYING THE JET DATABASE ENGINE

The ability to execute database queries quickly and efficiently is probably one of the most important functions of any database. Jet contains an advanced query engine that carries out the definition, compilation, optimization and execution of all database queries in a number of phases.

Jet will attempt to perform the execution of a query on the data server if it is used in a network environment. This will save network traffic and, in most sites, a server is quicker when it comes to processing large amounts of data.

There are some exceptions to this:

- Non-supported SQL Syntax. Jet has the ability to do some fairly complex queries which use SQL syntax that other database servers would not understand, for example PIVOT, TRANSFORM and TOP nn PERCENT
- Heterogeneous joins. Joining two server data sources may result in the data being brought to the local Jet engine for the join to take place. If a join is to occur between local tables with small numbers of rows and a larger server table then Jet will attempt to optimize the query and send it to the server for processing. If the remote server table does have an index on the join column then Jet will create a query for each row and send that to the server for execution.
- SQL Statements which cannot be contained in a single ANSI SQL statement such as nested GROUP BY queries.

14.5.1 Query Definition

Jet can receive the query definition from a number of different sources. Access users can create queries with the graphical query by example screen, typing in SQL directly to the SQL window or by embedding SQL into Access Basic. Visual Basic users are slightly more restricted and will generally have embedded SQL within specific code blocks. Which ever method is used to create the initial query, Jet will receive it as a SQL statement.

14.5.2 Query Parser/Binder

The syntax of the SQL statement is examined at this stage. Any common parts of the query string will be replaced with mnemonic tokens and the query will be placed into its first common data structure format. This format is similar to an inverted tree with the results set at the top of the tree (roots) and the underlying tables to be queried at the bottom (leaves).

The query folder mechanism will then move the expressions up the tree structure to as close to the root as possible to prevent unwanted calculations on any rows which may be discarded at a later stage.

The data structure is then broken down into its discrete components and the overall structure is removed from the tree in reverse order from the leaves to the root. The query flattener will then combine the joins as much as possible.

14.5.3 Query Optimization

Jet uses a cost based optimizer. The database statistics are used to form a best guess method of execution for the query. The costs are based upon two key database components, the tables and the table joins. There are three different mechanisms for accessing the table data:

- Index ranges
- Rushmore restriction
- Full table scan.

Hint: Compacting a Jet database will reset the database statistics. For heavily used databases it is advisable to compact on a regular basis.

The decision as to the best method depends upon the number of rows, data pages and location of the table. Indexes are examined for their selectivity, number of index pages and the presence or otherwise of nulls and duplicates. Any restrictions that may be placed upon the search criteria will also have a direct impact on any optimization that takes place.

The remote post processor will move along the query tree looking for subtrees that can be sent remotely. If so, the optimizer will generate SQL strings for remote queries and build additional data structures. The post processor will take this segment and copy components to create smaller execution segments.

14.5.4 Join Strategies for Multi-Table Queries

When Jet needs to perform a join between tables it has to establish a base table access strategy. The estimated number of records are returned and a cost calculated as to how expensive the operation was to read the table. Jet will then generate combinations of pairs of tables and cost each individual join strategy, adding tables to joins until the cheapest strategy is found.

- A base table scan is generally the least efficient access method as all data pages must be read and single table restrictions are checked for each row. Using an index range scan the table is opened with a particular index which includes one of the single table restrictions. Remaining restrictions are checked for any row which is left.
- Rushmore restriction uses bookmarks which are gathered together if they meet the restriction generated. Set operators are then used to compare lists of matching bookmarks for matching records.
- Nested iteration joins are only used as a last resort to join tables, generally when there are few rows, and no indexes.
- Index joins are used when the inner table has an index on the join column and is probably fairly small, with no data returned. The outer table will be highly restricted and probably only contain very few rows.
- Lookup joins are similar to index joins except that the inner table will be sorted before the join takes place.
- Merge joins are used when the tables are of a similar large size and where the output of a certain join can save another sort process.
- Index merge joins are used when each table is a native Jet table, with indexes on the join column and one of the indexes prevents nulls if there is more than one join condition.

14.5.5 Query Pitfalls

There are a number of areas to avoid if you wish to ensure that any Jet queries you compose are executed efficiently:

- Ensure that there are no redundant tables in the query
- Avoid any expressions in the query output

- GROUP BY before joining the tables and use as few columns as possible
- Index all of the join columns
- Use COUNT(*) instead of COUNT(column_name)

14.5.6 Rushmore Query Optimization

Rushmore is the name for the patent pending query optimization technology originally developed for Microsoft FoxPro and integrated into Jet from Version 2.0 onwards. It is used on queries that involve multi-column indexed restrictions, resolving the query with index restriction, probably the most obvious Rushmore feature. Rushmore will only work against native Jet and ISAM files, ODBC queries being processed by the specific data source.

Here are some examples where Rushmore can be used:

Index intersection - used where two indexes are intersected:

```
where county = 'Surrey' and country = 'UK'
```

Index union - used where the two indexes are unioned:

```
where county = 'Surrey' or country = 'UK'
```

Index counts - used where row count only is returned:

```
select count (*) from employees where county = 'Surrey' and
country = 'UK'
```

14.5.7 Dynasets verses Snapshots

Microsoft Access was the first commercial database product to fully support the use of dynasets or updatable views. Whilst not a new concept, the Jet implementation of the dynaset model is fairly advanced.

Most traditional databases will store the result of a query or other result set in a static table or view which does not allow the user to dynamically update the data or observe data changes that other users may have made. The dynaset allows dynamic population of data in real time and as such enables the developer to use the dynaset as a basis for forms and other queries saving a large amount of extra coding.

Jet also supports the more traditional result set view, the static table, in the form of snapshots.

When a dynaset query is initiated the result set is created as a keyset which is stored in memory (or disk if memory is full). Each unique key points to an underlying row, therefore creating a keyset driven cursor model. The keyset model is extremely efficient as the underlying rows do not need to be read until needed. A snapshot query will require the entire query to be completed and the rows stored to memory which will adversely affect database performance.

14.5.8 Connecting to External Data Sources

One of the versatile aspects of the Jet engine is the ability to integrate into a heterogeneous data environment. This data may reside in a common ISAM format such as dBASE or Paradox or a more complex relational structure such as Oracle or SQL Server.

In Jet version 2.0 the four ISAM formats supported are:

- Paradox v3.x and 4.x
- Btrieve v5.1x and 6.0
- dBASE III plus dBASE IV
- Microsoft FoxPro 2.x

These data sources can be accessed by attaching to the datasource or by using the simple import options. Once the data source has been opened, Jet will treat it as a native Jet table with one or two minor exceptions. Key differences involve the use of indexes. Index statistics may be difficult to maintain or access and a number of ISAM databases will not support the Jet primary or unique indexes.

Once connected to a data source Jet will undertake datatype matching from the underlying ISAM formats to a native Jet format. The actual data type matching process can be customized using the appropriate ISAM section in the Access .INI file. The example below shows some typical ISAM entries:

```
[Paradox ISAM]
ParadoxUserName=Nigel Stanley
ParadoxNetPath=C:\ACCESS
ParadoxNetStyle=3.x
CollatingSequence=Ascii
```

```
[dBase ISAM]
CollatingSequence=Ascii
Century=Off
Date=American
Mark=47
Deleted=On

[Btrieve]
Filter=Btrieve (file.ddf)|file.ddf|
Extension=ddf
OneTablePerFile=No
IndexDialog=No
CreateDbOnExport=Yes

[Btrieve ISAM]
DataCodePage=OEM
```

14.5.9 Jet and ODBC

Once the appropriate driver has been instaled using the ODBC driver administrator, Jet is automatically aware that the data source exists. Table attachment is the preferred method of accessing ODBC data from within Jet as Jet will optimize any actions on the datasource, including off loading as much processing as possible to the server, in true client/server fashion. Jet will not override any server based security or data integrity rules.

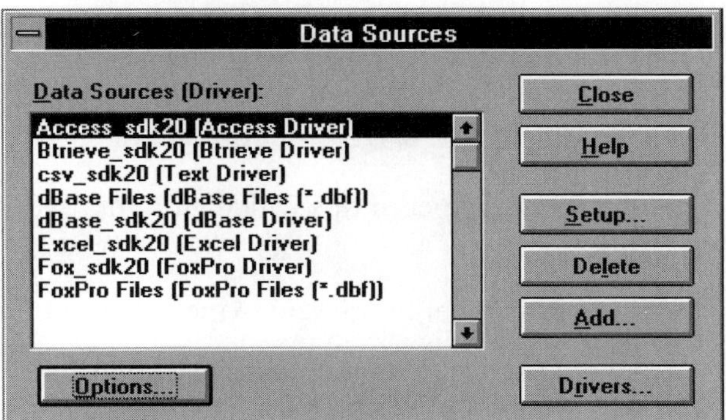

Figure 14-4 Typical ODBC Data Source Entries

Specific database queries may be required that use very specific server syntax that ODBC does not support. To facilitate this Jet supports the use of a pass through query. Whilst Jet Version 1.0 had to call a separate pass through DLL, from Jet version 2.0 this facility is built in.

Examples of using a pass through query include initiating a stored procedure on a server. Any data returned from a pass through query is always stored as a snapshot or static view as the user is effectively by-passing the Jet functionality.

Jet will map any ODBC data types as shown in Table 12.

ODBC Data type	JET Datatype
SQL_TINYINT/SMALLINT	Number-integer
SQL_INTEGER	Number-long integer
SQL_REAL	Number-single
SQL_FLOAT/DOUBLE	Number-double
SQL_TIMESTAMP/DATE	DateTime
SQL_BIT	Yes/No
SQL_TIME	Text
SQL_VARCHAR/CHAR	<=255 characters text, >255 characters memo
SQL_BINARY/VARBINARY	<=255 characters binary, >255 OLE object
SQL_LONGVARBINARY	OLE Object
SQL_LONGVARCHAR	Memo
SQL_DECIMAL/CURRENCY	Integer/Double/Longinteger/Currency depending on precision

Table 12 ODBC and Jet Datatype Mappings

Any other datatype will be treated as a text field with a size of 255 characters.

14.5.10 Optimizing the ODBC Connection

There are a number of tips which will improve the performance of an ODBC connection:

- Ensure that queries are sent to the server for processing whenever possible.
- Do not use large combo boxes or list boxes. Populating a large combo box will significantly reduce the performance of your database. A form which contains many combo boxes or list boxes will need to execute a separate query per list/combo box used reducing an application's performance.

- Use the FIND function wisely. FIND is not particularly rapid when used against large record sets on remote servers. The Query or Filter functions will improve your performance.
- Only ask for as much data as you actually need from the server.
- Use attached tables for remote data access.

14.5.11 Jet Server Connections

Jet has the ability to maintain more than one connection to a data source at any one time. The use of these multiple connections is dependent on the type of application that has been built and the data server used. For example, a server which closes any active statements after an insert, update or delete will need to have other connections in place to ensure the integrity of the remaining statements. It can, therefore, be seen that the number of simultaneous connections depends on the type of server being used and the number of active statements that will be open at anyone time.

Earlier versions of Jet had considerable problems in this area, especially with server software that limited the number of concurrent connections. Microsoft SQL Server was a particularly bad offender in this area, with each user only being allowed an average of 2.5 concurrent connections, leading to some rather difficult problems with connection hungry Access applications.

Jet version 2.0 overcame some of these problems by multiplexing connections and Dynaset objects or queries returning less than 100 rows now only use 1 connection. Snapshots only ever needed one connection as they were not updated.

Jet will share connections when connecting to a database with the same DSN (Data Source Name) and DATABASE value. Generally if a data retrieval operation is utilizing two tables a third connection would be shared - one connection to manage each of the table keys and a third to carry the data.

Connections are cached to save the time of recreating them when required by the user, a default of 600 seconds is used before the cached connection is terminated. This time can be altered by placing the appropriate entry into the MSACCESS.INI file as shown in Table 13 below.

Entry	Value	Effect
TraceSQLMode *	0	No SQL Tracing
	1	Trace SQL Statements and output to SQLOUT.TXT
QueryTimeout	n	Cancel queries that are not completed in n seconds
LoginTimeout	n	Cancel login attempts that are not completed in n seconds
TraceODBCAPI	0	No ODBC API tracing
	1	Trace ODBC API output to ODBCAPI.TXT
DisableAsync	0	Use asynchronous query execution
	1	Use synchronous query execution
ConnectionTimeout	n	Close cached connections in n seconds
AsyncRetryInterval	n	Ask query if it has completed every n milliseconds
AttachCaseSensitive	0	Attach to table regardless of case
	1	Only attach to table if case is correct
SnapshotOnly	0	Call SQL Statistics at attach time to allow dynasets to be created
	1	Forces snapshots as SQL Statistics not called
AttachtableObjects	string	Lists of server objects that can be attached
TryJetAuth	1	Try the Jet user ID and password before prompting (allows single stage login)
	0	Does not try Jet user ID and password.
PreparedInsert	0	Uses custom INSERT to INSERT all non null values
	1	Use prepared INSERT to INSERT all columns
PreparedUpdate	0	Uses custom UPDATE to only SET changed columns
	1	Use custom UPDATE to SET all columns

* *(SQLTraceMode for version 1.x compatibility)*

Table 13 Typical Jet ODBC Entries as used in MSACCESS.INI

1.5.12 Jet Security and Data Integrity

The integrity and security of the underlying data is critical to any database management system.

Jet supports a fully programmable workgroup based security model for all data access control. Each user and group account has their passwords stored within a separate MS-DOS file called SYSTEM.MDA along with a special unique security id number.

Jet has support for database specific rules, primary keys, foreign keys and referential integrity all at the engine level, helping the developer to avoid writing

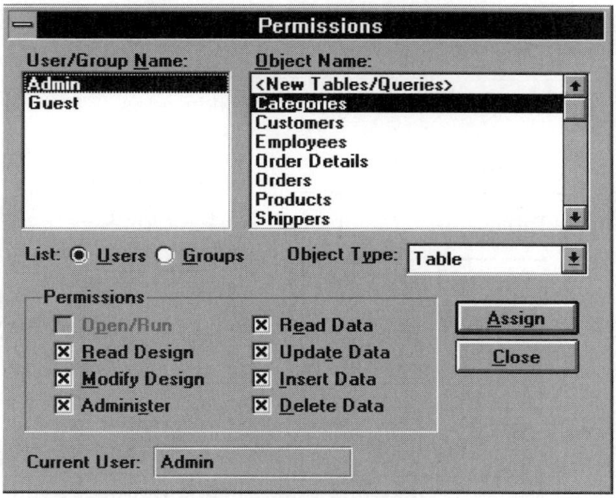

Figure 14-5 The Microsoft Access Security Dialog

complex code. These rules are also carried forward with any object created on a data set, therefore forms users are unable to override any engine rules.

Jet also supports the cascading update and deletion of data.

14.5.13 Data Access Objects

Data Access Objects (DAO) provide the developer with the ability to design and manage a number of database objects, including forms, reports, relationships and indexes using a high level programming technique.

Main Data Access Objects

The three main objects within the Data Access Object model are:

- DBEngine
- Workspaces
- Databases

DBEngine is the overall container. *Workspaces* can be created from the DBEngine and contain Users, Groups and Databases. *Databases* created by Workspaces contain Tabledefs, Querydefs, Recordsets, Relations and Containers.

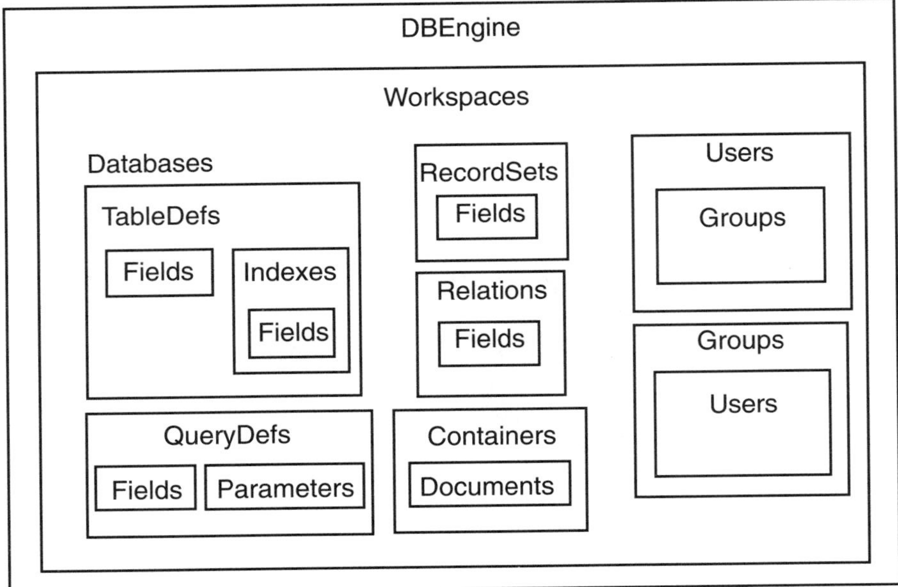

Figure 14-6 The Data Access Objects Hierarchy

There are four key elements to consider with Data Access Objects:

Properties

Every object has properties which define the state of an object. Properties are similar to the columns in a database and can be read only, read write or write only. The object can be made to undertake a specific action when a value is entered into a property.

Methods

Procedures are always kept with the data they work on. These methods are the only way to interact with an object, for example, to change the color of a screen object you would call the color method:

```
TextBox.Color
```

The object's properties cannot be changed directly, only via the methods that an object might have.

Navigation

Navigation is the way of determining the object specifier for a container objects containee. For example, db.TableDefs("Customers") refers to the table named "Customers" contained in the db database. The '.' is the navigation operator in Object Basic. This process can be used to determine the value or property of a containee:

```
NameValue$ = Recordset.Name
```

NameValue$ will contain the recordset name.

Containment

Objects can contain other objects in a nested manner. For example, a database contains TableDefs which contain Fields and so on. The database engine is the outermost container or data access object, and is therefore not contained by any other object.

14.5.14 Compacting a Jet database

Inevitably a Jet database will become fragmented through use and will need to be compacted or defragmented on a regular basis. Before compacting a Jet database it is advisable to defragment the host device or hard disk so that any data can be written to sequential disk areas. The person undertaking the compaction must have modify and design permission for all the database tables and the database must be opened exclusively.

- Compacting a Jet database will order a table's rows so that they reside on adjacent pages ordered by the table's primary key. Any sequential scan consequently undertaken should be faster as less pages will need to be read to retrieve the data.
- Any counter data types will be reset so any missed numbering following row deletions will be removed.
- All space that was filled by deleted rows or objects will be reclaimed. This is only marked as available when the objects are deleted, the .MDB file growing in size until the compaction is undertaken.
- Database statistics are regenerated.

15 Microsoft Access and SQL Server

15.1 INTRODUCTION

The *Microsoft Access Upsizing Tools* are designed for developers who wish to upsize an existing Microsoft Access application to a Microsoft SQL Server client/server application or create a new Access/Microsoft SQL Server application.

15.2 WHY UPSIZE?

Microsoft Access is a file server based database as are most, if not all, PC based databases in use today. A file server database is useful for creating applications designed for moderate amounts of data access, perhaps less then 100 Mb, and for moderate numbers of concurrent users, perhaps less than 20. This is due to the database mechanisms that come into play when used in a PC network environment.

If a user executes a query or some other table access action, then the entire contents of that table may be brought across the network and loaded into memory on the client PC. This action is enough to bring an active PC network to its knees in no time at all! Multiply this by a number of users and the end result is obvious.

To overcome this type of performance limitation it is necessary to re-look at the access of data across the network. This is where client/server computing comes into its own. Reduction of network traffic is one of the important benefits from implementing an efficient client/server system.

Instead of entire tables of data brought over the network, client/server implementations are generally more intelligent and will return only the data that the users actually require.

15.3 ACCESS UPSIZING TOOLS

With the performance limitations of a PC network in mind Microsoft undertook the development of the Upsizing Tools to assist developers moving from the Access environment to a Microsoft SQL Server and Microsoft Access client/server one.

The tools consist of two separate components:

- Upsizing Wizard
- SQL Browser

The *Upsizing Wizard* will take the developer through the steps of exporting the local table definitions, populating the remote tables with data and re-attaching the tables to the original forms. The *SQL Browser* is a utility used to browse remote data on the SQL Server.

Once installed the Access .INI file is changed to include the SQL Server Browser and Upsizing Tools Add-ins menu and the following files are copied to the client PC:

- WZCS.MDA – Library file containing the wizard and browser applications.
- WZCS.HLP – Help file for the upsizing tools.
- SQLDRVR.DLL – New SQL Server ODBC Driver.
- SWU2016.DLL – Version checking file to detect the version of SQL Server.
- README.TXT

15.4 THE UPSIZING PROCESS – PREPARING SQL SERVER

The target SQL Server will need to be configured correctly to successfully complete the upsizing process. This section looks at some of the tasks that should be completed on the target SQL Server.

Hint: As with any data sensitive task, back up the data prior to upsizing!

15.4.1 Permissions

It may seem obvious, but the SQL Server needs to be configured to accept the login from the client Access application.

For upsizing an existing database then the user requires CREATE TABLE and CREATE DEFAULT permissions. For creating a new database, the user requires CREATE DATABASE and SELECT permissions on the system tables in the master database.

New device creation can only be undertaken by the system administrator (SA).

15.4.2 Database and Device Size

The Access MDB file contains objects such as forms and reports as well as tables containing data. Prior to upsizing, the developer must estimate the typical growth rate of the proposed database. The more disk space available the better, and a rule of thumb is to multiply the number of megabytes of Access data by 1.5 to establish the likely size of the SQL Server database.

A SQL Server device, which is a storage area needed to hold the physical database and log file, must be selected that contains enough room for the Access file data. The Upsizing Tools allow the creation of further devices if required.

Hint: Always have enough space on your SQL Server. If you do run out of space on the SQL Server while upsizing, the Wizard will halt. You will then need to drop any tables, data or devices that have been created.

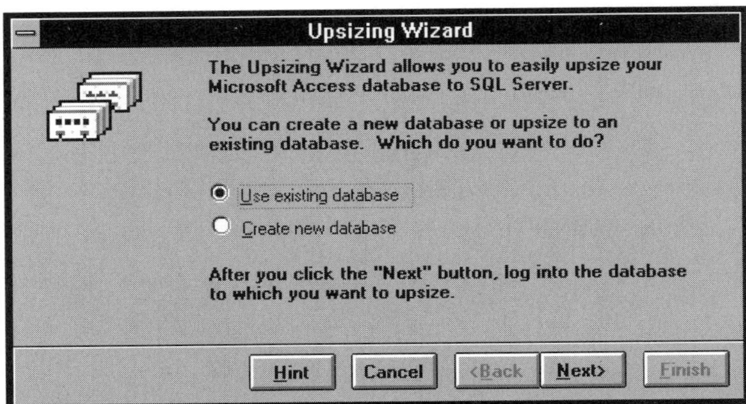

Figure 15-1 Upsizing the Database

15.4.3 Upsizing the Database

The basics of the Upsizing tools are remarkably straightforward. Object mapping, the process of converting Access data, tables, fields, indexes and defaults is a simple one-to-one mapping of the object types.

Complications arise with objects such as validations and relationships which are enforced within the Access Jet engine and form part of the data dictionary. SQL Server must take these and map them onto a type that it understands.

Upsizing Wizard
The Upsizing Wizard can export table attributes in addition to data; it can also attach the upsized tables in your local database.
What table attributes do you want to upsize?
[X] Indexes
[X] Table relationships
[X] Validation rules
[X] Add timestamp fields
[X] Defaults
[ ] Structure only, no data
How should your Microsoft Access database be modified?
[X] Attach newly created SQL Server tables
[ ] Save password and user ID with attached tables
Hint | Cancel | <Back | Next> | Finish

Figure 15-2 Upsizing Options

15.4.4 Table Objects

Table objects are mapped directly to SQL Server table objects, excluding most of the data dictionary elements. Any illegal characters or spaces are automatically replaced with an underscore "_" character and with the SQL Server names having a 30 character limit, the name may be concatenated. Objects containing keywords will have an appended underscore, such as "GROUP_".

Figure 15- 3 Upsized Table is Attached as Tablename_remote

15.4.5 Indices

Access primary keys are converted to clustered unique indexes on SQL Server and named "aaaaa_PrimaryKey" to ensure that they are selected first when attached to by Access as a remote table. Again illegal characters are replaced by the underscore "_" and unique/non-unique indices are mapped to SQL Server unique/non-unique indices. SQL Server does not support either ascending or descending indices.

15.4.6 Fields (Columns)

Column data types are mapped according Table 14.

Microsoft Access	Microsoft SQL Server
Yes/No	bit
Byte	smallint
Integer	smallint
Long Integer	int
Single	real
Double	float
Currency	money
Date/Time	datetime
Counter	int
Text(n)	varchar(n)
Memo	text
OLE Object	image

Table 14 Column Data Type Mappings

15.4.7 Defaults

Unlike Access, SQL Server treats defaults as objects that may be bound to any field in any table. Defaults that are created by the Upsizing Wizard are named after the table which they are bound to and a number which indicates the position of the column in the original Access table definition.

Any fields which contain a zero as default are automatically bound to a default named UW_ZeroDefault and YES/NO fields with no default are automatically assigned as a "NO" bound default.

15.4.8 Triggers

A SQL Server trigger is a set of Transact-SQL statements associated with a SQL Server table that is executed if certain conditions are met. Access counter fields, validation rules and inter-table relationships are all mapped to SQL Server triggers, with the appropriate Transact-SQL created automatically.

A SQL Server table can have up to three triggers, to react to either an UPDATE, DELETE or INSERT operation.

Table 15 indicates the mapping that is carried out between Access and SQL Server.

Microsoft Access	SQL Server Triggers
Record and field validation, required property, referential integrity	UPDATE
Record and field validation, required property, referential integrity for child tables and counter data type	INSERT
Referential integrity	DELETE - Parent tables only

Table 15 Trigger Mappings

The triggers are named according to the table which they are bound to and the type of trigger being implemented, in a simple naming convention as shown in Table 16.

Trigger Name	Trigger Type
Customers_Utrig	UPDATE
Customers_Dtrig	DELETE
Customers_Itrig	INSERT

Table 16 Trigger Naming Conventions

15.4.9 Validations

When the Upsizing Wizard encounters an Access validation, it takes the validation and converts it directly to Transact-SQL. If there is a required property on the Access table, an error message is created in Transact-SQL to replicate the Access error message. These Transact-SQL components are then combined and an UPDATE and INSERT trigger attached to the SQL Server table.

Hint: Any violation of a validation rule will always generate a user defined error number 44444.

15.4.10 Counter Fields

SQL Server does not support the counter data type as does Access (it does support the Identity Statement in SQL Server 6.0). To overcome this the Upsizing Wizard will create an INSERT trigger which automatically increments the counter number, as well as a default named UW_ZeroDefault which is bound to the counter field.

15.4.11 Table Relationships

SQL Server 4.21 enforces referential integrity by the use of triggers, Access supports declarative referential integrity at the engine level within Jet. To manage this the Upsizing Wizard will automatically create two triggers for the parent table and two triggers for the child table. If only one table in a relationship is upsized then the relationship is not exported and no triggers are created.

The parent table will have an UPDATE trigger to prevent changes to the primary key or cascade any changes, depending on the way the relationship was established within Access. There will also be a DELETE trigger to prevent deletion of a record with related children if this was established within Access.

The child table will have an INSERT trigger to prevent the creation of a new record with no parent and an UPDATE trigger to prevent any changes to the foreign key which would orphan a child record.

The developer can trap error messages created by an attempted relationship violation, with the following custom error numbers placed into a @@ERROR variable as shown in Table 17.

Attempted Action	Error
Delete	44445
Update	44446
Insert	44447

Table 17 Errors Due to Relationship Violations

15.5 MOVING THE UPSIZED APPLICATION FORWARD

The Upsizing Wizard will not instantly create a finely tuned client/server solution. There are a number of jobs that need to be undertaken to optimize the SQL Server and Access application.

15.5.1 Fine Tuning the Client

Transactions

Access supports a fairly complex transaction model of up to five levels, SQL Server only supports one transaction level. If there is a set of Access transactions then only the outermost one is executed, the others are ignored and no error message generated.

Methods and Objects

Not all methods and objects are supported in both Access and SQL Server. Refer to Table 18 and remove objects or methods which may not be supported.

Unsupported Objects	Unsupported Methods
Database Container	CompactDatabase
Documents	CreateDatabase
Index	CreateField
QueryDef	CreateQueryDef
Relation	DeleteQueryDef
	ListParameters
	ListTables
	OpenQueryDef
	RepairDatabase
	SetDefaultWorkspace
	Seek

Table 18 Unsupported Items

Record Locking

The Record Locks property of any form used must be set to No Locks or Edited Record as any Dynaset used from a server cannot be opened in exclusive mode. Server tables are used with optimistic locking, with the appropriate page only being locked for the duration of the commit.

Event Ordering

Access validation occurs when the user leaves the appropriate field, but SQL Server triggers are not fired until the user leaves the row when used as attached tables. Applications that rely on validations when the user tabs from a field may need to be rewritten. Similarly counter datatypes are incremented on field entry in Access and after row insert in SQL Server.

15.5.2 Fine Tuning the Server

A number of jobs need to be completed on the SQL Server. Access tables that need to be updated must have a unique index, if there was a unique index on the original table then it would have been exported otherwise the SQL Browser may be used to create it.

None of the users, groups or permissions on the original database would have been exported so these will need to be set by either using the SQL Server tools or the appropriate stored procedures *sp_adduser* or *sp_addgroup* in Transact-SQL. Any objects created will have default permissions allowing the system administrator or database owner to access them.

Access cannot override the security model of SQL Server, so although the Access application may not be explicitly aware of SQL Server security it cannot violate it. Indeed this is one of the strengths of this type of application - a strong security model. Users can log onto Access and then SQL Server separately or alternatively Access will default to logging the user in with the Access login password and username and only prompt for another if this fails.

Passwords can be stored locally with the Access table but this may not be suitable for a secure application. To overcome this the developer must create a configuration table called *MSysConf* on the SQL Server with appropriate values which avoids the local storage of passwords. The *MSysConf* table must be created with the structure shown in Table 19.

Column Name	Datatype	Required	Description
Config	SMALLINT	No	Number of the configuration option (create a unique index on this field)
chValue	VARCHAR(255)	Yes	Text value of the configuration option
nValue	INT	Yes	Integer value of the configuration option
Comment	VARCHAR(255)	Yes	Description of the configuration option

Table 19 The MSysConf Table

Hint: This table may be created on the SQL Server by using the SQL Browser tool. Once created, attach to the table using the Access table attach function.

Once created the values in Table 20 may be entered into the table to achieve the desired effect.

Config	nValue	Function
101	0	Prevents the storage of UserID and Password in attachments
101	1	Allows the storage of User ID and Password in attachments
102	D	Delay time D in seconds between background fetches by Access
103	N	Number of rows N fetched each time by Access

Table 20 Values for MSysConf

Fine tuning the rate at which Access reads data from the SQL Server will directly impact the performance of the network. If the server is generating excessive read-locks then the background population speed can be increased. If the network is too busy then slow down the background population.

Hint: Recordset objects in Access Basic are not populated during idle time, SQL Server places read locks on records as they are retrieved. Consequently it is not advisable to remain on a record or page for any length of time. By only partially populating Recordset variables in Access Basic you can prevent users from updating until the read locks are removed. Small recordsets can be cleared by using the MoveLast method to clear the locks. Large record sets may require the use of the Timer event procedure to replicate background population.

15.6 OPTIMIZING AN ACCESS AND SQL SERVER SOLUTION

Microsoft Access gives the developer a number of ways of integrating with SQL Server, and indeed any other RDBMS via ODBC. Once an Access application has been upsized the developer will need to optimize the system to ensure that it performs well. The Upsizing Tools will take away most of the tedious work but will not immediately fine tune the system to take advantage of the client/server architecture.

15.6.1 Attached Tables

Using attached tables is the easiest to use and most efficient method of using remote data. Once the tables have been attached, they may be treated as local Access tables. The Upsizing Wizard will automatically create attached tables during the upsizing process.

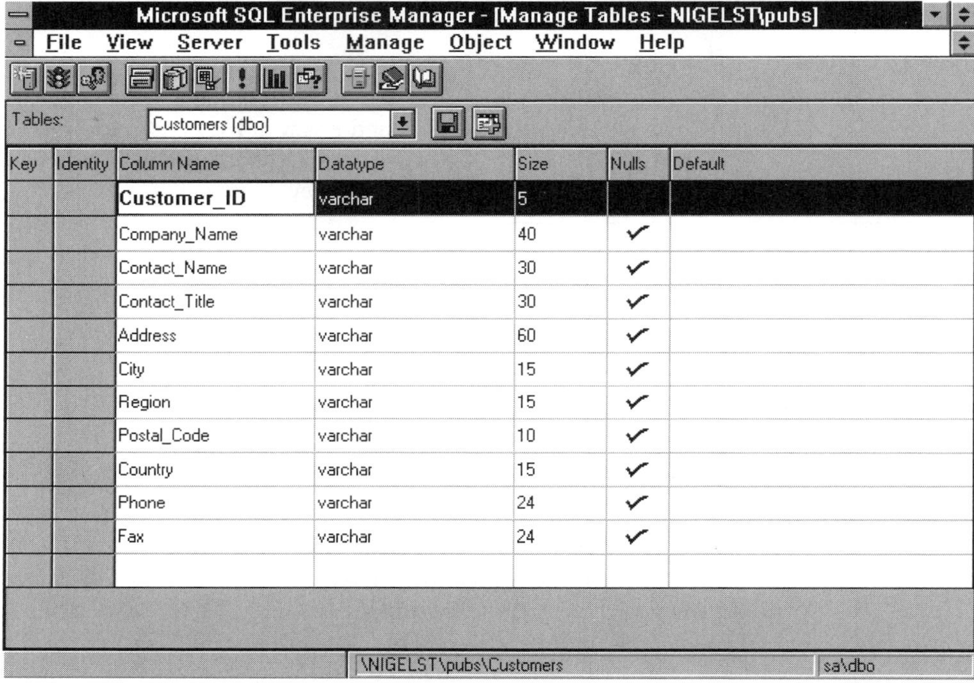

Figure 15-4 The Upsized Table as seen from within SQL Enterprise Manager

15.6.2 SQL Pass Through

Pass through is functionality that enables queries to be sent directly to the remote RDBMS, bypassing the Access query compilation process. This has a series of advantages and disadvantages that need to be taken into account before embarking on this route:

Advantages:

- Server based functions, such as stored procedures with no Access equivalent, can be used directly.

- Queries are executed on the server, with less local processing and network traffic.
- Heterogeneous data sources can be joined at the SQL Server, reducing amount of data returned locally to perform the join.
- Delete, Update and Append queries using pass through are faster than action queries on attached tables.

Disadvantages:

- The code to access functions has be typed in directly to the pass through window, with no syntax checking.
- Data is returned in Snapshots which are read only views.
- Pass through queries cannot prompt a user for a parameter.

15.7 OPTIMIZING ACCESS CONNECTION UTILIZATION

Developers need to be aware of the connection techniques used by Access in a client/server application to improve performance of the system.

A connection is different to a user login - one user may have multiple connections or threads to the server database which may, in some instances, prevent other users from logging onto the SQL Server as the maximum number of concurrent connections has been exceeded. Generally, the design of SQL Server allows an average of 2.5 connections per user logged on. For example a 64 user version of SQL Server allows up to 128 concurrent connections, which as a worst case scenario may all be used by one user!

Hint: Access version 1.0 had considerable problems in some Access/SQL Server combinations due to over use of available connections. This problem was overcome in later versions with the use of multiplexing within Jet to release unused connections.

15.8 DYNASETS

The best way of using a dynaset is to reduce the number of returned rows to less than 100. This way Access uses one connection, as opposed to two when data chunks of larger than 100 rows are returned – one connection for the key values and one for the returned data. Normally 100 rows are adequate for most applications. If other dynasets are created then they can share the *data* connection but must create their own *key* connection.

Connections can be forced to close by using a TOP 100 PERCENT query to return all of the data or using an OPEN EVENT procedure in a form to explicitly close the data connection.

If a default time of 10 minutes expires with no activity between the client and the server then the connection will be closed automatically. The connection will not be closed if a transaction or the results of a query are pending.

Hint: The connection timeout can be changed by setting the ConnectionTimeout in the [ODBC] section of MSACC20.INI, the Access initialization file. To keep the connection closed, increase the Refresh Interval setting of the multi-user/ODBC category in the Options dialog box. The default setting is for 25 minutes (1500 seconds).

15.9 OPTIMIZING QUERIES

The key to obtaining better performance in queries is to use indexes wisely and ensure the server is doing all or most of the processing.

Access tables that have primary keys will automatically get a SQL Server clustered index once they have been upsized. Index any join fields in multitable queries or fields used in the WHERE clause of the query. Chapter 7 describes the options available for choosing indexes.

15.10 INCREASING SERVER PROCESSING

When Access is required to query SQL Server it will attempt to send all of the query to be processed to the server, after evaluating any query clauses or expressions locally. To ensure that the query is processed on the server there are some simple steps that can be taken:

- Avoid constructs that contain functions or operators specific to Access, such as TOP queries and multi-level grouping in reports.
- Avoid any user defined Access Basic functions which use remote fields as their arguments.

- Avoid mixing text and numeric data types in UNIONS or expressions.
- Avoid heterogeneous joins, that is, those between different ODBC data sources. Access will either request all of the data from the remote table and perform the join locally or perform a remote index join where each key in the local table will be matched for data on the SQL Server.
- Avoid operations that cannot be contained in a single SQL statement, such as a FROM clause containing a totals query.

15.11 DELETIONS AND UPDATES

Tables with many columns can have their performance improved by using the SQL Server timestamp column type. The SQL Server Browser can be used to add the timestamp field to a table, and once added and reattached (if the SQL Browser is not used) it should improve application performance.

Writing the data to the SQL Server in batches, by using Access Basic transactions, will improve both multi-user concurrency and the performance of updates. Transactions are effectively units of work, which either succeed or fail - never half completing. They should be kept as short as possible as a SQL Server lock will be generated preventing users from updating or reading the affected data used in the transaction.

An alternative application design is to have a holding table, in Access, to which all updates are written. These records can then be written to the SQL Server in a single Access Basic transaction.

Whilst useful, transactions also have some limitations. SQL Server does not allow data definition, back up or permission related commands in a transaction. SQL Server does not support nested transactions - only the first level from an Access transaction is ever sent. Also server specific transaction commands in pass through queries should be avoided has it may lead to problems with Jet.

15.11.1 Recordset Caching

The CacheSize property of a recordset allows the storage of between 5 and 1,200 records in memory, which will spill into a temporary table should memory be filled. This caching will greatly improve the performance of datasheets and forms as cached records are retrieved from the client as opposed to the server and therefore reduce network traffic. To recover memory used in a cache then the CacheSize method can be set to 0.

15.11.2 Error Trapping the Server

As Access is connected to the SQL Server via ODBC two error messages will be generated if an error is encountered - the first from Access and the second from SQL Server. The Access *Error$* function can be used to concatenate the Access and server error message together. This can then be parsed to determine the error created by the server.

15.12 THE SQL SERVER BROWSER

SQL Server Browser is the second component of the Access Upsizing Tools. It enables the developer to manage SQL Server using more or less the same user interface paradigm that Access uses for the Database Container. With this tool the SQL Server can be browsed, objects created and edited and SQL statements passed directly to the server.

Figure 15-5 SQL Browser

The SQL Server Browser is not designed to replace SQL Server administration tools, rather it is designed to offer the Access developer some flexibility from within Access without the need to exit the application.

There are inevitably some restrictions on the functionality of the SQL Server Browser. Stored procedures must be executed to drop or increase the size of databases, bind or unbind rules and defaults. Ad hoc Transact-SQL commands will need to be executed to manage devices, segments, backup, security, server configuration and user administration.

16 Visual Basic and SQL Server

16.1 INTRODUCTION

Microsoft Visual Basic (VB) is a very popular application development environment based upon BASIC , one of Microsoft's key development languages. Based on the success of Visual Basic, the Microsoft long term goal is to provide a pan-application development language using this core technology.

Visual Basic consists of an Integrated Development tool suite with a forms designer where the developer effectively *paints* a graphical screen and then attaches code behind screen objects, such as buttons or text fields. Visual Basic uses an event driven model as Windows applications, by their very nature, can offer users a number of possible code paths at anyone time. Using a procedural languages to create this type of application is very complex and often not possible.

Visual Basic comes in two flavors – Standard and Professional.

- Standard Edition contains introductory tools to allow developers to create straightforward applications.
- The Professional version contains extra tools including the Microsoft Jet database engine that is also found in Microsoft Access.

Visual Basic is largely written using Visual C++ instead of Intel specific assembler code and consequently it is able to execute on the Windows NT 32 bit operating system.

The Visual Basic for Applications (VBA) edition is a new version of the Basic language engine designed to be embedded with other applications such as Excel or Project. The embedding of the language element gives the developer access to an application's objects using VBA as a macro language, therefore freeing the developer from having to learn a multitude of different macro languages to link applications together.

16.2 VBA ARCHITECTURE

The VBA code is organized into three separate components:

- Procedures
- Modules
- Projects

16.2.1 Procedures

Procedures are called using their name, and once called, the code block in the procedure is executed until the end of the procedure is reached. VBA has three different types of procedure:

- Sub
- Function
- Property.

16.2.2 Sub Procedures

Sub procedures are excellent general purpose code blocks which do not return any values. They are often used for tasks such as performing runtime screen changes and data input. A Sub procedure will always start with the *Sub* keyword followed by the Sub name and parenthesis which contain any arguments used in the procedure. If no arguments are used then the parenthesis are left empty. The code block to be executed then follows, with the procedure terminating with an *End Sub* keyword:

```
Sub Procedure:

Sub Name (arguments)
    ...Code
End Sub
```

16.2.3 Function Procedures

The key difference between a Function and Sub procedure is that a Function will return a value to the calling code. An obvious use for this would be in mathematical calculations. Indeed users of Excel are able to define functions and then call them as if they were native to the spreadsheet.

The Function construct is similar to a Sub:

```
Function Name (argument) As Returntype
    ...Code
    Name = value
End Function
```

One of the key differences between the Sub and the Function is that the Function can define the data type to be returned using the *As* keyword. The returning value is named after the Function name.

16.2.4 Property Procedures

Property procedures are an advanced feature of VBA. They enable a developer to call them by using the same syntax as used to set the value of a property.

16.2.5 Passing Arguments

Arguments can be passed to procedures using either conventional or named arguments.

Conventional arguments pass the arguments to the procedure in the order in which they were defined, with any omitted argument being replaced by a space contained in commas:

```
DemoAddress (Town, County, Country)
```

This contains all of the arguments needed to allow the procedure DemoAddress to operate. If the developer decided not to include the County argument then the example would look like this:

```
DemoAddress (Town, ,Country)
```

The alternative method is to use named arguments. Generally named arguments are easier to read and allow the arguments to be passed in any order irrespective of the order in which they were defined:

```
DemoAddress Country:="UK", Town:="Epsom"
```

Note the ":=" operator before any argument.

16.2.6 Variables

Variables are memory areas used to store information on a temporary basis by an application. Anything that contains a value has a data type which determines the type of, and legality of, data stored in that variable. Table 21 shows a sample of the data types available in VBA.

Data Type	Description
String	1 byte text characters, maximum about 2 billion
Integer	2 byte, non fractional numbers ranging from -32,768 to 32,767
Single	4 byte single precision floating point numbers
Boolean	2 byte true or false
Currency	8 byte scaled integer

Table 21 Key VBA Data Types

If a data type is not assigned to a variable then the variant data type is used by default. The variant data type can contain any numeric value up to the double range limit or any text character. Any change in the type of value stored in the variant data type is automatically managed by the code.

Any variables used in VBA are declared either explicitly in code written by the developer or implicitly when they are automatically given the variant data type.

Statement	Comment
Dim	Used by variables shared in a module and to declare variables in procedures that are removed from memory when a procedure ends.
Static	Used for variables that are not removed from memory when a procedure ends
Public	Used for all variables shared by all procedures in a project. This is the same as the Global statement in VB Professional and Standard which it replaces.
Private	Used for variables that are available only in the module containing the procedures where it was declared.

Table 22 Declaration Statements

Variables can be scoped, or made visible, at either the local, module or public level. During execution the variables are evaluated according to scope, starting with local variables, through the module level and then finally the public level.

Local variables are useful for temporary data storage in a procedure. As they have a narrow scope they are only visible to the procedure in which they were created. Either the Dim or Static statements can be used to declare these variables, with the Dim variable not remaining in memory after the procedure has ended. Variables declared with the Static statement will remain in memory and can be used the next time the procedure is called.

Module Level variables are declared with the Dim, Static or Private statements at the top of a module prior to the first procedure. This variable is then visible to all of the procedures in the module. If there is a conflict with a Local variable of the same name then the Local variable will take precedence over the Module Level variable which will be ignored.

Once declared with the Public statement, a Public variable is visible to all procedures in a project, irrespective of the module in which it was created.

16.3 OBJECTS IN VISUAL BASIC FOR APPLICATIONS

Each application supporting VBA has a file called an object library which contains information about the application's objects which are accessible from within VBA. These objects can be components of the application or other OLE objects from other external applications.

The interaction of these objects is the key to VBA. These objects can be manipulated by altering object properties, which are key attributes that control an object's behavior or appearance.

The setting of properties is a straightforward task. The object is named, with a period separating the object and the property which is to be altered. The new value of the property is entered after the "=" sign:

```
Form1.Visible = Yes
```

This will ensure that Form1 is visible.

16.3.1 Methods

A method is a characteristic of an object that it knows how to perform. Every object has a set of methods attached to it. An often cited example of a method is the Save method with Microsoft Excel which, when executed, will save the existing workspace or workbook changes. These methods may take arguments in the same way as a procedure, so a developer may, for example, specify the actual file name to be saved by the method.

16.3.2 Containment

Visual Basic offers the developer a framework for containment with the ability for a form to contain controls such as buttons and check boxes. VBA offers similar containment. For example Excel is an object which contains workbook, worksheet and range objects in, effectively, an object hierarchy.

16.3.3 Collections

A group of related objects can be contained in one object called a collection. Excel is a good example of this as the Worksheets collection object has a property which can be interrogated to establish some information about the worksheet, for example how many worksheets in a workbook

16.3.4 Object Browser

The object browser is a special dialog that enables browsing of an application's objects, showing the names of all the objects and their associated methods and properties, names of projects, procedures and modules.

16.3.5 Control Structures in VBA

VBA supports various code structures, including control and looping functionality. Probably the most commonly used control structures are the *If...Then*, *If...Then...Else* and *Select Case* structures.

If...Then enables conditional execution of code based upon the validity of an expression, with false validity skipping code execution. The additional *Else* statement enables an extra scenario if all expressions are false, often used at the end of the code block if all expressions effectively fail.

Select ...Case is more focused on identifying matching values rather than a testing process used in If...Then.

Looping structures allow the iterative use of code that will be repeatedly executed until conditions are met.

For...Next enables use of a counter to determine the number of code cycles executed with the developer specifying the number of cycles in a counter variable. Normally used in an incremental counting mode, decrementing is possible with the *Step* clause with a "-" sign prior to the step value.

Do...Loop will continue to process a code block iteratively without the need for a counter until a determined condition is satisfied. The addition of the clause *Until* or *While* will ensure the code is executed until conditions are met, which can lead to interesting application functionality unless catered for by the developer!

16.4 SQL SERVER DISTRIBUTED MANAGEMENT OBJECTS

Initially called SQL-OLE, the SQL Server Distributed Management Objects (SQL-DMO) bring the world of objects to the management of SQL Server. SQL Server has an object model with 40 separate objects containing 600 32-bit OLE interfaces which support the Visual Basic programming language.

The object model is a hierarchy, with the primary SQL Server object containing databases which in turn contain tables, views and stored procedure objects. Figure 16-1 shows a small part of the SQL Server Object Hierarchy.

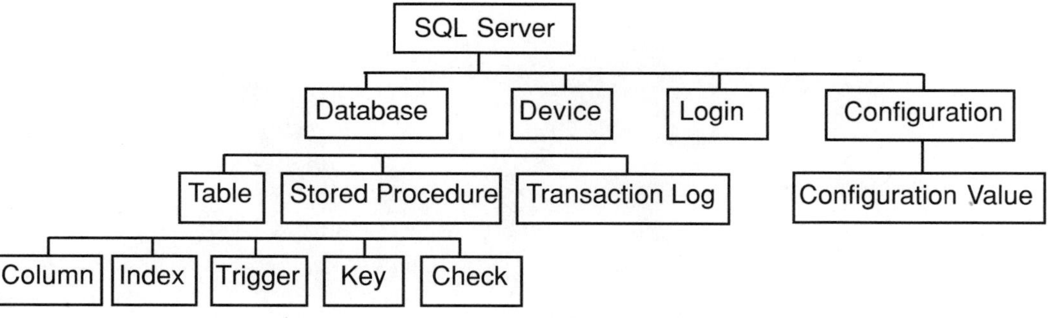

Figure 16- 1 Part of the SQL Server Object Hierarchy

16.4.1 Using SQL DMO

Developers familiar with Visual Basic will find the syntax for using SQL DMO straightforward. The following example uses Visual Basic to determine the name and space available for databases on a given server:

```
Dim NetServer as SQLServer
NetServer.Name = “AURIGA”
NetServer.Login = “sa”
NetServer.Connect
For each NetDB in NetServer.Databases
    Print NetDB.Name, NetDB.SpaceAvailable
    Next NetDB
NetServer.Disconnect
```

This example will declare the SQL Server object, connect to the server and then for each database within the server print the database name and the amount of available space remaining. The application will then disconnect from the server.

Each object has a multitude of methods and properties. The database object, for example, has many methods such as Dump and Load and many properties such as its Name and Owner. The Index object has methods such as Rebuild and UpdateStatistics and properties such as Name and FillFactor. Given the power and flexibility of VBA and the SQL DMO it can be seen that database administrators will be able to write very sophisticated scripts to assist them in their database administration tasks.

17 The Future of SQL Server

17.1 INTRODUCTION

The computer industry is undergoing a revolution. Between 100 and 150 million people world-wide use a PC each and every day. The growth in client server products and tools has fueled the dramatic reassessment of corporate computing requirements and evaluation of the need for mainframe-centric computing. Even so, 80% of the world's data is still resident on flat file data storage systems and the number of companies that have actually gone through the process of re-engineering their business from top to bottom and actively leverage client server technology is remarkably small.

The Microsoft company strategy is based on the decision to focus on key areas:

- Desktop computing
- Consumer "Microsoft at Home" brand
- Information Superhighway
- Enterprise computing

We will discuss the enterprise computing market, of which SQL Server is key, in this chapter.

17.2 WHAT IS THE ENTERPRISE?

Microsoft are determined to build the type of software that will run on any size of networked based personal computer. Alongside this comes a need to build additional software to compliment the existing portfolio, including transaction monitors, development tools and repositories.

But what exactly is the enterprise? The classical view is the typical mainframe based system, of which there are approximately 300,000 systems world-wide and 300,000 or so smaller mini type systems such as AS/400 and larger VAX based systems. The traditional playground for DB2, Oracle and Sybase and a weaker area for Microsoft.

The alternative view to the traditional enterprise arena is radical. Lets look at some interesting figures.

In the US alone there are about 29 million offices, 11 million of which have at least one employee working full time each day. Eventually, as time goes by, most of these work places will have a server of some description. That is an incredible number of servers and is the enterprise market that Microsoft is targeting with second generation products such as Windows NT.

Windows NT has been called a true "1/2 hour OS" – you buy the software from the local computer store, install it, and within 1/2 hour you have a fully featured 32-bit operating system, up and running. Try doing that with UNIX!

This radical philosophy extends down to the hardware. The days of large single box solutions comes to an end, being replaced by a cluster of smaller servers which grow over time to produce an infinitely scaleable solution.

But large boxes will be present for many, many years. Microsoft are focusing on producing software that can integrate into that environment in a seamless fashion. And to this over all end, Microsoft have hired 20 or so of the world's top database experts to create a truly formidable expert team.

This ultimate enterprise architecture is not going to be released this year. Nor next. Instead, based on the 18 month product cycles that Microsoft employs, various elements will be made available in steady increments with the full architecture in place in about 5 years. These 5 years are going to be interesting.

17.3 SQL SERVER DIRECTIONS

The next major feature release of Microsoft SQL Server is cited for the "Cairo" time frame, estimated to be available in 1997. "Cairo" is the next major feature release of Windows NT and will provide users with a fully object oriented operating system based upon a distributed model of OLE with tools to manage the enterprise network and applications.

There will certainly be incremental releases of SQL Server before 1997 containing some new features but Microsoft have publicly listed the following features as being under consideration for the new version:

- Parallel query/indexing
- Distributed joins
- OLE data access
- Versioning, row locking
- ANSI-92 conformance
- Cairo security, directory
- User-defined functions
- Object repository
- Hierarchic datatypes
- OFS integration
- Transaction co-ordination

A large number of these features are closely tied into the object orientated functionality provided by "Cairo".

17.4 DATABASE AND DEVELOPER TOOLS FUTURES

As discussed, Microsoft make no secret about their ambitions to move their desktop expertise into the enterprise arena. Windows NT, Back Office and SQL Server 6.0 have created a firm basis for that move but what about the general database and developer tool product range?

The first move in reaching the future architectural goal was to re-evaluate the product development teams. The days of having parallel teams at Microsoft working on near identical product features such as screen designers and query tools have come to an end. The development teams have been stream lined to focus on building a component based development environment.

The future architecture is proposed to look something similar to Figure 17-1.

An example of this future architecture in action is, maybe, a forms designer and query tool which can be shared by any one of the three key programming languages of xBASE for FoxPro developers, Visual Basic technology for Microsoft Office applications and Visual C++ for high end object developers.

It is proposed that developers will select their language of choice and "plug" in various components via a standard OLE interface to build their project.

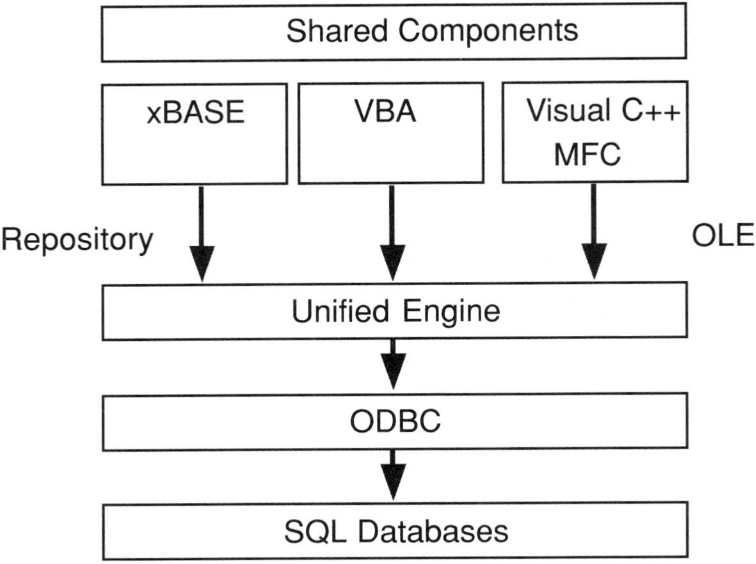

Figure 17-1 Next Generation Microsoft Database Architecture

The database engines are undergoing a review and work has started on creating a single unified database engine which will be scaleable from a single processor PC to a multiprocessor server running Windows NT.

All of these components need somewhere to be stored, and this will take the form of a software repository which is currently under design with teams from Microsoft and Texas Instruments, who are generally acknowledged to be the leaders in repository based technology.

Although the products are essentially undergoing a componentization process Microsoft will still be selling shrink wrap software in a box to end users – none of the products will disappear from the shelves, instead the developer will benefit from this ultimate plug and play architecture.

The engineering effort to create such a complex architecture should not be underestimated, but once delivered should offer an exciting array of development possibilities.

The authors await it eagerly!

Glossary

Aggregate Functions Functions in SQL which return a single value as a result of grouping together many rows, such as SUM or COUNT.

Allocation Unit A unit of data storage consisting of 256 pages (32 extents).

Alias A facility used to treat a number of people as the same user inside a database. Often used to associate a number of people with the database owner role.

ANSI The American National Standards Institute, a leading force behind the SQL standard.

Article A table or part of a table that can be replicated.

Ascending Order A sorting order that starts with the lowest key value and proceeds to the highest.

ASCII A computer character set and collating sequence. Acronym for *American Standard Code for Information Interchange.*

Attribute Another name for a column in a table.

B-tree A balanced tree or sorted index structure for a specified table.

Batch File A set of Transact-SQL statements executed together either interactively or from a file.

BCP See *Bulk Copy Program.*

Bldmastr A utility used for recovering a damaged master database.

Blob Binary Large Object. A datatype used for storing unstructured data such as pictures, sound or video. The actual datatype used in SQL Server is the *image* datatype.

Boolean Expression A string that specifies a condition that is either true or false.

Boolean Operator A symbol or word that facilitates joining two or more Boolean expressions. Typical Boolean operators are AND, OR, NOT.

Bulk Copy Program A command line utility for transferring data between SQL Servers and/or files.

Call Interface A mechanism for a program to access components of a software product.

Cardinality The number of rows in a table.

Catalog Stored Procedure Stored procedure added to SQL Server to provide a uniform catalog interface.

Checkpoint A mechanism which ensures that completed transactions are written from cache to the database at frequent intervals.

Clustered Index A type of index where the physical order of the data in the table is the same as the order in the index. There can only be one clustered index per table.

CODASYL Acronym for *Conference on Data Systems Languages*. A network model database management system.

Collating Sequence The sequence in which characters are ordered for merging, sorting, and comparisons.

Column A relational model term that equates to a field. Also called an *attribute*.

Commit A statement that ends a transaction and makes all changes upon the database permanent.

Composite Key Any type of key that comprises of one of more columns.

Computed Column A virtual field that appears in, for example, a table or view definition, but not physically in the table, therefore it occupies no space in the database.

Concurrency The simultaneous use of a database by a number of users.

Consistency The level to which a database system guarantees that tables being read by a user cannot be changed by another user at the same time.

Check Constraint A rule that defines the permitted values a column may take.

Cross Operation See *Join*.

Cursor An object used to store the output of a query for subsequent row by row processing.

Data Definition Language The statements that describe the metadata definitions.

Data Manipulation Language The statements that allow data in a SQL Server database to be stored, retrieved, modified, or deleted.

Data Table See *Table*.

Database A collection of data in which usually more than one user can access the data at the same time. The database maintains its own data integrity and security. There can, and typically will be, be a number of databases per SQL Server.

Database Administrator A person whose responsibility is the smooth running of the SQL Servers in a corporation and the underlying databases. Typically responsible for ensuring the database is backed up, DBCC is run regularly, performance is satisfactory and there are no nasty surprises about to happen. Can be recognized by the bags under their eyes. Usually have the same expression on their face as that on the parents of 3-week old quadruplets. See *System Administrator*.

Database Cache An area of memory set aside to hold data and index pages read in from disk.

Database Consistency Checker A database administration utility with many uses and options, such as checking database consistency and transaction log space usage.

Database Device An area of hard disk used to store databases and transaction logs. A database device typically equates to an operating system file.

Database Page The structure used to store data or indexes within a SQL Server database. The database page size is fixed at 2Kb.

Datatype An attribute assigned to a column or field such as char or int. The datatype determines the storage space taken by the column and a range of allowable values. Datatypes that come with SQL Server are known as system supplied datatypes, whereas datatypes that are not created by SQL Server are known as user-defined datatypes.

DBA See *Database Administrator.*

DBCC See *Database Consistency Checker.*

DDL See *Data Definition Language*.

DML See *Data Manipulation Language*

Deadlock The situation where two or more transactions request the same resources in an order that results in a deadly embrace. Nothing can be done to resolve the conflict, except aborting one of the transactions.

Default A value stored in a column if no value is otherwise specified.

Denormalization The reverse process of normalization.

Descending Order A sorting order that starts with the highest value of a key and goes down to the lowest.

Device Mirroring A facility within SQL Server whereby a second database device is written to as well as the original one. If a device then fails, SQL Server can continue to use the surviving one, thus keeping the system available.

Distribution Database An SQL Server database used as a staging post for those transactions that are being sent to subscription servers.

Distribution Server An SQL Server where the distribution database resides.

Dump Device An area of hard disk, diskette or tape used to store databases and transaction log backups.

EBCDIC Acronym for Extended Binary Coded Decimal Interchange Code, the computer set and collating sequence for IBM systems.

Equi-join A join operation that matches a column from one table with a corresponding column in another table.

Embedded SQL SQL code that is embedded in an application and pre-compiled before execution.

Error Log The file in which SQL Server writes error and informational text, especially on SQL Server startup.

Extended Stored Procedure A special kind of stored procedure that provides a means of dynamically loading and executing functions.

Extent A unit of data storage consisting of 8 contiguous pages.

Foreign Key A field in one table that is a primary key in another table.

Free Space The space on a database page that is available for new data.

Group A useful means of granting and revoking permissions. Users can be assigned to groups and then the group can have permissions granted and revoked. If no other group assignment is made, users belong to the public group.

Index A structure within the database that locates a row based on a key value.

Index Fill Factor A parameter that controls the initial fullness of an index page.

Index Key A column or columns that make up an index.

Integrated Security The security model where SQL Server uses Windows NT security to authenticate users and bypasses the SQL Server login process. This is available for users who use the default named pipes protocol.

Integrity The correctness of the information in a SQL Server database. There are three types of integrity control: integrity constraints, concurrency control, and recovery during or after a system failure.

Isolation Level Specifies how a transaction is affected by other transactions accessing the same data.

ISQL A utility for command line based SQL Server administration.

ISQL/w A graphical utility for executing Transact-SQL and examining query plans.

Joint Engine Technology (JET) The database engine underlying Microsoft Access and Microsoft Visual Basic Professional Edition.

Join Operation A relational operation that selects a row from a table, associates it with a row from another table, and present them as though they were one table.

Journaling The process of recording all operations applied to the database.

Key A column in a table that is used to locate one or more tables.

Livelock The situation where a request for an exclusive lock keeps getting denied because shared lock requests keep slipping in first.

Locking A mechanism for protecting transactions against interference from concurrently executing transactions. In SQL Server pages or tables can be locked.

Log Reader Process A process that takes the relevant transactions from the transaction log of a publication database and moves it to a distribution database.

Logical Name A user-specified name for a database or dump device.

Metadata Data that is used to describe other data.

Master Database The heart of a SQL Server installation, holding configuration information about the SQL Server and the objects in it. Also holds system tables and system stored procedures.

Mixed Security The security model where SQL Server uses Windows NT security to authenticate users who use the default named pipes protocol and standard security if they do not.

Model Database A template database used when SQL Server is asked to create a new database. A database administrator can modify some of the attributes of the model database which will then be copied to any databases created afterwards. Such attributes include database configuration options, user-defined datatypes, rules, defaults and privileges. There is one model database per SQL Server.

Multi-statement Transact-SQL See *Batch File.*

Nonclustered Index A type of index where the physical order of the data in the table is not the same as the order in the index. There can be 249 nonclustered indexes per table.

Normalization The process of reducing a database to its simplest form and eliminating data redundancy.

Null An indicator in SQL used to indicate that a value has not been supplied.

Object There are many objects in a SQL Server such as database devices, login IDs, databases, tables, columns and indexes.

ODBC Microsoft's de-facto standard for PC client access to database servers. Acronym for Open Database Connectivity.

On-line Transaction Processing (OLTP) An environment that supports many users performing the same critical business functions. Typically, an OLTP system has many simultaneous users, all performing the same function such as order taking or seat reservation.

Permissions The permissions system determines which users can access which objects and execute which Transact-SQL statements.

Physical Name An operating system name for a database or dump device.

Primary Key A column or group of columns that uniquely identifies a row. A primary key cannot be null or contain duplicates.

Privileges See *Permissions.*

Procedure Cache An area of memory set aside to hold stored procedures read in from disk and their query plans.

Publication A set of tables that have been specified as being candidates for replication.

Publication Database An SQL Server database from which replicated data originates. Sometimes known as the *primary* or *source* database.

Publication Server An SQL Server where a publication database resides.

Pubs Database The example database shipped with SQL Server representing a publishing business.

Pubs Buildings, sometimes quaint, sometimes not, found in Great Britain where beers, spirits and ales are consumed. A British Institution. Also the location where this book was conceived. No connection with the *pubs* database shipped with SQL Server.

Query Optimizer The component of SQL Server that works out the most efficient way to execute a query.

Query Plan The method the query optimizer has decided is the most efficient way to execute a query.

Record A table row.

Reflexive Join An operation that joins a table upon itself.

Relation Another name for a table.

Relational Database A database model that describes data as a set of independent tables. Within each table, the data is organized into rows and columns.

Remote Server An SQL Server on the network accessible from the user's local server.

Replication The process of copying data from a primary table to secondary tables around the network at various intervals.

Restore The process of rebuilding a database from a database dump using LOAD DATABASE.

Rollback The Transact-SQL statement used to undo all changes made to the database since the last transaction was started.

Rollforward The process of re-applying committed transactions from the transaction log to the database.

Row The relational-model term for a record.

Rule Integrity constraints that define the permitted values a column may take.

SA See *System Administrator*.

Security The protection of the data held in the database against unauthorized access.

Segment A portion of one or more database devices on which tables and indexes can be explicitly placed.

Select Operation The Transact-SQL operation for specifying which rows should be retrieved from the database.

Sort Key A column used for sorting a table.

Sorted Index An index structure where the key values are maintained in sorted order in a B-tree.

SQL Structured Query Language. The standard query language for accessing relational databases. It is an official standard. Comprised of both a data definition and a data manipulation language.

SQL2 The name for SQL-92 while it was a working standard.

SQL3 The next revision to the SQL standard that is under discussion and review.

SQL 86 The original SQL standard.

SQL 89 Further enhancements to the original SQL standard.

SQL 92 A major enhancement to the SQL standard which defines many new features and incorporates a number of features that have already been introduced into commercial relational database management systems. There are three levels to this standard, entry level, intermediate and full.

SQL Distributed Management Objects (SQL-DMO) A layer of management objects forming a hierarchy, with the primary SQL Server object containing databases which in turn contain tables, views and stored procedure objects. Used by the SQL Enterprise Manager and Visual Basic for Applications.

SQL Enterprise Manager The graphical SQL Server management tool. Can be used to administer SQL Servers distributed around a network and to create and edit SQL Server objects such as databases, tables and login IDs.

SQL Executive The component of SQL Server responsible for the management of administrative tasks such as the alerting of operators.

Standard Security The security model where SQL Server uses a login ID and password to authenticate users.

Stored Procedure A set of Transact-SQL statements defined as a procedure and stored in the system metadata.

Subscriber See *Subscription Server*.

Subscription Database A SQL Server database to which replicated data is sent. Sometimes known as the *secondary, destination* or *target* database.

Subscription Server A SQL Server where a subscription database resides.

System Administrator The name often given to the database administrator of a SQL Server installation. Usually abbreviated to SA. SA is also the privileged login ID on a SQL Server system that bypasses normal SQL Server security checking.

System Stored Procedure A group of Transact-SQL statements defined as a procedure and stored in the system metadata in the master database. Supplied by Microsoft and typically used for managing a SQL Server and its underlying databases.

System Table A table that contains information required for the operation of the SQL Server.

Table A collection of rows and columns. Will typically contain the user data.

Temporary Table A table created in the tempdb database which will be removed when the user connection terminates. Temporary tables can be local or global.

Tempdb Database A temporary storage area that can be used for temporary tables and other scratch space requirements. There is one tempdb database per SQL Server. The database administrator can map tempdb into memory for extra performance.

Transaction The grouping of a number of Transact-SQL statements together such that all their changes are applied to the database or none of them are.

Transaction Log A file that contains all the data structures modified during a transaction. The journal file is used to reconstruct the database and maintain integrity during a system or application failure.

Transaction Processing A style of computing supporting multiple users performing predefined tasks against a shared database.

Trigger A type of stored procedure that is automatically executed when a table is changed. Triggers are associated with particular tables and there can be different triggers that execute if a row is inserted, updated or deleted. Triggers are useful for maintaining integrity and keeping audit logs.

Tuple Relational database terminology for a row or record.

User-Defined Datatype A datatype not supplied by SQL Server but named and designed by a database administrator or database designer. User-defined datatypes are based on system supplied datatypes.

Windows NT Microsoft's 32 bit server operating system.

View A logical definition of a table that includes rows and columns from one or more physical base tables.

Windows NT Performance Monitor A graphical utility for monitoring various aspects of Windows NT and SQL Server performance.

WORM Write Once Read Many device.

X/Open An independent, world-wide, open systems organization that is supported by most of the leading information system suppliers, software companies and user organizations.

Index

D

E

F

G

H

I

T

X